Introduction to Development Studies

Introduction to Development Studies

B.K. Pattanaik
Indira Gandhi National Open University, New Delhi

SAGE | TEXTS
www.sagepublishing.com
Los Angeles | London | New Delhi | Singapore | Washington DC | Melbourne

First published in 2016 by

SAGE | TEXTS

SAGE Texts
B1/I-1 Mohan Cooperative Industrial Area
Mathura Road, New Delhi 110 044, India
www.sagepub.in

SAGE Publications Inc
2455 Teller Road
Thousand Oaks, California 91320, USA

SAGE Publications Ltd
1 Oliver 's Yard, 55 City Road
London EC1Y 1SP, United Kingdom

SAGE Publications Asia-Pacific Pte Ltd
3 Church Street
#10-04 Samsung Hub
Singapore 049483

Published by Vivek Mehra for SAGE Publications India Pvt Ltd, typeset in 10/12 pt ITC Stone Serif by Diligent Typesetter India Pvt Ltd, Delhi, and printed at Saurabh Printers Pvt Ltd, Greater Noida.

Library of Congress Cataloging-in-Publication Data

Name: Pattanaik, B. K. (Bikram K.), author.
Title: Introduction to development studies / B.K. Pattanaik School of Extension and Development Studies, Indira Gandhi National Open University, New Delhi.
Description: New Delhi ; Thousand Oaks : SAGE, 2016. | Includes bibliographical references and index.
Identifiers: LCCN 2015041357 | ISBN 9789351508205 (pbk.)
Subjects: LCSH: Development economics. | Economic development–Developing countries. | Political development–Developing countries. | Social planning—Developing countries.
Classification: LCC HD82 .P285 2016 | DDC 338.9—dc23 LC record available at http://lccn.loc.gov/2015041357

ISBN: 978-93-515-0820-5 (PB)

The SAGE Team: Amit Kumar, Indrani Dutta, Sudeshna Nandy, and Rajinder Kaur

CONTENTS

List of Abbreviations ix
Preface xiii
About the Author xix

1. Introduction to Development **1**
Concept of Development 2
Development and Growth 6
Characteristics of Less Developed Countries 9

2. Classical and Neo-classical Theories of Development **16**
Classical Theories 16
Marxian Theory 20
Neo-classical Model of Development 22
Harrod–Domar Model 22
Robert Solow's Model 24

3. Developmentalist Theory of Development **29**
Balanced Growth Theory 30
Unbalanced Growth Theory 34
Rostow's Stages of Economic Growth 36
W.A. Lewis' Theory of Unlimited Supply of Labour 37
Developmental State Theory 39
Harris–Todaro Model of Labour Migration 43

4. Heterodox Theories of Development **49**
Modernization Theory of Development 50
Dependency Theory of Development 56
Neo-Liberal Theory of Development 60
Human Capabilities Theory 63
Gandhian Theory of Development 66
Sarvodaya 68
Gandhian Doctrine of Trusteeship 68
Gandhi Methodology of '*Nai Talim*' for Development 69
Gandhian Villagism and Gram Swaraj for Total Development 69
Gandhian Model of Balanced Growth 70
Gandhian Model of Sustainable Development 70
Gandhian Model of Population and Development 71

5. Dimensions of Development **76**
Economic Dimension of Development 77
Human Development Dimension 79
Social Development Dimension 81
Cultural Development Dimension 85
Political Development Dimension 88
Gender Dimension 90
Ethical Dimension of Development 95

6. Market, State, and Heterogeneous Actors **104**
The Market 105
The State 108
The Market vis-à-vis State Partnership 110
The International Agencies 112
The Non-governmental Organizations (NGOs) and Civil Society Organizations (CSOs) 113
The Local Self-government (LSGs) Institutions 115
The Sectors of Development 118

7. Paradigms of Development **126**
Poverty Reduction and Basic Needs Paradigm 127
Inclusive Development Paradigm 128
Sustainable Development Paradigm 132
Poverty 134
Governance 134
Health 135
Education 135
Demography 136
International Economic Relationship Paradigm 137
Decentralization and Participatory Development Paradigm 139

8. Development Administration **145**
Concept and Meaning 146
Role and Functions of Development Administration 147
Challenges of Development Administration 150

9. Development Governance **158**
What Is Development Governance? Why Is it Essential for Development? 159
Dimensions of Development Governance 161
Decentralized Governance 161
e-Governance 164
Participatory Governance 167
Attributes of Good Development Governance 168
Accountability 169
Transparency 170
Responsiveness 170

Equitable and Inclusive 170
Effectiveness and Efficiency 171
Rule of Law 171
Participatory 171
Consensus Oriented 172
Pluralistic 172
Issues of Development Governance 173

10. Development Planning **180**
Meaning of Planning 181
Role of Development Planning in Development 182
What Are Different Types of Development Planning? 184
Principles of Development Planning 187
Development Plan Formulation 188
Decentralization Development Planning: Indian Experiences 189

11. Development Management **195**
What Is Development Management? 196
Functions of Development Management 197
System Approach to Development Project Management 202
What Are the Issues in Development Project Management? 208

12. Development Communication **215**
What Is Development Communication? 216
Development Communication Theories 219
Principles of Development Communication 220
Approaches to Development Communication 222
Development Communication Strategies 230

Glossary G–1
Index I–1

LIST OF ABBREVIATIONS

ADB	Asian Development Bank
ADS	Area Development Societies
AFR	Adolescent Fertility Rate
AICD	Africa Infrastructure Country Diagnostic
AIDS	Acquired Immuno Deficiency Syndrome
ASPA	American Society for Public Administration
BMF	Bio Mass Fuel
CAG	Comparative Administrative Group
CAN	Communication Need Assessment
CBO	Community-based Organization
CCP	Committee on Comparative Politics
CDC	Continuous Discharge Certificate
CDS	Community Development Societies
CEO	Chief Executive Officer
CIDA	Canadian International Development Agencies
CIP	Competitive Industrial Performance
CPR	Common Property Resources
CSO	Civil Society Organization
CSR	Corporate Social Responsibility
DFID	Department for International Development
DPC	District Planning Committee
EDI	Education Development Index
EU	European Union
FAO	Food and Agriculture Organization
FDI	Foreign Direct Investment
FPAI	Family Planning Association of India
GAID	Global Alliance for ICT and Development
GAIN	Global Alliance for Improved Nutrition
GDN	Global Development Networks
GKN	Global Knowledge Networks
GDI	Gender Development Index
GDP	Gross Domestic Product
GEM	Gender Empowerment Measure
GII	Gender Inequality Index
GNI	Gross National Income
GNP	Gross National Product
GWP	Global Water Partnership

HCI	Head Count Index
HDI	Human Development Index
HDR	Human Development Report
HIV	Human Immuno Virus
HPI	Human Poverty Index
HRST	Human Resource in Science and Technology
IAY	Indira Awas Yojana
IBI	International Broadcast Institute
IBRD	International Bank for Reconstruction and Development
ICDS	Integrated Child Development Services
ICIDI	International Commission on International Development Issues
ICS	Indian Civil Service
ICT	Information and Communication Technology
IFAD	International Fund for Agricultural Development
IFLA	International Federation for Library Association
IFOAM	International Federation of Organic Agriculture Movement
IFPRI	International Food Policy Research Institute
ILC	International Land Coalition
IGI	Income Gap Index
ILO	International Labour Organization
IMF	International Monetary Fund
IOM	International Organization for Migration
ISIC	International Standard Industrial Classification
IT	Information Technology
JICA	Japan International Cooperation Agency
LDC	Least Development Countries
LGC	Local Government Code
LSG	Local Self-government
MDG	Millennium Development Goals
MEA	Millennium Ecosystem Assessment
MMR	Maternal Mortality Rate
MORD	Ministry of Rural Development
NABARD	National Bank for Agriculture and Rural Development
NCEA	National Classification of Economic Activities
NCPPP	National Council for Public Private Partnership
NGO	Non-governmental Organization
NHG	Neighbourhood Group
NHS	National Health Services
NREGA	National Rural Employment Guarantee Act
NRHM	National Rural Health Mission
ODI	Overseas Development Institute
ODII	Organization for Development and International Institute
OECD	Organization for Economic Co-operation and Development
PDG	Political Development Group
PDS	Public Distribution System
PGI	Poverty Gap Index

POA	Programme of Action
PPL	Popular Participation Law
PPP	Purchasing Power Parity
PRI	Panchayati Raj Institutions
PSE	Poverty and Social Exclusion
PURA	Provision of Urban Amenities in Rural Areas
PVO	Private Voluntary Organization
R&D	Research and Development
SAP	Structural Adjustment Programme
SEWA	Self-employed Women's Association
SGSY	Swarnajayanti Gram Swarojgar Yojana
SIDA	Swedish Agency for International Development
SIEZ	Special Industrial Economic Zone
SMEs	Small and Medium Enterprises
SPC	Secretariat of the Pacific Community
SSA	Sarva Shiksha Abhiyan
SSI	Small Scale Industry
STD	Sexually Transmitted Diseases
TEK	Traditional Environmental Knowledge
TSC	Total Sanitation Campaign
UK	United Kingdom
ULBs	Urban Local Bodies
UNCHS	United Nations Centre for Human Settlements
UNCTAD	United Nations Conference on Trade and Development
UNDESA	United Nations Department of Economic and Social Affairs
UNDP	United Nations Development Programme
UNEP	United Nations Environmental Programme
UNESCAP	United Nations Economic and Social Commission for Asia and Pacific
UNESCO	United Nations Educational Scientific and Cultural Organization
UNFPA	United Nations Fund for Population Activities
UNICEF	United Nations Children's Fund
UNIDO	United Nations Industrial Development Organization
USA	United States of America
USAID	US Agency for International Development
WCCD	World Congress on Communication for Development
WFP	World Food Programme
WHO	World Health Organization
WSIS	World Summit on the Information Society
WTO	World Trade Organization
WWF	World Wildlife Fund

PREFACE

'Development' is one of the most dynamic and multidisciplinary concepts in social sciences. Although the concept of 'development' is most frequently used in the common discourse, yet it has not been comprehensively defined to universal satisfaction. Defining 'development' is as challenging as that of descriptions given by five blind men trying to tell about an elephant: the first man, who touched the elephant's leg, said it is a pillar; the second man, who touched its tail, said it is like a rope; the third man, who touched its trunk, argued that it is like a thick branch of a tree; and so on. Here, each man is right from his own perspective because they all touched different parts of the elephant, and actually, an elephant has all these features which were defined by the blind men. Likewise, a student of economics may describe 'development' as an increase in gross domestic product (GDP) and per capita income and a reduction of poverty; while a student of sociology may argue that 'development' means social development in terms of increase in education and health status, reduction of social inequality, and proliferation of social capital; a student of political science may counter both of them and can say development means upholding democratic and political values, good governance, a responsible and accountable political system, and so on. From these descriptions, it can be deduced that all of them are right from their own perspective because 'development' being a multidimensional concept has all these features and dimensions. Truly, 'development' is a versatile concept having many dimensions—economic, social, political, human, and cultural. Further, 'development' from the perspective of developed countries may vary from that of the underdeveloped or developing countries.

The subject 'development' in the discourse of social sciences is the most exciting and versatile one than any other subject in social sciences. Looking at the multidisciplinary nature, the coverage of the subject would be vast, having contents on theory as well as action-related course materials such as development planning and management, development governance, development administration, and development communication, all of which hold much significance in development. The present book *Introduction to Development Studies* gives a holistic description of various important aspects of development, which have relevance to the contemporary developing countries.

Chapter 1, 'Introduction to Development', introduces the concept of 'development' and gives a description about the meaning of 'development'. It also introduces the different definitions of development given by various exponents and the definitions given by the various development agencies, i.e. World Bank, United Nations Development Programme, and other United Nations organizations which are providing technical and financial assistance to various development projects and programmes in the developed as well as developing countries. This chapter also covers the distinction between growth and development as well as various characteristics of developing countries.

Chapter 2 describes 'Classical and Neo-classical Theories of Development'. Different types of theories covered in this chapter are classical theories of development; Marxian theory; and the neo-classical theories propounded by Harrod–Domar and Robert Solow.

Chapter 3 is on 'Developmentalist Theory of Development', and it covers a large number of theories put forward by various developmentalists of the 19th century. Prominent among them are Ragnar Nurkse, Paul Rosenstein-Rodan, Albert Hirschman, Arthur Lewis, Harvey Leibenstein, W.W. Rostow, Gunnar Myrdal, and the Harris–Todaro model of labour migration.

Chapter 4 is on 'Heterodox Theories of Development' and covers a number of heterogeneous theories given by the economists and social scientists. These are basically non-economic theories. This chapter broadly covers modernization theory, dependency theory, neo-liberal theory, human capability theory, and Gandhian theory of development.

Chapter 5 is on 'Dimensions of Development'. This chapter covers the various dimensions of development. Customarily, it is accepted that 'development' is a multidimensional concept and various dimensions of development are—economic development dimension—measured in terms of GDP, national income, and per capita income; social development dimension emphasizes on the development of education and health, reduction of social inequality, and propagation of social capital for development; and the human development dimension as universally measured in terms of literacy, life expectancy, and per capita income. In the political dimension of development, a narration has been made on political governance, political values, political freedom, democratic decentralization, and political empowerment of the disadvantaged. The cultural dimension of development emphasizes on the importance of cultural economy, cultural pluralism, cultural rights and freedom, and cultural investment and tourism in the process of development. The gender development dimension of development deals with the significance of women workforce participation, education, health, and political empowerment in acceleration of development in the developed as well as developing countries. Last but not the least, is the ethical dimension of development in the discussion on dimensions of development, which is one of the influencing factors of development in the socially and culturally sensitive developing countries, where market is too much imperfect and the corporate sector is searching for a social space to promote economic and social well-being of the disadvantaged section of society.

Chapter 6 describes the 'Market, State, and Heterogeneous Actors' playing an important role in development. This chapter describes the role of market as an important actor of development, playing an important role in the capitalist countries of USA and Europe. However, the failure of market mechanism to provide a solution to the Great Depression of 1930s gave rise to the emergence of the 'State' as an actor of development both in developed as well as developing countries. The State is also playing a leading role in the socialistic countries, popularly known as the Second World. Besides, the importance of 'State' as a welfaristic actor of development resorted to largely by the Third World countries independent from the colonial rule after the Second World War. The 'Market' is keen to maintain 'equilibrium', while 'state' is engaged in promoting 'equity'. However, failure of the 'Market' because of market imperfections and shortcomings of the 'State', i.e. bad governance and corruption in the Third World countries has promoted the involvement of other actors of development, i.e. international agencies, non-governmental organizations

(NGOs), and local self-government institutions in their development process. Moreover, international agencies and the NGOs are also playing an equally important role in the development process of the developed nations.

Any analysis on an overview of 'development' will remain incomplete if it fails to discuss the various sectors of development. In this chapter, the role of three important sectors of development, i.e. primary, secondary, and tertiary or service, has been illustrated briefly. From the perspective of developing countries, the role of informal sector in the socio-economic development of the developing countries has been narrated, and it is felt that this informal economy in the developing countries poses a challenge to all these three sectors of development and is instrumental in perpetuating poverty and underdevelopment in the developing countries.

Chapter 7 deals with the 'Paradigms of Development'. It is pertinent to note here that various models and development strategies have been successfully experimented on pilot basis during the initial phases of the development process in many developing countries by the international agencies and also by the government and non-governmental organizations of these countries. These are documented and found to be replicated by other countries and these experimentations in the social science may be termed as 'paradigms of development'. A few important paradigms of development discussed in this chapter from the standpoint of the development of the developing countries are as follows: basic needs and poverty reduction paradigm, decentralization paradigm, international economic relationship paradigm, inclusive development paradigm, and sustainable development paradigms.

Chapter 8 gives an account of the 'Development Administration'. Development administration is one of the indispensable and important arms of the developmental state. Development administration as a component helps the nation-state to streamline the processes, approaches, and strategies of development. It helps to facilitate effective implementation of development activities, projects, and programmes undertaken for the accomplishment of developmental goals. An accountable, transparent, and honest bureaucratic system is sine qua non for the management of the development affairs of a nation. The administrative system and bureaucratic system needed to be oriented from time to time about the changes in the developmental system and a clear and transparent nexus between the bureaucracy and political system on the one hand and the bureaucracy and the people on the other will be helpful in the effective implementation of planned developmental projects and programmes at the grassroots level for the attainment of developmental goals and objectives. Various aspects of development administration covered in this chapter are as follows: concept and meaning of development administration, scope of development administration, features of good development administration, and challenges of development administration.

Chapter 9 'Development Governance' is an important wing of development, which has been extensively discussed in this chapter. Why the developmental endeavours have not yielded the aspired results in developing countries? One of the reasons is bad governance. Accountability, transparency, and honest political and bureaucratic system are essential features of good governance, which is utterly lacking in most of the developing countries. This chapter covers the meaning and scope of development governance and its functions and components. Besides, it also comprises a discussion on features of good governance, attributes, and challenges of good development governance. As 'development' is a multidisciplinary concept, any discussion on the anatomy of 'development' will be half-baked if it does not take into account development governance.

Chapter 10 is on 'Development Planning'. Whether written or unwritten, planning is essential for the attainment of development goals and objectives. Particularly for the developing countries having scanty resources and a large number of unfinished development agenda, planning is very crucial to make the systematic use of resources in a balanced way in different sectors of development in order to achieve holistic development. Planning is a process of setting of goals, formulation of objectives, development of strategies, and outlining activities and tasks for the accomplishment of the developmental goals within a particular time period. In recent years, many nations, both developed as well as developing, are in the process of implementation of decentralized planning for the effective implementation of developmental projects and programmes at the grassroots level with the help of local self-government institutions. The development planning section in this chapter broadly covers the following aspects: meaning and concept of development planning, significance of development planning, types of development planning, preparation of development plan, and decentralized planning.

Chapter 11 is on 'Development Management'. Development management is an emerging area in development. It is needless to say that even if you have abundant resources but not properly managed, then both the resources and the endeavour would not yield satisfactory results. Therefore, an effort has been made to integrate an analysis on development management in the anatomy of development. In a holistic sense, development management refers to effective management of money, manpower, and materials deployed in performing development activities, projects, and programmes in an efficient, effective, systematic, and sustainable way for the attainment of development goals. This chapter on development management comprises the following aspects, i.e. meaning and concept of development management, aim and scope of development management; development management cycle; and requisites of effective development management.

Chapter 12, the last and final chapter of the book is 'Development Communication', another vital aspect of 'development' important for the developing countries having sizeable number of illiterate and lower educated population. Different aspects covered in this chapter are meaning and importance of development communication and approaches to and strategies of development communication.

This book is based on my research and teaching experiences of more than two and a half decades of handling projects on various sectors of development. Exposure to various projects in development, particularly action research projects, monitoring and evaluation studies on different developmental programmes on rural development, sanitation, education, safe drinking water, health, and family welfare, functioning of local self-government institutions with extensive field work in the countryside had enticed me to write a book on anatomy of development. This book will be useful not only for the students pursuing courses on development and development studies but also for students of other related disciplines of social sciences such as economics, sociology, public administration, and so on. However, this book will also be useful for development practitioners, NGOs, research scholars, and persons interested to know about the development. I take this opportunity to thank my colleagues who are currently working in different national level organizations, i.e. NCERT, NIHFW, CRRID, and also in IGNOU. I highly appreciate the work of Sumit Kumar and Manish Kumar, two young colleagues of mine, in helping me in computer work. I am also thankful to SAGE Publications and two young editors, Amit and Indrani, for giving valuable suggestions during the process of updating the manuscript. Last but not the least, I underscore the invisible blessings of my late father (a primary school teacher), which has always been a support in disguise to undertake any assignment and complete it with full dedication.

ABOUT THE AUTHOR

B.K. Pattanaik possesses Master's Degree in Analytical and Applied Economics, MA in Human Resource Management, and PhD in Economics. He has to his credit more than 25 years of experience in research and teaching in various national level organizations, for example, National Council of Educational Research and Training (NCERT), New Delhi; National Institute of Health and Family Welfare (NIHFW), New Delhi; Centre for Research in Rural and Industrial Development (CRRID), ICSSR Centre, Chandigarh; and so on. At present, he is a Professor in the School of Extension and Development Studies at Indira Gandhi National Open University (IGNOU), New Delhi. He has to his credit 26 projects sponsored by various international agencies, such as the World Bank, USAID, Ford Foundation, UNICEF, European Commission, UNFPA, Bill Gates Foundation as well as projects sponsored by various government departments, for example, the Department of Panchayati Raj, Rural Development, and Health and Family Welfare of Government of India. He has also completed projects and studies sponsored by various departments of state governments of Punjab, Haryana, and Himachal Pradesh in different areas of development, such as drinking water and sanitation, border area study, migrant labour, contract farming, study on Scheduled Castes and Scheduled Tribes, health and family welfare, Panchayati Raj, education, rural development, and decentralized planning.

So far, Prof. Pattanaik has authored two books, co-authored four books, and edited a book published by Springer. He has published more than 125 papers (research papers, articles, editorial columns, and book reviews) in various national and international journals; currently, he is the Editor of the *Political Economy Journal of India*. He is also on the editorial board of *Journal of Economics and Development Studies*, American Research Institute for Policy Development, New York, and *Asian Journal of Social Sciences and Humanities*, Oyama, Japan.

He is also guiding PhD students on different areas of Development Studies and two candidates have already been awarded a PhD degree. He is instrumental in designing MA programme in Development Studies and PG diploma programme in Urban Planning and Development. He has attended international seminars, conferences, and study tours and has visited countries such as USA, China, Spain, and Finland. He has conducted an international conference on Diaspora and Development at IGNOU in which more than 100 participants from 25 different countries had participated. Prof. Pattanaik has been awarded the Distinguished Leadership Award, 1999 by the American Biographical Institute, USA and the International Man of the Millennium by the International Biographical Centre, Cambridge, London.

1 Introduction to Development

Development never will be and never can be defined to universal satisfaction.

— Brandt Commission (1980)

Development is probably one of the most depreciated terms in social science literature, having been used more than it has been understood.

— Uphoff and Ilchman (1972)

Development means upward movement of the whole social system by providing better living conditions, viz. adequate food, better housing, improved facilities for health, education and training, and the general improvement of cultural facilities which are all desirable.

— Gunnar Myrdal (1968)

The ultimate purpose of development is to provide increasing opportunities to all people for a better life to bring about a more equitable distribution of income and wealth for promoting both social justice and efficiency of production, to raise substantially, the level of employment, to achieve a greater degree of income security, to expand and to improve facilities for education, health, nutrition, housing, and social welfare and to safe guard the environment.

— The United Nations General Assembly Resolution (1970)

Development has to be more concerned with enhancing the lives we lead and the freedoms we enjoy.

— Sen (1999)

The challenge of development, in the broadest sense, is to improve the quality of life.

— World Development Report (1991)

Development is a commonly confabulated word being aggressively and frequently used in the political and economic landscape of developing countries. The use of the term development by the planners, policy-makers, economists, social scientists, politicians, international funding agencies, and common men in the developing countries is phenomenal. Frequent deliberations, discussions, and debates on 'development' in the print and electronic media as well as through meetings, rallies, seminars, conferences, and symposia is considered as an imperative means and a way well intentioned to urge and put pressure on the government of the developing countries to improve the human well-being and the quality of life of the vast majority of its impoverished population. For the developing countries, 'development' is the means as well as the end, because through the development policies, plans, and programmes, it is intended to achieve the development goals of increased access to basic necessities, like food and nutrition, housing, sanitation, and safe drinking water, and make provision of infrastructure for various sectors so that the performance of the agriculture, industry, and services sector of the economy is improved, and the problems of illiteracy, ill health, insanitation, poverty, unemployment, and inequality are addressed. Development is a big fight, as in recent years, in the developing countries, the election to national as well as provincial and even local self-governments are being fought on the promises of delivering on the development front, such as reduction of poverty, provision of employment to youth, housing, drinking water, road, sanitation, education and health care facilities, control of inflation, and so on. A recent United Nations report (The State of Food Insecurity in the World, 2015), which says that India is a home to the highest number of hungry people in the world at 194 million, is a 'development' challenge for India, to mitigate poverty and hunger from its landscape. The governments of different countries, particularly developing countries are investing their resources—natural, human, financial, etc.—to achieve the development goals. As the goals, objectives, and variables as well as dimensions and indicators of development are many, it is very difficult to define the concept of 'development' precisely to universal satisfaction. One of the opinions on development can be 'development is what development means', which makes the meaning of development wide open and leaves it to the perception of an individual and his or her expectations from development. Per se for a beggar, development may mean access to two square meals a day, clothing, and shelter; while for a farmer, it may mean the availability of irrigation facility, better technology, and enhanced agricultural productivity; and for an impoverished man staying in rural areas, it may mean better food, housing, sanitation, drinking water, employment opportunity, etc. So, anticipation of people from the word 'development' varies. Therefore, for centuries, the concept of development, its meaning and its process, approaches, and strategies have remained a widely debated topic at least in the developing countries.

After reading this chapter, you will be able to:

(i) Explain the meaning of development and also be able to distinguish between growth and development.
(ii) Able to describe why developing countries are underdeveloped.
(iii) Able to understand what, between growth and development, is more important for the developing countries and how.

CONCEPT OF DEVELOPMENT

If we carefully dissect the word 'development', we will know that it is a combination of two words, 'develop' and 'ment'. The dictionary meaning of 'develop' is 'to grow' or 'to move to a more advanced state' and 'ment' as a suffix means 'the process' or 'the action'. If the meanings of these two terms are combined together, development can be defined as the process or action required to take a nation to a more advanced state or towards modernization and advancement. To be more argumentative, the term 'development' is a relative term and can be better defined and understood when it is compared with the concept of 'underdevelopment'. The development status of an underdeveloped country from South Asia, Africa, and Latin America can be better assessed when it is compared with the development status of a developed nation from Europe and America. To be comical, one can enjoy or recognize the glamour and beauty of the 'glittering moon' and 'twinkle, twinkle little star' in the sky, only when there is darkness on the earth. In other words, one is being recognized because of the presence of the other. In other words, the concept of 'development' can be effectively defined and assessed when it is compared with the concept of 'underdevelopment' in terms of achievement in various development indicators. Per se, the underdevelopment or development status of Ethiopia will be better understood when it is compared with the developed nations like USA and UK. Similarly, in India, the level of underdevelopment or development status of Jharkhand and Chhattisgarh will be better understood when it is compared with the comparatively more developed states like Punjab and Kerala. The United Nation Development Programme (UNDP) in its Human Development Report has categorized the development of the nations of the world into four types, i.e. very high development, high development, medium development and, low development on the basis of their values on Human Development Index (HDI). To be more precise, development means a positive change or qualitative and quantitative advancement in different spheres of a nation, i.e. economic, social, political, human, technological, infrastructural, etc. and empowerment of a nation in such as way so as enable it to reduce poverty, hunger, inequality, unemployment and control inflation and to effectively deal with socio-economic distress and discrimination and raise the quality of life of all the people, especially the impoverished, irrespective of caste, creed, ethnicity, gender, and colour. The International Labour Organization (ILO, 1976) while defining development insisted on incorporating the following development plans for developing countries: First, a plan should include the minimum requirements of a family for private consumption: adequate food, shelter, and clothing and the necessary household equipment and furniture; and second, it would include essential services provided by and for the community, such as safe drinking water, sanitation, public transport, and health and education facilities. Another social scientist, Todaro (1977) described development as a multidimensional process involving changes in structures, attitudes and institutions as well as the acceleration of economic growth, the reductions of inequality, and the eradication of absolute poverty. Todaro's definition of development runs as "development is both a physically reality and a state of mind in which society has through some combination of social, economic, and institutional process, secured the means for obtaining a better life". He advocated that in order to achieve development, all societies must have at least the following three objectives: (a) to increase the availability and widen the distribution of basic life-sustaining goods such as food, shelter, health, and protection of all members of society; (b) to raise the level of living, higher incomes, provide more jobs, better education, and more attention to cultural and humanistic values; and (c) to expand the range of economic and social choice to individuals and nations by freeing them from servitude and dependence. Development is a dynamic concept and its basic aim is to raise the quality of living of people through various interventions in different dimensions of development such as economic, social, political, human, cultural, and so on and through the development of various sectors, i.e. agriculture, industry, and services and through the efforts of different actors such as market, state, international agencies, NGOs, and civil society organizations (CSOs).

Its objective is to reduce poverty, inequality, unemployment, illiteracy, ill health, and insanitation and provide access to each and every family healthy housing, safe drinking water, sanitation, energy for cooking and lighting, surface and e-communication, primary education, and primary health care services through good governance. A country which fails to provide all these basic amenities to its population, irrespective of caste, class, ethnicity, religion, and gender, is categorized as underdeveloped.

Multidimensional development aims at improving the performance of an economy on various dimensions, i.e. economic, social, human, cultural, and political, which results in the enhancement of the quality of life of its population. The economic dimension of development broadly emphasizes on the rise in GDP and per capita income, reduction of poverty and increase in employment, raising agricultural and industrial productivity, controlling inflation and deflationary pressure, improving the balance of payment situation, and raising the standard of living and quality of life of the people. While, the social dimension of development aims at improving the status of education, health, and social and human well-being; empowerment of women and other marginalized sections of the society, reduction in social inequality and discrimination, promotion of social justice, strengthening social capital, social networking, and inclusive social development. The objectives of the social development in the developing countries are to reduce illiteracy, raise the level of education, decrease infant and maternal mortality rates and malnutrition, with focused emphasis on the socially and economically backward sections of population. The political dimension of development largely intends to strengthen political system, deepen democracy and democratic decentralization, encourage participation of people in political processes and political empowerment of women and marginalized, and inculcate political ethics and values among the masses, political and bureaucratic good governance, formulation and implementation of effective rule of laws to restrain corruption at all levels, and so on. The human development dimension embodies three main targets, i.e. longevity: through a healthy life; knowledge: through organized education, and a decent living standard: through access to income, resources, and services. The cultural dimension of development expects to recognize and strengthen the role of culture in the processes and strategies of development, pursue a development model which acts in consonance with the cultural milieus, and is intricately linked to the society where it is pursued. It further expects that the cultural beliefs and values do not act as a stumbling block in the process of modernization and development. The gender dynamics of development emphasizes on the social, economic, and political empowerment of women, and actions on mainstreaming of women in the development process. The development actions need to be sustainable and inclusive, have to and must carry along the marginalized and disadvantaged in the mainstream process of development, with the aim 'development of all and all for development' and the present action on development must take into consideration its impact on the outcome in the future. A few important aims of development in the developing countries are to:

(i) Increase human well-being and quality of life of the people and provide highest benefits to the greatest numbers who are being deprived.

(ii) Ensure basic amenities, i.e. healthy housing, sanitation, safe drinking water, elementary education, primary and referral health care, road, electricity, recreation facilities, etc. to all people staying in both rural as well as urban areas.

(iii) Reduce poverty, inequality, and unemployment. At the same time, restrain inflation that imposes economic stress on the impoverished and control population.

(iv) Reduce illiteracy, raise level of education, reduce infant and maternal mortality and morbidity, and control HIV/AIDS and other communicable and non-communicable diseases.

(v) Enhance productivity of the agriculture, industrial, and service sectors. Attempt has to be made so that all the sectors contribute to their best capabilities towards economic growth and development of the nation-state. Provide skills to the manpower for enhancement of productivity and economic growth.

(vi) Bring structural changes in the economy thorough the provision of infrastructure and technology. Transference of surplus manpower from the agriculture to the industrial and services sector. Modernization of agriculture, industry, and service sectors to enhance their contribution to economic growth and development.

(vii) Achieve inclusive development and see that the benefit of growth and development reaches to the unreached and to the poorest of the poor. All the community and people share the fruits of development without any discrimination adhering to the principle, i.e. 'development for all with the involvement of all'.

(viii) Achieve sustainable development by promoting healthy interaction between the people, environment, and the society. At the same time, enhance the capabilities of dry land, desert, and hilly areas to contribute towards national development. Enhance the contribution of differently abled people, women, and aged population towards economic growth and development.

(ix) Augment the process of effective and sustainable urbanization and make available the provision of urban facilities in rural areas and synchronize the gulf between rural and urban areas.

(x) Enhance the capabilities, open up choices and opportunities for all irrespective of caste, colour, creed, ethnicity, and gender.

(xi) Formulate appropriate fiscal and monetary policies with judicious allocation of planned budget for various sectors of the economy, carefully dealing with the fiscal deficit, taxation policy, and interest rate policy. Both the fiscal and monetary policies need not be only growth oriented, but necessarily be development oriented in the developing countries.

The Millennium Development Goals

The Millennium Development Goals (MDG) declared by the United Nation General Assembly on 8 September 2000 has delineated a few important development goals, which are as follows:

- Eradication of extreme poverty and hunger
- Achieve universal primary education
- Promote gender equity and empower women
- Reduce child mortality
- Improve maternal health

- Combat HIV/AIDS, malaria, and other diseases
- Ensure environmental sustainability
- Develop a global partnership for development

MDG Achievement of South Asian Countries, 2011

Countries	MDG Score (2011)
Bangladesh	4.5
Bhutan	4.0
India	4.5
Maldives	4.5
Nepal	5.5
Pakistan	4.0
Sri Lanka	6.0
Average	4.7

Source: UN (2012) Governance and Development, UN system Task Team on the Post-2015 UN Development Agenda, thematic think Peace, UNDESA, UNDP, UNESCO, see http://www.un.org/millenniumgoal.pdf/Think%20

The MDG indicators are judged against a maximum score of 8. Barring Sri Lanka, most South Asian nations are only half way near the move. The performances of South Asian nation states are very poor in MDG achievement.

Source: www.un.org/millenniumgoals

DEVELOPMENT AND GROWTH

Growth is what we understand, development what we do not.

— Lucas (1988)

To understand 'growth' we must understand 'development'.

— Romer (1990)

It is conceptually possible for an economy to grow without developing, however, development without growth is a little harder to imagine.

— Higgins (1990)

For several decades, development was equated with economic growth, which is measured purely in terms of economic variables such as GDP, gross national product (GNP), per capita income, capital formation, rate of investments and savings, and rise in agricultural and industrial productivity. From the standpoint of the developing countries, it was felt that defining development and setting the goals and objectives of development with sheer achievement in terms of quantitative economic growth may do more for GDP and GNP, but will not do enough justice for the poor. Therefore, majority of the development scientists were no longer impressed by the growth performance of the economy reflected in terms of rise in GDP and GNP. Rather, they emphasized to concentrate more on development process and achievements in terms of various development indicators such as literacy, life expectancy, mortality and morbidity, sanitation, safe drinking water, and so on, which are critical to standard of living of the people. The important distinctions between growth and development are that growth is a unidimensional quantitative phenomenon meaning economic growth, and, on the contrary, development is a multidimensional quantitative and qualitative concept. Growth is a discontinuous change, while development is a continuous change in a positive direction. The quantitative aspects of development relates to various quantitative dimensions of development such as percentage increase in literacy, decrease in infant and maternal mortality rates, rise in life expectancy, reduction in percentage of population living below poverty line, increase in agricultural and industrial productivity, and so on. On the contrary, the qualitative dimension of development emphasizes upon the quality of education and health care, quality of food and nutrition, and quality of life depending on the accessibility to healthy housing, sanitation facility, safe drinking water, and quality energy for cooking and lighting.

Growth and development are not necessarily same, and at any point of time, higher growth can be achieved amidst less development. In India, Bihar, a socio-economically backward state, had achieved higher economic growth rate during 2009–10 even with less development. The growth rate of Bihar, during 2009–10 was 10.42 higher than that of Punjab, 6.61, one of the most socio-economically advanced state of India (Table 1.1). However, the various development indicators, i.e. literacy rate, per capita income, health, sanitation, housing, etc. of Punjab are much better than Bihar. Bihar's achievement of higher growth rate at certain point of time amidst underdevelopment shows that growth can occur even with less developmental achievements. Similarly, an inter-country comparison of growth rate given in Table 1.2 shows that the growth rate of India is +6.3 while that of Japan is –0.6 in 2013. This status of growth rate might not lead us to conclude that

Table 1.1 *GDP Growth (Annual %) of Selected States of India, 2009–10*

India/States	Growth Rate
India	8.39
Maharashtra	10.47
Gujarat	12.87
Haryana	11.00
Punjab	6.61
Bihar	10.42
Himachal Pradesh	14.76
Madhya Pradesh	10.50
Kerala	8.95

Source: Ministry of Statistics and Programme Implementation, Government of India.

Table 1.2 *GDP Growth (Annual %) of Selected Countries*

Countries	Growth Rate
Bangladesh	6.7
China	9.3
Denmark	1.1
Ethiopia	7.3
India	6.3
Japan	–0.6
UK	1.0
USA	1.8

Source: World Bank, World Development Indicators, 2013.

India is more developed than that of Japan. Thus, from these two examples, it is amply clear that higher economic growth rate is not a true indicator of higher development. In other words, higher growth rate is not a clear passport to higher development and higher growth rate can occur even with less development.

The term, 'growth' is being frequently used by the developed countries, while 'development' is a buzz word in the developing countries. The urge to achieve higher economic growth rate has become a cruel proposition for the developing countries, because, in the recent past, it is being observed that the developing countries are trying hard to achieve higher economic growth rate by giving priority and incentives to the private and corporate sectors, downsizing the role of public sector. Similarly, the developed countries achieved higher growth rate during 1970s and 1980s through a capitalist model. England and other Western countries could have failed to achieve higher growth rate and prosperity in the initial phase of their development without the exploitation of the poor countries of Asia, Africa, and Latin America. Internationally, it is widely recognized that the realization of economic growth and accumulation at the early stage of capitalism was inseparable from the worldwide colonial intervention involving political repression, forced labour, and drainage of resources from South and Southeast Asia, Africa, and Latin America (Chopra, 1983; Furtado, 1983). It is perceived that instead of expanding people's democratic rights, economic growth has usually been accompanied by internal repression and control (Seers, 1979). Haque (2004) was of the opinion that in order to enhance the GNP figures, premarket policies such as privatization, deregulation, and liberalization were introduced by states through executive power without popular mandate. Pereira, Maravall, and Przeworski (1993) in their study have mentioned that in Argentina, Brazil, and Peru, the neo-liberal policy approach has usually been based on presidential decrees without any public support, legislative debate, and discussion with opposition parties (Pereira, Maravall, and Przeworski, 1993). In India, elected governments laid by different political parties in power at various point of time have also tried to push their economic reforms agenda of liberalization and privatization through ordinances in order to give a boost to economic growth. If the motive of the achievement of high growth rate is through the means of exploitation of the poor and through the expansion of profit-mongering privatization and is pushed through undemocratic means, then it is a cruel proposition. Therefore, the mainstream development has gradually been moving away from the preoccupation with economic growth towards a people-centred definition of development (Pieterse, 1998). In recent years, government of the developing countries through the process of corporate social responsibility (CSR) is trying to involve private and corporate sectors in the socio-economic development. Moreover, this benevolent capitalist approach aims at giving a humane face to growth-centric and profit-making attitude of the private and corporate sectors and to encourage and involve them in the development-centric human well-being activities. No doubt, at the initial phase of the development of the developing economy, high growth rate is desirable; however, the gains acquired from the higher growth rate are to be utilized for the development of the impoverished and socio-economically marginalized. Per se the rise in agricultural productivity, which is a growth factor, will raise the income of farmers. The higher income will enable them to spend on the education of their children, better housing, and access to quality health care and other household amenities, which can ultimately raise the quality of their life. Further, the higher agricultural productivity of the agriculturist will also benefit the agricultural labourer, who works in the land of the agriculturists and gets food grain and wages in lieu of his work. Indirectly, it will be helpful to mitigate hunger among the farm labourers through 'tickle down' effect. The agriculture in Punjab has benefited a lot of migrant labourers from the less developed states like Bihar and Uttar Pradesh as they are able to meet their livelihood and improve their standard of living back home. The investment in infrastructure, technological upgradation, and modernization of the agriculture, industry, and service sectors are all growth-boosting initiatives. Whereas launching various development programmes such as Indira Awas Yojana, Mahatma Gandhi Rural Employment Guarantee Act, National Rural Health Mission, Swajal Dhara, Swachh Bharat Abhiyan, and Sarva Shiksha Abhiyan by the Government of India at different points of time aiming at improvement of education, health, social security, and human well-being are development-boosting initiatives. From the point of view of the developing countries, both 'growth' and 'development' are indispensable; however, 'development' is more imperative than 'growth' as a majority of people in these countries are suffering in poverty, inequality, illiteracy, malnutrition, ill health, insanitation, lack adequate housing facilities, and astoundingly low quality of living.

CHARACTERISTICS OF LESS DEVELOPED COUNTRIES

Undeveloped countries are those which, compared to advanced countries, are underdeveloped with capital in relation to their population and natural resources.

— Nurkse (1953)

Underdeveloped economy is that economy in which there are low levels of living, absolute poverty, low per capita income, low consumption levels, poor health services, high death rates, high birth rates and dependence on foreign countries.

— Todaro (1977)

> *An underdeveloped country is that country in which there is a constellation of numerous undesirable conditions of work and life, output, income, and levels of living are low; many modes of production, attitude and behaviour patterns are disadvantageous and these are unfavorable institutions.*
>
> — Myrdal (1968)

The continual discourse on development was seriously started after the Second World War, when many countries belonging to Asia, Africa, and Latin America got independence from the colonial rule. These newly independent nations suffering from a multitude of socio-economic problems, such as poverty, inequality, unemployment, illiteracy, ill-health, and insanitation, were labelled variously as the 'Third World', 'underdeveloped', 'less developed', and 'developing' nations. The Third World is the English translation of *le tiers monde*, developed in France in the 1950s, with the heightened anti-colonial consciousness that arose with the coming of the new nation-states in Africa and Asia. The underdeveloped countries were being called the Third World countries in order to differentiate these nations from the First World and Second World nations. The First World consisted of the capitalist's world or the world of advanced market economies, and the Second World largely comprised of the centrally planned economies of Eastern Europe and the Soviet Union. The Third World consisted of all other impoverished nations usually belonging to Africa, Asia and Caribbean, the Pacific, and South and Central America. Besides these terminologies, one of the other important terms used to distinguish between the developed and developing nations was 'North' and 'South'. The 'North' comprised the developed countries of Europe and America, and the 'South' comprised the poor nations belonging to Asia, Africa, Latin America, and the Caribbean.

Customarily, the developing countries are those countries in which greater percentage of people is living below the poverty line, being devoid of basic amenities. The population growth rate is high, and a large percentage of people are found to be dependent on agriculture and allied activities for earning livelihood. There is deficiency in development of infrastructure, inequality between rich and poor is high, and majority of people lead inferior quality of life. The informal sector plays an important role in the economic activities of these nations. They are predominantly labour-intensive, agriculture-based economies, with a huge percentage of economy's labour force being agriculturists, farmers, and farm labourers. Although the contribution of agriculture to the gross domestic product in many developing countries is found to be declining in recent years, yet the number of people engaged in agriculture and its allied activities has not declined proportionately, as the agriculture sector is found to be predominated with disguised unemployment and under-employment. The agriculture sector in most parts of these countries follows traditional practices. There is poor adoption of advanced technology in this sector and mechanization of agricultural activities is also in a low state. Besides low irrigation facilities, poor adoption of high-yielding variety (HYV), and its package of practices, tardy implementation of land reform measures and poor investment in agricultural research, training, and extension are other factors affecting the agricultural productivity in underdeveloped countries. There is hardly any structural transformation and shifting of surplus manpower from agriculture to industrial and tertiary sectors.

Developing countries are featured with high population growth rate and high fertility among the lower income group of population, which affects the per capita income and standard of living of the majority of lower middle and poor sections. It is putting pressure on the scanty infrastructure and basic facilities like housing, sanitation, drinking water, education, health care, etc. available in both rural and urban areas and particularly in urban areas, where the high density of population is leading to the growth of slum and squatter population. Endurance of poverty, inequality, illiteracy, and low level of literacy, poor health condition with morbidity, mortality, and high unemployment rate, as well as lower per capita income are an outcome of high population growth. Although the demographic dividend of high percentage of youth population in a few economies sounds ecstatic, yet the burgeoning number of child population and gradual increase in ageing population would depress their per capita income and standard of living.

The developing countries are suffering from low capital formation and poor entrepreneurial qualities and innovations. They are characterized with the vicious circle of low capital formation, low capital formation leads to low investment, low investment results in less employment opportunity, less employment opportunity results in lower income, which leads to lower savings, ultimately resulting in low capital formation. Further, these economies have poor capacity to invest in the modernization of agriculture, industries, and manufacturing activities and lack financial capabilities to create quality social overhead capital, which fails to attract the investment by the private and corporate sector in these economies. The contribution of agriculture sector to economic growth is declining, while that of industrial sector is more or less stagnant. Although the contribution of tertiary sector to economic growth is rising, yet it has failed to absorb adequate amount of labour force in it. In other words, there is either job stagnant or jobless growth of the service sector in the developing countries. According to ILO (2010), the service sector in the developed economies and European Union makes up 72.8 per cent of the total employment, while in the South Asia and Sub-Saharan Africa, which are constituted of developing countries, service sector comprise only 27.6 and 30.4 per cent of total employees, respectively. In India, in the year 2012 service sector contributed 56.9 per cent to the GDP; however, it shares only 28.1 per cent of total employment. It is pertinent to mention here from another angle that excessive emphasis and growth of the service sector in these economies without adequately strengthening primary and secondary sectors is one of the reasons for fluctuations in the economic growth rate in these countries. Job creation in the secondary and tertiary sectors is a central challenge before the developing countries in order to provide employment to their growing youth population. Dualism scenario, i.e. existence of traditionalism versus modernism in various spheres of development is another important feature of developing countries. There exists a small modern sector and a vast traditional sector. Those people who are living in urban areas get access to all modern amenities and education and more per capita income. Less percentage of people live below poverty line as compared to the traditional rural sector. The rural sector has a higher percentage of people living below poverty line, level of education is low, and quality of life is poor. Good educational institutions, quality health care institutions, and modern service sector are found in the urban areas, while rural sector is largely devoid of these facilities. Another example of dualism is the formal versus informal sector. Developing economies are characterized by vast informal sector, where more than 90 per cent of people are earning their livelihood. The people working in the informal sector, i.e. with the petty businessmen, individual entrepreneurs, contractors, private practitioners, large landlords, etc. are getting lower wages, and they work for long hours with poor or no social security. On the other hand, people working in the formal public and private sectors are well paid and have better social security provisions. The developing countries are facing the challenge of how to reduce the urban rural divide and curtail the size of informal economy.

The social development indicators of the developing countries such as adult literacy rate and gross enrolment ratio are low, whereas infant and maternal mortality rates and morbidity rate are high as compared to that in developed countries. The malnutrition and nutritional anaemia are high among children and women, particularly pregnant and lactating women as compared to their counterparts in developed countries. Most of the developing countries are found to be stratified society on the basis of class, caste, religion, and ethnicity, which prevent the socially backward sections of the society to have equal access to developmental opportunities. Per se in India, the Scheduled Castes and Scheduled Tribes are having lower socio-economic status than the general castes. The developing countries are deficient in social capital. The Human Development Index, which is measured by three important variables such as per capita income, life expectance, and the literacy rate, is low as compared to the developed countries. The UNDP Human Development Report 2013 shows that USA, with an index value of 0.937, occupies third place and is in the category of Very High Human Development; on the other hand, Nepal, a developing country with an index value of 0.463, is positioned on 157th place, in the category of Low Human Development. Low human development is an indicator of lower quality of living and poor standard of living.

Many developing countries belonging to Asia, Africa, and Latin America are featured with cultural paradox. The cultural beliefs and values are a hurdle in the path of development; on the other side, the cultural trade and tourism earn sizable revenues to the nation-states of the developing countries and provide livelihood to the millions of indigenous people in these countries. Many developing countries, because of lack of cultural investment, are not able to exploit the potential of cultural trade and businesses. However, cultural taboos and traditional beliefs and values have created obstruction in the path of modernization and technological advancement of these countries. In other words, culture is a source of livelihood as well as a mean of obstruction to modernization, industrialization, and development. Therefore, conventionally and also contemporarily, cultural livelihoods and development-related activities and actions are in contradictions in the forest and hill areas of the developing countries.

Poor political development and weak political governance are also critical features of the developing countries. Many developing countries of Asia, Africa, and Latin America are marred with political instability, and many of them are still struggling after decades of their independence from the colonial rule to establish a representative democratic system. Multiparty system, supremacy of dynastic politics and authoritarianism in representative democracy, weak political governance, lack of political values and rights, criminalization of politics, and growth of regionalism within the representative democracies are some of the emerging problems that are affecting the political development and, ultimately, the economic development of the developing nations. The culture of developmental experimentation with the change of guard from one political party or one coalition government to the other and the resultant change in the development policies, processes, and approaches is affecting growth and development of the developing countries. The weak governance, i.e. bribe and corruption, in the political and bureaucratic system, political indecisiveness, nepotism, red-tapism, poor decision-making, shifting of responsibility, and lack of accountability are affecting the growth and development process of these countries. Abeyasinghe (2004) was of the opinion that political instability can have serious consequences on economic growth.

The inclusive development process is very weak in the developing countries. The exclusion on the basis of caste, class, ethnicity, gender, and religion very much exists in these countries. Although exclusion and discrimination on the basis of above criterion are prohibited through law, yet these exist in the heart and mind of the people and also in the social sphere of these countries among the dominating sections of population, thereby creating hurdles for inclusive development. The stratified societies in the developing countries are still struggling to be socially, economically, culturally, and politically inclusive. The exclusion of a certain group of population from the labour as well as land market is one of the reasons for endurance of poverty and inequalities in these countries. According to UNDP, development can be inclusive, and it can reduce poverty only if all groups of people contribute to creating opportunities, share the benefits of development, and participate in decision-making.[1]

Not only inclusive development but also the sustainable development has posed a big challenge to the developing countries. These countries are poor in green governance as there is lack of effective coordination in the society, economy, and environment. The society and the economy are careless about the impact of their action on the environment. Tardiness and lack of honesty in the formulation and implementation of environmental policies and poor political and bureaucratic will power deal with environment laws and absence of community awareness on environmental-related developmental issues. This leads to faulty actions without paying adequate attention towards the impact of environment on development in the developing countries. Per se construction of more number of hydroelectric projects in Himachal Pradesh and Uttarakhand in India are adversely affecting the environment and climate. The occurrences of frequent cloudbursts in these regions, which has taken away a lot of lives, are the outcome of environmental degradation. Further, these countries lack a coherent policy on sustainable development, and as a result, their endeavour and action in agriculture and industrial development front is adversely affecting environment and producing negative effect on development, health, and human well-being. The rising population, urbanization, poverty, inequality, and urge for higher economic growth in the developing countries is further going to make the achievement of sustainable development difficult for them in the coming years. Balanced economic, social, and environmental development is a requisite for sustainable development, which is lacking in these countries. The UN in its World Economic and Social Survey Report, 2013, has urged that a developing economy needs to pursue the goal of greening their catch-up growth.

The Sum Up

Development is a continuous process and a relative concept which has given rise to many relative terminologies, such as 'more developed', 'less developed', 'underdeveloped', and 'developing', making its meaning and measurement more involved and entangled. It is true that the term 'development' has sprouted the concepts of the 'First World', the 'Second World', and the 'Third World'. Over a period of time, it has also overcome the era of 'isms', so now virtually there are two worlds, one is 'developed', where the people are enjoying good quality of life, and the other is 'developing', where people are relentlessly trying to achieve the better quality of life for its population. No doubt 'development' will remain a debated and spicy concept both for the developed as well as the developing countries; and, particularly in developing countries, it will remain a big issue and challenge in the years to come.

Keywords economic growth rate, development, basic needs, capital formation, Third World country, sustainable development, inclusive development, political governance, human development, social development.

REVIEW QUESTIONS

1. What do you mean by development? How is development a multidimensional phenomenon? Explain.
2. What are the differences between growth and development? Which is more beneficial to the underdeveloped countries and why?
3. Explain why developing countries are underdeveloped.
4. Explain five key features of underdeveloped countries. What are the measures to be taken to promote development of the underdeveloped countries?
5. The capital formation is central to the development of the underdeveloped countries. Explain.
6. Economic growth is possible without development. Explain how growth can be promoted in an underdeveloped economy.
7. Basic needs are important for the development of underdeveloped countries. Explain various basic needs which are central to the development of the underdeveloped countries.
8. Distinguish between developed and underdeveloped countries. What are the measures needed to be taken to make underdeveloped countries developed?

NOTE

1. The UNDP statement is quoted from http://www.undp.org/content/undp/en/home/ourwork/povertyreduction/focus_areas/focus_inclusive_development/ (accessed on 15 February 2016).

REFERENCES

Abeyasinghe, R. 2004. "Democracy, Political Stability and Developing Country Growth: Theory and Evidence." Honors Projects, Paper 17, Illinois Wesleyan University. Available at: http://digitalcommons.iwu.edu/econ_honproj/17 (accessed on 12 May 2014).

Brandt Commission. 1980. *North–South: A Programme of Survival*, 48. London: Pan Books.

Chopra, P. 1983. "Development and Society: An Overview of the Indian Experience." In *A Society for International Development Prospectus*, edited by A. Mattis, 1984, 215–26. Durham, NC: Duke University Press.

Furtado, C. 1983. *Accumulation and Development*. Oxford: Martin Robertson and Company.

Haque, M.S. 2004. "The Myths of Economic Growth (GNP): Implications for Human Development." In *Hand Book of Development Policy Studies*, edited by G. Mudacumura and Haque M.S., 1–24. New York: Marcel Dekker.

Higgins, B. 1990. *Economic Development Problems, Principles and Policies*. New Delhi: Universal Book Stall.

ILO. 1976. *Employment, Growth and Basic Needs, One World Problems*. Geneva: International Labour Organization.

———. 2010. Trends Econometric Models, October, International Labour Organization, Geneva.

Lucas, R.E. 1988. "On the Mechanics of Economic Development." *Journal of Monetary Economics*, 22: 3–42.

Myrdal, G. 1968. *Asian Drama*. New York: Pantheon.

Nurkse, Ragnar. 1953. *Problems in Capital Formation in Underdeveloped Countries*. New York: Oxford University Press.

Pereira, L.C.B., J.M. Maravall, and A. Prezeworski. 1993. "Conclusions." In *Economic Reforms in New Democracies: A Social Democratic Approach*, edited by L.C.B. Pereira, J.M. Maravall, and A. Prezeworski, 199–220. New York: Cambridge University Press.

Pieterse, J.N. 1998. "My Paradigm or Yours? Alternative Development, Post Development or Reflective Development." *Development and Change*, 29: 343–73.

Romer, P.M. 1990. "Endogenous Technical Change." *Journal of Political Economy*, 98: S71–S102.

Seers, D. 1979. "The Meaning of Development." In *Development Theory: Four Critical Studies*, edited by D. Leham, 9–30. London: Frank Cass.

Sen, A.K. 1999. *Development as Freedom*. Oxford: Oxford University Press.

Todaro, M.P. 1977. *Economics for a Developing World*. London: Longman.

United Nations. 1970. *2626(XXV) International Development Strategy for the Second United Nations Development Decade*, Twenty-fifth session, Agenda Item 42, UN. Available at: www.un-documents.net/a25r2626.htm (accessed on 4 October 2013).

Uphoff, Norman T. and Warren F. Ilchman, eds. 1972. *The Political Economy of Development: Theoretical and Empirical Contributions*. Berkeley, CA: California University Press.

World Development Report. 1991. *World Development Report 1991, World Bank*. New York: Oxford University Press.

2 Classical and Neo-classical Theories of Development

Development theories were originally dominated by the economists.

— Sano (2000)

The classical and neo-classical theories of economic growth and development emerged during the rise of capitalism in the West, and the discussions on the processes of economic growth and development in these theories are based on the analysis of the capitalist economic system. At the outset, Adam Smith's work on economic growth and development in the capitalist system, which is given in his illustrious book, *An Inquiry into the Nature and Causes of the Wealth of Nations*—popularly known as *The Wealth of Nations*—is one of the pioneering classical works on economic growth and development. J.S. Mill, David Ricardo, and T.R. Malthus are the other exponents of the classical theories of economic growth and development. The illustrious work of Karl Marx, who analyzed the dynamics of capitalist system, predicated its downfall and advocated the advent of socialism, constitutes another milestone in the perspectives on classical theory of development. The classical theories of development have basically analyzed the functioning of the capitalist system which has enabled the countries of the West to attain higher economic growth and development.

After reading this chapter, you will be able to:

(i) Describe classical theories of development and their criticisms.
(ii) Critically explain Marxian theory of development.
(iii) Narrate various neo-classical theories of development.

CLASSICAL THEORIES

The classical theorists believed that the growth and development of an economy are determined by the increase in output or national productivity, which depends on four important factors, i.e. (a) size of labour force (L); (b) the stock of capital (K); (c) the amount natural resources available (N), or the land; and (d) available technology (T). The functional relationship between the dependent variable, i.e. Output = O; and the independent variables such as L, K, N, and T are represented as:

$$O = f(L, K, N, T)$$

The rate of economic growth over time $\left(\frac{dO}{dt}\right)$ depends on the productivity and the rate of expansion of these four important factors of production over time. The economic growth rate as propounded in the classical model can be put in the form of an equation below, where '*d*' represents change and '*t*' represents time.

$$\frac{dO}{dt} = f_N \frac{dN}{dt} + f_L \frac{dL}{dt} + f_K \frac{dK}{dt} + f_T \frac{dT}{dt}$$

According to classical proposition, the increase in output depends on the availability of land, labour, capital, and technology in an economy. The output and productivity gained through the united application of land, labour, capital, and machinery is divided among these actors of development, i.e. the proprietors of land, the owner of capital, and the labourers who contribute in the production process. The challenge of the economy, as deemed by the classists, is how to raise the productivity of land and distribute income acquired from the productivity of land among these three different actors of production, i.e. landlords, capitalists, and labourers. The economic growth and development of an economy largely depends on the dynamics and efficiency of these three actors of development and in the effective use of factors of production. Labour is a critical input and the growth and development of an economy rest on the shoulder, skill, and dexterity of the labourer and the prudent use of labour by the landlord in the process of production. Adam Smith emphasized on the 'Division of Labour' as a vital process to stimulate economic growth and development and advocated breaking the total labour effort of an economic activity into different specialized components so that each division works to the best of its potential to enhance productivity. The division of labour enhances productivity in three ways: (a) it increases dexterity (skill) of the labourer, (b) it saves labour times, and (c) it helps in the invention of labour-saving machinery. Smith (1976) has nicely described the division of labour by giving the following example:

> ...the woolen coat, for example, which covers the day-labourer, as coarse and rough as it may appear, is the produce of the joint labour of a great multitude of workmen. The shepherd, the sorter of the wool; the wool comber or carder, the dyer, the scribbler, the spinner, the weaver, the fuller, the dresser, with many others, must all join their different arts in order to complete even this homely production.

Apart from labour, capital is another vital input of production. The classists believe that all economic activities will smoothly continue as long as capital is accumulated and new technology is introduced into the process of production. The capital accumulation enables the entrepreneurs or producers to introduce the latest and modern technology into the production system, which enhances the efficiency of capital and maximizes output and profit. Higher profit leads to higher savings, leading to higher investment, and further leading to more capital formation; this cycle continues which ultimately promotes sustainable growth and development of the economy. In order to enhance capital accumulation, the classical economists, particularly David Ricardo, laid stress on the reduction of unproductive consumption by the landlords as unproductive consumption is deterrent to capital accumulation. The other source of promoting capital accumulation and stimulating economic growth and development of an economy according to the classists is the free trade. Classical theorists were the votaries of free trade and against imposition of any restriction on free trade. They were of the view that the free trade needs to be based on the principle of comparative advantage and the country needs to export those products for which it enjoys comparative cost advantage. They were against the imposition of taxes on capitalists, landlords, and labourers as it would demotivate them and reduce their income, profit, and capital accumulation, which would ultimately affect the performance of the economy in terms of economic growth and development. Here, Adam Smith's principle of *laissez faire* is worth noting as the policy of left alone or '*laissez-faire*' allows the producers to produce as much they like, earn as much income as they can, and save as much as they wish, in accordance to the free play of demand and supply in the economy. In Adam Smith's view, *laissez-faire* promotes 'self-interest', which energizes the capitalists and landlords to be intensely involved in their business and production activities, which ultimately stimulate economic growth and development process in the economy. The invisible hand of market operates through the forces of demand and supply and the free play of demand and supply would ensure an efficient level of production, consumption, and distribution of goods in the society. It is the 'invisible hand' which creates automatic equilibrium between demand and supply in the perfectly competitive market. Last, but not the least, the vital factor of production is land, which is an important natural resource and an indispensable resource of an economy, and economic development depends on the productive capacity of the land and on the advancement of agriculture and enhanced contribution of agriculture towards economic development. Enhancement of agricultural productivity is done by the effective use of land as well as by doing improvement in the skill and dexterity of labour and use of machinery in the production process. Increase in productivity will lead to acceleration of profit, and enhanced profit will promote savings and capital accumulation. Ricardo believed that greater productivity on the existing land could be achieved over the long run with the adoption of technology. The economy will achieve higher productivity from the land with the introduction of machinery and application of technology in agriculture. Ricardo was against the Corn Law, which was imposed to protect the farmers against foreign competition and he considered Corn Law as an obstacle to economic growth.

In the classical development analysis, capital accumulation, technological progress, division of labour, and free trade are the factors influencing the economic growth and development in an economy. The key players of an economy's economic growth and development are the farmers, producers, and businessmen. The free trade, enterprise, and competition empower the farmers, producers, and businessmen to expand the market and enhance productivity of the economy. The economic growth also continues as long as capital accumulation persists and new technologies are being introduced in the economy. This stage of momentum in the direction of higher and higher economic growth and development is called the 'progressive state'. However, the classists were of the view that the progressive state would not endure for long. The population growth and the competition for employment would reduce wage rate to the subsistent level in the market. In the same coin, competition among the capitalists in the economic system could bring down their profit. When this happens, the capital accumulation comes to halt and there is stagnation in income, savings, and investments in the economy. This state of affairs ultimately affects productivity and economic growth as a result; the economy then reaches the state of stagnation. This is known as 'Stationary State', which gradually moves towards 'Declining State'. The 'Stationary State' is dull and life of the people in this state becomes more or less standstill and monotonous; while in the 'Declining State', it becomes miserable. J.S. Mill in his wage fund theory suggested that a fund is to be created by the economy through the accumulation of capital for payment of wages to the labourer, called 'wage fund'. He was of the opinion that before undertaking any economic activities, adequate amount of capital must be acquired in the form of wage fund so that it would not be difficult on the part of the producer to pay the wage to the labourer. However, an increase in population can lower the wage rate unless it is accompanied by a corresponding increase in capital accumulation. Therefore, creation of wage fund is *sine qua non* in order to maintain a subsistence level of wage rate. However, because of diminishing return, it is always difficult on the part of the economy to maintain a wage fund, which ultimately affects capital formation, economic growth, and development of the economy. Almost all classical economists had a scathing attack on population growth as one of the factors that retards economic growth in the economy. Malthus was quite critical of population growth and was of the view that population growth is the core and the end product of the whole process of economic development and a high population growth in an economy would adversely affect its economic growth and development. Malthus' population theory is based on his famous formulations that population increases in a 'geometric progression (2,4,8,...)' and productivity grows at arithmetic progression (1,2,3,...). This formulation produces adverse effect on the economic growth and development of a nation. In order to check population growth, Malthus advocated 'Positive Checks' and 'Preventive Checks'. The positive checks are automatic and happen due to famine, starvation, and spread of epidemic, which cause deaths resulting in automatic reduction of population. On the other hand, preventive checks are those checks, which are pursued in the form of population control measures like adherence to small family norms, adoption of family planning methods, delayed marriage, and similar kind of population control measures.

To sum up, in the classical model, the high economic growth and development which is achieved with the dynamics of land, labour, capital, and technology ultimately ends in a 'stationary state'. The 'stationary state' in the opinion of classical economists is a stage where the development of an economy come to a halt. Some of the criticisms leveled against the classical theories are:

(i) It is based on the unrealistic assumption of perfect competition, particularly in the developing economies where the market is too much imperfect, the assumptions postulated by the classical economists will hardly work.

(ii) It ignores the role of state in development. The guided capitalism in Japan has proved to be the best role the state can play to guide the private and corporate sectors and engage them in economic growth and development process. Minimizing the role of the state in the economic growth and development process is too much impractical at least in the resource poor developing countries.

(iii) It ignores the role of human capital as it is supreme to all capital and the efficiency and effective functioning of all other capital depends on the skill, ingenuity, and dexterity of human capital. Without proper training and skill upgradation of manpower, it is difficult to achieve higher growth and development.

(iv) Last but not the least, a stationary state is an unrealistic one and is possible in the *laissez faire* economies. In the recent years, almost all economies are mixed economies, where the state is playing a proactive role in economic policy-making. As the state will take appropriate measure to drag the economy out of the state of stagnation and depression and it is happening in both developed as well as developing countries, the imagination of a stationary state is a distant possibility.

Marxian Theory

Karl Marx, the celebrated author of *Das Kapital* is one of the most influential classical thinkers, writers, philosophers, and development economists of the 19th century. The contribution of Marx to the contemporary world of development theory is stupendous and is well acclaimed. Marx was the only economist who equivocally predicated the downfall of capitalism and yearned for the advent of socialism. Marx, an ardent votary of socialism, said that capitalism is destined to collapse, not because of population growth, diminishing returns, or stagnation, but because of the inherent problem of class struggle. In Marxian theory of economic development, Marx has attempted to explain how contradiction in the capitalist system will lead to the downfall of this system, which will be replaced by socialism. The three important edifices of Marxian theory of development are the 'materialistic interpretation of history', 'the surplus value', and 'theory of the falling rate of profit and decline of capitalism'.

The materialistic interpretation of history is the starting point of Marxian theory of development. According to Marx, "Foundation and evolutionary cause of all social life is materialism". In the Marxian materialistic interpretation of history, all the historical events are influenced and determined by the economic conditions, while non-economic forces exert only meagre influence on historical developments. To Marx, every society passes through four different stages of transformation before it ultimately reaches an ideal state. The four different stages are the primitive communism, ancient slave stage, feudalism, and capitalism. In the first stage, the factors of production are owned and controlled by the community and individuals. While in other three stages, the group and particularly the influential group controls the factors of production and also the society. In the aforesaid three stages, the society is broadly divided into two groups such as dominant and suppressed or dominated. The dominant group owns all the means of production, while the suppressed contribute their labour in the process of production. Those dominant groups which capture all means of production are called 'capitalist' or 'bourgeois', and those which own only their labour and contribute labour in the production process are known as the 'labourer' or 'proletariat'. Capitalists accumulate enormous wealth by exploiting the labourer during the process of carrying out production. Which in the words of Marx's quotable quote is, "Accumulate, accumulate, that is Moses and prophet of capitalism". This disproportionate acquisition of wealth by a certain group of population in the society leads to class struggle between the 'haves', i.e. the capitalists, and the 'have nots', i.e. the labourers. This class struggle is inevitable in the capitalist society because of uneven distribution of resources and the accumulation of wealth by a certain section of the population who are small in number. Too much of exploitation and suppression will lead to the outburst, leading to the class struggle and ultimate collapse of the system.

According to Marx, the capitalist system is broadly classified into two classes, i.e. the capitalists and the labourers, and the capitalists own all the means of production and carry out production by deploying labourers in the production process. The labourer contributes labour, earns wages, and profit goes to the capitalists or in other words, one is bread owner and the other is bread earner. The foundation wall of the capitalist economy is constructed on the hard work of the labour and the hard work of the labourer produces 'surplus value', which is unscrupulously appropriated by the capitalist. The surplus value, which is over and above the wage and appropriated by the capitalist, is the extra labour of the worker for which he or she does not get any wage. In other words, the labourer toils not for enhancing his or her income but for accelerating the income and profit of the capitalists. The idea of 'surplus value' is a well thought out mechanism adopted by the capitalist to exploit labour. The profit motive is the Moses and prophet of capitalism. The profitability of the producer or capitalist depends directly on his capacity to exploit labour and indirectly on the organic composition of capital.[1] Surplus value is appropriated and enhanced by the capitalists in different ways: (a) by reducing the wage rates; (b) by extending the working hours, and (c) by increasing the productivity of labour through technological improvement. As the first two methods cannot be pursued for a long period, the capitalist, therefore, adopts the third method, increasing the productivity of labour by introducing technological improvements. The labour saving tool, 'the technology' adopted by the capitalists to enhance their profit creates an army of unemployed, which Marx calls 'industrial reserve army'. Technological change for enhancing labour productivity and for the acceleration of profit in the capitalist system is an inherent feature of Marxian theory of development. This is the main cause growing misery of the working class or the pauperization of the labour and enhanced affluence of the capitalists. The higher and higher capital accumulation and technological improvements increase the total output in the economy and enhance the surplus values for the capitalist.

Marxian theory predicts that there is an inherent limit to the increase in profit produced by each worker for the capitalists and exploitation mechanism adopted by the capitalist in the process of economic growth and development of the capitalist economy. According to Marx, this economic development path is self-destructive. In order to reap greater profits and ensure their existence in the economy, the capitalists tend to accumulate more and more capital by introducing technology into the production process, which can become disastrous for the capitalists in the long run. This will lead to the growing pauperization of the working class, which will ultimately lead to falling rates of profit. The desire to accumulate more and more profit, which acts as a boon for the capitalist in the short run, becomes a bane in the long run. The decline of the rate of profit is the result of capitalism's own internal dynamics, characterized by continual 'labour saving' technological change, which replaces workers with machines. The gradual decline of profit is the beginning of the downfall of the capitalism. According to Marx, all these measures adopted by the capitalists to enhance the rate of profit prove to be self-defeating and self-destructive for the capitalists. In the short run, it will produce economic fluctuations and in the long run, these factors lead to the breakdown of the capitalist system, as Marx put it 'capitalism is doomed to decay'. As Marx rightly put it, "The true barrier to capital is capital itself". The downfall of capitalism will lead to the advent of the socialistic economic system.

Some of the criticisms labelled against Marxian theory are as follows: (a) the materialistic interpretation of history as given by Marx is too much idealistic; (b) as far as the theory of surplus value and calculation of surplus value is concerned, it is quite cumbersome as in recent years, everything is calculated in terms of tangible prices; and (c) lastly, in the words of Marx, capitalism is doomed to decay is not true and most of the economies in the world are mixed economies with features of both capitalism and socialism. The capitalist systems nowadays are economically more powerful and people are enjoying a good quality of living.

NEO-CLASSICAL MODEL OF DEVELOPMENT

HARROD–DOMAR MODEL

The Harrod–Domar model gives an account of the economic mechanism, which proclaims that more savings in an economy lead to more investment and more investment accelerates the pace of growth rate. Harrod–Domar model propounded that the economic growth rate of an economy fundamentally depends on two things: (a) The level of savings: higher savings enables higher investment which leads to higher income and higher growth rate; (b) the level of capital-output ratio: capital output ratio, which implies efficiency of investment. The capital-output ratio means a unit of capital required to produce a unit of output over a given period of time. Lower is the capital-output ratio more efficient is the invested capital. In other words, the lower the ratio, the better the investment. On the contrary, the higher the ratio, the costlier the investment, and it does not entice the investors to invest in the economy. According to Harrod–Domar model, the economy must do investment of such an amount of saving which would maintain full employment level of income, and the growth of an economy is directly related to savings, the more the economy is able to save out of a given GDP, the greater will be the GDP growth rate. Harrod–Domar model added the concept of capital-output ratio, which is essentially intended to measure the efficiency in productivity in terms of capital invested in an economy. If the capital output ratio is low, then the economy can produce a lot of output with the help of a small amount of capital; and on the contrary, if capital-output ratio is high, then the economy requires a lot of capital for production of a certain quantity of output. In other words, the invested capital will not get as much value of output as desired out of the invested amount of capital. Thus, the growth rate of an economy has an indirect relationship with the capital-output ratio, that is the higher the capital-output ratio, the lower the growth rate, and vice versa, and direct relationship with saving, i.e. the higher the saving, the higher is the capital formation, which will lead to higher growth rate. The Harrod–Domar model is based on the notion that increased amount of savings increases the investment, which will enhance the capital stock, and increased capital stock raises output and income and ultimately affects the growth rate of an economy. To put the increase in output in equation is $\frac{\Delta Y}{Y}$ and in the Harrod–Domar model of economic growth is the rate of growth of GDP, which is jointly determined by the net national saving ratio, symbolically which is 's', in an economy and the national capital output ratio, which is symbolically is 'k', and the famous relationship between them to put it in the form of an equation is $\frac{s}{k}$. The equation depicts that the growth rate of an economy is directly related to savings that is higher is the rate of saving higher will be the economic growth rate; and inversely related to capital output ratio means lower is the capital output ratio higher will be the economic growth rate and vice versa.[2]

Harrod–Domar model has devised three distinct types of growth rate, i.e. actual growth rate, warranted growth rate, and natural growth rate. The actual growth rate is determined by savings and investments, and this is the growth rate which the economy actually achieves with its volume of saving and investment in its hand. The warranted growth rate is the growth rate which the economy is required to achieve in order to fully utilize its manpower and machines, it is otherwise known as 'equilibrium growth rate' where planned saving becomes equal to planned investment. According to Harrod, it is the rate 'at which producers will be content with what they are doing'. At the warranted growth rate, the demand for goods produced by the businessmen is high, which encourages them to sell their produce as it is primarily related to the profit-maximizing behaviour of businessmen. The warranted growth rate is necessary to absorb society's savings into various investment projects in order to accelerate its pace of economic growth rate. The natural growth rate is the maximum possible growth rate, which the economy is required to achieve with the existing stock of capital, labour force, natural resources, and the state of technology in the long run in order to attain full employment. It is otherwise known as 'full employment growth rate'. The equality between these growth rates can ensure full utilization of manpower and technology in an economy. However, any divergence from the equilibrium of these three types of growth rate will lead to a state of instability, which according to the Harrod–Domar model is called 'knife-edge equilibrium' problem.

Harrod–Domar model predicts that it is very difficult on the part of the economy to maintain equilibrium among these three different growth rates and particularly between the actual and warranted growth rate and once the equilibrium is disrupted, the economy would persistently move away from the equilibrium. Therefore, according to Harrod–Domar, the economy will not be able to automatically attain equilibrium as proclaimed by the classical economists. The major task of the economy or the government is to prevent divergence between these three different types of growth rates in order to maintain long-run stability in the economy. The criticism leveled against Harrod–Domar model is that it has not addressed issues like quality of infrastructure, institutional capacity, attitudinal conditions, the bureaucratic efficiency and effectiveness, and the political stability in the economy. Most of the developing countries are lacking in these spheres. The Marshall Plan worked for Europe because the European countries receiving aid possessed the necessary structural, institutional, and attitudinal conditions (e.g. well-integrated commodity and money markets, highly developed transport facilities, a well-trained and educated workforce, the motivation to succeed, an efficient government bureaucracy) to convert new capital effectively into higher output (Todaro and Smith, 2012). Despite shortcoming, the Harrod–Domar model is beneficial to developed countries to overcome secular stagnation and a lesson for underdeveloped countries to augment economic growth by introducing fiscal and monetary policy measures to accelerate savings in the economy. According to Kurihara (1959):

> Harrod–Domar model is a stimulating attempt not only to dynamic and secular Keynes's static short-run saving investment theory, but also it is capable of being modified so as to introduce fiscal policy parameters as explicit variables in the economic growth of an underdeveloped country.

Kurihara (1959) further noted that:

> ...these growth models have the positive lesson for underdeveloped economies that state should be allowed to play not a stabilizing role but also a developmental role in these economies to industrialize more effectively and rapidly than the new industrialized economies did in condition of *laissez faire*.

Robert Solow's Model

Robert Solow is one of the outstanding and well-acclaimed classical economic growth and development theorists. The departure of Solow's neo-classical theory from the Harrod–Domar model is that the economy can achieve a steady state of growth, instead of 'knife-edge equilibrium' as perceived in Harrod–Domar model. According to Solow, the growth process is a stable one and not unstable as propounded by Harrod–Domar. It is remarked that Solow's model is one of the most influential neo-classical growth models and one that has shaped much modern thinking about the processes of economic growth (Cypher and Dietz, 2006). It is well extolled that the second wave of interest in growth theory was launched by the development of the neo-classical model propounded by Robert Solow (Hagemann, 2009).

The important aspects of Solow's growth model are: (a) capital is fundamental to economic development; (b) exogenous technological changes; (c) convergence of income per capita; and (d) diminishing return and steady state. According to Solow, acceleration of capital formation through savings and investments is fundamental to economic growth and development of an economy. The countries which are poor or not growing fast may be because of the reason that they might not be saving and investing a sufficient proportion of their gross national income. Higher rate of savings and investment are critical inputs for higher economic growth rate. Therefore, higher capital formation through the higher rate of savings and investments needs to be the developmental motto of the nation intending to enhance the economic growth rate and through it aim at raising the standard of living of its population. Solow considers that technological changes are exogenous factors to influence economic growth rate of an economy, because he assumes that the technological changes are available to the economy, both developed as well as underdeveloped, at the same rate. It is this exogenous technological factor, which is central to the higher level of income per capita over time. If the technology and the rate of increased use of labour force remain constant, a Solow type of growth model predicts that with an increase in the saving and investment, the economy will achieve a steady rate of growth in income. The Solow model assumes that two types of economy, i.e. rich or developed economy and poor or underdeveloped economy, will converge to the same level of income if they have the same rates of savings, investments, and population growth rate. He also went to the extent of predicting that assuming the equal rate of saving, investment, and growth rate of population, the poorer nations will grow faster than the richer nations. The model further predicts that the closed economy having lower rate of savings and investments will enjoy lower growth rate and converge to lower per capita income, while an open economy with the higher rate of savings and investments will have higher growth rate and will converge to higher income. Solow's neo-classical model like the classical model assumes that diminishing returns will ultimately set in to the factors of production used in the production process in an economy. It believes that any amount of increase in the level of savings and investments and any addition to the physical capital, i.e. machinery or technology, to the production process after a certain point of time, that is where the input and output combination is at equilibrium, will not lead to higher growth rate in income, this is otherwise known as the 'steady state' as also predicted even by the classical economists. After this stage of 'steady state' of the economy, any further increase in application of capital will not lead to growth of income; rather, it will start to diminish. Thus, diminishing return will set in after the phase of the 'steady state' of an economy.

The Solow model provides an important and vital basis for the analysis of growth process, which has a lot of implications for both developed as well as developing countries of the world. According to Solow formulation, countries which are poor and not growing faster are thus poor because they are not saving and investing a sufficiently high proportion of their gross national income. Countries wanting to attain faster economic growth rate and intending to raise the standard of living of its population have to save and invest an increasingly high proportion of their national income. Solow's model has been and continues to be an important starting point for many economists in theorizing about the underlying forces at work, which influence the process of economic growth in the real-world economies (Cypher and Dietz, 2006). However, Solow model has also been criticized for its unrealistic assumptions. The neo-classical growth model has several weaknesses, and important criticism labelled against is the assumption that the technological change is exogenous to development and the level of technology is the same throughout the world and is unrealistic. Even the technology is equally available for both a developed and an underdeveloped country, and even two underdeveloped countries, the country having *techno-sauve* and technologically skilled manpower, will attain faster economic growth rate and development than the one which is deficient of the same. By predicting the 'steady state' and diminishing return, the Solow model also succumbs to the same conjecture like those of the classical theorists. Romer (1986) also argued that the tendency towards diminishing returns, which is the central feature of the neo-classical growth model, is perhaps exaggerated.

The Sum Up

The classical and neo-classical theories are the cornerstone of development theories. These are the foundation stones on which all other theories of development have been largely constructed. The classical theories of development given by Adam Smith, David Ricardo, T.R. Malthus, and J.S. Mill advocated that the development of an economy means increase in output or national productivity, which depends on four factors, i.e. (a) size of labour force (*L*); (b) the stock of capital (*K*); (c) the amount of available natural resources (*N*) or the land; and (d) available technology (*T*). The classical theorists believe that increase in output depends on the availability of land, labour, capital, and technology in an economy. The application of all these factors of production and technology in the land enhances productivity, which in turn, depends on the level of saving, investment, and capital formation. In the classical model, the end result of economic progress is 'stationary state'. The 'stationary state' in the opinion of classical economists is a stage where the development in an economy came to halt. The Marxian theory of economic development explains how internal contradiction in the capitalist system may lead to downfall of this system, which will be replaced by socialism. Marx, an ardent votary of socialism said that capitalism is destined to collapse, not because of population growth, diminishing returns, or stagnation, but because of inherent problem of class struggle. According to Harrod–Domar model, the economy must invest such an amount of saving which would maintain full employment level of income in order to accelerate its economic growth rate and development. The model denotes that the growth of an economy is directly related to savings, the more the economy saves out of a given GDP, the greater will be the GDP growth rate. Harrod–Domar model added the concept of capital-output ratio, which is essentially intended to measure the efficiency of productivity in terms of capital invested in an economy. The proponent of neo-classical theory advocated that capital formation is fundamental to economic growth and development, which ultimately depends on savings and investment. Solow type of growth model predicts that with an increase in the saving and investment, the economy will achieve a steady rate of growth in income. The Solow model assumes that two types of economy, i.e. rich or developed economy and poor or underdeveloped economy, will converge to the same level of income if they have the same rates of savings, investments, and population growth rate. He also went to the extent of predicting that assuming the equal rate of saving, investment, and growth rate of population, the poorer nations will grow faster than the richer nations. Like the classical theorists, Solow expounded that the economy will reach the 'steady state' because of diminishing returns. Many of the interpretations of both classical and neo-classical theories have contemporary relevance to both developed and developing countries.

Keywords surplus value, invisible hand, Say's law of market, *laissez faire*, razor-edge equilibrium, steady state.

REVIEW QUESTIONS

1. Critically discuss the classical theory of development.
2. Explain the various features of Marxian theory and discuss its relevance to the underdeveloped countries.
3. How is Harrod–Domar model relevant for the underdeveloped countries? Discuss its relevance by critically analyzing its features.
4. Write short notes on the following:
   (i) Theory of surplus value
   (ii) Malthus view on population and development
   (iii) Knife-edge equilibrium
   (iv) Features of neo-classical theory of development
   (v) Analyze the stage of stationary state in classical theory
   (vi) Materialistic interpretation of history
5. Critically analyze the Solow's theory of economic growth and development.

NOTES

1. Marx's theory of surplus value can be explained by the following set of equations:

   (i) $Y = C + V + S$
   (ii) $s = S/V$
   (iii) $k = C/(C + V)$
   (iv) $\pi = S/(C + V) = s(1 - k)$*

Where Y = total income, C = constant capital, V = variable capital, S = surplus value, s = rate of surplus value, k = organic composition of capital (capital intensity), and π = rate of profit.

This equation shows that π is directly related to s and inversely related to k. It means that the profit of the producer directly depends on his capacity to exploit labour and indirectly on the organic composition of capital. The 'organic composition of capital' is the ratio of fixed capital that is machinery to the variable capital that is labour power. Due to competition, the capitalist tries to raise productivity through the application of more and more technology into the production process and, thus in turn, the organic composition of capital grows. It means that the rate of profit increases with the rise in exploitation of labour and falls with the rise in constant capital. Therefore, the capitalist suffers from continual reduction of his profit and profitability with the increased application of technology into the production process.

The equational representation of surplus value is as follows:

*$\pi = s(1 - k)$ can be proved through equational representation as formulated below:

$$\pi = \frac{S}{(C+V)}$$

By multiplying both the numerator and denominator by V, the equation becomes:

$$\pi = \frac{SV}{V(C+V)}$$

Then, by adding and subtracting SC in numeration, the equation becomes:

$$= \frac{SV + SC - SC}{V(C+V)}$$

$$= \frac{S(C+V) - SC}{V(C+V)}$$

$$= \frac{S(C+V)}{V(C+V)} - \frac{SC}{V(C+V)}$$

$$= \frac{S}{V} - \frac{SC}{V(C+V)}$$

$$= \frac{S}{V}\left[1 - \frac{C}{(C+V)}\right]$$

$$= s\,[1 - k]$$

2. From the Harrod–Domar model, we learn that if an economy wishes to achieve higher growth rate, the most fundamental strategy is to increase the proportion of national income saved. For example, if a developing economy has low capital-output ratio, say 2, and the aggregate net saving ratio is supposed to be 8 per cent of GDP, then the country can grow at the rate of 4 per cent [equation (i)]

$$\frac{\Delta Y}{Y} = \frac{s}{k} = \frac{8\%}{2} = 4\% \tag{i}$$

Now, suppose the national saving rate of the country with the endeavour of the government measures through i.e. the increased in taxes, forced savings measures, foreign aid and general consumption sacrifices increased from 8 to 16 per cent—the GDP growth will shoot up from a lower rate of 4 per cent to a higher growth rate of 8 per cent [equation (ii)]

$$\frac{\Delta Y}{Y} = \frac{s}{k} = \frac{16\%}{2} = 8\% \tag{ii}$$

REFERENCES

Cypher, James M. and Dietz, James L. 2006. *The Process of Economic Development*. New York: Routledge.
Hagemann, H. 2009. "Solow's 1956 Contribution in the Context of the Harrod–Domar Model." *History of Political Economy*, 41(1): 67–87.
Kurihara, K.K. 1959. *The Keynesian Theory of Economic Development*. New York: Columbia University Press.
Romer, P. 1986. "Increasing Returns and Long-run Growth." *Journal of Political Economy*, 94(October): 1002–37.
Smith, A. 1776. *An Inquiry into the Nature and Causes of the Wealth of Nations*. Chicago, IL: University of Chicago Press.
Todaro, M.P. and Smith, S.C. 2012. *Economic Development*. Tenth edition. New Delhi: Pearson.

SUGGESTED READINGS

Domar, E.D. 1957. *Essays in the Theory of Economic Growth*. Oxford and New York: Oxford University Press.
Harrod, R.F. 1948. *Towards a Dynamic Economics: Some Recent Developments of Economic Theory and Their Application to Policy*. London: Macmillan.
Malthus, T.R. 1798. *An Essay on the Principle of Population*. London: St. Paul's Church-Yard.
Marx, K. 1977. *A Contribution to the Critique of Political Economy*. Moscow: Progress Publisher.
———. 1853. "The Future Results of the British Rule in India." *New York Daily Tribune*, No. 3840, 8 August.
Mill, J.S. 1948. *Principles of Political Economy with Some of their Application to Social Philosophy*. First edition. London: John W. Parker.
Nafziger, E.W. 2012. *Economic Development*. Sixth edition. New York: Cambridge University Press.
Ricardo, D. 2001. *On the Principles of Political Economy and Taxation*. Kitchener, Ontario, Canada: Batoche Books.
Romer, P.M. 1990. "Endogenous Technical Change." *Journal of Political Economy*, 98(5): S71–S102.

3 Developmentalist Theory of Development

The idea of developmentalism and the developmental state is often referred to as a post World War II phenomenon.

— Reinert (2010)

The post Second World War approach towards development was primarily developmental in nature, aimed at dealing with the development problems of the underdeveloped countries, in contrast to the orthodox classical and neo-classical theories, which were largely economic growth theories based on the scenario of the developed economies of the West. The classical and neo-classical economists have largely emphasized that economic growth of an economy can be accelerated through capital formation, which is possible through the enhancement of the savings and investment. On the contrary, the developmentalist theorists have propounded various ways and processes by which not only the economic growth rate but also the holistic multidimensional development of the underdeveloped economies can be promoted. They have propounded various ways, such as modernization, industrialization, infrastructure development, technological advancement, transfer of labour from the primary sector to the secondary sector, a strong developmental State, development of rural areas, and good governance through which the underdeveloped countries can achieve higher economic growth rate and development. Most of the developmental theories as propounded by various exponents are based on their research work in the developing countries of Latin America, Africa, and Asia.[1] The leading developmentalists of the post-Second World War period were Ragnar Nurkse, Paul Rosenstein-Rodan, Albert Hirschman, Arthur Lewis, Leibenstein, and W.W. Rostow.

Just as a war cannot be won without a suitable battle strategy, similarly the objective of higher economic growth rate and rapid development cannot be attained without the formulation and adoption of appropriate development strategies. The development strategies would help the nation to search for resources and formulate appropriate planning and implementation mechanisms. The development theories propounded by the developmentalists have advocated different development strategies for the development of the underdeveloped countries. Two important strategies advocated by the developmental theorists are balanced and unbalanced growth theories. Balanced growth theorists were of the view that for the attainment of the higher economic growth rate and faster development, underdeveloped countries have to follow a balanced investment approach in the various sectors of the economy whereas the propounders of the unbalanced theories advocated that as the underdeveloped countries have paucity of financial resources and hence are incapable of investing in a balanced way in various sectors of the economy, therefore, the appropriate strategy for them would be, to invest in a selected sector in an unbalanced manner, which would gradually provide impetus to the investments in other sectors and facilitate holistic development of the underdeveloped countries.

After reading this chapter, you will be able to:

(i) Explain balanced and unbalanced growth theories and their thrust areas.
(ii) Analyze Lewis theory of unlimited supply of labour and Harris–Todaro labour migration theory and explain how labour and development are interrelated.
(iii) Discuss the developmental theories propounded by Peter Evans and Gunnar Myrdal and understand the Harris–Todaro model of labour migration.

BALANCED GROWTH THEORY

Paul Rosenstein-Rodan is an illustrious propounder of balanced growth approach and his big-push theory is considered as an outstanding piece of work in development economics.[2] The big-push theory is based on his studies conducted on a number of poor Eastern and South-East European nations during the period of the Second World War. The big-push theory is based on the premises that in the countries where growth and development has not taken place or is yet to take place, a certain amount of big investment and a big economic push is required, in order to pull these economies out of the clutches of the economic backwardness and underdevelopment and propel them towards the state of economic prosperity and progress. Rosenstein-Rodan was of the view that if the economic development programme was to be initiated in the true and effective sense in the underdeveloped countries, where development is in a nascent stage, the governments of these nations have to follow a 'big-push' approach.[3] The theory advocates that the large-scale investments through big-push approach, are able to create effectively an entire developmental structure in one go. However, any attempt to investment in 'piece meal' would not produce the desirable result and would fail to provide the impetus to drag these countries away from the despondency of underdevelopment. The large-scale investment in the field of 'social overhead capital', i.e. investment in roads, bridges, railways, docks, hospitals, schools, colleges, irrigation, communication networks, and so on will provide necessary infrastructural support to the economy, augment economic growth, and enhance employment opportunities. These huge amounts of investments are required because of 'the indivisibilities' characteristics of social overhead capital and these are abiding physical assets necessary for economic development of the underdeveloped economies. It will also create positive externalities in these economies. Besides construction of infrastructure, huge investment is also required for the industrialization of the these economies and industrialization through big-push approach will not only facilitate structural transformation but also enable these economies to transfer a huge surplus manpower from agriculture sector to the industry sector and as a result the persistent problem of disguised unemployment prevalent in agriculture sector would be mitigated. However, construction of infrastructure and establishment of industry is not possible through small and piecemeal investments and endeavours by the individual entrepreneurs, but needs a big-push investment by the government. The big-push theory advocated that a large amount of investment requires a high volume of savings, the high volume of savings in the developing countries would be made possible only through the large-scale investments concurrently undertaken by the market, by the government, and also through foreign investment. These large-scale investments, if undertaken by the various sectors of development will create employment, boost productivity, and increase income and consequently enhance savings in the economy. As 'big push' of investment in the industrial sector would bring technological revolution in these economies, training of workforce is vital for the augmentation of this developmental momentum. Therefore, Rosenstein-Rodan's big-push theory suggested the capacity building of the workforce employed in both primary and secondary sector. In the words of Rosenstein-Rodan (1944):

> The first task of industrialization is to provide for training and 'skilling' of labour which is to transform peasants into full-time or part-time industrial workers...although it is not a good investment for a private firm it is the best investment for the State.

Although the big-push theory propounded by Rosenstein-Rodan has many limitations, such as resources' inadequacy in the underdeveloped countries, attracting foreign investment, and too much emphasis on indivisibilities. yet it has much relevance for the underdeveloped economies.

Ragnar Nurkse was a well-acclaimed developmental economist and is well known for his work on theory of balanced growth. The balanced growth theory propounded by Ragnar Nurkse states that the underdeveloped economies are unable to develop because of three reasons, i.e. vicious circle of poverty, low capital formation, and small size of its market. These economies are basically poor, because their productivity per worker is low and the low productivity is due to low investment and low investment happens because of low savings, which creates a vicious circle. Because of this vicious circle, the circular constellation of forces tends to act and react upon one another in such a way as to keep a poor country in a state of poverty and economic backwardness. This vicious circle happens to operate from both sides:

(i) On the demand side: low demand for goods leads to low investment, low investment leads to low production, low production results in low employment, low employment leads to low income, and low income finally leads to low demand.
(ii) On the supply side: low supply of capital leads to low investment, low investment leads to low production, low production results in low employment, low income, and low savings, low savings ultimately results in low investment and low investment will lead to low capital formation.

A quotable quote that says, "A country is poor because it is poor" well fits the case of underdeveloped countries. In these vicious conditions, a paltry dose of increase in investment and small amount of capital formation would not be able to lift these economies out of the trap of vicious circle of poverty. In the same coin, any market based strategy of promoting capital formation with the help of individual entrepreneurs or single industry in any particular sector may not be capable enough to find a solution to the development problems of these underdeveloped countries. Nurkse like Rosenstein-Rodan, favoured a large dose of investment with balanced growth approach spread across a broad range of sectors in order to break the vicious circle of poverty existing in underdeveloped economies.[4]

For the successful achievement of balanced growth, developing economies have to, firstly, promote their export potential of finished high-value products, because the export of tropical products or raw materials and import of finished product, i.e. machinery, equipment, and manufactured consumer goods by the underdeveloped economies from the developed countries would create trade imbalance and consequently have adverse impact on economic development of the developing countries. Secondly, he was in favour of a dynamic fiscal policy and advocated forced saving through taxes on upper income group, public borrowing, and deficit financing to meet the financial requirement in order to pursue and implement the strategies of balanced growth. Thirdly, he was of the view that in the developing countries the domestic industries must be encouraged to increase their capital formation and raise their productivity and enhance their market. To quote Nurkse (1953), financing for development has to come mainly from within the country as there is a clear danger that significant amounts of foreign financing would end up funding private consumption patterns emulating Western living standards and thus creating balance of payment problems. Finally, Nurkse was of the opinion that the role of government is critical to balanced development and he advocated that the government of the underdeveloped nations must initiate appropriate steps and measures to promote public cooperation and participation in the process of economic development. Like Rosenstein-Rodan, Nurkse strongly believed that underdeveloped economies have immense potential for progress and it must be properly harnessed, so that they can move on the path of balanced growth and development. Although Ragnar Nurkse has given one of the most illuminating theories of development, yet balanced development of developing countries with huge investment is practically impossible especially in the era of globalization where most of the developing countries are dependent on foreign direct investment (FDI); Nurkse's emphasis on country's own investment capabilities without depending on FDI is a difficult proposition.

Harvey Leibenstein's critical minimum effort theory advocates that in the underdeveloped economies, in order to achieve the transition from the state of backwardness to a state of more development, where the economy can expect steady secular growth, it is necessary, that these economies should receive a stimulus to growth that is greater than a certain minimum size, because, these economies are largely suffering from 'vicious circle of poverty', which is negatively affecting their income, savings, investments, and growth rate. A critical minimum level of investments and savings would be helpful to overcome the inertia of underdevelopment and pull these economies out of the trap of underdevelopment. In the opinion of Leibenstein, every economy is influenced and affected by two vital forces namely 'stimulant forces' and 'forces of shocks'. Stimulant forces give impetus and generate drive which increases level of savings, investments, income, and output in an economy, while, the 'forces of shocks' act as distractors to development which reduces the level of output, income, savings, and investments of an economy. The former are treated as income-generating forces and the latter as income-depressing forces. In an underdeveloped economy, the forces of shocks outstrip forces of stimulants, therefore, in the long run, economic development either does not takes place, or even if it takes place, it cannot sustain for a long period because of the meagre magnitude of stimulants. To break the vicious circle of poverty, hunger, socio-economic backwardness, and economic imperfections in underdeveloped economies, critical minimum effort is *sine qua non* for dragging the economy from the shocks and put the economy on the path of sustained economic growth and development. Certain factors influencing the stimulant forces according to Leibenstein are: (a) attitude, motivation, and incentives to actions deployed in the process of development and (b) role of growth agents in the development process and relationship between population growth rate and economic growth rate. The growth agents are critical mass of actors who carry forward the message of growth throughout the economy. He promotes, encourages, and sustains positive-sum activities which are essential for the growth of the country. The growth agents of various sectors of an economy are entrepreneurs, inventors, discoverers, teachers, and trainers of new knowledge and skills required for development of an economy. According to Leibenstein, growth agents are those individuals who have the capacities to carry out the growth contributing activities. In the Leibenstein growth model, economic growth does not take place automatically, it is rather to be instigated and stimulated. The actors involved in the economic growth process, i.e. the entrepreneurs, the inventors, the discoverers, and the innovators have to be given zero-sum incentives for those activities which produce zero effect on economic growth and positive-sum incentives for those activities which exert positive impact on economic growth. The zero-sum incentive consists of trading risks, non-trading or speculative activities, and transference of income and profit from one section of people to another. On the other hand, positive-sum incentives include the productive investment, use of technical know-how, exploration and exploitation of new market, and use of scientific discoveries and innovations. The positive-sum activities raise the savings, investments, income, and employment opportunities in the economy; while the zero-sum activities do not produce conducive effects on the national income and growth rate. Some of the factors which produce depressing impact on economic development are conservative attitude, lack of innovations among entrepreneurs, high capital-output ratio, population growth, resistance to charge, and unproductive expenditure. Leibenstein considered that population growth and economic growth are intrinsically related, as high population growth causes economic backwardness. High population growth necessitates greater minimum effort to provide basic minimum needs and employment to the large population. According to Leibenstein, "The point at which fertility decline sets in will determine the height of the critical minimum level". In his view, the role of population growth is an increasing function of per capita income up to certain level income, after that it is a decreasing function of income, because of high cost of rearing a family. Therefore, he was of the opinion that the economy need not to wait till the decline in population growth act as a drag on economic development. Controlling population growth in necessary but not a precondition to economic growth, as the economic growth depends on many other factors other than population growth, such as availability of natural resources, capital, and so on. In Leibenstein's view, the relationship between population growth and economic growth is based on Dumont's 'social capillarity thesis' which says that as income increases, the desire to have additional children among the population declines, resulting in rise in per capita income of population in the economy. The critical minimum effort theory propounded by Leibenstein exerts that minimum effort strategy is the only answer to the economic backwardness of an underdeveloped economy. It can help the economy to come out of the clutches of vicious circle of poverty and put economy on the path of sustainable economic development. However, as most of the countries are facing the problem of capital formation, therefore, investment in social overhead capital is found to be very low. Although Leibenstein's theory of critical minimum effort sounds well for the underdeveloped countries, yet in these resource-poor countries, arrangement of critical minimum of capital for investments is a herculean task.

UNBALANCED GROWTH THEORY

One of the leading developmentalists of the unbalanced growth theory was Hirschman. Hirschman was one of the pioneers in the field of development economics, who was involved in the process of reconstruction of devastated European economies after the Second World War. His practical experience and involvement in the economic affairs in the reconstruction of the economy of Colombia provided him with adequate food for thought on economic development. He propounded the doctrine of 'unbalanced growth' in his illustrious book *Strategy of Economic Development*. The basic idea behind suggesting a model of unbalanced growth for the development of underdeveloped countries according to Hirschman is that as the underdeveloped countries have paucity of capital and other resources, therefore, they cannot be in a position to invest huge amount of capital required for holistic development of all sectors of their economy at one go. Therefore, it is wise on their part to invest their scarce resources in a selected few priority sectors and later on, the benefits derived from these sectors can be further utilized for the development of other sectors. This process will enable the economies of the underdeveloped countries to gradually move from the path of unbalanced growth to balanced growth and from the situation of underdevelopment towards path of higher growth and development. Therefore, he suggested that in order to achieve balanced development, an economy has to create a series of imbalances which would be constantly created and adjusted and it is the imbalance between different sectors which will later create balanced economic growth and development. As has been maintained by Hirschman (1958) that:

Development is a chain of disequilibria that must be kept alive rather than eliminate disequilibrium of which profits and losses are symptoms in a competitive economy. If economy is to be kept moving ahead, the task of development policy is to maintain tensions, disproportions and disequilibria.

The two vital components of Hirschman theory of unbalanced growth are: (a) social overhead capitals (SOCs) and directly productive activities (DPAs) and (b) backward and forward linkages. The SOCs includes all public services, i.e. law and order, education, public health, road transportation, communications, power, water supply, irrigation, drainage, etc. which are required for development and provide boost to the take-off of the economy. DPAs are the consequences of SOCs which adds to the flow of final goods and services. As the SOCs are infrastructure-related activities, therefore these have to be provided by the government, and obviously private sector being guided by the profit motive will be least interested to invest in SOCs. However, the investment in SOCs by the public sector will boost DPAs by the private investors in agriculture and industrial sectors and also in tertiary sector. The DPAs in the agriculture will enhance food grain productivity and in industrial sector, per se steel industry sector will increase productivity of steel items, which will ultimately boost employment and economic growth rate of the economy and in the tertiary sector it will enhance education, health, banking, and insurance sector activities.

The four characteristics that distinguish SOC from DPA are:

(i) SOC is basic to (and facilitates) a great variety of economic activities and provides stepping stone to economic growth and development.
(ii) It is typically provided by the public sector or by regulated private agencies as it requires huge investment.

(iii) It cannot be imported, as it has to be built within the economy.
(iv) It is 'lumpy' in the sense of technical indivisibilities which is a unique feature of SOC.

It is argued that the function of SOCs investment is to 'ignite' DPAs and the investment in SOC is advocated not because of its direct effect on final output, but because it permits and in fact invites and encourages DPAs to come in. Thus, by this process, the imbalance in the economy can be created by initiating actions on SOCs which ultimately put pressure on DPAs to come in: and there it is argued and even assumed that from the standpoint of resource crunch, in underdeveloped economies SOCs and DPAs cannot be expanded simultaneously. The expansion of the SOCs needs to be done vigorously, so that it would maximize induced decision making in DPAs. In short, the best strategy to promote economic development is to create deliberate imbalances in the economy.

The second important aspect of Hirschman theory of economic development is forward and backward linkages. He argued that investments should occur in industries that have the greatest backward and forward linkages: the backward linkages will enhance the selling of inputs by the entrepreneurs to the industries, while the forward linkages will boost up units that buy output from the industries. For example, establishment of steel industry would enhance the demand for coal and iron ore and related goods. This linkage is called 'Backward Linkages', which will promote activities and employment in the coal and iron sector as well. In the same coin, expansion of steel industries would also lead to expansion of industries making use of steel product such as steel furniture, steel home appliances, and steel machine and tools. This linkage is called 'Forward Linkages'. In Hirschman's unbalanced growth process, the size of potential of backward and forward linkages was of paramount importance in evaluating where to locate the initial investment (Cypher and Ditez, 2006). Development strategies and investments in the developing countries needed to be built around and be made in those key strategic sector or industry that produces maximum amount of forward and backward linkages. Hirschman believes that the undeveloped countries have immense potential to achieve higher growth rate and advocated that these countries can be put on the economic growth path through unbalanced growth process. It is but natural that while unbalancing development in one sector, the other sector becomes worse off, leading to what Hirschman termed as an 'antagonistic growth', but gradually the balance will be restored and both the sectors will grow at an equal pace. In the words of Hirschman (1958), economic development typically follows a path of uneven growth, where balance is restored as result of pressure, incentives, and compulsions, which is the efficient path towards economic development. One of the disadvantages of the Hirschman theory is that it lays too much emphasis on big investment which most of the underdeveloped countries may not be able to meet. Also, it does not spell out the degree of imbalances to be created in an economy, in order to attain sustainable economic growth. In the words of Streeten (1963), in so far as unbalance does create desirable attitudes, the crucial question is not whether to create unbalance, but 'what' is the 'optimum' degree of unbalance, 'where' to unbalance, and 'how much', in order to accelerate growth, which are the 'growing points', where should the spearheads be thrust, on which slope would snowballs grow into avalanches?

ROSTOW'S STAGES OF ECONOMIC GROWTH

Many developmental economists were of the view that a country passes through many stages during its process of development. To begin with, Adam Smith believed that the underdeveloped countries went through the stages of hunting, pastoral, agricultural, and manufacturing before they reached the high level of economic growth. Karl Marx, in his materialistic interpretation of history also envisaged that the society passes through various stages, i.e. the primitive society, ancient slave stage, feudalism, capitalism, and socialism. One of the profound protagonists of stages of economic growth was W.W. Rostow. Rostow in his classic book *The Stages of Economic Growth: A Non-Communist Manifesto* published in 1960, propounded that countries would pass through five stages of development process before they achieve the hallmark of high economic growth.

The five stages are: (a) the traditional society, (b) the pre-conditions of take-off, (c) the take-off, (d) the drive to maturity, and (e) age of high mass consumption.

According to Rostow (1960):

> The stages are not merely descriptions. They are not merely a way of generalizing certain factual observations about the sequence of development of modern societies. They have an inner logic and continuity; they have an analytical bone-structure rooted in a dynamic theory of production.

Rostow's theory is considered as one of the variants of unbalanced growth theories. The key features of Rostow's stages of economic growth are:

(i) The Traditional Society: The traditional societies are customarily the primitive societies, where the main occupation of the people is agriculture. Agriculture is basically done with the help of primitive technology and people usually lack basic knowledge about the use of science and technology. The traditional knowledge system governs the way of living. However, it could be mentioned that although the development process in the traditional society was not static, yet, was very slothful in terms of adoption of technology and therefore the level of productivity and income was low. The knowledge and attitude of people towards development is poor and rigid. Rostow has described traditional society, "...as one, whose structure is developed within limited production functions based on pre-Newtonian science and technology and Pre-Newtonian attitudes towards physical world". The 'framework of mind' conducive to modern science was non-existent in these pre-Newtonian societies, which possessed a 'long-term fatalism' and a 'ceiling on the productivity of their economic techniques' (Rostow, 1960). It is believed and even emphasized that the knowledge about the traditional societies would provide critical inputs to diagnose the problems of future development.

(ii) The Precondition of Take-off: During the precondition of take-off stage, social, economic, and political changes take place in the traditional societies. The economic progress is triggered off with the development of transport and communication system and advancement of science and technology. The adoption of technology in agriculture brings radical changes in agriculture enabling it to enhance productivity. Later on, emphasis on industrialization and foreign trade bring in more stride into the economy. At this state, change in knowledge, attitude, appreciation, and values of people towards transition takes place, which provide the necessary impetus to economic development process. According to Rostow, "The essence of transition can be described legitimately as a rise in the rate of investment to a level, which regularly, substantially, and perceptibly outstrips population growth".

(iii) The Take-off: Rostow considers this stage as one of the important stages of economic growth. It is the most decisive stage in the evolution of any society. At this stage, growth becomes a normal process of development in a society. This becomes possible because of agricultural and industrial revolution, application of scientific and technological innovations into the agricultural and industrial sector of the economy, being corroborated by the supportive international environment. The economy marches towards self-sustaining growth and the obstacles and resistances to steady growth are being removed and the forces of economic development dominate the society. Rostow calls it as 'great watershed in the life of modern society'. Rostow advocated that this stage can be accomplished with a high rate of investment, i.e. over 10 per cent of national income.

(iv) The Drive to Maturity: It is a stage of self-sustained growth, in which, saving and investment in an economy reaches to such a magnitude that economic growth becomes self-sustaining. According to Rostow, "It is a period when a society has effectively applied the range of modern technology to the bulk of its resources". The three important changes that take place at this stage are: (a) The composition of the workforce in the economy changes. (b) The characteristics of leadership also changes. (c) People become accustomed to the process of change and development. The economy becomes capable enough to carry out economic development activities effectively so that high economic growth rate is attained and developmental activities are smoothly carried forward.

(v) The Age of High Mass Consumption: It is a stage, where an economy after attaining maturity moves towards high mass consumption. At this stage, the attention of the economy is dragged from production towards consumption and from accumulation towards welfare. The mature economy is also known as welfare state. According to Rostow, "The emergence of the welfare state is one manifestation of a society's moving beyond the technical maturity".

The critics of Rostow's theory of economic growth were of the view that stages were not possible always and economies need to possess some other conditions such as well-developed commodity and money market, institutional mechanism, infrastructure facilities, trained and educated manpower, and, over and above, an efficient and effective government.

W.A. LEWIS' THEORY OF UNLIMITED SUPPLY OF LABOUR

The theory of unlimited supply of labour is a noteworthy contribution of W.A. Lewis to development economics. Arthur Lewis' seminal paper 'Development with Unlimited Supply of Labour' in 1954 embodies his views on the existence of surplus labour force in the primary sector and its adverse impact on the economic growth and development of the underdeveloped countries. However, Lewis was quite optimistic about the development potential of underdeveloped countries in the form of unlimited supply of labour and considered that if the unutilized and underutilized potentials of the surplus labour force are effectively tapped and utilized it would have significant contribution to the economic growth and development of these countries.

Three important dynamics of Lewis theory are:

(i) Labour is the engine of economic growth and development.
(ii) The underdeveloped countries can overcome poverty and augment their economic and social development through industrialization and shifting of excess labour force from the agriculture to the industrial sector.
(iii) Augmentation of export from the underdeveloped countries to the developed countries will boost economic growth and development of the underdeveloped countries.

Lewis was an 'export optimist' and believed that the export of tropical products from the developing countries to the developed nations should not face any barriers, and could be easily dispersed throughout the global economy, as the underdeveloped countries enjoy comparative advantage in these areas. Besides these, countries also have hidden potential in some types of manufacturing goods; those should be exploited not only for their own benefit and own consumption but also for the export of those products to the developed nations.

Lewis was of the view that the economy broadly comprises two sectors, one is the scintillating sector called the capitalist sector and other is the subsistence sector or the traditional sector. The capitalist sector is capital intensive and more productive as compared to the subsistence sector which is comparatively dull, labour-intensive and less productive. Lewis believed that the growing disparities between these two sectors were because of differences in their production structures. The wage rate is higher in the capitalist sector and astoundingly low in the subsistence sector where it also stagnates at the subsistence level. This dualistic nature of underdeveloped countries, where there is hardly any interconnection between the technologically advanced capitalist or industrial sector and the traditional low-productivity rural and predominantly agriculture sector is a cause of concern for the economic development of the underdeveloped countries. He advocated that there is a need for capital formation in the subsistence sector for the gainful employment of surplus labour in this sector also transferring some labour from agriculture to industry, so that it would enable the remaining work force in the agriculture sector to work longer hours, as a result the total agricultural productivity could either remain constant or even increase. This process of self-sustaining economic growth and employment expansion and transfer of labour force from the agriculture to the industrial sector would continue until all of the surplus labour is transferred from the traditional agriculture sector and gainfully absorbed in the industrial sector. As long as there is surplus labour in agriculture sector, the wage rate in the subsistent agriculture sector will remain low, on account of which it will be convenient on the part of the capitalist class to appropriate a gigantic share of national income or profit, which will create a gap in income between the workers working in the industrial sector and the agriculture sector and it will escalate economic disparities within the economy. It will also escalate the glut of labour force or disguised unemployment in agriculture sector. Lewis was in favour of the adoption of modern technology in the primary sector which would propel the 'modernization' of agriculture and enhance productivity and capital formation in the economy through more income, saving and investment. Lewis was in favour of the balanced development of both agriculture and industrial sector.

An important observation of Lewis was that a large percentage of profit earned by the capitalists that was supposed to be saved is squandered by way of conspicuous consumption. He was totally against the unproductive expenditure and wasteful consumption done by the upper strata of society that are largely unproductive classes and control significant amount of economic resources. Therefore, he proposed imposition of tax on the rich and capitalists by the State and whatever income earned through taxation needed to be spent for the socially productive purposes. The Lewis theory concludes that the effective utilization of surplus labour and prudent use of surplus income are vital to economic development of the underdeveloped countries.

One of the drawbacks of the Lewis theory observed in the underdeveloped economies is that the transfer of labour force from the agriculture to the industrial sector is very difficult in the underdeveloped countries as these countries are incapable to invest in the industrial and manufacturing sector. As the process of economic reform is very slow in the underdeveloped countries, transfer of labour force from primary to secondary sector is slow and even stagnant. Even the modernization of agriculture is too slow in the underdeveloped countries resulting in declining contribution of agriculture to GDP of these countries. It was commented that although the Lewis two-sector model of development was too simple and was in conformity with the historical experience of growth in the Western countries, however, its key assumptions do not fit to the institutional arrangement and economic realities of the most of the contemporary Third World countries (Todaro and Smith, 2012).

DEVELOPMENTAL STATE THEORY

The developmental state approach has been and was popular during 1990s mostly in Asia, Africa, and Latin American countries, where the State played a pro-active role in the development of the underdeveloped economies. From the UNCTAD (2009) point of view, the State is defined as developmental, if the economy is developing, economic success is equated to State strength, and the latter is measured by the presumed outcomes. According to Bolesta (2007), developmental state, positioned between free-market capitalist economic system and centrally planned socialist economic system, makes it neither capitalist nor socialist in texture. Two outstanding propounders of developmental state theory are Peter Evans and Gunnar Myrdal.

Peter Evans' 'developmental state' is based on his urge to seek an answer to a pertinent question, "What kinds of State structure facilitate industrial transformation?" From his study conducted in four countries, i.e. Zaire, South Korea, India, and Brazil. Peter Evans made an important contribution to the development model and his concepts of three archetypes of State are illustrious works in the field of economic development.

The three types of State as conceptualized by Evans are: (a) the predatory state, (b) the intermediate state, and (c) the developmental state. Evans (1995) viewed that states are the result of complex historical forces and relationships, but they are also actors of agents potentially capable of shaping and influencing the ongoing process of historical evolution.

The first category of State is the Predatory state and some of the important characteristics of predatory State are:

(i) In predatory state the public sector functionaries are guided by the sale motive and government employees try to maximize their wealth in minimum shortest possible time.
(ii) The cardinal motives of the political offices in the predatory state are not to serve the society but to amass wealth for their personal benefit.
(iii) Corruption is endemic in the society and prevalent in all spheres.
(iv) Characteristic features of pre-capitalist societies are vividly seen.
(v) There is scarcity of trained bureaucrats; in other words, bureaucracy lacks capability.

Some of the most notorious features and results of the predatory state as stated by Evans (1995) are:

(i) The predatory state extracts at the expense of society, undercutting development even in the narrow sense of capital accumulation.
(ii) The predatory state lacks the ability to prevent individual incumbents from pursuing their own goals.
(iii) Personal ties are the only source of cohesion and individual maximization takes precedent over pursuit of collective goals.
(iv) The predatory state deliberately disorganizes civil society.

The second category of archetypes states is the intermediate state. Some of the attributes of intermediate states according to Evans (1995) are as follows:

(i) The intermediate state depicts a mixed bureaucratic achievement where professionalism predominates in certain sectors, while in some other sectors, personal ties and corruption are routine affairs for which Evans coined that intermediate state falls victim to 'bureaucratic fragmentation'.
(ii) Some sectors demonstrate better achievement and public sector work in tandem with private sector in order to successfully implement development projects and programmes.
(iii) Intermediate state lacks the means to consistently transform society.
(iv) This society is observed to suffer from scarcity of efficient bureaucrats.

In the intermediate state, the role of the government in performing development functions is comparatively better than in the predatory state. Some of the sectors having efficient bureaucrats perform better and are found to have involved in less corruption, while some other sectors they are observed to be more engrossed with corruption. The intermediate state depicts mixed attributes of government functioning blended with good and bad features. One of the important features of intermediate state is that state provides space to the private sector to work in tandem with the public sector for the effective implementation of development projects and programmes. Like the predatory state, the intermediate state also lacks efficient and transparent bureaucrats.

The third type of Evans' archetype state is the development state. The important characteristic of the development is 'embedded autonomy'. Evans argued that development outcomes of any country are largely conditioned by the form of state organization, the bureaucratic elements as well as the nature of its ties with dominant societal interests (Evans, 1989). Through embedded autonomy, the actors of development such as state, private sector, the CSOs, and the bureaucracy coordinate and collaborate in the effective implementation of development projects and programmes. Evans' developmental state is endogenous and is broadly embedded in civil society through a chained network. According to Cypher and Dietz (2006) an embedded state possesses a variety of institutionalized channels, where in the State apparatus and the private sector continually interact in a constructive manner via a 'joint project' for fostering development. Evans (1989) has outlined four roles for developmental state:

(i) The Custodian Role—to formulate and enforce rules and regulations.
(ii) The Demiurge Role—directly compete with the private investors, rather than simply playing a complementary role.
(iii) The Midwife Role—act as a facilitator by steering, assisting, and inducing challenges in areas which are of higher priority.
(iv) The Husbandry Role—creating necessary environment for the successful emergence of new industries.

The developmental state will continue to play a crucial role in economic growth and social transformation in the 21st century as it did in the latter half of the 20th century (Evans, 2008). The features of development state as tried out in African context by Meyns and Musamba (2010) are: (a) development-oriented political leadership, (b) autonomous and effective bureaucracy, (c) production-oriented private sector, and (d) performance-oriented governance.

It is remarked that the developmental state stems from the amalgam 'embedded autonomy' in which the developmental state is linked intimately with the private sector but preserves sufficient distance from the renegotiation of goals and policies when capitalist interests are inconsistent with national development (Charlotte, 2008). The key actors in the development state are the government, the private sector, and the bureaucracy and synergy of action between these three are crucial for economic growth and development in a developmental state. According to Evans (1989) the efficiency of developmental state depends on a meritocratic bureaucracy with a strong sense of corporate identity and a dense set of institutionalized links with private élites. Further, in the developmental state, the state capacity in respect of the relationship between the state and private enterprise is critical in determining the developmental role of state (Evans, 1995). The developmental state is the stage of improved performance and governance capabilities of the bureaucracy to run the affairs of the economy in collaboration with other actors of development. As compared to other two states, such as predatory and intermediate state, the performance of the government in activating growth and development of an economy in the development state is better.

One of the outstanding propounders of the Developmental State is Gunnar Myrdal. The contribution of Gunnar Myrdal to contemporary development economics is stupendous. His illustrious book *The Asian Drama* and the other book, *Economic Theory and*

Undeveloped Regions together give insights on his argument about the caves of underdevelopment in underdeveloped countries and how the role of State through institutional reforms can promote development in the underdeveloped regions. The two key terms Myrdal used in his development analysis are 'cumulative causation' and 'backwash effect'. Cumulative causation means a change in one form of institution will lead to successive changes in other institutions. According to Myrdal, cumulative causation is one of the factors responsible for affecting an underdeveloped region within a nation to progressively move away from equilibrium. Myrdal argued that the underdeveloped nation suffers from 'dualism' of developed and underdeveloped regions, as a result, what happens, when these nations receive stimulus to growth, is that stimulus largely flows towards the more prosperous region of the economy. In other words, the benefits of development initiatives in the developing countries go to more developed regions. As a result the more developed region becomes more prosperous and surges further ahead and the more economically deprived region lags behind and dips down towards more underdevelopment. This is what is called the 'cumulative causation'. Another reason of cumulative causation in the underdeveloped countries is the migration of population and the movement of capital from less developed region to more developed region for better returns and opportunities. When more ambitious and better trained people migrate from less developed region for better employment opportunities available in the more developed region, the less developed regions are left with unskilled and dependent population. This further adds to their agony. In addition to migration, the rising fertility also reduces per capita income, enhances poverty, and sustains the low level of development in the underdeveloped regions of the underdeveloped countries. In the same vein, when the capital moves from the poorer region to the prosperous region, the rate of return to capital becomes high in the developed region and the developed region becomes secure and underdeveloped region faces capital crunch. Myrdal, from his studies conducted in many countries, said that when the banking system is not regulated, it acts differently and tends to become an instrument for siphoning off the savings from the poorer regions to richer and more progressive ones where returns to capital are high and secure. These cumulative movements, which tend to economically weaken a region, were termed as 'backwash effect'. Contrary to 'backwash effects', Myrdal advocated 'spread effects'. Myrdal perceived that with the help of 'spread effects', industrial expansion in more developed region of the underdeveloped countries will have positive repercussion on its less developed region in terms of demand, market avenues, and technology through the transfer of surplus capital from the more developed region to the less developed region. These favourable effects, which the more developed regions produce on the socio-economic development of the less developed regions, are termed as 'spread effects' and the positive impact of the 'spread effects' will help to neutralize the negative impact of 'backwash effects' to a great extent. However, according to Myrdal, the spread effect in underdeveloped countries is weak and is not capable to balance the backwash effects, as a result regional imbalances continue. Myrdal was of the opinion that it is not possible to attain equilibrium between backwash and spread effects in underdeveloped countries and as a result, regional inequalities are much wider within various regions of the poorer countries than those of the richer countries; and also regional inequalities are increasing in poor countries and diminishing in the rich countries. Thus regional disparities and imbalances in terms of socio-economic development in underdeveloped countries are the outcome of cumulative causation.

According to Myrdal, a crucial difference between the advanced countries and the poor countries, is the existence of strong State in the former and the weak (or soft) State in the latter. With the help of strong State, advanced nations formulate and implement coherent national policies which help these nations to achieve balanced economic growth and development across the regions of the country, while the weak State in the poor countries lacks effective policies and willpower to implement them honestly which act as deterrent to their economic growth and development. Myrdal observed that in the underdeveloped countries political power is largely concentrated in the hands of top social strata of the society and these elite groups through their money and muscle power accumulate all power and do not fear even to violate State power through muscle, money, and political manoeuvering. Myrdal advocated institutional metamorphosis in the underdeveloped countries in order to hasten the process of balanced economic growth and development in these countries. Attitudinal changes among people and institutional reforms are necessary for the development of the underdeveloped countries. Examples of some of these institutional reforms as advocated by Myrdal are fight against corruption, land reforms, and displacement of elite from the commanding heights of state policy. Proactive, pragmatic, and less corrupt institutional arrangements are needed to augment economic growth and development of the underdeveloped countries.

The description of developmental state as given by these two exponents is based on the empirical analysis; therefore, it holds sufficient ground of reliability in its applicability on the Third World countries. Routley (2012) has remarked that the term, developmental state was initially and is still, frequently used to describe countries such as Japan, South Korea, Taiwan, Singapore, and Vietnam, which have experienced rapid economic growth through State led policies and interventions. In developmental state, the State plays an important role in directing and associating the role of other actors such as private sector, NGOs, and local self-government institutions in the process of development through policies.

HARRIS–TODARO MODEL OF LABOUR MIGRATION

John Harris and Michael Todaro developed a model of labour migration during 1960s in order to find out an answer to the problems and challenges of growing informal sector and unemployment in Kenya. In development economics, this model is known as Harris–Todaro model of labour migration. Harris–Todaro model tried to answer one of the pertinent questions pertaining to the rural to urban migration of labour in the developing countries, which is affecting not only the development of the urban areas but is also having repercussions on the development process of the rural areas and also encouraging the growth of informal sector in the urban areas. In this model, Harris and Todaro have endeavoured to find out why despite the lower wage rate and a difficult lifestyle in urban informal sector, people of the rural areas are migrating to the urban areas. Customarily, the labourer migrates from the rural areas to the urban areas with a hope to get a formal sector job in the urban areas which carries higher wage rate than the rural areas jobs.

Anticipation of higher wage rate and a formal sector job entices the people of rural areas to migrate to urban areas.

The important assumptions of rural to urban migration in Harris–Todaro model are:

(i) Migration has a positive relationship with the real income difference between a job in rural area and a job urban area.
(ii) Migration is an increasing function of the probability to get a formal sector job in urban areas, in other words, migration increases when the probability of getting a job in the urban sector increases.
(iii) Duality in urban labour market, that is, existence of both formal and informal sector. In the urban formal sector job is more secure and carries higher wage rate as compared to the urban informal sector where job is less secure and wage rate is low.
(iv) Rural to urban migration takes place in two stages, at the first stage migrant workers get jobs in the urban informal sector and later on move to the urban formal sector job.

The presentation of the model in the form of an equation will give a better understanding of the Harris–Todaro model. The connotations run as:

(i) Let L_{uf} be the number of jobs in the urban formal sector
(ii) Let L_{if} be the number of jobs in the urban informal sector
(iii) Let w_{if} be the wage rate in urban informal sector
(iv) Let w_{uf} be the wage rate in urban formal sector
(v) Let w_r be the wage rate in rural sector

Then total number of jobs available in the urban sector is the sum total of jobs available in the urban formal sector and urban informal sector which is: $L_{uf} + L_{if}$.

As the number of jobs available in the urban formal sector is $L_{uf,}$ the probability of getting an urban formal sector jobs if interpreted in the form of a ratio then it becomes:

$$\frac{L_{uf}}{(L_{uf} + L_{if})}$$

However, after migrating from rural to urban areas, when a rural migrant worker does not get a job in the urban formal sector, he or she hangs on in the urban areas and starts working in the urban informal sector, with a hope to get a formal sector job in the near future. Generally the minimum wage rate in the urban formal sector would be higher than the wage rate offered in the rural sector, which is $wu_f > w_r$.

However, in Harris–Todaro model, the expected wage rate of the migrating worker from rural to the urban areas is:

$$\frac{(L_{uf})}{(L_{uf} + L_{if})} w_{uf} + \frac{L_{if}}{(L_{uf} + L_{if})} w_{if}$$

Then the people from rural areas will keep migrating to urban areas till the wage rate in urban areas is higher than rural areas, that is:

$$\frac{(L_{uf})}{(L_{uf}+L_{if})}w_{uf}+\frac{L_{if}}{(L_{uf}+L_{if})}w_{if}>w_{r}$$

The equilibrium will be reached at a point when people will cease to migrate from rural to urban areas:

$$\frac{(L_{uf})}{(L_{uf}+L_{if})}w_{uf}+\frac{L_{if}}{(L_{uf}+L_{if})}w_{if}=w_{r}$$

This is known as the Harris–Todaro equilibrium condition. At this stage, migration from rural to urban areas will cease to continue.

According to Harris and Todaro, the informal sector exists in urban areas for two reasons:

(i) As everybody does not find a job in the urban formal sector, therefore, they continue to stay and work in the in urban informal sector, with a hope to get a formal sector job in future, many of them hang on in the urban informal sector and as a result the urban informal sector continues to persist.

(ii) However, this migration and engagement of workforce in urban informal sector continues till expected wage rate from migration to urban areas equalizes with the rural wage rate. Therefore, in the developing economies, urban informal sector is an upshot of rural to urban migration. The urban informal sector largely comprises frustrated job seekers who not only get low wage rate but also are devoid of job security and social security benefits.

The Harris–Todaro model offered two policy options:

(i) At the outset, the creation of formal sector jobs in urban areas would increase the formal sector labour force through the migration of more and more workers from rural to urban areas, thereby, further worsening, urban unemployment problem. Thus, according to Harris–Todaro model, the solution to urban unemployment problem is certainly not the creation of urban employment.

(ii) The second policy option was to promote rural development. Launching effective rural development programmes which would raise rural sector real wage rate will check rural to urban migration and thus reduce the growth of informal sector in urban areas.

Therefore, in the Harris–Todaro model, the solution to urban unemployment would be rural development. Soon after the model was published, the government of Kenya followed the Harris–Todaro precepts by putting into place an integrated rural development programme, which was successful in reducing unemployment in Kenya. However,

Harris–Todaro model has not delineated the rural to rural migration, i.e. migration taking place from the rural areas of the underdeveloped State to the rural areas of developed State. One of the illustrious examples is the migration of labour from the rural areas of Bihar and Eastern Uttar Pradesh to Punjab and Haryana to work in their agriculture and allied sectors. With the effective implementation of MGNREGA by Bihar government during certain period, it was found that the seasonal migration of labourer from rural Bihar to rural areas of Punjab, Haryana and other northern Indian states was reduced. However, faster rural development and provision of urban amenities in rural areas will certainly check migration of rural population to urban areas. Moreover, it is not only the wage rate that attracts migration of labour from rural to urban areas; many young people from the economically weaker states migrate to urban areas for higher education and prepare for competitive examinations but settle down in the informal sector if they fail to get a formal sector job.

The Sum Up

The developmentalist theorists have tried to provide solutions to the economic growth and development problems of the underdeveloped countries. The two outstanding theories offered by the developmentalists are balanced and unbalanced growth theories. The advocates of balanced growth theory laid emphasis on the large-scale investment across different sectors in the underdeveloped countries, while the unbalanced growth theorists believed that the underdeveloped countries having paucity of resources may resort to unbalanced growth approach for their development. Leibenstein advocated that minimum effort strategy is the only answer to the economic backwardness of an underdeveloped economy, which can help these economies to come out of the clutches of vicious circle of poverty and put economy on the path of sustainable economic development. The Lewis theory of unlimited supply of labour suggested that for the development of the underdeveloped countries transfer of surplus labour from the agriculture to the industrial sector, modernization of agriculture, industrialization, and improvement in the export potential of these country are sine qua non. The Harris–Todaro model of labour migration advocated that the underdeveloped countries can make economic growth and development possible through effective rural development which can not only check migration of rural population to urban areas but also promote holistic economic growth and development of the developing countries. The developmental state theory of Gunnar Myrdal advocated a strong State for the effective development of the developing countries and the government has to play a proactive role with a focus on the effective development of the underdeveloped regions of the underdeveloped countries.

Keywords big push, social overhead capital, vicious circle of poverty, capital formation, directly productive activities, backward and forward linkages, stimulant forces, forces of shocks, positive-sum incentives, zero-sum incentives, take-off stage, drive to maturity, backwash effect, spread effect.

REVIEW QUESTIONS

1. Explain Rosenstein-Rodan's big-push theory. How it is different from Nurkse's theory of balanced growth?
2. Discuss the Leibenstein's theory of critical minimum effort. How it is relevant for the developing countries?
3. How Hirschman's theory of unbalance growth is relevant for the underdeveloped countries?
4. Vicious circle of poverty is central to Nurkse's theory. How can the underdeveloped countries overcome this?
5. Explain in detail Rostow's stages of economic growth.
6. Unlimited supply of labour is deterrent to development of the underdeveloped countries. Explain.
7. Explain the Harris–Todaro model of labour migration and development. How is it relevant for the developing countries?
8. Write short notes on:
   (i) Vicious circle of poverty
   (ii) Drive to maturity
   (iii) Backward and forward linkages
   (iv) Social overhead capital
   (v) Directly productive activities

NOTES

1. Santos has stated that from the end of the Second World War, a group of scholars supporting the existence of serious discrepancies between the development models of advanced nations in relation to the underdeveloped ones prevailed in Latin America.
2. To quote Bhagwati and Eckwas (1972), for thirty years, Paul Rosenstein-Rodan has been a leader in the efforts of the economics profession to understand the problems of the poor nations of the world and to assist in their development. He has not merely been the doyen of development theorists; he has also dedicated much of his life to policy making by international organizations for development of domestic policy formation within many of less developed countries.
3. While explaining the theory, Rosenstein-Rodan (1957) said, "there is a minimum level of resources that must be devoted to... a development programme, if it is to have any chance of success. Launching a country into self-sustaining growth is a little like getting an airplane off the ground. There is a critical ground speed which must be passed before the craft can become airborne".
4. This proposition as described by Nurkse (1953) is that in development programmes, "all sectors of the economy should grow simultaneously, so as to keep a proper balance between industry and agriculture and between production of more consumption and production for exports...the logic of this proposition is as unassailable as its simplicity".

REFERENCES

Bolesta, A. 2007. "China as a Developmental State." *Montenegrin Journal of Economics,* No. 5. Also see Bolesta, A. "China as a Post-socialist Developmental State: Explaining Chinese Development." Available at: www.repec.mnje.com/mje/2007/v03-n05/mje_2007_v03-n05-a16.html (accessed on 15 February 2016).

Cypher, James M. and Dietz, James L. 2006. *The Process of Economic Development.* New York: Routledge.

Evans, P. 1989. "Predatory, Developmental and Other Apparatuses: A Comparative Political Economy Perspective on the Third World State." *Sociological Forum*, 4(4): 561–87.

———. 1995. *Embedded Autonomy: States and Industrial Transformation*. Princeton: Princeton University Press.

———. 2008. "In Search of the 21st Century Development State." Working Paper No. 4, Centre for Global Political Economy, UK.

Hirschman, A. 1958. *The Strategy of Economic Development*. New Haven: Yale University Press.

Leibenstein, H. 1957. *Economic Backwardness and Economic Growth*. New York: John, Wiley & Sons.

Meyns, P. and C. Musamba. 2010. "The Developmental State in Africa: Problems and Prospects." Institute for Development and Peace, University of Duisburg-Essen.

Nurkse, Ragnar. 1953. *Problems in Capital Formation in Underdeveloped Countries*. New York: Oxford University Press.

Reinert, Erik S. 2010. "Developmentalism." The Working Paper in Technology Governance and Economic Dynamics, No. 34, The Other Canon Foundation, Tallinn University, Tallinn. Available at: hum.ttu.ee/wp/paper34.pdf (accessed on 15 February 2016).

Rosenstein-Rodan, Paul N. 1944. "The International Development of Economically Backward Areas." *International Affairs*, 20(2): 161–62. Available at: http://www.rrojasdatabank.info/pioneers8a.pdf (accessed on 14 February 2016).

Rostow, Walter W. 1960. *The Stages of Economic Growth: A Non-communistic Manifesto*. Cambridge: Cambridge University Press.

Routley, L. 2012. Developmental States: A Review of the Literature, ESID Working Paper No. 03, University of Manchester, UK. Available at: http://r4d.dfid.gov.uk/PDF/Outputs/ESID/esid_wp_03_routley (accessed on 15 February 2016).

Todaro, M.P. 1969. "A Model Labour Migration and Urban Unemployment in Less Developed Countries." *American Economic Review*, 59: 138–48.

Todaro, M.P. and Smith, S.C. 2012. *Economic Development*, Tenth Edition. New Delhi: Pearson.

UNCTAD. 2009. *The Least Developed Countries Report 2009*. New York and Geneva: United Nations Publication.

SUGGESTED READINGS

Bhagwati, J.N. and Eckaws, Ricard S. 1972. *Development Planning: Essays in Honour of Paul Rosenstein-Rodan*. London: Allen and Unwin.

Chilcote, Ronald H. 1974. "Dependency: A Critical Synthesis of the Literature." *Latin American Perspectives*, 1(1): 4–29.

Cypher, James M. and Dietz, James L. 2009. *The Process of Economic Development*. New York: Routledge.

Harris, J.R. and M.P. Todaro. 1970. "Migration, Unemployment and Development: A Two Sector Analysis." *American Economic Review*, 60: 126–42.

Myrdal, G. 1984. "International Inequalities and Foreign Aid in Retrospect." In *Pioneers in Development*, edited by G. Meier and D. Seers. London: Oxford University Press.

Myrdal, G. 1957. *Economic Theory and Underdeveloped Region*. London: Gerald Duckworth.

———. 1970. *The Challenge of World Poverty*. New York: Vintage Books.

———. 1984. "International Inequality and Foreign Aid in Retrospect." In *Pioneers in Development*, edited by G. Meir and D. Seers, 151–56. Oxford: Oxford University Press.

Nurse, K. 2006. "Culture as the Forth Pillar of Sustainable Development." Paper prepared for the Commonwealth Secretariat. Available at: www.fao.org/sard/coommon/ecg/2785/en/cultureas4pillarSD.pdf (accessed on 26 November 2013).

Rosenstein-Rodan, Paul N. 1957. MIT Centre for International Studies, Special Committee to Study the Foreign Aid Programme, The Objectives of US Economic Assistance Programmes, Washington DC. Available at: http://www.rrojasdatabank.info/pioneers8a.pdf (accessed on 14 December 2013).

———. 1943. "Problem of Industrialization of Eastern and Southeastern Europe." *Economic Journal*, 53(210–211, June–September): 202–11.

Santos, T.D. 1968. "El Nuevo Character de la Dependencia Santiago: Cuadernos de Estudios Socio-economico." (10) Centro de Estudios Socio-economicos (CESO), Universidad de Chile.

———. 1971. "The Structure of Dependence." In *Readings in US Imperialism*, edited by K.T. Fann and D.C. Hodges. 226. Boston, MA: Porter Sergeant.

Streeten, P. 1979. "From Growth to Basic Needs." *Finance and Development*, 16(3): 28–31.

4 Heterodox Theories of Development

For the heterodox economists, the changes required to propel the development process forward are more fundamental, more sweeping and more profound.

— Cypher and Dietz (2006)

Heterodox economics provides a descriptively richer, contextually subjective, and fuller illustration of the individual than that given by the orthodoxy's rational, optimizing, economic man.

— Wrenn (2006a)

The development theories as propounded by the classical, neo-classical, and developmentalists were constructed on various approaches, for example, how to promote economic growth and development of a nation with natural, financial, human, and technological resources at its disposal. The postulates of the classical and neo-classical theories were mainly based on the economic growth and development experiences of the developed countries, while the propositions of the developmentalists were largely based on their research works relating to the development problems of the underdeveloped countries. As development is a multidimensional phenomenon, the other dimensions such as social, political, cultural, and human, besides economic dimensions, also need attention for the holistic development of the underdeveloped countries, and therefore, the propounders of the 19th century while analyzing the economic growth and development, particularly of the underdeveloped countries, considered heterogeneity in approach to deal with the economic growth and development problems of the underdeveloped countries. The heterogeneity in approach towards holistic development of the underdeveloped countries has been well recognized by the social scientists across the world. Wrenn (2006b) noted that heterodox economic thought includes a diverse range of streams or 'schools' of thought which can best be described as 'not orthodox' and the non-orthodox component includes a different theory, a different methodology, a different research agenda, varied historical and cultural approaches, general criticisms, rejection of rationality, interdisciplinary approach, a different political learning, and rejection of positivism. The heterodox theories are in favour of pluralism (Garnett, 2006) and heterodoxy involves both sociological and intellectual aspects.[1] The heterodox theory of development emphasizes on the importance of various non-economic aspects which are playing and would play a critical role in the development process of the developing countries, i.e. modernization and social change; role of communication media; role of human capabilities in development, traditionalism, and cultural obstacles; political leadership and governance; economic dimension of neo-liberalism; and dependency model of development. In other words, the heterodox approach to development is pluralistic in nature of which economic dimension is one of the components. Some of the leading heterogeneous theories on development propounded in the 19th century are modernization theory, dependency theory, neo-liberal theory, and human capabilities theories, and from the standpoint of the holistic development of the underdeveloped countries of Asia, Africa, and Latin America, Gandhian approach to development has substantial relevance.

After reading this chapter, you will be able to:

(i) Describe modernization theory of development and its relevance to the developing countries.
(ii) Explain dependency theory and how the developments of the developed countries were based on the exploitation of the underdeveloped countries.
(ii) Discuss the human capability theory propounded by Amartya Sen and Martha Nussbaum.
(iv) Analyze the neo-liberal theory of development.
(v) Narrate the Gandhian theory of development and how holistic development can be achieved through various approaches advocated by Mahatma Gandhi.

MODERNIZATION THEORY OF DEVELOPMENT

The modernization theory of development originated in America and Europe during the period 1945 to 1960. It remained one of the most potent forces of development during the period 1950 to 1970. The main propounders of modernization theory were Max Weber, Emile Durkheim, Talcott Parsons, David McClelland, W.W. Rostow, and Daniel Lerner. The main proposition of modernization theory is that the underdeveloped economies can also become developed economies through the adoption of modernization approach as was adopted by the developed economies of the West. The primary intention of the modernization theorists is to provide ways and approaches for bringing modernity to the Third World countries of Asia, Africa, and Latin America, in order to break the jinx of 'underdevelopment' which they are suffering since centuries so that they will be put on the path of development. Modernization theory advocates that the modernization process experienced by USA and several Western European countries has provided a model which could be applied to other countries to enable them to develop through modernization (Kreutzmann, 1988). The modernization school of thought believed that the problem of underdevelopment of the Third World countries was mainly because of internal shortcomings of prevalence of traditionalism and their resistance towards modernism. Therefore, at the heart of modernization theory is the idea that economic growth can be stimulated in any country by following a USA/European model (Green, 2008). To common understanding, modernization means transition from the traditional society to the modern advanced society, from a static agrarian economy towards more dynamic industrial economy, and from rural to urban way of life. According to Lerner (1967), modernization is the social process of which development is the economic component. Moore (1963) was of the view that modernization is the total transformation of a traditional or pre-modern society into the types of technology and associated social organization that characterize the 'advanced', the economically prosperous, and the relatively stable nations of the Western world. Some of the characteristics of modernization are:

(i) Readiness by the underdeveloped and traditionally rigid society to accommodate the process of transformation and social change resulting from metamorphosis occurring due to modernization and impact of the Western culture.
(ii) Continuous upgradation of life experiences, knowledge, and attitude towards the modern system and social change.
(iii) Continuous planning and readiness to act upon and to put these changes planned out in different spheres into practice.
(iv) Changing attitude towards kinship, family roles, family size, and the role of religion and traditional beliefs and values from the perspective of modernization.
(v) Attempts to be made to attain the societal goal of holistic development by applying modern technology, methods, approaches, and strategies.
(vi) Ready to accept and put into practice technical knowhow and modernization principles in the production process of the various sectors of economy, i.e. agriculture, industry, and service sector.
(vii) Changing consumer behaviour, attitude, and perspectives towards modernization and acceptance of modern products and practices.

Max Weber one of the prolific propounders of modernization theory of development, while basing his analysis of growth of capitalism in both Western world and Eastern world, viewed that the growth of capitalism and modernization of economic system depends on three things: (a) their capability to overcome the trait of traditionalism which tends to put hurdle in the way of development of trade and commerce of a nation; (b) to overcome internal impediments like traditional beliefs and values and cultural practices prevailing in an economy which resist the acceptance of modernity for development; and (c) to overcome the restrictions being imposed by the 'gain spirit' in the economic relationship of an economic system with other countries (Weber, 1954). By 'gain spirit', Weber meant a system of conduct based on ethical norms which govern and influence commercial activity. This brings the economic system and religious beliefs and values and ethical spheres into a relationship with each other, which interface and act as deterrent to free trade and commerce in the Eastern economies. While pointing out the differences between the Eastern and Western economies, he was of the opinion that eastern economies are mostly inland and closed economies which impose restriction on free trade and profit-making actions of the capitalist and business classes; while on the other hand, the Western economies believe in free trade and are more propitious to the dynamic entrepreneurial behaviour of capitalists and entrepreneurs. Weber believed that the combination of economic, political, and legal aspects of the citizen was unique to the functioning of Western capitalism. The effective coordination and combination of all these have enabled the Western nations to build an economic system formed around a rationale state and city life. The rational state is guided by the law and officialdom, which has effectively emerged and has been fittingly functioning only in the modern society. The traditional underdeveloped societies are lacking in the features of a rationale state. Max Weber's theory states that the development of a nation depends on a few important non-economic factors, i.e. (a) the emergence of a system of rationality and religiously putting it into practice; (b) the development of a system of calculable law and forms of citizenship which is more favourable to modernity; (c) the rise of a rational state and city life; and (d) the growth of the 'gain spirit' and a system of development ethics which promotes commerce and trade

(Morrison, 1995). One of the important distinctions between the underdeveloped and developed economic system as perceived by Weber is that the former is ritualistic, restrictive, and based on magical beliefs, while the latter is more rational and pragmatic and hardly has any faith in belief and magic. The Western system is more progressive because it believes in modernity and the countries belonging to the Eastern world are underdeveloped because of their faith in beliefs and values of traditionalism.

Emile Durkheim is another outstanding propounder of modernization theory. The key concept in Emile Durkheim's modernization theory of development is 'social solidarity'. It is 'social solidarity' which distinguishes a developed country from that of the developing one. Durkheim viewed the 'solidarity' feature as vital for the social and economic development of a nation. The concept, 'solidarity' refers to the system of social bonds which link individual to the society and widen the individual's thinking, vision, and approaches towards the society. Without social link and effective social networking, individuals would be isolated, unrelated, and would remain detached from the social mainstream and his or her growth will be ultimately restricted. Solidarity is broadly categorized into two types, i.e. mechanical solidarity and organic solidarity. The characteristic features of underdeveloped nations are akin to mechanical solidarity, while those of advanced nations are in proximity to organic solidarity.

Some of the features of mechanical solidarity of a society are:

(i) A homogenous population, which is small and isolated, besides the density of population is also high.
(ii) The division of labour in the society is based on the principle of social cooperation, with little or no specialization.
(iii) A system of social institutions in which religion is dominant and people are guided by the religious beliefs and values.
(iv) The society is based on a system of social, religious, and cultural beliefs and values which are uniformly diffused throughout the society, and individual actions and attitudes are guided by these beliefs and values.
(v) The degree of individual autonomy is meek and the place of an individual in the society is determined by the kinship.
(vi) Individualism is in a low state and an individual has little voice in the society. In other words, it is society which influences to a great extent the individual behaviour.
(vii) Social links between individuals is based on customs, traditions, obligations, cultural and religious beliefs and values, and the individual's sentiment and relationships is based on kinship and marriages.
(viii) There is resistance to technological advancement because of the predominance of traditionalism and traditional beliefs and values.

On the other hand, the main characteristics of organic solidarity are:

(i) Large populations spread over broader geographical areas and the density of population is low.
(ii) Complexity of division of labour and the economic functioning is guided by the division and specialization of labour.

(iii) Individuals are linked to each other by contract or through social networking rather than by sentiments and obligations.
(iv) Individuals obtain their place and are known in the society by their occupation and not by his or her inheritance or by kinship affiliation.
(v) Individual autonomy is based on a system of law, and individual action is regulated by law. The law also recognizes the rights and freedom of an individual.
(vi) Technological advancement enhances the productivity and efficiency of the economy.

Durkheim believed that the structure of advanced societies is firmly formed with a system of organs. These organs are more specialized and segmental and based on the competency of the individual. Durkheim was of the opinion that 'individualism is a direct product of industrial and advanced society'. It is individualism which entices an individual to achieve and contribute towards the development of the society. Durkheim believed that society exerts a powerful influence on individuals and creates an enabling environment for individuals to perform for the economic development of the society. According to Durkheim, modernization is an upshot of three factors: (a) the population density—growth of population in an area and its size; (b) the 'moral density'—that is development of more complex interaction among individuals in the society that is the status of social networking of an individual in the society; and (c) increasing specialization—that is division of labour. Because of impact of these factors, a society will move from traditionalism to modernity and from mechanical solidarity to organic solidarity. To Durkheim, social development and the role of individual in the society is central to the acceptance of modernization and social change, which are fundamental requirements of development of an underdeveloped society. The importance of social development analysis in development is being termed by Durkheim as 'social pathology', and 'social backwardness' is an inherent feature of underdeveloped society, which is responsible for slower economic growth and development. The underdeveloped nation-state can move to the advanced nation-state by injecting social pathology to their social system.

Another strong protagonist of the modernization theory is Talcott Parsons. Talcott Parsons (1964) noted that the developing societies are guided by the 'traditional' beliefs and values, which is the greatest obstacle to development. People belonging to the traditional society are perceived to be bounded by the traditional beliefs and values and were committed and obliged to the customs, rituals, and practices and, consequently, are fatalistic and less progressive. However, he argued that as a society evolves towards full modernity 'stratification often becomes a predominantly conservative force' (Parsons, 1964). Parsons viewed that modernity can be brought to the traditional underdeveloped society through the evolution of administrative bureaucracy and money and market. The crucial feature of bureaucracy is to institutionalize the authority of the office. While the role of money and that of the market is to emancipate the resources from the ascriptive bonds. Sociologically, ethnicity is defined as an ascriptive bond.

Parsons argued that a modern society is characterized by its positioning based on five criteria:

(i) Criteria of achievement over aspiration: Modern societies are largely democratic states rather than aristocratic or monarchical states and, hence, political, occupational, and social power is achieved through popular participation rather than inherited or ascribed by birth.

(ii) Pluralistic over universalistic criteria: Modern societies are pluralistic and diverse in nature and no one group in society is favoured, or in other words, these pluralistic societies follow the principle of 'unity in diversity'.

(iii) Specific over diffused criteria: Modern societies require individuals to master certain bodies of basic knowledge and the ability to specialize in specific competencies, and there is division of labour and individual has to acquire a certain skill to perform the task assigned to him or her.

(iv) Emotional neutrality over affectivity criteria: In modern societies, there is a differentiation between public (e.g. work occupation) and private (e.g. family) spheres and their respective normative orientations to emotion and an individual in a modern society balances his or her family private life and public office work and timing. In other words, familial emotions are being kept neutral so that it does not have any repercussion on his or her official performance.

(v) Self-orientation rather than collective orientation criteria: In modern societies, individuals are expected to follow their desires in choosing an occupation, a marriage partner, lifestyle, etc. unlike the traditional societies where they are being restrained by the kinship. In other words, in the traditional society, family, ethnicity, and religious affiliation impose constraints on individual choices and preferences (Dillon, 2010).

The developed countries have undergone a high degree of modernization in terms of democratization, industrialization, urbanization, and technological revolution compared to their counterpart underdeveloped countries which are still characterized by dominance of agriculture, low degree of industrialization, and technological backwardness. Therefore, modernization is essential for the development of the underdeveloped countries.

McClelland (1961), one of the prolific protagonists of modernization theory, was of the view that societies having high achievement motivation will produce more energetic entrepreneurs who will bring rapid economic development in an economy. He advocated that the developing countries need to have high achieving and motivated entrepreneurs who are capable of transforming foreign aid into productive investment. The need for achievement denotes 'desire to do well, not so much for the sake of social recognition or prestige, but to attain an inner feeling of personal accomplishment'. It is not the economic, political, or social structure of a society that shapes the nature and direction of its development, but rather the values, motives, or psychological forces that ultimately determine the rate of economic and social development. In order to promote rapid development, the developing nation has to adapt modernity, give stress on technology, promote specialization and division of labour, and acquire energetic and motivated entrepreneurs and workforce in their industrialization process. McClelland's ideology concerning development runs as:

> ...unless we learn our lesson and find ways of stimulating that drive for achievement under freedom in poor countries, the Communists will go on providing it all around the world. We can go on building dikes to maintain freedom and improving ourselves to feed and arm the people behind those dikes, but only if we develop the entrepreneurial spirit in those countries will we have a sound foreign policy. Only then can they look after their own dikes and become economically self-sufficient. (McClelland, 1964)

Another profound propagator of the modernization theory is Daniel Lerner. To Lerner (1967) "modernization is the social process of which development is the economic component". From his work on Western economies, he emphatically asserted that Western modernization can be used as a model of global applicability. He opined that those who cannot see themselves in the shoes of others will not be able to develop themselves. Development is a learning process and the underdeveloped nations in order to promote themselves into a developed state have to continuously observe, learn, and adopt change as it is occurring in the Western world. While highlighting the role of media in development process, he said that media plays a crucial role in the modernization of a nation. In his illustrious book, *The Passing of Traditional Society: Modernizing Middle East*, Lerner (1958) noted that "...as people are more exposed to media, the greater is their capability to imagine themselves as strange persons in strange situations, places, and time than did people in any previous historical epoch".

Social development model of Lerner (1958) consisted of the following components:

(i) A core of dynamic individuals whose psychological orientation make them forward-looking to accept rapid changes in their personal lives and overall social system.

(ii) An omnipotent and pragmatic mass media system that reinforces and accelerates social and individual change by disseminating the new ideas and attitudes conducive to modernization in the society across all sections of population.

(iii) Correlation and continuous interaction between important indices of urbanization, media literacy, media exposure, and economic and political participation system supportive to establish a modern, Western-type society.

Lerner considers that in modern society, people are more advanced, educated, and media savvy and are mostly urbanized. Lerner in his study categorized individuals into two types, i.e. 'traditional' and 'transitional or modern' and found that the modern individuals are better informed, happier, and relatively younger and forward-looking as compared to traditional individuals who are less awarded and conservative in nature. While identifying characteristics of modern individuals, he said, to be modern, one should be empathetic, pragmatic, and change-oriented.

Modernization theorists believe that modernization is a gradual process which all the underdeveloped world would experience while attaining the glory of development over a period of time. They were of the view that the developed countries have achieved economic development through modernization and that could be very much applicable to underdeveloped countries in order to enable them to attain the status of developed nations. The underdeveloped nation-states in recent years are experiencing the value of being democratic nations and democracy is on the rise. Besides, the processes of industrialization and modernization through the growth of manufacturing and service sector are giving rise to economic development and social change in the underdeveloped world. Modernization theory remained mainstream theory of development in the Western countries between 1950s and 1960s and remained in force but not aggressively in the subsequent decades of the 19th century. However, the relevance of modernization theory cannot be overemphasized in the contemporary world, and many of the nation-states are seen to have reached development state by accepting and adopting the ideals of modernization.

However, the modernization theory has been criticized on different grounds. Inglehart (1997) said that modernization theory is now less deterministic and as it absorbs post-modern ideas, and cultural diversity and aspects of tradition are seen as beneficial, rather than obstacles to development. The role of culture and cultural goods and trade in the economic system of many countries of the world, particularly in the developing countries of South Asia and Africa, is visible and is being emphasized and encouraged by the government of these countries for promotion of holistic regional development. Haynes (2008) was of the opinion that the modernization theory is being criticized on the ground of being caught in the dichotomy between the 'traditional' and 'modern' and its resulting treatment of cultural issues. According to Haynes (2008), the biggest critique of modernization theory came from dependency theory; as the latter gained momentum, the former diminished. Dependency theory viewed that it was because of the developed world and its exploitation of developing countries that caused them to remain underdeveloped and considered that external barriers were the main obstacles for development and not the internal ones (Green, 2008).

DEPENDENCY THEORY OF DEVELOPMENT

The dependency theory came after the modernization theory and remained in force as an important development theory during 1970s. It is a critical reaction to the conventional approach to development emerged in the aftermath of the Second World War. Hout (1993) was of the opinion that one of the most conspicuous perspectives that have been developed as an alternative to the orthodox approach certainly was dependency theory, and over the last two decades, this theory has proven to be a successful theoretical approach to the study of international relations. The two important approaches to dependency are: (a) Marxist approach to dependency and (b) structuralist approach to dependency. The main protagonists of Marxist approach to dependency are Paul Baran, Andre Gunder Frank, Samir Amin, Arghiri Emmanuel, and others; while the leading propounders of structuralist theory of dependency are Raul Prebish, Celso Furtado, Fernando Henrique Cardoso, and others. Dependency theory is not a homogenous theory; however, one of the unanimities among the dependency theorists is that in order to deal with the problem of underdevelopment of the developing countries, one has to take into cognizance the development process of developed countries and analyze how it has happened through adoption of the process of exploitation of the underdeveloped countries by the developed countries. According to Santos (1968), by dependency, we mean a situation in which the economy of certain countries is conditioned by the development and expansion of another economy to which the former is subjected. To Sunkel (1969), dependency can be defined as an explanation of the economic development of a state in terms of the external influences—political, economic, and cultural—on national development policies. The dependency theorists believe that the development of developed countries is intrinsically related to the underdevelopment of underdeveloped countries. The protagonists of dependency theory were of the view that underdevelopment is not a condition; rather it is an active process of impoverishment link to development. Some parts of the world are underdeveloped because others are developed and thus development and underdevelopment are interlinked. The development policies adopted by the developed nations, North

America, and Europe were based on the premises of the systematic perpetuation of the developing countries by the developed countries. The foundation wall of the development of developed nations has been built on the grabbing up of natural resources, cheap labour, and capturing volatile market conditions of the underdeveloped countries. For their own development, the developed nation created a condition of economic, political, and cultural dependency of the underdeveloped countries on the Western world. Paul Baran (1957) in his illustrious book, *Political Economy of Growth,* has argued that the way in which imperialism penetrated into underdeveloped countries had destroyed the social formation and distorted the economic development process of the underdeveloped countries. It has created ground of lasting conditions of dependency of the underdeveloped countries on the developed countries. Baran's study on less developed countries, which were reeling under colonialism, led him to argue that the economic surplus created by the developed countries through the exploitation of natural resources and the potential of the labour of the underdeveloped countries could have been used by these underdeveloped countries to meet their basic needs and prosperity otherwise. The reason of poverty and miseries in the underdeveloped countries is attributed to the richness of developed nations. Baran was of the view that the countries belonging to the underdeveloped world have shipped off a large part of their economic surplus to more advanced countries on account of interests and dividends. Baran also argued that the internal conditions of the underdeveloped countries are responsible for their backwardness. The common characteristics of underdeveloped nations, in the view of Baran, are:

(i) Imperialism and predominance of imperialistic society
(ii) Low per capita income of the majority of people
(iii) Low level of socio-economic development
(iv) Internal and external obstacles to development resulting from the history of colonialism/imperialism (Foster, 2007)

Besides the exploitation by the developed nations, the potential surpluses of the underdeveloped economies are appropriated by a group of dominant class, i.e. landlord, moneylenders, and small and monopolistic industrial bourgeoisie. Because of all these conditions, the potential surpluses of underdeveloped countries are being plundered and appropriated by the dominants from within and also from outside the nation, what he termed as 'the morphology of backwardness'.

Another exponent of dependency theory, Andre Gunder Frank perceived development and underdevelopment as the opposite sides of the coin and the development of the industrialized world has been made possible only by the corresponding underdevelopment inflicted by the developed nations on the underdeveloped nations. A.G. Frank in his work, *The Development of Underdevelopment,* envisaged that the underdeveloped countries of Latin America and other similar underdeveloped countries would be able to gain, owing to the foreign competition and the introduction of free trade, which was in the interest of the ruling groups of the economically developed countries. Frank used two famous connotations, i.e. 'metropolis' and 'satellite' nations; the former are the developed countries and the latter are the underdeveloped countries. The 'metropolis' have accelerated their development by sucking the capital or economic surplus of the latter group of nations, the 'satellite'. He was of the view that underdevelopment is not an original state, but rather, it is a consequence of the economic capture and control of backward countries by the advanced metropolitan capitalist nations.[2]

Samir Amin, another leading exponent of the Marxian dependency theory, based on his extensive work in the African countries, propounded the illustrious 'centre' and 'periphery' idea, i.e. at the 'centre' are the key developed nations, while the 'periphery' consists of the poor underdeveloped countries roaming around the centre. The determining aspect of the periphery's dependence on the centre is that the peripheral economies are only the producers of basic products, and for the import of the advanced finished industrial products, they are dependent on the industrial developed economies at the centre.

According to Amin (1976), all peripheral countries have four main characteristics in common:

(i) First, at the outset, the periphery countries are featured with the predominance of agrarian capitalism, which implies that there is usually a dominating class of large landowners, cultivating their land for the production of agricultural goods for the world market.

(ii) Second, the existence of a comprador (literally: trading) bourgeoisie—this class is directly tied to the bourgeoisie in the centre, and they are largely dependents and are not in a position to develop independently from the latter.

(iii) Third, the peripheral countries have been commanded and guided by the dominant bureaucracy, either civil or very often, military origin, which tries to take over the role of bourgeoisie in developing country.

(iv) Fourth, the periphery nations are characterized by extreme inequality in the distribution of income because of widespread unemployment and underemployment. He believed that one of the important ways for the development of the peripheral countries is that these nations have to 'de-link' their economies from the world system and come out of the clutches of the exploitation of the developed nations.

One of the leading propounders of structuralist dependency school was Raul Perbisch, a well-known Latin American structuralist economist. The central point on which the Perbisch theory revolves around was centre-periphery—at the centre are the rich European countries and USA, and at the periphery are the impoverished Latin American, Asian, and African nations. According to Perbisch, the centre exploits the periphery to its own advantage or development. In other words, the development of the rich centre is built on the exploited resources of the periphery poor. Perbisch–Singer hypothesis tried to explain whether the trade relationship between the centre and periphery will benefit all participating nations or prove detrimental to one and favour the other. It states that as the existing economic conditions, productive process, and labour market structure of both the groups are highly different, the trade engagement would be detrimental to peripheral nations and beneficial to the 'centre' developed nations. The centre nations would gain doubly and the periphery nations would lose in equal proportion and become the worst sufferers. As the periphery nations are primarily suppliers or exporters of low value raw materials and importers of high cost finished product from the centre nations; therefore, most of the benefits from the trade would be accrued by the centre nations. With the acceleration in the trade relationship, the inequality of per capita income between the centre-developed nations and the periphery-underdeveloped nations would be elongated than it being reduced. Perbisch advocated for the industrialization of the periphery nations as this will reduce their vulnerability, synchronize the difference between the underdeveloped nations and the developed nation, and would ease international crisis. He suggested the imposition of tax on the export of primary products and also proposed a set of duties on manufacturing imports by the underdeveloped nations. This will help them to switch over resources from the production of primary goods for export to industrial activities. He was not against expansion of the export in the periphery countries as long as it helped them to reduce their labour surplus, push up wages, and boost export prices.

F.H. Cardoso, another influential structuralist, had a different opinion about the 'economic gain' to the centre and 'economic loss' to the periphery.[3] He viewed that the internal dynamics of a nation and its link with the external forces is a complex whole and the gains of the periphery nations are being influenced not only by the external factors but also by the internal social, political, and economic forces prevailing in the periphery nations. He was of the opinion that dependency is not a 'zero sum' game for the periphery underdeveloped nations and absolute gain to the centre developed nations. It is rather a 'positive sum' game in which both the developed and underdeveloped nations gain from each other. The gain of capital by the underdeveloped countries from the developed countries through the export of raw materials also economically enables these countries to invest in various productive sectors thus help them to promote their economic growth and development. Cardoso and Faletto (1979) argued that not only was capitalist development in the periphery possible, but foreign capital also had a tendency to be reinvested in the host country so that foreign investment might in fact stimulate domestic investment. This dependency is not a relationship between the raw material exporter underdeveloped countries and finished goods supplier industrialized developed countries, but that between countries with different degrees of industrialization.

Dependency theory was popular in the Western world during 1950s–1960s. The dependency theory characterized that the international system comprised two sets of states variously described as 'dominant/dependent', 'centre/periphery', and 'metropolitan/satellite'. The dominant nations are the advanced industrialized nations, while the dependents are the poor nations belonging to Latin America, Asia, and Africa. The dependency theory commonly believes that the development of developed nations has been possible due to the 'exploitation of the economic surplus' of the periphery underdeveloped nations. It has benefited rich centre nations at the cost of the poor periphery nations. Prebisch advocated that the only way for the periphery underdeveloped countries to overcome their disadvantage position was to reform the structure of their economies by promoting industrialization and relying less on the production and export of primary products to the developed nations. Lal (2000) has nicely commented that the gist of the dependency thesis seems to be that the 'centre' has exploited the 'periphery' for over 400 years, first through 'colonialism' and 'imperialism' and more recently through the neo-colonial form of 'dependent capitalism' and has endangered the Third World. One of the criticisms levelled against the dependency theory of development is that it treats all the LDCs as a homogeneous entity; however, there are many variations among the developing countries in terms of their development. Further, technological and economic dependency of the developing countries, the role of FDIs, and outsourcing and remittances from the developed countries to the underdeveloped countries have enabled these countries to develop along different dimensions of development. This has not been adequately dealt with by the exponents of dependency theory. Per se remittances have brought a lot of changes in the quality of life of people in the Indian states of Kerala and Punjab.

NEO-LIBERAL THEORY OF DEVELOPMENT

Neo-liberal theory of development emerged during 1980s, as a panacea to the economic crisis being faced by the developed countries, i.e. USA and the UK.[4] Over the past 30 years, neo-liberalism has become the dominant hegemony in USA and much of the world (Harvey, 2005). According to Pieterse (2006), the onset of neo-liberalism is the confluence of the economic ideas of the Chicago school and the policies of Ronald Regan and Margaret Thatcher and a further step is the Washington Consensus, the economic orthodoxy that guided the International Monetary Fund (IMF) and World Bank in their policies through the 1990s and turned neo-liberalism into a global policy. The neo-liberalism theory, policies, and practices are also being encouraged by the international agencies, i.e. World Bank, IMF, World Trade Organization (WTO), and European Union. According to Saad-Filho and Johnston (2005), 'we live in the age of neo-liberalism.

Neo-liberalism has been divided into three phases:

(i) An early phase of Porto-neoliberalism from the 1940s to the 1970s in which the main idea took shape.
(ii) A phase of roll-back neo-liberalism in the 1980s, when it became government policy in USA and the UK.
(iii) A phase of roll-out neo-liberalism in the 1990s when it became hegemonic in the multilateral institutions (Tickell and Peck, 2003).

The distinction between 'liberalism' and 'neo-liberalism' or 'classical liberalism' and 'modern liberalism' is a matter of degree of the role of state in the affairs of the country. The 'classical' liberals favour *laissez faire* economic policies, because it is thought that it leads to more freedom which encourages the entrepreneurs to invest more and more, in order to gain more and more profit, which is further reinvested, which ultimately promotes economic growth and development. However, the modern liberals believe that besides market, the state has to play a significant role in the economic development process of the economy. They were of the view that size of the government is to be determined by the degree of failure of the market forces in an economy. When the market fails to perform its assigned functions, then the government action is clearly called for, to reconstitute and reinvigorate the competitive forces and fulfil the gap left out by the market. Besides, in the developing countries, market, which is guided by the profit motive, cannot solely be able to provide social and economic justice to the poor and act upon to reduce economic inequality between haves and have-nots. The neo-liberal believes that for the effective growth and development of the nation, state should play the role of a night watchman, and need to intervene in the economic affairs of a nation only when the market fails to perform or to provide a helping hand to the market to perform its functions effectively and efficiently.[5]

Harvey, one of the strong proponents of neo-liberal theory, defined neo-liberalism as a theory of political economic practices which believes that human well-being can best be accelerated by promoting individual entrepreneurial freedoms and skills within an institutional framework which assigns importance to strong private property rights, free market, and free trade. The role of the state is to create and preserve an enabling institutional framework which preserves, protects, and promotes such practices. Harvey, in his book, *A Brief History of Neo-liberalism*, while advocating the role of state, has noted that it is the duty and responsibility of the state to guarantee the quality and integrity of money. It has to set up military, defense, police, and legal structures and administer and manage their functioning. It needs to secure private property rights and its guarantee through the law. The state also needs to look at the proper functioning of markets, and if markets do not exist in certain areas such as land, water, education, health care, social security, or environmental pollution in any country, it is the duty of the state to create them and enable them to function effectively and efficiently and provide services with equity. However, the state should not venture beyond these tasks. Finally, he was of the opinion that the state intervention in the affairs of the market must be kept to a bare minimum.

Bauer (1984) another protagonist of neo-liberalism attacked the intervention of government in the affairs of the economy. He was of the view that the major investment in infrastructure by the government would not necessarily accelerate or push the development forward. He believed that it is the desire for profit by the individual mediated by the market would promote economic growth and development in an economy.

Bauer and others have criticized the state intervention in the growth and development affairs of the economy on three grounds:

(i) At the outset, the role of public sector has become overextended and overemphasized because of perceived attitude towards private sector in the economy.
(ii) The public sector many times over emphasizes and even over estimates the quantum of capital formation and scale of mega investment projects, which is certainly intended to look down the role of market.
(iii) The rise of the size of public sector leads to the proliferation of economically distorting controls in the economy, which creates an inefficient production structure in the economy (Cypher and Dietz, 2006).

He is all praise for Adam Smith's invisible hand which governs market forces and the process of capital accumulation by the individual entrepreneurs with *laissez faire* principle which pushes economy to the higher growth and development. He admonished Gunnar Myrdal's viewpoint, that the underdeveloped countries are poor because of vicious circle of poverty and was of the opinion that they are poor because of too much interference of government. The functions of the government in his view are to ensure the basic provision of health and education to the people and to perform the duty of effective and efficient management of monetary and fiscal system of the economy. Milton Friedman and Peter Bauer[6] who influenced the Thatcherian and Reganian liberal economic policy during 1980s was in the favour of market against government. Milton Friedman argued that government should not be involved in the economy except for main functions: (a) defence; (b) law and order; (c) provision of necessary public works that private enterprises does not find profitable to produce; and (d) protection from members of the community who cannot be regarded as 'responsible individuals'. Deepak Lal, another protagonist of neo-liberalism believes that market is an essential component of any well-functioning economy. He was of the view that the development economics suffers from a 'dirigisme dogma', i.e. a preference for state-led development strategy. In his best-known book, *The Poverty of Development Economics*, he criticized the views of the development economists that the price and market system should be "supplanted (and not just supplemented) by various forms of direct government control...to promote economic development". He believed that government failure is worse than market failure and that imperfect planning is even worse than an imperfect market. In his view, the market fails to achieve equilibrium not due to its inefficiency but because of the rent-seeking behaviour of the producers who capture the government to stifle market. He has strongly argued that market reform has lifted hundreds of millions of people out of poverty. He was against all kinds of government interventions; however, he favoured government policy as an instrument of economic growth and development.

In essence, neo-liberalism is a political economic theory, committed to *laissez faire* market fundamentalism and a minimalist role for state intervention in the economic affairs of the nation.

From all the earlier discussions on neo-liberalism, some features of neo-liberalism can be deduced:

(i) Market is the key economic player, and its proper functioning would hasten economic growth and development in developed as well as developing countries.
(ii) Neo-liberal policies aim at privatization, liberalization, and globalization.
(iii) Privatization of public sector unit will enhance their efficiency and raise their contribution to economic development.
(iv) Government role in the process of economic development must be minimal and its action in correcting market imperfection will act as stimulant to economic development.
(v) The economy needs to 'open up' and there should be minimum protection and maximum free trade.
(vi) Deregulation and disinvestment of public sector unit are the recommended measures for economic development.
(vii) Individualism and individual urge for profit is a driving force for hastening pace of development.
(viii) The *laissez faire* philosophy is a fundamental feature of neo-liberalism.
(ix) State role should be confined to the public goods such as defense, health, education, and infrastructure promotion in different sectors, which will enable the private sector to run efficiently and effectively to contribute towards country's economic growth and development.

Neo-liberalism has been criticized as not being friendly to the Third World countries. It is considered a boon for the developed countries where the market has taken a deep-seated root and a bane for developing countries where the market is highly imperfect. Pieterse (2006) remarked that neo-liberalism is crisis-prone rather than crisis-proof is no news to most of the world but a novel experience for the United States. The neo-liberalism is found to be tilted towards the benefits of rich nations and the underdeveloped countries are not being much benefited from neo-liberalism.

HUMAN CAPABILITIES THEORY

Human capital or skill, capabilities and dexterities of human beings, in the late 19th century, was being considered as one of the fundamental aspects to growth and development of a nation. To Poolman (2012), the capability approach has been the subject of an increasingly enthusiastic enquiry in development studies over the last two decades and has been hailed as a suitable theory of development (Deneulin and Shahani, 2009). However, the importance of capability approach in development was very well stressed by Aristotle, Adam Smith, and Karl Marx in their respective areas of work on development.[7] The international organizations in recent years have also stressed on the human capability as an engine of economic growth and development. UNDP (2001) considered, 'people are the real wealth of a nation' and therefore, envisaged that "the most basic capabilities for human development are to lead long and healthy lives, to be knowledgeable, to have access to the resources needed for a decent standard of living, and to be able to participate in the life of the community". Two nations with equal amount of natural, financial, and technological resources but endowed with different quantum and quality of human capital would certainly perform differently in the sphere of development and people living there will enjoy different levels of quality of life. Of late, the Asian countries, i.e. Japan and Singapore, are illustrious examples.

The two prominent propounders of human capability approach to development are Amartya Sen and Martha Nussbaum. Capability approach puts people and their capabilities at the centre stage of development. The human capabilities approach considers human beings and the freedom they enjoy as a means to achieve the ends of developmental goals in the developing countries. Amartya Sen in *Inequality Re-examined* said that "A person's capability to achieve functions that he or she has reason to value provides a general approach to the evolution of social arrangements, and this yields a particular way of viewing the assessment of equality and inequality" (Sen, 1992). The two aspects important to Sen's human capability are 'evaluative aspect' and the 'agency aspect'. The former is concerned with evaluating the human achievements, the key indicators of progress, and the latter is concerned with what human beings can do to achieve such achievements. The key idea of the capability approach is that social arrangements in a country should aim at expanding people's capabilities and should also try to enhance individual's freedom in order to enable him or her to achieve valuable beings and doings. The aim of development is to improve the capabilities of an individual so that he or she will be able to do a range of things, such as to be healthy and well- nourished, to be knowledgeable and to participate in community life. Sen treats endurance of poverty in a society as 'capability deprivation' and as a result wants to place human beings at the centre of development, enabling them to fight against poverty. Capability is freedom and freedom includes a person's ability to get systematically what he would choose to do, no matter who actually controls the levers of operation. Freedom enhances people's ability to be effective and influential. Freedom is not only the basis of the evaluation of success and failure, but it is also a principal determinant of individual initiative and social effectiveness. Greater freedom enhances the ability of people to help themselves and also helps them to `function in a way to influence the world. The capability approach is generally conceived as a flexible and multipurpose framework, not only to promote human well-being, but also to enable a nation to achieve higher level of development.

The key components of capability approach as propounded by Sen are: (a) functioning, (b) capability, and (c) agency.

Functioning: To Sen, functioning is 'the various things a person may value doing or being'. The examples of 'being' are being well-nourished, being housed in a healthy house, being educated, being part of a supportive network, being groomed in a healthy environment, etc. An achievement or outcome will not be treated as functioning if it is not something that is valued by the person concerned, who has achieved the milestone. For example, a young man who has just completed computer qualification on the instruction of his father, despite the fact that he is a passionate and talented artist who wished to study fine arts, would not necessarily view his computer qualification as a functioning or an achievement that he has reason to value.

Capabilities: Capabilities are the alternative combinations of functioning that are available to an individual which enable him or her to achieve. Put differently, capabilities are 'the substantive freedoms' that an individual ought to enjoy in order to lead the kind of life he or she has reason to value or wants to lead (Sen, 1999). Capabilities are a kind of freedom of opportunity. For example, a person with a handsome income can choose to buy different things; in the same coin, a person having many skills and capabilities could choose a suitable activity from many different available activities and pursue a life path which is best suited to his or her capabilities. With capabilities, an individual could overcome the constraints which he or she is facing in his life. Capabilities enable an individual to avail or grasp opportunities. The capability set is like a budget set. To put it simply, 'a functioning is an achievement [outcome] whereas a capability is the ability to achieve [potential]' (Sen, 1985; Walker and Unterhalter, 2007).

Agency: The third important concept in Sen's capability approach is agency. According to Sen, agency refers to a person's ability to pursue and realize goals that he or she values and has reason to value. An agent is someone who acts and brings about change. The agency aspect is important 'in assessing what a person can do in line with his or her conception of the good'. Agency in Sen's term is a powerful concept in capability formulation which stresses on self-determination, self-reliance, empowerment, raising voice, and so on.

In Sen's account, agency comprises the following things:

(i) Agency is exercised with respect to goals the person values and has reason to value.
(ii) Agency includes effective power as well as direct control, that is, it includes not just individual agency, but also what one can do as a member of a group or collectively or as a political community.
(iii) Agency may advance well-being or may address other related goals, for example, relating to the good of one's family or community or of other people and of art and the environment.

(iv) Identifying agency entails an assessment of whether the agent's goals are in some way reasonable; a person who harms or humiliates others would not, in this view, be the existing agency.

(v) The agent's responsibility for a state of affairs should be incorporated into his or her evaluation of it (Sen, 1985; Alkire, 2008). It is agency which brings changes in the society through innovations. Human capability is central to Sen's approach of development. Capability is freedom, which enables a person to effectively contribute not only for the well-being of his or her family but also for the development of the society in which he or she lives, and collectively it ultimately promotes development of the nation-state.

Another influential propounder of capability approach to development is the feminist philosopher Martha Nussbaum. Nussbaum's analysis of capability is heavily tilted towards the philosophy of Aristotle and Karl Marx. Nussbaum advocated a capabilities approach that could fully express human powers and not just provide opportunities for people to perform certain functions. The capability must enable a person to perform his function in a truly human way and not in just any way. She was of the view that if a person lives a life where she cannot exercise her human power and freedom of expression, this means she is living her life in a sub-human way. Nussbaum (2000) capability approach to development differs from Sen's approach in two ways: First, her capabilities analysis tilts more towards gender perspective and second, it takes copiously into account the psycho-social aspects of capabilities building. In her book, *Women and Human Development: The Capabilities Approach*, she has listed out ten capabilities, which are as follows:

(i) Life: Able to live to the end of a normal length human life, and do not have one's life reduced to not worth living.

(ii) Bodily health: Able to have a good health which includes (but is not limited to) reproductive health, nourishment, and shelter.

(iii) Bodily integrity: Able to change locations freely, in addition to having sovereignty over one's body, which includes being secure against assault (for example, sexual assault or domestic violence), and having opportunities for sexual satisfaction and choice in matters of reproduction.

(iv) Senses, imagination, and thought: Able to use one's senses to imagine, think, and reason in a 'truly human way', informed by an adequate education. Furthermore, the ability to produce self-expressive works and engage in religious rituals without fear of political ramifications. The ability to have pleasure experiences and to avoid unnecessary pain and to lead a meaningful life.

(v) Emotions: Able to have attachments to things outside of ourselves; this includes, being able to love others, grieve at the loss of loved ones, and be angry when it is justified.

(vi) Practical reason: Able to form a conception of the good and critically reflect on it.

(vii) Affiliation: (a) Able to live with others and show concern for others, empathize (and show compassion for) with others and have the capability of justice and friendship. Institutions help to develop and protect forms of affiliation and (b) able to have self-respect and not be humiliated by others, that is, being treated with dignity and equal worth. It entails (at the very least) protections of being discriminated on the basis of race, sex, sexuality, religion, caste, ethnicity, and nationality. In work, this means entering relationship of mutual recognition.

(viii) Other species: Able to have concern for and live with other animals, plants, and the environment, at large.

(ix) Play: Able to laugh, play, and enjoy recreational activities.

(x) Control over one's environment: (a) political—able to effectively participate in the political life which includes having the right to free speech and association; and (b) material—able to own property, not just formally, but materially (that is as a real opportunity). Furthermore, having the ability to seek employment on an equal basis, as others, and freedom from unwarranted search and leisure (Nussbaum, 2000).

Nussbaum has justified this list by arguing that each of these capabilities is needed for a human life. Without these capabilities, a human being is not worth living. She argued that these capabilities needed to be the moral entitlements of every human being on the earth. Nussbaum argues that this list of capabilities should be enshrined in every country's constitution. The citizens of a nation should be guaranteed a social minimum whereby capabilities can be realized. It is the duty and responsibility of the state-led institutions to ensure that a threshold level of central capabilities is realized. However, the most important challenge before capability approach, as propounded by Nussbaum in development policy, is about deciding which capabilities are important and require immediate attention towards development perspectives. Capabilities of an individual are largely dependent on social, economic, psychological, and environmental factors and even on the political and bureaucratic factors, particularly in a stratified developing society, which pose challenge before the nation-state for its achievement.

GANDHIAN THEORY OF DEVELOPMENT

Mahatma Gandhi was neither an economist nor a development scientist; however, Gandhian thoughts and philosophy provide vital inputs to development theories and approaches and is quite relevant to the development of the underdeveloped countries. Even today, it is being admired and realized by both the developed as well as underdeveloped countries that the Gandhian philosophy of development has a lot of relevance in this globalized and neo-liberal world of the 21st century. Gandhian model of development is based on his advocacy on development ethics and philosophy rather than hardcore economics. As J.B. Kripalani (1971), one of the ardent supporters of Gandhian philosophy, pointed out that Gandhi did not recognize the separation of economics from ethics, rather he wanted to achieve an ethical ordering of the economic life of society. Gandhi was against 'economics' which lays stress on the creation of wealth, builds a paradise of material plenty, hypes standard of living, benefits a few, and only aims at optimizing the production at the cost of human well-being. He considered that the gospel of the creation of economic abundance through exploitation of many by a few through following unscrupulous and unjust practices is a delusion and a snare. Gandhi advocated that true national economy leads to social justice and adds to the good of all, and reduces inequality and promotes well-being of the poorest of the poor. The one-sided raising of the standard of living of a small number capitalists, entrepreneurs, and businessmen leads to a world of struggle and misery of many which is unfair and is unacceptable to an undeveloped country with the vexing problem of a large number of people reeling under poverty and hunger. Morality means, from the social point of view, that everyone will be able to share the general welfare and the general welfare must not be confined to the benefit of a few. The ideal society as visualized by Gandhi, therefore, is not a materially or economically affluent society, as conceived by mainstream economists, but a just and egalitarian society. The concepts for the promotion of holistic development as popularized by Gandhi during his socio-political *yojana* (planning) in India's freedom and prosperity is as follows: (a) truth, (b) ahimsa, (c) prohibition, (d) self-control, (e) worship, (f) eradication of untouchability, (g) women's emancipation, (h) national integration, (i) village uplift, (j) *khaddar*, (k) swadeshi, and (l) manual labour (Gangrade, 1991). To Gandhi, economic development and social development must go hand in hand and promotion of economic development without social development is irrelevant for the development of poor countries. Holistic development is achieved only when there is simultaneous development in all spheres, i.e. economic, social, political, human, cultural, and so on.

The three important factors of economic development, i.e. land, labour, and capital as prescribed by the hard-core classical economists were critically analyzed by Mahatma Gandhi. Gandhi believed in the principle of land to the tiller approach for the agricultural development and was against concentration of land in the hands of a few villagers (landlords) and advocated distribution of land among the landless. He said, "Land belongs to God—it belongs to all or none. Nobody created the land, so why should anyone claim to possess it?" In his view, air, water, sunshine, forests, hills, rivers, and all other natural resources on the earth are part of our planetary heritage and each and every individual has right over them. Therefore, no one group or individual has a right to own it, possess it, spoil it, pollute it, or destroy it. He was in favour of transfer of surplus land from the landlord to the landless and was ardent supporter of 'Bhudan Movement' (land gift movement) launched by Vinoba Bhave. From its interpretation, it is observed that Gandhi was an ardent supporter of land reform, particularly ceiling on land holding which intends to limit the size of land to be possessed by a family. Gandhi was strongly against the exploitation of labour by the feudal and considered it as an evil act. He defined that whenever a labourer is paid less than the basic wage rate or minimum living wage rate, he or she is said to be exploited. According to Gandhi, capital is the source of all wealth. However, he thought that both capital and labour need to be coherently coordinated and capital cannot work independently considering the significance of labour, and a proper mix of labour and capital is required to avoid unemployment in the society. Gandhi believed that employment is critical to eradicate poverty and a vital factor to promote development. The problem of unemployment can be tackled only by developing villages and cottage industries. He told, "Village economy cannot be complete without the essential village industries such as hand grinding, hand pounding, soap making, paper making, match making, tanning, oil pressing, etc.". (Gandhi, 1981). He said that:

> The people of India are forced to remain idle at least four months in a year. People who are thus forced to remain idle cannot be revived. For crores of people, the spinning wheel is the only occupation which can supplement their income for the fields, most emphatically they have no other one. (Gandhi, 1967)

He was against the exorbitant use of technology in the process of development. He was not in favour of the modern type of capital-intensive industrialization which squeezes the employment of labour force. Gandhi was vehemently against the 'soulless machine' and 'soulless state' which enslave human beings. He used to say that mechanization is good when the hands are too few for the work intended to be accomplished and an evil when hands are too many to be deployed for the intended assignment. Although Gandhi had recognized the need for some large industries for the development of the underdeveloped economy, yet he advocated that those are to be organically related to the needs and requirements of agriculture and cottage and small industries. Some of the important edifices of Gandhian philosophy of development are discussed as follows.

Sarvodaya

Gandhi advocated *sarvodaya* for holistic development. To him, *sarvodaya* is an important means of development and it intends to make the development process 'of the people, by the people and for the people' and to promote welfare of all. By welfare of all, Gandhi did not mean that greatest good of the greatest number, but for prioritizing the welfare of 'the last man', the most deprived and the weakest and the poorest of the poor. He advocated that it is the duty of the society, to give priority to the care of the poorest of the poor. In the *sarvodaya* system, basic needs always get precedence over other needs that are not so basic, i.e. largely the needs for attainment of comfort and luxury. Gandhi considered the whole world as a single family and, therefore, his perspective, ideal, and concept were to develop everything that is popularly known as *sarvodaya*. He was against the affluence of a few and pauperism of many. In his opinion, human greediness is the main cause of poverty, inequality, and economic disparities. He summarized all these facts and truths in his often-sighted statement, "the earth provides enough to satisfy every one's need but not for anybody's greed" (Gandhi, 1967). He argued that happiness is a mental condition by quoting "a man is not necessarily happy because he is rich or unhappy because he is poor. The rich are often seen to unhappy and the poor to be happy" (Gandhi, 1908—*Hind Swaraj*).

Gandhian Doctrine of Trusteeship

Gandhi propounded the doctrine of trusteeship as a way to realize social change and development through non-violent means. Gandhi was critical to both capitalism and socialism, as he believed that the former emphasizes on the private ownership, while the latter advocates state ownership of means of production and distribution. He advocated a new method that would substitute both capitalist and socialist forms of ownership, called 'trusteeship'. Trusteeship provides a means of transforming the present capitalist order of society into an egalitarian one. It emphasizes the legislative regulation of ownership and use of wealth and was not in favour recognition of any right of the private ownership of property except in as much as it may be permitted by society for its own welfare. Under the state-regulated trusteeship, an individual will not be free to hold or use his wealth for selfish satisfaction or in disregard of the interest of society. The Gandhian economic order believes that the character of production will be determined by social necessity and not by personal whim or greed. Gandhi advocated that the best method of development is participatory method and advised that the development functionaries have to work along with the people.

The four important steps to work with the people are: (a) involve the villagers in systematic discussion of their felt needs, (b) systematic planning to carry out the first self-help project selected by the community, (c) harness the resources of the community for carrying out the concrete project, and (d) creation of community appreciation and determination to take up additional projects to maintain enthusiasm and spirit of the people. Gandhi 'considered' that any strategy of development which does not consider people's participation is not a genuine strategy of development.

Gandhi Methodology of '*Nai Talim*' for Development

Gandhi advocated the *Nai Talim* (new education) approach to education in 1937. It emphasizes on total personality development of an individual including body, mind, and spirit. The basic principles of *Nai Talim* are:

(i) Education or learning in mother tongue along with handicraft work.
(ii) Work should be linked with most useful vocational needs of the locality.
(iii) Learning should be linked with vocational work.
(iv) Work should be socially useful and productive needed for living (Panse, 2007).

This approach of work-centric education with technology will promote skill among the rural youth. Gandhi emphasized on life-long learning by linking education with work, yoga, and cooperative development. Life skill education among youth will enable them to get employment and promote rural development.

Gandhian Villagism and Gram Swaraj for Total Development

Gandhi said, "Our cities are not India. India lives in her seven and half lakhs of village and the cities live upon the villages". According to Gandhi, the real India lives in its villages. It is there that our producers live, voters live, and the poor and illiterate live. It is the village that holds the key to the country's problems and, therefore, the vision of future India cannot be greater than that of rebuilding its villages. The first concern of an ideal village as propounded by Gandhi is to grow its own food crops and cotton for clothing. It should have fodder reserve for its cattle, and recreation and playground for adults and children. If there is more land available, it will be used for growing cash crops, but not products like *ganja*, tobacco, opium, and the like. The village needs to have a village theatre, school, and public hall. It should have its own water works, for ensuring clean water supply to all sections of its population. Basic and primary education needs to be compulsory for all children. The village should try to conduct every activity on cooperative basis. The government of the village needed to be run by a panchayat of five persons annually elected by the adult villagers. Panchayats will be endowed with legislative, judiciary, and executive powers. A self-reliant village must be self-sufficient in regard to food, clothing, and other necessities. He dramatized the problem of city vs. village antagonism, "the blood of the villages is the cement with which the edifice of the city is built. I want this blood that is today inflating the arteries of the cities to run once again in the blood vessels of the village" (Gandhi, 1946). Gandhi philosophy of rural and village development was based on *Gram Swaraj*. This notion of Gram Swaraj contains threefold revolution: land to the villagers, industries and economic activities to the villages, and political power to the villages. He wanted independent India to be a union or republic of self-sufficient but interrelated village republics. Gandhi was of the view that only a rural civilization based on the principles of self-reliance, self-sufficiency, simplicity and limited wants, mutual aid and cooperation, participation and sharing, and finally caring and mutual empowerment through meaningful community interaction is sustainable and helpful for human spiritual evolution (Mathew, 2010). In Gandhi's view, a sustainable village economy is essential for the total development of the nation-state. Gandhi was against unbridled urbanization as it will lead to the devastation of the austerity of rural life.

Gandhian Model of Balanced Growth

Gandhian principle of balanced growth and development is constructed with the combination of both economic growth and mental and moral growth of the population of a nation. Gandhian doctrine of economic growth believes that economic growth cannot be meaningfully formulated without moral and spiritual growth.

The balanced growth model is characterized with the following types of balance:

(i) Philosophical balance: A balance between economic progress and moral progress.
(ii) Structural balance: A balance between rural and urban structure of the economy. The growth of urban sector must not take place at the expense of the rural sector.
(iii) Ecological balance: A balance in the relationship of man and environment. Environment is crucial for development and it must not be exploited for the selfish benefit of the society.
(iv) Technological balance: A balance between small- and large-scale technologies. The use of technology be made for raising productivity and not to enhance unemployment. He was against the indiscriminate use of Western technology to economize labour and to expand production at the cost of rural deindustrialization. He endorsed a proper mix of technology in order to optimize the social benefits of science and technology. He was of the opinion that unlimited growth is impossible with the limited amount of natural resources.

Gandhian Model of Sustainable Development

The Gandhian model of sustainable development is based on his philosophy that "The earth has enough resources for our needs not for our greed". Gandhi emphasized that the sustainable development must bank on economy, society, and environment intrinsically. He told that the present lifestyle of human beings has to be changed for sustainable development.

Gandhi suggested the following steps in order to attend sustainable lifestyle:

(i) Sustainable agriculture: Less use of chemical fertilizers and pesticides and more use of organic methods, i.e. bio-manures and bio-pesticides.

(ii) *Khadi* and village industries: Emit fewer pollutants and are eco-friendly. Generate employment for the rural masses and help in poverty alleviation.

(iii) Renewable energy sources: Gandhi emphasized on the use of renewable energy sources like solar energy which is limitless and inexhaustible. Harnessing water and wind energy for producing electricity.

(iv) Sylviculture: Gandhi emphasized on planting of trees for protection of environment and also for fuel wood and construction of houses. Gandhian concept of sustainable development advocated the more natural way of living which can be more sustainable.

Gandhian Model of Population and Development

Gandhi was in support of population control; however, his opinion regarding population and development was different from that of Malthusian fear of overpopulation. Gandhi advocated that if suitable improvements could be made in the laws relating to land and the state of agriculture and an allied occupation could be provided, India could support twice its population (Suman, 1969). Gandhi had two observations regarding birth control: (a) the burden of large families falls on the poor and middle class; and (b) of course, women do not want many children, however, they cannot resist their husbands. If they could do so without causing bitterness, birth control would be possible without any coercive measures. The principal aspect of Gandhian theory of population is that Gandhi outrightly rejected artificial methods of birth control. He was in favour of practicing *brahmacharya* (celibacy) rather than using family planning methods for restriction of family size. He suggested that the population workers must propagate the value of *brahmacharya* among men and women. However, he advocated sterilization in certain circumstances, where a person is suffering from incurable or sexually transmitted diseases and wanting sterilization. Gandhi was in favour of raising the age at marriage in India and opined that "any sensible legislation in the direction of raising the age of consent will certainly have my approval" (*Young India*, 27 August 1925). To Myrdal, Gandhi was a radical liberal who denied that India was overpopulated and derived his position from Gandhi's statement that if all laboured for their bread, there would be no cry of overpopulation, no disease, and no misery (Myrdal, 1968). Gandhi was in favour of raising the status of population in the society to deal with population and development problem. He emphasized on the change in public opinion about the age at marriage, widow remarriage, education of women, and equality of status between men and women. Gandhi was critical to the Western opinion that population growth in developing countries slow down the pace of development. Rather, he was of the opinion that population must be effectively used for the development of the nation.

Gandhian philosophy on development has a lot of relevance for the developing countries trying to achieve MDGs. Gandhian approach to bring holistic development through a participatory means is quite relevant for democratic developing countries. Gandhi was a true developmentalist and his principles of development have a lot of relevance for the holistic development of the developing countries even in the present globalized world. However, Gandhian theory of development is criticized on the ground that he did not emphasize on the modernization and liberalization which is playing important role in development of developing countries in recent years. His views of industrialization and technological interventions on development are also too much conservative in nature. Besides, many of his advocacies on development are idealistic in nature, and it is very difficult to put them into practice.

The Sum Up

The heterogeneous theories comprise economic and non-economic theories of development. The modernization theorists believe that besides economic aspects, the other socio-psychological, human, cultural, and political aspects are needed to be given emphasis for the holistic development of the developing countries. Dependency theory is not a homogenous theory; the dependency theory is based on the argument that in order to deal with the problem of underdevelopment of the developing countries, one has to take into cognizance the development process of developed countries. For the proponents of the neo-liberal theory, the free market and free trade are critical to ensure freedom, democracy, and sustainable economic growth and development of the developed as well as developing countries. The human capability theorists have given emphasis on human capabilities and freedom for facilitating development of the developing nations. Last but not the least, Gandhian theory of development is basically based on Gandhi's viewpoints on development, which are heterogeneous in character and his emphasis on social, economic, political, human, and cultural development aspects has a lot of relevance for the sustainable and holistic development of developing countries.

Keywords organic solidarity, social solidarity, ascriptive bond, morphology of backwardness, centre and periphery, neo-liberalism, functioning, agency, *sarvodaya*, trusteeship, *nai talim*.

REVIEW QUESTIONS

1. What is modernization theory? Explain its features and how far these are relevant for the developing countries.
2. Critically discuss the Weber and Learner theory of modernization. How are they different and relevant for the developing countries?
3. Discuss the McClelland theory of modernization. How far is it relevant for the developing countries?
4. Explain the features of dependency theory. How far is it relevant for the developing countries in a globalization era?
5. Neo-liberal theory has benefited more to the developed countries rather than the developing countries. Illustrate the argument.
6. What is human capabilities theory? Explain Amartya Sen's theory of human capabilities.
7. Critically explain Nussbaum theory of human capabilities. How is it different from Amartya Sen's concept of human capabilities?

8. Critically explain the Gandhian concept of balanced and sustainable growth.
9. Explain four important features of the Gandhian theory of development. How are they relevant for the developing countries?
10. Write short notes on the following:
    (a) Social pathology
    (b) Ascriptive bond
    (c) Westernization
    (d) Morphology of backwardness
    (e) Marxian approach to dependency
    (f) Capability is freedom
    (g) Agency
    (h) Functioning
    (i) *Sarvodaya*
    (j) Trusteeship

NOTES

1. The statement was quoted from Ramona, B.N., V.A. Iolanda, and B. Sanziana, "Orthodoxy, Heterodoxy and Mainstream Theory of Economic Growth". Available at: http://steconomiceuoradea.ro/anale/volume/2009 (accessed on 29 July 2015).
2. Frank (1969) has commented that no country which has firmly tied to the metropolis as a satellite through incorporation into the world capitalist system has achieved the rank of an economically developed country.
3. Cardoso and Faletto (1979) in their pioneering work have analyzed the changing relationship between internal and external factors which have determined the development process in Latin America.
4. Hahn (2007) have noted that neo-liberalism in the past three decades have a tremendous impact on both thought and practice throughout most of the world and has dominated international development since the early 1980s.
5. Blomgren (1997) arguments of state role as a night watchman also emphasizes the internal diversity of neo-liberal thought in the following words: "neo-liberalism is commonly thought of as a political philosophy giving priority to individual freedom and the right to private property. It is not, however, the simple and homogenous philosophy it might appear to be. It ranges over a wide expanse in regard to ethical foundations as well as to normative conclusions. At the one end of the line is 'anchro-liberalism' arguing for a complete *laissez faire* and the abolishment of all government. At the other end is 'classical-liberalism' demanding a government with functions exceeding those of the so-called 'night watchman state'."
6. New Right (neo-liberal) Theory on Development, 03d New Right Theory. Available at: http://resource.download.wjec.co.uk.s3.amazonaws.com/vtc/2009-10/Sociology/a2-cynnal/index.html (accessed on 17 February 2016).
7. Aristotle made extensive use in his analysis of 'the good of human being' and this he linked with his examination of 'the functions of man' and his exploration of 'life in the sense of activity' (Ross, 1980). Adam Smith and Karl Marx explicitly discussed the importance of functioning and the capability to function as determinants of well-being (Smith, 1976; Marx, 1977).

REFERENCES

Alkire, S. 2008. "Concepts and Measures of Agency." OPHI Working Papers, ophiwp010, Queen Elizabeth House, University of Oxford.

Amin, S. 1976. *Unequal Development*. New York and Hassocks: Harvester Press.

Baran, P. A. 1957. *The Political Economy of Growth*. New York: Monthly Review Press.

Blomgren, A.M. 1997. Nyliberal politisk filosofi, En Kritisk Analys av, Milton Friedman, Robert Nozick och F.A. Hayek, Nora: Bokforloget Nya Doxa. Also quoted in Thorsen, D.E. "The Neoliberal Challenge: What is

Neoliberalism?" Working Paper, Department of Political Science, University of Oslo. Available at: http://folk.uio.no/daget/neoliberalism2.pdf (accessed on 11 October 2015).

Cardoso, F.H. and Faletto, E. 1979. *Dependency and Development in Latin America*. Berkley, CA: University of California Press.

Cypher, J.M. and Dietz, J.L. 2006. *The Process of Economic Development*. New York: Rutledge.

Deneulin, S. and Shahani, L., eds. 2009. *An Introduction to the Human Development and Capability Approach: Freedom and Agency*. London: Earth Scan.

Dillon, M. 2010. *Introduction to Sociological Theory: Theorists, Concepts and their Applicability to the Twenty-first Century*. UK: Wiley-Blackwell.

Frank, A.G. 1969. *Capitalism and Underdevelopment in Latin America: Historical Studies of Chile and Brazil*. London: Monthly Review Press.

Gandhi, M.K. 1908. *Hind Swaraj or Indian Home Rule*. Ahmedabad: Navajivan Publishing House.

———. 1946. *Harijan*, 23 April 1946, 198.

———. 1967. *The Collected Works*. Delhi Publication Division, Ministry of Information and Broadcasting, Government of India.

———. 1981. *Constructive Programme: Its Meaning and Place*. Navijivan Publishing House, Ahmedabad.

Gangrade, K.D. 1991. *Gandhian Ideal Development and Social Change*. New Delhi: Northern Book Centre.

Garnett, R.F. 2006. "Paradigms and Pluralism in Heterodox Economics." *Review of Political Economy*, 18: 521–46.

Green, Phil. 2008. "Are Development Theories of the 1950s, 1960s and 1970s still Relevant Today? Discuss with Reference to Modernization Theory." Available at: https://philmgreen.files.wordpress.com/2010/08/modernisation-theory-today.pdf (accessed on 15 February 2016).

Harvey, D. 2005. *A Brief History of Neo-liberalism*. New York: Oxford University Press.

Haynes, J. 2008. *Development Studies*. Cambridge: Polity.

Hout, Wil. 1993. *Capitalism and the Third World, Development, Dependence and the World System*. England: Edward Elgar Publishing Company.

Inglehart, R. 1997. *Modernization and Post-modernization: Cultural, Economic and Political Change in 43 Societies*. Princeton: Princeton University Press.

Kreutzmann, H. 1998. "From Modernization Theory towards the 'Clash of Civilizations': Directions and Paradigm Shifts in Samuel Huntington's Analysis and Prognosis of Global Development." *Geo Journal*, 46: 255–65.

Kripalani, J.B. 1971. *Gandhi: His Life and Thought*. New Delhi: Publication Division, Government of India.

Lal, Deepak. 2000. *The Poverty of Development Economics*. Cambridge, MA: MIT Press Edition.

Lerner, D. 1958. *The Passing of Traditional Society, Modernizing the Middle East*. Glencoe, IL: Free Press.

———. 1967. *The Passing of Traditional Society: Modernizing the Middle East* (Paperback edition), Toronto.

Marx, K. 1977. *A Contribution to the Critique of Political Economy*. Moscow: Progress Publisher.

Mathew, J. 2010. Available at: Shodhganga.inflibnet.ac.in/bitstream/10603/10166/.../17_chapter%206.pdf (accessed on 11 December 2015).

McClelland, D.C. 1961. *The Achieving Society*. Princeton, NJ: Van Nostrand.

———. 1964. "Business Drive and National Achievement." In *Social Change*, edited by A. Etzioni and E. Etzioni. New York: Basic Books, 165–78.

Moore, Wilbert. 1963. *Social Change*. New Jersey: Printice-Hall.

Morrison, K. 1995. *Marx Durkheim Weber Formations of Modern Social Thought*. London: SAGE Publications.

Myrdal, G. 1968. *Asian Drama*. New York: Pantheon.

Nussbaum, M. 2000. *Women and Human Development: The Capabilities Approach*. Cambridge: Cambridge University Press.

Parsons, T. 1964. "Evolutionary Universals in Society." *American Sociological Review*, 29: 339–57.

Pieterse, J.N. 2006. "Neo-liberal Globalization." In *Globalization and After*, edited by S. Dasgupta and P. Kiely. London: SAGE Publications.

Poolman, C. 2012. "Humanity in the Capability Approach to Development." *POLIS Journal*, 7: 366–408.

Ross, D. 1980. *Aristotle, the Nicomachean Ethics, the World's Classics*. Oxford: Oxford University Press.

Saad-Filho, A. and Johnston, D. 2005. "Introduction." In *Neoliberalism: A Critical Reader*, edited by A. Saad-Filho and D. Johnston, London: Pluto Press, 1–6.

Sen, A. 1985. "Well-being, Agency and Freedom." The Dewey Lectures 1984, *Journal of Philosophy*, 82: 169–221.

———. 1992. *Inequality Re-examined*. Oxford: Clarendon Press.

———. 1999. *Development as Freedom*. Oxford: Oxford University Press.

Smith, A. 1976 [1776]. *An Inquiry into the Nature and Causes of the Wealth of Nations*. Chicago, IL: University of Chicago Press.

Suman, R. 1969. *Samaj Sudhar: Samasyayen aur Samadhan*. Allahabad: Gandhi Sahitya Prakashan.

Sunkel, O. 1969. "National Development Policy and External Dependence in Latin America." *The Journal of Development Studies*, 6(1): 23.

Tickell, A. and Peck, J. 2003. "Making Global Rules: Globalization and Neo-liberalization." In *Remaking the Global Economy*, edited by J. Peck and H. Yeung. London: SAGE Publications, 163–81.

UNDP. 2001. *Human Development Report*. United Nations Development Programmes, New York.

Walker, M. and Unterhalter, E. 2007. "The Capability Approach: Its Potential for Work in Education." In *Amartya Sen's Capability Approach and Social Justice in Education*, edited by M. Walker and E. Unterhalter. New York: Palgrave Macmillan.

Weber, M. 1954. *Law in Economy and Society*. Cambridge: Harvard University Press.

Wrenn, M.V. 2006a. "Agency and Mental Models in Heterodox Economics." *Journal of Economic Issues*, 40: 483–91.

———. 2006b. "On the Nature of Heterodox Economics: A Survey Study." *History of Economic Review*, 43: 123–45.

SUGGESTED READINGS

Alkire, S. and Debeulin, S. 2009. "Human Development and Capability Approach." In *An Introduction to the Human Development and Capability Approach: Freedom and Agency*, edited by S. Deneulin, and L. Shahani. London: Earthscan.

Cardoso, F.H. 1973. "Associated Dependent Development: Theoritical and Practical Implementations." In *Authoritarian Brazil*, edited by A. Stepan. New Haven, CT: Yale University Press.

———. 1977. "Consumption of Dependency Theory in the United States." *Latin American Research Review*, 12(13): 7–24.

Frank, A.G. 1967. *Crisis in the Third World*. New York: Holnes and Meier.

———. 1972. "The Development of Underdevelopment." In *Monthly Review*, edited by J.D. Cockcroft, A.G. Frank, and D.L. Johnson, 18(4).

Gandhi Book Centre. 2002. "Gandhi on Villages Selected and Compiled with an Introduction by Divya Joshi." Mumbai: Gandhi Book Centre.

Inglehart, R. 1999. "Trust, Well-being and Democracy." In *Democracy and Trust*, edited by M.E. Warren, 88–120. New York: Cambridge University Press.

Inkeles, A. and Smith, D.H. 1974. *Becoming Modern—Individual Change in Six Developing Countries*. Cambridge: Harvard University Press.

Lal, Deepak. 1985. *The Poverty of Development Economics*. Cambridge, MA: Harvard University Press.

———. 2003. "Is Democracy Necessary for Development?" In *Development and Democracy New Perspective of an Old Debate*, edited by S. Ramaswamy and J.W. Cason, 17–42. London: University Press of New England.

Marx, K. 1853. "The Future Results of the British Rule in India." *New York Daily Tribune*, No. 3840, 8 August.

McClelland, D.C. 1963. "The Achievement Motive in Economic Growth." In *Industrialization and Society*, edited by B.F. Hoselitz and E. Moore, Paris: UNESCO-MOUTON, 74–96.

———. 1976. *The Achieving Society*. New York: Irvington Publishers.

Parsons, T. 1951. *The Social System*. New York: Free Press.

Pieterse, J.N. 1998. "My Paradigm or Yours? Alternative Development, Post Development or Reflective Development." *Development and Change*, 29: 343–73.

———. 2001. *Development Theory Deconstructions/Reconstructions*. London: SAGE Publications.

Prebish, R. 1950. *The Economic Development of Latin America and Its Principal Problems*. New York: United Nations, Department of Economic Affairs.

———. 1959. "Commercial Policy in the Underdeveloped Countries." *American Economic Review*. Papers and Proceedings, 49(2): 251–73.

———. 1968. *Towards a Dynamic Development Policy for Latin America*. New York: United Nations.

Pyarelal. 1948. *Mahatma Gandhi: Last Phase*, Vol. II. Ahmedabad: Navajivan Publishing House.

———. 1965. *Towards New Horizon*. Bombay: Navajivan Publishing House.

Rostow, Walter W. 1960. *The Stages of Economic Growth: A Non-communistic Manifesto*. Cambridge: Cambridge University Press.

5 Dimensions of Development

While many definitions of 'development' focus on economic aspects, it is crucial to recognize that the social and cultural variables not only affect economic growth but also those social and cultural norms and expectations need to be considered in their own right.

— Willis (2005)

Development incorporates the diverse and broad aspirations of what might be called the 'good life' in all its economic, social and political dimensions.

— Cypher and Dietz (2009)

There can be no substitute for interconnection between social, political and economic sectors and long-standing relationships between the key institutions and actors that will constitute the base of action for attaining developmental goals.

— Zafarullah and Huque (2006)

For a layman, 'development' may be a simple word, but for the political economy of the developing countries, it is a heavily loaded and an extremely elastic concept having many dimensions. In fact, development is not a simple proposition as it is being confabulated in common parlance or seems to be, but is the most complex and challenging phenomenon having many dimensions—social, political, economic, cultural, etc. known as 'economic development', 'political development', 'social development', and so on. Any discussion on 'development' or, to effectively say, holistic development will remain incomplete if it neglects or does not take into consideration various dimensions of development. As the story in the Preface to the book mentions, different individuals or groups tend to look at and understand development from a different angle and widely varied dimensions. The achievement of development goals is intimately connected with the performance of a nation on its various dimensions.

After reading this chapter, you will be able to:

(i) Explain what economic development is, and what are the factors responsible for the poor economic development of the underdeveloped countries.
(ii) Describe human and social development, why they are critical to development, and how they can be strengthened.
(iii) Analyze why political development is essential for development and how political development can be strengthened.
(iv) Discuss why gender development is critical to development, how it is measured, and what are the factors responsible for gender development.

(v) Critically analyze why ethical aspects are important for development, what does it mean, and how it can be promoted.

ECONOMIC DIMENSION OF DEVELOPMENT

Conventionally, economic dimension of development is considered as a stepping stone to promote and energize all other dimensions of development, i.e. social, human, and political. Economic development means improvement in economic health of a nation, which is commonly assessed in terms of percentage increase in GDP, increase in national and per capita income, and reduction in percentage unemployment and percentage of people living below the poverty line. According to Kindleberger (1975), economic development implies both more output and changes in technical and constitutional arrangements by which it is produced. While, Todaro and Smith (2012) see economic development in terms of the reduction or elimination of poverty, inequality, and unemployment within the context of a growing economy, to Nafziger (2006), economic development refers to economic growth accompanied by changes in output distribution and economic structure. Gross domestic product (GDP) and gross national income (GNI) are two popular measures of economic development. GDP measures the total value for final output produced by an economy, by both its residents and non-residents, while GNI is the total income created by an economy by both its residents and non-residents.[1] For developing countries, the GNP measures seem to be more realistic, because in these countries, profits or incomes made by foreign investors are much more common and significant than profits made by their residents in foreign countries (Cobb et al., 1995). Another yardstick used to measure the economic development of a nation is the per capita income of the people. While GDP determines the economic strength of a nation, per capita income indicates the economic strength of its people. If the per capita income is calculated for the household, it determines the economic health of a household. Generally, per capita income measures how much do the individuals of a nation earn in an accounting year generated through productive activities. In other words, it is a measure of the share of each individual when the income from the productive activities is divided equally among the citizens.[2]

Economic development is vital to the holistic development of a nation. The underdeveloped countries are found to be economically weak because of various reasons, i.e. high population growth rate, excessive dependence on agriculture, and weak industrialization resulting in small percentage contribution of the manufacturing sector to the GDP. Service sector is less proactive in creating employment in these economies, because of low capital formation, less use of technology in different sectors of the economy, poor economic governance, and ineffective implementation of economic development policies and programmes. At the outset, agriculture plays an important role in the economic development of the underdeveloped countries as it provides a gigantic percentage of employment in these economies. Over the period, it is observed that although the contribution of agriculture towards GDP in developing countries has drastically declined, yet the percentage of workforce engaged in agriculture has not proportionately diminished. Besides, the impoverishment of farming community, lack of innovations in agriculture, fragmentation of landholdings, poor access to farm credit, poor extension of training and research activities in agriculture are some of the factors responsible for lack of modernization of agriculture in the developing countries. Agriculture, despite playing a key role in development, is at the crossroads. Mellor (1969) has rightly remarked, as compared to high-income modernized agriculture, the low-income traditional agriculture of much of Asia, Africa, and Latin America, employs high proportion of their economies' resources at low levels of production and the output per man, per acre of land, and even per unit of capital is low. In order to enhance contribution of agriculture to GDP, the economic reforms in the developing countries need to stress on structural transformation, shifting of labour force from agriculture to industrial and service sector, mechanization, and use of technology in the agriculture sector at all levels. The secondary sector is the wheel of economic development. The economic history of developed countries establishes that their development has been the result of simultaneous growth of large- and small-scale industries (Kashyap and Shah, 1989). The illustrious examples are Asian giants, Singapore, Korea, Taiwan, and Hong Kong. To Kniivila (2007), industrial development has had an important role in the economic growth of countries like China, The Republic of Korea (Korea), Taiwan Province of China (Taiwan), and Indonesia. Moreover, it is also seen that the contribution of industrial sector towards the GNP of China is higher compared to the contribution made by agriculture and service sector. Therefore, it is said that industrialization is the main hope of most of the poor countries trying to increase their level of income (Chenery, 1955). The proactive role of service sector is concomitant to higher economic development. Thus, service not only needs to contribute towards the GDP, but also needs to provide employment and sustainable income to the people employed in the sector. Poor capital formation is a cause of slow economic development of the underdeveloped countries because of low savings and low investments. The role of capital formation in the process of economic growth and development cannot be overemphasized in the resource-poor Third World countries trying to augment their investments in infrastructure and in the implementation of various development projects and programmes. The economic development strategies of the Peoples' Republic of China during the three decades beginning in the early 1950s is characterized by high rate of capital accumulation at the expense of consumption and the promotion of industry at the expenses of agriculture (Chow, 1990). Economic development is influenced by market imperfection which is a factor responsible for the underdevelopment of the underdeveloped countries. Key features of market imperfection are price rigidity, factor immobility, buyer and seller ignorance about market conditions, etc. which hinders smooth functioning of market in an economy. Market imperfection does not allow flow of resources from the less productive sector to the more productive sector, which results in underutilization and ineffective utilization of resources. Ineffective utilization of resources influences the production possibility curve of an economy which operates below the potential level. In the neo-liberalized world, economic growth rate and development of the developing countries of Asia, Africa, and Latin America are influenced by the FDIs.[3] Morrissey (2001) pointed out that there are number of mechanisms through which aid can contribute to economic growth:

(i) Aid increases investment, in physical and human capital.
(ii) Aid increases the capacity to import capital goods or technology.
(iii) Aid does not have indirect effects that reduce investment or savings rates.
(iv) Aid is associated with technology transfer that increases the productivity of capital and promotes endogenous technical change.

Like FDI, the remittances from the developed countries to the developing countries are also influencing the investment pattern and economic growth rate of the developing countries.[4] For many developing countries, however, remittances represent a major part of international capital flows, surpassing FDI, export revenues, and foreign aid (Giuliano and Ruiz-Arranz, 2005). In India, the remittances of the Malayali and Punjabi diaspora are found to have been used in raising the quality of life of the people in rural areas, i.e. construction of beautiful houses with all amenities, purchase of durable assets such as refrigerators, motor cars, air conditioners, and other luxury household appliances, and giving better quality education and health care facilities to their children and other family members. The investment in business and industrial promotion activities by the Gujarati diaspora has certainly contributed to the state GDP. Countries have to formulate effective monetary and fiscal policies, to have sound capital and money markets and must effectively implement economic development policies and programmes, i.e. wage and self-employment programmes, poverty eradication programmes, housing, sanitation and drinking water programmes, social security and small savings programmes, etc. in order to place their economy on a higher economic growth and development path. Good economic governance is a prerequisite to faster economic growth and development.

HUMAN DEVELOPMENT DIMENSION

Human beings are the prime assets of a nation and human capital is the supreme and primary capital that facilitates faster economic growth and development as compared to all other forms of capital, as the performance of all other forms of capital depends on the knowledge, skill, dexterity, and quality of human capital. Certainly, a country which is unable to develop the skills and knowledge of its people and utilize them effectively in the national economy will not be able to develop anything else. UNDP considers people as the real wealth of a nation and has laid stress on human development which is a process of enlarging the people's choices. The most critical of these wide-ranging choices are to live a long and healthy life, to be educated, and to have access to resources needed for a decent standard of living (UNDP, 2001). Human development aims at enriching the people's lives by widening choices, expanding human capabilities, boosting their education, income and life expectancy, building of confidence and skill, enhancing freedom, and fulfilment of human rights. Human development is measured by the Human Development Index (HDI) with the key indicators, i.e. education, health, and standard of living.[5] Over the period of time, more and more variables are being added to the human development measures. Table 5.1 shows the HDI of a few countries.

The Delhi Human Development Report 2013 emphasizes on improving lives and promoting inclusion and these themes encompass all the fundamental concerns of human development.

- (i) Improving people's capabilities, segmenting the choices available to them.
- (ii) Assuring the progress of all segments of society in terms of income, education, and health care.
- (iii) Ensuring widespread access to basic civic amenities.
- (iv) Fostering a safe and enabling environment for the various population groups in the city (Institute for Human Development, 2013).

Table 5.1 *Human Development Index of a Few Selected Countries*

Country	Value	Rank
Very High Human Development		
Norway	0.955	1
Australia	0.938	2
USA	0.937	3
Japan	0.912	10
Singapore	0.895	18
Barbados	0.825	38
UAE	0.818	41
High Human Development		
Kuwait	0.790	54
Mexico	0.775	61
Malaysia	0.769	64
Sri Lanka	0.715	92
Medium Human Development		
China	0.699	101
Kyrgyzstan	0.622	125
India	0.554	136
Low Human Development		
Pakistan	0.515	146
Senegal	0.471	153
Nepal	0.463	157

Source: UNDP, Human Development Report, 2013.

Human development, which is critical to the holistic development of a nation, is influenced by a host of factors, i.e. income, poverty, inequality, quality of living, education and health, nutrition, and overall good governance. Income, employment, and poverty are the key influencing factors which affect the household standard of living and human development status by impacting access to health care, nutrition as well as education. UNDP (1990) observed that the extent to which people can improve their capabilities depends largely on their income and the access they have to basic goods and services. The unequal distribution of income in a society disproportionately affects the access to quality health care and education by different strata of society. In developing countries, there is a wide inter- and intra-regional disparity in terms access to employment, per capita income, and even wage rate. Higher income over and above the sustainable income after meeting the basic needs enables a household to spend on other capability enabling goods and services such as education and health care. The provision of sustainable employment and income-earning activities, eradication of poverty, and higher per capita income can augment qualitative human development in a nation-state. Quality education and health care institutions are important for human development in two crucial areas, health and education; the countries having a high percentage of population with lower level of education and with a high infant rate are found to be positioned in low HDI group. The amount of skilled population to the total population in a country is a vital factor to boost HDI. Besides, human development significantly influences and is influenced by environment and UNDP considers sustainable environment essential for human development. Environmental factors affect health and remain a major cause of sickness and death in many regions, particularly developing regions of the world. Economic development and human development efforts are increasingly constrained by environmental concerns, including degradation of forests and fisheries, lack of fresh water resources, and poor human health because of air and water pollution (Banister, 1998). Therefore, achieving environmental sustainability requires carefully balancing human development activity while maintaining a stable environment that predictably and regularly provides resources and protects people from natural calamities (Melnick et al., 2005). Last but not the least, women's social, economic, and political empowerment would lead to higher human development and gender equality is a necessary condition for sound human development (UNDP, 1995). UNDP (2010) has concluded that there is a tight coupling between gender equality and human development, that is, "countries with unequal distribution of human development also experience high inequality between women and men and countries with high gender inequality also experience unequal distribution of human development". There is a positive rank correlation between HDI and GDI that means the nation-state ranking higher in GDI will also have higher rank in HDI. A comparative analysis of HDI and GDI values and rank of Indian states (2006) shows that Goa with HDI and GDI values of 0.764 and 0.747, respectively enjoys the 2nd rank in both the indices at all-India level, while, on the contrary, Bihar with GDI and HDI values of 0.507 and 0.479, respectively, is positioned in both the indices with the 35th rank at the all-India level. Customarily, there is a positive rank correlation between gender development and human development indices. In the same vein, the UNDP, Human Development Report, 2013 shows that Sweden with HDI and GII (Gender Inequality Index) values of 0.916 and 0.056, respectively, closely ranks 7th and 2nd among the countries; while India with GII and HDI values of 0.610 and 0.554, respectively, ranks 132nd and 136th, respectively, among the countries. This also reveals that the country with more gender inequality also ranks poorly in human development. Thus, generally, there is a negative co-relationship between gender inequality and human development, that is, the higher the gender inequality, the lower the human development, and vice versa.

SOCIAL DEVELOPMENT DIMENSION

Social development is an inseparable and a vital dimension of development, as it is remarked by Higgins (1990) that the day will no doubt arrive when the distinction between 'economic' and 'social' development will disappear from the literature. Midgley (1993) was of the opinion that economic growth is typically viewed as a necessary condition for social development. Faster social development in terms of education, health care, social empowerment of women, reduction of social inequality and discrimination on the basic caste, ethnicity, religion, and gender will promote economic justice and enhance the contribution of socially marginalized sections towards growth and development. 'Sabake Sath Sabka Vikas' (development of all with the cooperation of all) can be possible only through faster social development and social development is an important instrument of inclusive and sustainable development. Bilance (1997) stated, "Social development is the promotion of a sustainable society that is worthy of human dignity by empowering marginalized groups, women and men, to undertake their own development, to improve their social and economic position, and to acquire their place in society…". Social development and economic development are intimately interconnected. Beverly and Sherraden (1997) said that social development as a complement to economically oriented development aims to improve the well-being of people, to integrate social improvements with economic growth, and to ensure that all people participate in the process and the benefits of development. Social development dimension of development emphasizes on the role and vitality of social aspects such as education, health, women empowerment, social equalities, social inclusion, social networking, and social capital formation in development of a nation, particularly developing nations. Social development also emphasizes on social inclusion in which people, irrespective of sex, caste, religion, ethnicity, and place of birth, get equal opportunity to participate in the development process as well as equally share the fruits of development. In many societies, institutionalized discriminatory and exclusionary practices trap certain groups of people on the basis of their race, ethnic origin, place of residence, or gender into poverty (Kabeer, 2000). World Bank (2000) emphasized that for social development, people should be put in the centre of development (inclusion), strengthening the social fabric of communities so that their members can work together (cohesion) and finding ways for people to exercise their voices to authorities (accountability).

While emphasizing the role of social capital in development, the World Bank (2000) has envisaged that:

(i) Social capital can 'bridge' different groups by enabling cross-cutting and inclusive ties.
(ii) Social relationships and networks are a form of capital that may bring benefits to their members.
(iii) The interplay of kin and communal bonding and bridging social relations shapes cross-cutting social capital and social cohesion.

Social development puts people and the society at the forefront of development and intends to overcome barriers through social networking so that people belonging to different communities and groups can share their views freely, participate in the decision-making process in the society, and enjoy the fruits of development equally without any fear, favour, or discrimination. It involves individuals, families, households, communities, CSOs, and government, each with specific roles to play for the well-being and development. Mahrey (2004) emphasized:

> …we need strong social institutions, strong families, and strong communities to thrive in a demanding global environment. We have to invest in people as a top priority, so that they

feel secure and are able and willing to participate in our society and to face the challenges arising from constant change.

Social development takes place when society moves in a positive direction and in a cohesive manner and the social tensions, communal violence, and terror activities which produce negative effect on development are shunned.

Social development is one of the most complicated dimensions of development, and as the variables and indicators of social development are many, it is difficult to accurately measure social development.

Some of the important indicators of social development are:

(i) Literacy and level of education
(ii) Literacy and education of socially disadvantaged (in the Indian context women, Scheduled Caste and Scheduled Tribes, minorities)
(iii) Infant and maternal mortality
(iv) Sex-ratio
(v) Formation and empowerment of social groups, i.e. *mahila mandals* (women groups), self-help groups, and other social networking institutions and their functioning and participation in social development activities
(vi) Discrimination based on gender, caste, religion, and ethnicity
(vii) Workforce participation and mobility
(viii) Political participation of disadvantaged
(ix) Crime and atrocities against women and other disadvantaged sections
(x) Child labour and bonded labour
(xi) Social security measures for old persons, widows, disabled, and other disadvantaged people
(xii) Availability and access to social development institutions such as education and health care institutions and gram nyayalaya (village court) for social justice, etc.
(xiii) Participation in social gathering and constitutionally provisioned local level institutions (in the Indian context, participation in gram sabha (village assemblies)

Social development is influenced by sundry of factors. Demographic indicators, such as fertility, mortality, age at marriage, sex ratio, and dependency ratio influence the rate of social development of a nation, region, or state. The declining sex ratio in northern Indian states of India has created gender and social imbalance, as a result, the society is reflecting the characteristics of male chauvanism and sex imbalance has promoted many social unrests. Besides, social discrimination on the basis of caste, clan, ethnicity, and religion also influences economic development and the benefits of development are being enjoyed by higher castes and socio-economically advanced among the backward castes, popularly known as 'creamy layer' of population and it has also created inter- and intra-state development disparities.[6] Paradoxically, it is envisaged that in a world which is rapidly globalizing, one of the most important determinants of well-being is still where a person is born; in which community, in what province within the country, and whether in a city or the countryside, within that province (World Development Report, 2009). The income disparities between the coastal and inland regions and between urban and rural areas in the People's Republic of China have become almost as widely known as the rapidity of its economic growth (Wan, 2008). Education and health are considered to be the two vital sectors that can play a crucial role in determining the level of social development of a region (Mukherjee and Banerjee, 2009). Dreze and Sen (1995) emphasized that education and health can play important empowerment and distributive roles by increasing people's ability (especially of disadvantaged groups) to resist oppression, to be organized politically, and to get a fairer deal. For instance, in India, Scheduled Castes and Scheduled Tribes are socially backward as compared to other caste groups of population. In terms of poverty, access to employment opportunity, education, and health, quality of life, and possession of basic amenities, these groups are in a disadvantaged position. Dreze and Sen (1995) opined that social development is the equality of social opportunities. Social development practice aims at the elimination of barriers to development which in every society, have been used to oppress historically disadvantaged population groups, and especially women, the aged, the poor, children, disabled persons, political and economic refugees as well as persons who have been disadvantaged on the basis of race, religion, ethnicity, social class, caste, and sexual orientation (Campfens, 1990; Meinert and Kohn, 1987). Social cohesion believes in universal brotherhood and the prevalence of fellow feeling among different sections of society, stratified on the basis of caste, class, religion, and ethnicity. One of the classical determinants of social development is social capital formation. Social capital customarily refers to social institutions, networking, racial–ethnic relations, and social values that underpin successful development. According to Putman (1993), social capital is characterized as, "...features of social organization, such as trust, norms and networks, that can improve the efficiency of society by facilitating coordinated actions and cooperation for mutual benefits". Social capital helps in the creation of human capital, produces public order, enhances people's participation, creates partnerships, and contributes to social and economic well-being and sustainable development (Thomas, 1996; Holm, 2004).

While emphasizing the role of social capital in development, the World Bank (2000) has envisaged that:

(i) Social capital can 'bridge' different groups by enabling cross-cutting and inclusive ties.
(ii) Social relationships and networks are a form of capital that may bring benefits to their members.
(iii) The interplay of kin and communal bonding and bridging social relations shapes cross-cutting social capital and social cohesion. Investments in social capital are an important requisite not only for raising social capital formation but also for promoting human, economic, social, and political development.

The six important related components of social capital, vital for the promotion of social development, are:

(i) Social beliefs and values, which are the main connecting links in the society.
(ii) Social and cultural practices that promote common understanding and are an important determinant of group behaviour in a traditional society.
(iii) Social norms that guide the behaviours of the social level institutions and individuals.

(iv) Social networking which is critical to social development. Social networking is an effective tool for enhancement of knowledge and understanding in the society.
(v) Social gathering for common cause which helps in promoting brotherhood and fellow feeling among different sections of population in a stratified society.
(vi) Social customs and traditions that are established social systems which guide social behaviour.

Social development places man and his social surroundings at the forefront of all development activities for achievement of development goals.

CULTURAL DEVELOPMENT DIMENSION

Culture and development are strongly interconnected at least in the countries of Asia, Africa, and Latin America, as it is perceived that culture acts both as a stimulant as well as a deterrent to development. Emphasizing the importance of culture, Willis (2005) noted that while many definitions of 'development' focus on economic aspects, it is crucial to recognize the social and cultural elements. This is not just because social and cultural variables affect economic growth but also because social and cultural norms and expectations need to be considered in their own right. Holistic development process must take care of cultural development, as culture is deeply associated with livelihood, well-being, and social and human development. The importance of cultural identities, i.e. cultural goods, cultural food and livelihoods, cultural trade and practices, etc. in the culturally sensitive areas particularly the tribal areas play an important role in tribal development and livelihood. The cultural development process is low cost, locally acceptable, and socially cohesive and can be economically sustainable in the long run. The cultural dimension of development emphasizes on culture-sensitive development, administration and governance, and political and economic system. According to Munck and Hearn (1999), the importance of culture to development discourse is seen to be that if development is to have real value at the local level, it requires a qualitative understanding of the complexities and dynamics of everyday life. The development must be an integral part of the existing cultural and social relations. It is said that development is inevitably culture bound and is, therefore, intricately linked to the society where it is pursued (Zafarullah and Huque, 2006). The cultural heritage, cultural and creative industries, sustainable cultural tourism, and cultural infrastructure can serve as strategic tools for revenue generation, particularly in developing countries, given their often-rich cultural heritage and substantial labour force (UNESCO, 2012). Cultural and creative industries represent one of the most rapidly expanding sectors in the global economy with a growth rate of 17.6 per cent in the Middle East, 13.9 per cent in Africa, 11.9 per cent in South America, 9.7 per cent in Asia, 6.9 per cent in Oceania, and 4.3 per cent in North and Central America (UNESCO, 2012). Promoting this sector requires capital formation in cultural development as it has direct impact on the tribal, vulnerable, and hilly rural population and on women, whose development is more culture sensitive. Culture-led development also includes a range of non-monetized benefits, such as greater social inclusiveness and rootedness, resilience, innovation, creativity, and entrepreneurship for individuals and communities, and the use of local resources, skills, and knowledge (UNESCO, 2012). Cultural development is

Ethnic and Cultural Diversity and Development in Singapore

Singapore, a developed nation in Asia, is comprised of diverse ethnic population. In 2012, the population of Singapore was 5.18 million consisting of 74 per cent Chinese, 13 per cent Malaya, 9 per cent Indian, and 3 per cent others. As far as religious composition is concerned, it comprised population belonging to Buddhists, Islam, Christianity, Taoism, and Hinduism. When Singapore got independence in 1965, it experienced severe racial conflicts among these three main ethnic groups. The post-colonial government of Lee Kuan Yew recognized that such divisions were not conducive to economic growth and development of the country and, therefore, he emphasized on ethnic harmony at the heart of its policies. Post-1965, throughout there has been a focus on promoting a Singaporean identity regardless of ethnic allegiance and diversities. This was put into practice through National Day celebrations of various groups. Some other attempts to promote inter-ethnic awareness and understanding include celebrating a range of religious and cultural festivals, such as Chinese New Year, Ramadan, and Hari Raya, with public holidays on the main festival days. It was felt by the government of Singapore that if people from different ethnic groups live in close proximity and harmony, this will help develop understanding, friendship, and greater social networking among them. This government measure has promoted inter-ethnic harmony and the Singapore's economic success is attributed to this cultural and ethnic integration.

Source: Willis (2005).

considered as the fourth pillar of sustainable development after economy, ecology, and society. The cultural identities, i.e. dress code, song, drama, food habits, languages, tangible and intangible heritage, cultural industries, cultural institutions, like marriages and festivals, cultural pluralism, and geo-culture are the fabrics of cultural development. According to Nurse (2006), the areas of culture has grown in salience in global development issues on account of the rising share of cultural goods, services, and intellectual property in world trade as well as the threats to cultural diversities and identities associated with contemporary globalization.

A few important factors influencing cultural dynamics of development are cultural rights and freedom, cultural goods and services, cultural industries, cultural trade and investment, cultural heritage and tourism, and respect for cultural values and identity. The most commonly understood meaning of culture is that it is a way of life being recognized in different forms, i.e. language, dress code, food, dance, customs, song, products, etc.[7] and cultural identity is identified through these means. One of the objectives of cultural development is to respect the ethos of cultural pluralism. The cultural identities of different cultures must coexist, and rather need not to compete, in such way that one culture does not annihilate but strengthens the other. In other words, cultural pluralism or diversity refers to the coexistence of people belonging to different cultural groups in a nation-state with peace, harmony, fellow feeling, and brotherhood, and there is mutual respect for each other's culture. Dabaghian (1970) stressed that the pride of any society lies in its culture since no society in the world could be considered great without reference to its tradition and culture. Cultural pluralism must be upheld in order to promote need-based, people-centred, and culture-specific development. Protection of cultural rights and freedom of the people belonging to different cultural groups is a critical determinant of cultural development. Implementing developmental projects and programmes within the ambits of cultural sensitivity will lead to its effective implementation and yield desirable outcomes.

UNESCO Declaration on the Principles of International Cultural Cooperation (1966) focuses on the following:

(i) Each culture has a dignity and value which must be respected and preserved.
(ii) All people have the right and the duty to develop their culture.
(iii) In their rich variety and diversity and in the reciprocal influences they exert on one another, all cultures form part of the common heritage belonging to all mankind.

People and the institutions must have the right to propagate and flourish their culture and the freedom to educate about their culture. Promoting cultural investment for the preservation of cultural arts, sculpture, heritage, and practices is the key to enhancing contribution of culture towards socio-economic growth and development through cultural tourism, trade, and business. With globalization and modernity, cultural arts and practices are vanishing day by day which is detrimental not only to cultural development but also to the social and economic development of the society, community, and nation-state having faith and belief in culture. Although cultural products, like traditional clothes and ornaments, organic vegetables and farm products, forest products, etc. are relatively costlier than their counterpart modern industrial products, yet these are high-value laden and less harmful. Hawkes (2001) argued that culture is the 'fourth pillar of sustainability' and an essential ingredient in public planning for a healthy and sustainable society. It is noted that "the cultural industries are increasingly seen as a tool for economic development and poverty reduction and as the assurance of cultural diversity. In addition, cultural industries are closely linked to participation in the post-industrial economy and the knowledge-based society. Accordingly, there is a new focus on the potential of mainstreaming cultural industries into national development plans as a means of achieving more sustainable development".[8] Besides public sector investment, encouraging private sector investment in cultural development in preservation of cultural heritage, beliefs and values, arts and practices at the local level are critical support for cultural development. A few countries have also encouraged involvement of NGOs and civil society groups for promoting culture and preserving cultural heritage and practices. Cultural tourism is an illustrious service sector in many of the culturally acclaimed nations and a few nation-states are earning a lot of revenue through cultural tourism.

In the World Decade for Cultural Development 1988–97, UNESCO earmarked on four key activities:

(i) Acknowledging the cultural dimension of development
(ii) Affirming and enriching cultural identities

(iii) Broadening participation in cultural life
(iv) Promoting international cultural cooperation[9]

Culture is an integral part of development and, therefore, cultural development is an important dimension of development.

POLITICAL DEVELOPMENT DIMENSION

Economic development of a nation truly depends on its political development, as frequent elections, lack of democracy, and poor political governance seem to adversely affect economic development. The term 'political economy' veritably signifies the effective integration of the two concepts, 'politics' and 'economics', for the achievement of economic growth and development of nation-states through better political governance. It is obvious that economic development will not take place in countries where the political power-elite is resolutely opposed to it (Higgins, 1990). It is argued that since development requires new configurations in the use and distribution of resources of land, money, and human energy, there will be disputes among individuals and groups which can only be sorted out by a political process (Leftwich, 2000). The institutions dealing with politics and its relation to development provide scope for policy innovation and entrepreneurship and for the acquisition, evaluation, and utilization of development ideas from the outside, contextualize and use them in policy formulation of development. Political development implies that the political system needs to be mature enough to deal with economic growth and development of a country. It emphasizes on the development of pluralistic political systems, strengthening of developmental education among the parliamentarians, legislators, and elected representatives of the local self-government institutions, the creation and empowerment of local political units through capacity building, encouragement of effective public interest groups, democratic decentralization, political modernization, equalization of power, protective discrimination in political empowerment of disadvantaged, gender political empowerment and good governance, and recognition of political federalism.[10] Political leadership, their ingenuity, acumen, style of governance, and commitment to the people's welfare determine the level of achievement on development front. Regional and sub-regional disparities in development in developing countries are compared with the achievement of political parties and the role of grass-roots level political institutions in power in those regions and states honestly monitoring the development projects and programmes with effective political governance. Political willpower to introduce economic reforms and play a constructive role as a responsible opposition is a prerequisite of the democratic processes to boost economic growth and development. It was well said that economic development is indeed difficult (although not completely impossible) where the country is ruled by a landed aristocracy with deeply embedded feudal attitudes, strongly opposed to industrialization, mass education, and technological change (Higgins, 1990).

Democracy, particularly a strong, stable, and vibrant participatory democracy is considered to be a deterministic measure of political development. Political democracy will enable the people to choose their leaders and government, instead of accepting the ruling of the authoritarians. Right to reject and right to recall an elected political representative if he or she commits a crime, indulges in corruption, and does not perform up to the expectations of the people of his or her area are now days being advocated in order to strengthen political democracy and bring honesty into political system. Millikan and Rostow (1960) had argued that our way of life is more secure in a world of 'mature democracies' than it is when we are surrounded by poverty-stricken countries with unstable governments. Political decentralization is another means to strengthen political development and the goal of political decentralization is to make decision-making process participatory, people-centred with a bottom-up approach. The advocators of political decentralization believe that decisions made with greater people participation through their elected representatives at the local level will be more relevant to diverse interests of the society than those made at the national and provincial level political institutions and by the national and provincial level elected representatives. According to Bardhan (2002), decentralization is widely believed to promise a range of benefits, particularly in making governance more responsive and efficient in meeting local needs and preferences and will be helpful in diffusing social and political tensions and enhancing social cohesion. Another barometer of political development is empowering the disadvantaged, such as women and socially and ethnically backward groups by electing them to national, provincial, and local self-government institutions. Political inequality is a deterrent to competitive political development and a drawback of representative democracy. Congregation of political power in the hands of elites and erudite will promote parochial and undemocratic political institutions and sometimes it may lead to authoritarian and autocratic functioning in a democratic set-up. Political inequality may retard development because elites who control politics may create rents for themselves and impede entry (Acemoglu, 2008). In states characterized by powerful local elites, neo-patrimonial and patronage relationships, decentralization risks the capture of resources by local elites (Manor, 1999; Tanzi, 2000). In much of the Sub-Saharan Africa, since independence, measured economic inequality has been quite low, but political inequality has been severe—with rule by long-rung autocrats or small clines most clearly in Sudan, Angola, the Congo, Maluri, Lote d'Ivoire, Togo, and Cameroon (Acemoglu et al., 2007)—which is affecting their development. Political values are central to political development. The rise and fall in the vote bank of political parties not only depends on their performance but also on political values like the importance they attach to the social groups, other aspects, like governance ethics, individualism, secularism, cleanliness in politics and social life, etc. Therefore, party identification and core political values represent two of the most central and enduring predispositions lying within the political belief systems of ordinary citizens (Goren, 2005). Use of religion, caste, and ethnic cards by various political parties in elections of the democratic countries of South Asia is a draconian spot on political values.

The creation and support of appropriate, stable, and responsive political governance framework is crucial to the attainment of each of the MDGs (SPC and UN, 2004). Adherence to governance principles, i.e. transparency, accountability, and rule of law by the political parties in the process of running the state is crucial to development.

Many of the developing countries are suffering from political governance deficiencies. Some of the features are:

(i) Cronyism, connection, favour to family members and relatives
(ii) Political parties accepting donations for political campaigns and party candidates spending huge amounts of money on election by bribing people for vote

(iii) Economic rent on government contracts and administrative and bureaucratic appointments, posting, and transfers
(iv) Frauds of all kinds, such as stamp paper, house booking, sale and purchase of properties, and so on.

This has led to growing dissensions among the common men and in small countries, it has led to collapse of civilian government and sabotage of democracy by coup. Therefore, political governance is an essential prerequisite for a stable democracy.

Political governance needs to rely on:

(i) Free and fair election and transition of power
(ii) Effective and constructive political opposition and representative government
(iii) Absence of political corruption and misuse of political power for personal and family gains
(iv) Dereliction of political pressure on executive, judiciary, and other investigating agencies in their function for political and personal gains
(v) Transparency and accountability in the implementation of development projects and programmes

The key challenge before the nation-state is to effectively utilize the political governance and wisdom of legislatures in the development affairs of the country. Besides political governance, protection of political right is crucial to strengthen political development. The protection of right of individuals to freely contest election and exercise their franchise freely without any fear in the electoral process are important political rights in a representative democracy. However, free and fair election and universal people's participation in general elections is still a problem in many countries.[11]

GENDER DIMENSION

Male and female are the two sides of a coin and their equal participation in development process is necessary to promote holistic and gender-inclusive development. It is advocated that development requires good governments that give men and women equal voices in decision-making and policy implementation (Parpart et al., 2000). However, the early development initiatives, which have begun to preoccupy economists and colonial officials in the 1930s, largely ignored women (Connelly et al., 2000). The role of women in development was vigorously invoked by the developmentalists as well as national and international agencies and by the nation-states of the Third World countries, particularly since 1970s. The third United Nation Development Decade gave rise to the trend towards seeing women as equals, as agents and beneficiaries in all sectors, and at all levels of the development process. The participation of women in the freedom struggle movement and fight against the colonial rule in different colonial nations of Asia, Africa, and Latin America has fortified the role of women in social and political movement and in the nation building development process. Traditionally, women were being sympathized with and were considered as the weaker gender to perform more arduous tasks in agriculture and industry sector. Denying empowerment to women means absolving contribution of around 50 per cent of population towards economic development. The economic participation of women in the workforce, in qualitative as well as quantitative terms, is important not only for lowering the disproportionate levels of poverty among women, but also for raising household income and standard of living and recognizing the contribution of women towards the national income and growth rate both at the national and provincial levels. Duflo (2012) was of the view that there is a bidirectional relationship between economic development and women's empowerment defined as improving the ability of women to access the constituents of development, in particular health, education, earning opportunities, rights, and political participation.

The UNDP, since 1990, at different points of time has formulated three indices for the measurement of gender development in different countries. These indices are: (a) Gender-related Development Index (GDI), (b) Gender Empowerment Measure (GEM), and (c) Gender Inequality Index (GII). GDI measures the achievement of women on the front of literacy, life expectancy, and income as used in HDI, however, take cognizance of inequality in achievement between women and men. GEM is being calculated by using three important indicators such as proportion of seats held by women in national parliament, percentage of women in economic decision-making positions, and female share of income. GII, a measure propounded by UNDP, has used three dimensions of women's backwardness for the calculation of GII: reproductive health, empowerment, and labour market participation. The two important indicators used in the determination of reproductive health are maternal mortality rate (MMR) and adolescent fertility rate (AFR); and indicators used in the measurement of empowerment of women are share of parliamentary seats held by men and women and higher education attainment level (secondary education and above) of women. The labour market participation indicators were: women's participation in paid work, unpaid work, and actively looking for work. Table 5.2 shows the GDI, GII, and GEM of a few countries.

Table 5.2 *Gender Development Index, Gender Inequality Index, and Gender Empowerment Index of Selected Countries*

	Gender Related Development Index (GDI)		**Gender Inequality Index (GII)**		**Gender Empowerment Measure (GEM)**	
Country	**Value**	**Rank**	**Value**	**Rank**	**Value**	**Rank**
Netherlands	0.951	6	0.045	1	0.859	6
USA	0.937	16	0.256	42	0.762	15
Denmark	0.944	11	0.057	3	0.875	4
Kazakhstan	0.792	65	0.312	51	0.469	69
Sri Lanka	0.735	89	0.402	75	0.369	85
China	0.776	73	0.213	35	0.534	57
India	0.600	113	0.610	132	NA	NA
Pakistan	0.525	125	0.567	123	0.377	82
Singapore	NA	NA	0.101	13	0.761	16
Brazil	0.798	60	0.447	85	0.490	70
Kenya	0.521	127	0.608	130	NA	NA

Source: Human Development Report 2007/2008, http://hdr.undp.org/en/media/HDR_20072008_GDI (GEM)

As far as economic empowerment of women and their role in economic development is concerned, it is observed that women are largely concentrated in low-skilled and low-paid occupations, face more unemployment and underemployment problems, and are majorly occupied in household work. Women labour forces are the victim of labour market imperfection and wage discrimination and physical and mental exploitation as women are largely being forced to be away from the labour market. Tzannatos (1999) noted that growth helps, as women seem to benefit from economic growth at large; inequality hurts, as welfare gains are lost through continuing gender discrimination and that public policy matter, as the state plays a crucial role in promoting gender equality.

Women's economic empowerment is a prerequisite for sustainable development and pro-poor growth (OECD, 2012). Economic empowerment is the capacity of women and men to participate in, contribute to, and benefit from growth processes in ways which recognize the value to their contributions, respect their dignity, and make it possible to negotiate a fairer distribution of the benefits of growth (Eyben et al., 2008). According to an international estimation, women represent 70 per cent of the world's poor. The statistics indicate that women are more likely to be poor and at risk of hunger than men because of the systematic discrimination they face in education, health care, employment, and access to and control of physical and financial assets. Poverty, assetlessness, and hunger are worse

Grameen Bank—A Tool for Women Empowerment and Participation in Development

The Grameen Bank grew out of a project undertaken by Dr Mahammad Yunus in 1976 in Bangladesh. During his fieldwork in villages, he came to the conclusion that people were poor because they lack access to credit at reasonable interest rates and are deprived of appropriate conditions and came to the conclusion that a specialized financial institution is needed that would provide small loans to poor to people with particular emphasis on women on terms and conditions that were appropriate to them. The Grameen Bank project, which was kick-started by him in Jobra village of Bangladesh in 1976, is now a gigantic institution having acquired the recognition of government of Bangladesh. It is an outcome of Dr Yunus' strenuous fieldwork. The central feature of the Grameen Bank is its credit programme providing small loans to the poor to be used for self-employment activities. After 30 years of its operation, today Grameen Bank has successfully provided loans to more than seven million people and services in over 73,000 villages in Bangladesh with 97 per cent of its members being women. Grameen Bank's participation has positively and significantly increased women's income and their contribution to family income (Bernasek, 2003). The credit programme participation leads to women taking greater role in household decision-making and having greater access to financial and economic resources, greater social networks, greater bargaining power vis-à-vis their husbands, and greater freedom of mobility (Pitt et al., 2003).

Source: Noble Lecture, Oslo, 10 December 2006. http://www.nobelprize.org/nobel_prizes/peace (accessed on 11 October 2015).

Kudumbashree—An Effective Programme of Women Empowerment for Development

Kudumbashree is a Malayalam term which means 'prosperity to the family'. It was conceived as a joint programme of the government of Kerala and NABARD and was implemented through community development societies (CDSs) of poor women. *Kudumbashree* differs from conventional programmes in which it perceives poverty not as the deprivation of money but as the deprivation of basic rights.

The grass roots of *Kudumbashree* are neighbourhood groups (NHGs) that send representatives to the ward level area development societies (ADSs). The ADSs send their representatives to the community development societies (CDSs), which completes the unique three-tier structure of *Kudumbashree*. Today there are 194,000 NHGs, over 17,000 ADSs and 1,061 CDSs in *Kudumbashree*. The programme has 3.7 million members and covers more than 50 per cent of the households in Kerala. Built around three critical components, micro-credit, entrepreneurship, and empowerment, the *Kudumbashree* initiative has today succeeded in addressing the basic needs of the less privileged women, thus providing them a more dignified life and a better future.

Kudumbashree programme has made substantial impact on various sectors of development such as health, education, agriculture, animal husbandry, dairy development, women empowerment, and rehabilitation of destitutes. It has succeeded in addressing problems related to revamping of traditional sector and improving basic amenities such as shelter, drinking water, safe latrines, and employment. It has not only built up the confidence and self-esteem of poor women but also enabled them to set up several enterprises (John, 2009).

Source: www.kudumbashree.org/?=homepage&aajeevika.gov.in/SPIP/NRLM-SPIP-Kerala.Final.pdf

among women-headed households belonging to socio-economically impoverished families. These sometimes push many single and deserted women to absolute poverty and even begging in many developing countries of South Asia. While cautioning the rising unemployment among women, the ILO estimates that the economic slow downturn could lead to 22 million more unemployed women in 2009, jeopardizing the gains made in the last few decades in women's empowerment (UN Women). The economic vulnerability of women flows from their weakly defined property rights to major productive assets such as agricultural land and houses, as in many countries' customs and traditions restrict their ability to own parental properties. Moreover, a gigantic percentage of working women are agricultural labourers, casual labourers, and self-employed in paltry income-earning activities and are employed in low-paid jobs. Women's economic empowerment faces three major challenges:

(i) Women are less likely to have a paid job.
(ii) Women's jobs are more likely to be concentrated in the informal economy and in low value-added sectors in low-paid jobs characterized by poor working conditions.

(iii) Women are mostly engaged in non-paid household activities and never being considered having any economic value; women are not even considered in national income accounting. However, as income rises and manufacturing sectors gain prominence, depressed female labour-force participation due to limited educational opportunities and social stigmas suggests that economic development should enhance women's status because it encourages societal integration, supports women's investment in human capital, and creates employment opportunities for women in relatively higher paying non-farm sector (Clark et al., 1991; Forsythe et al., 2000). Globalization has boosted the chances of educated women getting employment in the services sectors of the liberal democratic countries, particularly in tourism, IT, banking, and insurances, Business Process Outsourcing and other gender-sensitive service sectors, such as health care and education. Economic empowerment will open their doors to social and political empowerment. OECD (2012) advocated that economic empowerment increases women's access to economic resources and opportunities, including jobs, financial services, property and other productive assets, skill development, and market information. Women as legislators and executives and those in judiciary will not only gain as an individual but also act as role models for other women to follow and will enable them to raise their voices for women at different forums of development at national, regional, and local levels. Reservation for seats for women in legislative assemblies and parliament will enable them to be elected to these decision-making bodies and lead to gender political empowerment and equity in political participation. True et al. (2012) were of the view that gender quotas and reservations have significantly improved women's political representation at the national and local levels. Besides, their representation in executive and judiciary positions will help them to take up gender-related issues to the decision-making level. Some scholars argued that the presence of a few women on state supreme courts and high profile women lawyers could affect the reality of the status of women in the legal profession (Costello, 1997). Ironically, women are less in number in these positions. Education of women is a powerful tool to enhance the contribution of women towards economic growth and development. Decades of empirical evidences, practical experiences, and observations support the robust association between women's educational attainment and positive development outcomes.[12]

Some of the benefits of education with regard to the empowerment of women are:

(i) It is an enabling factor to promote social mobility, overcome social barriers, and improve decision making power and autonomy.
(ii) It can empower women to acquire knowledge and skill which will enhance scope of employment in the formal sector.
(iii) It will reduce social and economic dependency of women on men and other members of the family and society.
(iv) Educated women are more likely to nurture improved health, nutrition, and education in the family and are vital to a nation's economic success.

(v) It will enable women to fight for their social, economic, political, and human rights and reduce their subordinate status.
(vi) It will enhance their ability to support their family, raise their children well, and ensure the future educational and economic success of the next generation.
(vii) It will curtail domestic violence and gender related atrocities.
(viii) It will raise self-esteem of women and enable women to demand respect from the family and society.
(ix) It will reduce gender-based inequalities in the labour market.
(x) Finally, it will enable them to demand justice in lieu of injustices done to them because of being women. Education, in its widest sense, is a potential instrument that would empower women to reach their full potential and contribute significantly towards economic growth and development of nation.

ETHICAL DIMENSION OF DEVELOPMENT

In the cookbook of the philosophy of economics, 'development' is equally considered as an ethical, moral, benevolent, and humane concept. Goulet (1965) in his book, *The Ethics of Development* has envisaged that 'development' in the ultimate sense cannot be regarded merely as economic development or industrialization or modernization, nor even simply as the increase in productivity and argued that the concept of development is best expressed in the phrase 'the human ascents', which includes the economic, biological, psychological, social, cultural, ideological, spiritual, mystical, and transcendental dimensions. He insisted that the philosopher needs to be added to the development team, as without a clear concept of philosophy of development, the team becomes 'a simple *ad hoc* mission'. The aim of economic development is not only to raise productivity, enhance national and per capita income, but also to reduce hunger, poverty, inequality, and miseries, ensure social justice, and raise the moral of the people, particularly the deprived sections, so that they can lead a respectable life. In the poverty-stricken developing countries, development endeavours need more humanistic, compassionate, and benevolent approach from the side of the government as well as market mechanisms. According to Cypher and Dietz (2009) development is about realizing very fundamental human values and finding the means to extend the fruits of these values to the greatest majority of the world's population. While, Nordhaus and Tobin (1973) advocated that we must acquire a lifestyle which has as its goal maximum freedom and happiness for the individual, not maximum gross national product.[13] Here, it is worth noting to quote Gandhi (1967), a votary of ethical development: "I must confess that I do not draw a sharp or any distinction between economics and ethics. Economics that hurts moral well-being of any individual or nation is immoral and therefore sinful".

In *Hind Swaraj,* Gandhi (1908) apprehended:

> We notice that the mind is a restless bird; the more it gets the more it wants, and still remain unsatisfied. The more we indulge our passions, the more unbridled they become. Our ancestors, therefore, set a limit to our indulgences. They say the happiness was largely a mental condition. A man is not necessarily happy because he is rich or unhappy because he is poor. The rich are often seen to be unhappy, the poor to be happy. Millions will always be poor. Observing all this our ancestors dissuaded us from luxuries and pleasures.

Although there is no concrete way to measure the ethics of development, yet it aims at enhancing development with distributive justice, human well-being, and happiness. At the outset, the endeavour of the nation-state is movement from consumerism towards welfarism and establishment of ethics of a welfare state. The emphasis is to be less on consumerism and more on welfarism, and there should be a shift from accumulation of wealth to distribution of wealth for promoting greater well-being of the poorest of the poor and the deprived sections. The ethics of development believe that the consumerism is guided by selfish motives leading to malpractices and distortions of the market. The economic system guided by the principles of consumerism has transposed human beings to an economic species by making him more and more materialistic, individualistic, and self-centred. Consumerism leads to exploitation and greediness for profit and may even lead to corruption. The consumerism approach is parochial in nature and, therefore, cannot be effective in achieving holistic and inclusive development. Truly, consumerism is antithetic to the consumer and is the champion of producers (capitalists), in which, not the consumers, but the capitalists and businessmen are at the centre stage of economic system. It elongates the prosperity of a few, keeping majority at the periphery of development. On the contrary, welfarism leads to the well-being of the largest sections of the society and also aims at investing a portion of profit of the capitalists on social and human well-being of the common man, particularly the impoverished and marginalized sections of population. 'Welfarism' in the capitalist and mixed economic systems in recent years is variously termed as 'creative capitalism' or 'benevolent capitalism', a departure from the accumulative capitalism. The term 'corporate social responsibility' (CSR) is an illustrious mechanism to promote welfare in the capitalist and mixed economic systems. According to Bill Gates,[14] "We need a creative capitalism where business and non-governmental organizations work together to create a market system that eases the world's inequalities". Another votary of creative capitalism was JRD Tata,[15] who opined "Modern capitalism has changed beyond recognition from what it was century ago. It has shown a remarkable capacity to fit into the most modern concept of the welfare state, while creating wealth and prosperity unprecedented in human history". In the words of JRD Tata:

> ...Industrial enterprise, whether in the private or the public sector, can and could do much within their means to improve the conditions of life of the surrounding population, relieve distress where it exists, help find work for the unemployed and extend a helping hand to those who need it.

He further advocated that let industry be established in the countryside and 'adopt' the villages in their neighbourhood; let some of the time of its managers, its engineers, doctors, and skilled specialists be spared to help and advise the people of the villages and to supervise new developments undertaken by cooperative effort between them and the company. In the modern selfish society, man has become self-centred and there is lack of human concerns and the gluttonous individual never feels felonious to snatch the rights of others for their parochial gains. Development should serve the need of the masses rather than interests of a few. The State through its welfare measures needs to make provisions of subsidized basic necessities to the poorest of the poor and reach to the unreached, underprivileged, and marginalized. Once the basic necessities are fulfilled, people could afford other amenities required for the better quality of living.

The ethical dimension of development emphasizes on human happiness. Happiness is something eternal and can be truly gained holistically by caring for the well-being of all, keeping one's self-interest minimal. The mission of the ethical development is to facilitate development of all and involve all in the process of development. The United Nations (2011) in its resolution on "Happiness towards a Holistic Approach to Development" envisaged that "a fundamental human goal is the deep-abiding happiness that comes from living life in full harmony with the natural world and with our communities and fellow beings". The concept of development as happiness believes that GDP-based approach is outdated and a nation should be seen as succeeding not if its citizens are financially well off but rather if they are healthy and happy (Helliwell et al., 2013).

The goal of development is to promote happiness of the largest number and should aim at the following:

(i) Majority of people, particularly the marginalized section of society are satisfied with the employment and income which sustainably fulfils their basic needs.
(ii) The upper strata of the society, such as the corporate sector owners, industrialists, and business entrepreneurs spend a portion of their profit for the well-being of the poor and deprived section under CSR.
(iii) There is little or no physical, financial, and mental exploitation by the rich of the poor, political and administrative governance is free from corruption and the menace of child trafficking, and child labour is abolished.
(iv) Socio-economic inequality and discrimination in terms of class, caste, gender, and ethnicity is abolished.
(v) Corruption and red-tapism are removed from the executive, judiciary, and legislative system.
(vi) The society is free from communal riots, extremism, and terrorism.
(vii) People lead tension-free life, get sustainable employment, wage rate, and income, are free from the coercion of continuous inflation, and get public services benefits without paying any kickbacks.
(viii) There is less market imperfection and regulation of the informal economy by the government for the benefit of the poor.
(ix) There is inclusive development where State takes proactive steps for upliftment of the status of the disabled, disadvantaged, and deprived.
(x) There is sustainable development and all people enjoy a sustainable livelihood at their own levels and there is harmonious relationship among individual, society, economy, and environment.
(xi) Last but not the least, sustainable happiness depends on the balanced growth and development of all sectors of development, i.e. primary, secondary, and service sectors, so that economic shocks are kept at a minimum which create stagflation and burnout among the common masses. The various actors of development such as market, government, NGOs, bilateral and multilateral agencies, and the local self-government institutions work in tandem for the promotion of well-being and happiness in the nation-state.

The Sum Up

Development is a multidimensional and dynamic concept. Considering its dimensions, development can be best defined as 'development is what development does'. If it raises the GDP and standard of living, then it is considered as economic development; if any developmental initiatives promote education and health in a society then it is best regarded as 'social development'. Holistic development can be promoted only when there is effective synergy among various dimensions of development and all the dimensions function cohesively.

Keywords gross domestic product, gross national income, economic governance, Human Development Index, Gender Development Index, gender empowerment measure, Gender Inequality Index, political values, political governance, social capital, cultural tourism, corporate social responsibility, Gross Happiness Index.

REVIEW QUESTIONS

1. Economic dimension is critical to development. Discuss various factors influencing economic development of an underdeveloped country.
2. Political development influences economic development. Elucidate.
3. Education and health are critical dimensions of human development. Discuss the factors influencing education and health care sectors of underdeveloped countries.
4. Gender and development are interlinked. Discuss factors influencing gender development.
5. Culture is an important dimension of development. How and why? Explain.
6. Ethical dimensions are important for the development of the underdeveloped country. Critically discuss role of ethics in development.
7. Write short notes on the following:
   (i) Measures of economic development
   (ii) Human Development Index
   (iii) Gender Development Measure
   (iv) Cultural economy
   (v) Remittances and development
   (vi) Political values
   (vii) Corporate social responsibilities
   (viii) Happiness as a development determinant

NOTES

1. According to Cypher and Dietz (2009), GDP is the total value (= value of final output) of all incomes created within the borders of a country, regardless of whether the ultimate recipient of that income resides within or outside the country. On the other hand, GNP is the total value of all incomes (= value of final output) accruing to residents of country, regardless of the source of that income, that is, irrespective of whether

such income is derived from sources within or outside the country (Cypher and Dietz, 2009). GNP measures the money value of total annual domestic product of a country, plus income (e.g. investment earnings and remittance) earned abroad by its residents, minus payments made to non-residents and foreign institutions (e.g. interest on foreign loans and repatriated profits made by foreign investors) (World Bank, 1985; David, 1986). Thus, GNI (alternatively used as GNP) comprises GDP plus the difference between the income residents receive from abroad for factor services (labour and capital) less payments made to non-residents who contribute to the domestic economy (Todaro and Smith, 2012).

2. The two types of per capita that could be calculated for the purpose of measuring the economic health of a nation and a household are: (i) GNI per capita and (ii) household income per capita.

$$\text{GNI} = \frac{\text{Total national income}}{\text{Total population}}$$

$$\text{House per capita} = \frac{\text{Total gross household income}}{\text{Total household population}}$$

3. Karras (2006) study on correlation between foreign aid and growth in per capita GDP using annual data from 1960 to 1997 for a sample of 71 aid-receiving developing countries found that the effect of foreign aid on economic growth is positive, permanent, and statistically significant. In the same vein, Gomanee et al. (2005) by using a sample of 25 sub-Saharan African countries over the period 1970–97 found that foreign aid has a significant positive effect on economic growth.
4. Stahl and Arnold (1986) argued that the use of remittances for consumption may have a positive effect on growth because of their possible multiplier effect. The result of a study in African countries has shown that remittances do positively impact the economic growth of African countries and a 10 per cent increase in remittances leads to a 0.3 per cent increase in the GDP per capita income (Fayissa and Nsiah, 2008).
5. UNDP (1990) has developed HDI for the measurement of human development of a nation. HDI measures the average achievement of a country in three basic dimensions of human development, which are as follows:

   (i) A long and healthy life as measured by life expectancy at birth.
   (ii) Knowledge as measured by the adult literacy rate (with two-thirds weight) and the combined primary, secondary, and tertiary gross enrolment ratio (with one-third weight).
   (iii) A decent standard of living as measured by GDP per capita in purchasing power parity (PPP) terms in US dollar.

   The formula used in calculation of each dimensions of human development is as follows:

$$\text{Dimesion index} = \frac{\text{Actual value} - \text{Minimum value}}{\text{Maximum value} - \text{Minimum value}}$$

   The HDI is the simple average indices of all the above three dimensions.
6. According to Rao (2010), inter-state and intra-state disparities in development have not only persisted but have even increased in certain cases in the post-reform period in India, especially where backward regions do not have the necessary political clout in decision-making regarding public investment and provision of jobs has led to regional tensions and persistent demand for carving out of a separate state consisting of backward areas, Uttarakhand, Jharkhand, and Chhattisgarh and demand for Telangana are some of the recent examples.
7 Ukeje (1992) viewed that culture is the totality of a people's way of life as deduced from material and non-material aspects of their life such as clothing, values, beliefs, thoughts, feelings, and customs.

   To Granato et al. (1996) "... by culture, we refer to a system of basic common values that help shape the behaviour of the people in a given society. In most preindustrial societies, this value system takes the form of a religion and changes very slowly, but with industrialization and accompanying processes of modernization, this worldview tend to become more secular, rational, and open to change".
8. For UNESCO cultural industries, see http://documents.ms/documents/2009-02-culture-and-development-synexe-knowledge-note.html (accessed on 15 February 2016).
9. Quoted from Barakat, A. "Integrating Culture into the Development Agenda." Available at: http://www.unesco.org/new/fileadmin/MULTIMEDIA (accessed on 30 November 2013).

10. Pye (1965) has remarked that "no single scale can be used for measuring the degree of political development." However, he has provided a few aspects central to political development: (i) political development as a political prerequisite of economic development, (ii) political development as politics typical of industrial societies, (iii) political development as political modernization, (iv) political development as operation of a nation-state, (v) political development as administrative and legal development, (vi) political development as mass mobilization and participation, (vii) political development as building of democracy, (viii) political development as stability and orderly change, (ix) political development as mobilization and power, (x) political development as one aspect of multidimensional process of social change
11. According to an opinion poll conducted in 12 countries in Latin America, more than half the respondents regarded the electoral process in their country as distorted or unfair (World Bank, 1997). One of the studies conducted in Sub-Saharan Africa has also shown that in 17 of 33 countries of the region which held general elections, there was no change of government after the conduct of general elections and several leaders or ruling parties were accused of unfair election practices to enable them to stay in power (Bangura and Nakamura, 1999).
12. There is even evidence to suggest that in a setting where education is more gender equitable, economic growth is more robust (Wasen, 1999). The World Development Report, 2012 notes that "in both high and low income countries, gender difference in education has contributed significantly to the productivity and wage gap between men and women".
13. In the opinion of Panchamukhi (2004), "the concept of GDP and GNP all pertain to the material aspects of economic activities. However, the spiritual dimensions of man cannot be ignored in analyzing the totality of events around us. Concepts like happiness, welfare, prosperity, utility, etc. need to be defined and understood in a holistic framework".
14. For the detail about the Bill Gates' quotation refer to the website http://leaderswedeserve.wordprocess.com/2008/01/25/bill-gates-wants-creative-capitalism-but-what-is-it/ (accessed on 14 October 2013).
15. JRD Tata's views were quoted from his letters in the book edited by Mambro, Arvind 2004, *JRD Tata, Letters*, Rupa, New Delhi.

REFERENCES

Acemoglu, D. 2008. "Oligarchic vs Democratic Societies." *Journal of European Economic Association*, 4: 1–44.

Acemoglu, D., Bautista, M. A., Querubin, P., and Robinson, A. 2007. "Economic and Political Inequality in Development: The Case of Cundinamarca, Colombia." Available at: http://economics.mit.edu/files/3831 (accessed on 23 December 2015).

Banister, J. 1998. "Population, Public Health and the Environment in China." *China Quarterly*, (Special Issue: China's Environment), 156: 986–1015.

Bardhan, P. 2002. "Decentralization of Governance and Development." *Journal of Economic Perspectives*, 16: 185–205.

Bernasek, A. 2003. "Banking on Social Change: Gramin Bank Lending to Women." *International Journal of Politics, Culture and Society*, 16(3).

Beverly, S. and Sherraden, M. 1997 "Investment in Human Development as a Social Development Strategy." *Social Development Issues*, 19(1): 1–18.

Campfens, H. 1990. "Issues in Organizing Impoverished Women in Latin America." *Social Development Issues*, 13(1): 20–43.

Chenery, B.H. 1955. "The Role of Industrialization in Development Programmes." *American Economic Review*, 45(2): 40–57.

Chow, Gregory C. 1990. "Capital Formation and Economic Growth in China." Princeton University, Econometric Research Programme, Research Memorandum, No. 356.

Clark, R., Thomas, W. Ramsey, and Emily, S.A. 1991. "Culture, Gender and Labour Force Participation: A Cross-National Study." *Gender and Society*, 5(1): 47–66.

Cobb, C., Halstead, T., and Rowe, J. 1995. "If the GDP is Up, Why is America Down?" *Atlantic Monthly*, October: 67.

Connelly, Patricia M., Li, T.M., MacDonald, M., and Parpart, Jane L. 2000. "Feminism and Development: Theoretical Perspectives." In *Theoretical Perspectives of Gender and Development*, edited by Jane L. Parpart, Patricia Connelly, and V.E. Barriteau. Ottawa, ON: International Development Research Centre, 51–160.

Costello, M.A. 1997. "Women in the Legal Profession: You Have Come a Long way—or Have You?" *Law Review of Michigan State University, Detroit College of Law*, 909–15.
Cypher, James M. and Dietz, James L. 2009. *The Process of Economic Development*. London and New York: Routledge.
Dabaghain, J. 1970. *Mirror of Man: Readings in Sociology and Literature*. Canada: Little, Brown and Company.
Dreze, J. and Sen, A. 1995. *India Economic Development and Social Opportunity*. New Delhi: Oxford University Press.
Duflo, E. 2012. "Women Empowerment and Economic Development." *Journal of Economic Literature*, 50(4): 1051–79.
Eyben, R., Kabeer, N., and Cornwall, A. 2008. "Conceptualizing Empowerment and the Implications for Poverty Reduction." Paper for OECD-DAC Poverty Network, OECD.
Fayissa, B. and Nsiah, C. 2008. "The Impact of Remittances on Economic Growth in Africa." Working Paper Series, February. Department of Economics and Finance, Middle Tennessee State University.
Forsythe, N., Korzemiewicz, R.P., and Durrant, D. 2000. "Gender Inequalities and Economic Growth: A Longitudinal Evaluation." *Economic Development and Cultural Change*, 48(3): 573–617.
Gandhi, M.K. 1908. *Hind Swaraj or Indian Home Rule*. Ahmedabad: Navajivan Publishing House.
Gandhi, M.K. 1967. *The Collected Works*. Delhi Publication Division, Ministry of Information and Broadcasting, Government of India.
Giuliano, P. and Ruiz-Arranz. 2005. "Remittances Financial Development and Growth." IMF Working Papers, 2005, see WP/05/234. Available at: https://www.imf.org/external/pubs/ft/wp/2005/wp05234.pdf (accessed on 15 February 2016).
Goren, P. 2005. "Party Identification and Core Political Values." *American Journal of Political Science*, 49(4): 882–97.
Goulet, D. 1965. *La Ethica del Desarollo*. Madrid, IEPAL/Tstela.
Hawkes, J. 2001. *The Four Pillar of Sustainable Culture's Essential role in Public Planning*. Victoria, Australia: Common Ground Publishing.
Helliwell, J., Layard, R., and Sacha, J., eds. 2013. *World Happiness Report, 2013*. New York: UN Sustainable Development Solutions Network.
Higgins, B. 1990. *Economic Development Problems, Principles and Policies*. New Delhi: Universal Book Stall.
Kabeer, N. 2000. "Social Exclusion, Poverty and Discrimination." *IDS Bulletin* 31(4): 83–97.
Kniivila, M. 2007. "Industrial Development and Economic Growth: Implications for Poverty Reduction and Income Inequality." Available at: http://www.un.org/esa/sustdev/publications/in (accessed on 7 February 2014).
Leftwich, A. 2000. *States of Development: On the Primacy of Politics in Development*. Cambridge: Polity Press.
Mahrey, S. 2004. "Opportunities for All New Zealanders." Ministry of Social Development. Available at: www.msd.govt.nz/documents/about-msd.../opportunity-for-all.doc (accessed on 15 February 2016).
Manor, J. 1999. *The Political Economy of Democratic Decentralization*. Washington DC: World Bank.
Meinert, R. and Kohn, J. 1987. "Towards Operationalization of Social Development Concepts." *Social Development Issues*, 10(3): 4–18.
Mellor, John W. 1969. "Production Economics and the Modernization of Traditional Agriculture." *Australian Journal of Agricultural Economics*, No. 35, 13(1): 24–34.
Melnick, D., McNeely, J., Navarro, Y.K., Schmidt-Traub, G., and Sears, R.R. 2005. "Environment and Human Well-being: A Practical Strategy." UN Millennium Project, Task Force on Environmental Sustainability. Available at: http://www.unmillenniumproject.org/documents/Environment-complete-lowres.pdf (accessed on 15 February 2016).
Midgley, J. 1993. *Social Development: The Development Perspective in Social Welfare*. Thousand Oaks, CA: SAGE Publications.
Mukherjee, J. and Banerjee, S. 2009. "Education and Health: Strategic Sequencing in Social Development Contemporary Issues and Ideas in Social Sciences." Available at: www.worldwewant2015.org/file/300184/download/325641 (accessed on 28 September 2013).
Munck, R. and O'Hearn, Denis. 1999. *Critical Development Theory: Contributions to a New Paradigm*. London and New York: Zed Books.
Nafziger, E.W. 2006. *Economic Development*. New York: Cambridge Press.
Nurse, K. 2006. "Culture as the Fourth Pillar of Sustainable Development." Paper prepared for the Commonwealth Secretariat. Available at: www.citesseerx.ist.psu.edu/viewdoc/downbad?rep=rep_1&type=pdf&doi=10.1.1.1835662 (accessed on 15 February 2016).

OECD. 2012. *Women's Economic Empowerment, Poverty Pro-poor Growth: The Role of Empowerment*. Paris: OECD.

Parpart, Jane L., Connelly, Patricia M., and Eudine Barriteau, V. 2000. "Forward." In *Theoretical Perspectives on Gender and Development,* edited by Parpart, Jane L; Connelly, Patricia, M, and Eudine Barriteau, V. Ottawa, ON: International Development Research Centre, 65–134.

Pitt, M., Khandker, S.R., and Cartwright, J. 2003. "Does Micro-credit Empower Women? Evidence from Bangladesh." World Bank Policy Research Working Paper, 2998. The World Bank, Washington, DC.

Putman, R. 1993. "The Prosperous Community: Social Capital and Public Life." *American Prospect*, 13: 35–42.

Rostow, Walter W. 1960. *The Stages of Economic Growth: A Non-communistic Manifesto*. Cambridge: Cambridge University Press.

SPC and UN. 2004. "Pacific Islands Regional Millennium Development Goals Report." Noumea/Suva: UN-CROPMDG Working Group.

Tanzi, V. 2000. *On Fiscal Federalism: Issues to Worry About*. IMF Conference on Fiscal Decentralization, Washington.

Thomas, C. 1996. "Capital Markets, Financial Markets and Social Capital." *Social and Economic Studies*, 45: 1–23.

Todaro, M.P. and Smith, S.C. 2012. *Economic Development Third Edition*. New Delhi: Dorling Kindersley (India) Private Ltd.

True, J., Parashar, S., and George, N. 2012. "Women's Political Participation in Asia and the Pacific." SSRC Conflict Prevention and Peace Forum. Available at: webarchive.ssrc.org/working-papers/CPPF_WomenInPolitics_03_True.pdf (accessed on 15 February 2016).

Tzannatos, Z. 1999. "Women and Labour Market Changes in the Global Economy: Growth Helps, Inequality Hurt and Public Policy Matters." *World Development*, 27(3): 551–70.

UNDP. 1990. *Human Development Report*. United Nations Development Programmes, New York.

———. 1995. *Human Development Report*. United Nations Development Programmes, New York.

———. 2001. *Human Development Report, 2001*. United Nations Development Programmes, Oxford University Press, Oxford.

———. 2010. *Human Development Report*. United Nations Development Programmes, New York.

UNESCO. 2012. "Culture: A Driver and Enabler of Sustainable Development Thematic Think Piece." UN System Task Team on the Post-2015 UN Development Agenda, United Nations, Paris. Available at: en.unesco.org/post2015/sites/post20156/files/Think Piece culture.pdf (accessed on 10 December 2015).

United Nations. 2011. *Happiness: Towards a Holistic Approach to Development*. Resolution adopted by the General Assembly, Sixty-fifth Session, Agenda Item 13, 65/309, United Nations, New York.

Wan, G. 2008. *Economic Growth and Regional Disparities Inequalities and Growth of Modern China*. Oxford: Oxford University Press.

Willis, K. 2005. *Theories and Practices of Development*. USA: Routledge.

World Bank. 1985. *World Development Report 1985*. The World Bank, Washington, DC.

———. 2000. *New Paths to Social Development, Community and Global Net Work in Action*. Washington: World Bank.

World Development Report. 2009. *World Development Report 2009*. Spatial Disparities and Development Policy. The World Bank, Washington, DC.

Zafarullah, H. and Huque, A.S. 2006. "Introduction: Challenges of Governing Development." In *International Development Governance*, edited by A.S. Huque and H. Zafarullah. London: Taylor & Francis, 3–12.

SUGGESTED READINGS

Bangura, Y. and Nakamura, T. 1999. "Democratization Equity and Stability: African Politics and Society in the 1990s." Geneva: UNRISD.

David, W.L. 1986. *Conflicting Paradigms in the Economic of Developing Nations*. New York: Praeger Publishers.

Gomanee, K., Girma, S., and Morrissey, O. 2005. "Aid and Growth in Sub-Saharan Africa: Accounting for Transmission Mechanisms." *Journal of International Development*, 17(8): 1055–75.

Granato, J., Inglehart, R., and Leblang, D. 1996. "Effect of Cultural Values on Economic Development: Theory, Hypotheses and Some Empirical Tests." *American Journal of Political Science*, 40(3): 607–31.

Holms, A. 2004. "A (Social) Capital Idea: Making Development Work." *Harvard International Review*, 24–27. Available at: http://www.questia.com/library/1G1-112984254 (accessed on 27 September 2013).

Jones, N., Bhatta, B., Gill, G., Pantuliano, S., Singh, H.B., Timsina, D., Uppadhaya, S., and Walker, D. 2009. "Governance and Citizenship from Below: Views of Poor and Excluded Groups and Their Vision for a New Nepal." Working Paper 301, ODI, London.

Karras, G. 2006. "Foreign Aid and Long-run Economic Growth: Empirical Evidence for a Panel of Developing Countries." *Journal of International Development*, 18(7): 15–28.

Kashyap, S.P. and Shah, A. 1989. "Ailing Industrial Systems of India: A Diagnosis." *Economic and Political Weekly*, 24(21): 77–80.

Kindlebeger, C.P. 1975. *Economic Development*. New York: McGraw-Hill.

Panchamukhi, V.R. 1990. "New Paradigms of Development Some Thoughts." In *Development Perspectives*, edited by K.S. Ramachandran. New Delhi: Vikas Publishing House, 152–60.

Pye, Lucian W. 1965. "The Concept of Political Development." *The Annals of the American Academy of Political and Social Sciences*, 358: 11–13.

Rao, Hanumantha. 2012. *Regional Disparities, Smaller States and Statehood for Telangana*. New Delhi: Academic Foundation.

Stahl, Charles W. and Arnold, F. 1986. "Overseas Workers' Remittances in Asian Development." *International Migration Review*, 20(4): 899–925.

Ukeje, B. 1992. *Educational Administration*. Enugu: Four Dimension Publishing Company.

Wasen, S. 1999. *Does Gender Inequality Reduce Growth and Development? Evidence from Cross-country Regressions (Rep No. 7)*. The World Bank Development Research Group/Poverty Reduction and Economic Management Network, Washington, DC.

World Bank. 1997. *World Development Report 1997. The State in a Changing World*, Washington, DC.

6 Market, State, and Heterogeneous Actors

The failure of the market system to deliver results that are either economically efficient or socially acceptable, there is a legitimate role for government that most economists accept as necessary to improve the operation of the entire economy, including the private capitalist sector.

— Cypher and Dietz (2006)

The onus to realize development goals has fallen on the State, but it cannot achieve them alone, therefore, the involvement of civil society, non-governmental organizations and international development agencies becomes vital.

— Zafarullah and Huque (2006)

Fundamentally, the role of NGOs in development is considered as a paradigm shift in the process of development break from the conventional wisdom that social development is primarily the responsibility of states and markets.

— Fernando and Heston (1997)

The decentralization is a means to enhance government performance and ultimately to support economic development.

— Bahl and Smoke (2003)

The *laissez faire* principle advocated by the classical and neo-classical economists gave the market a free hand to play a key role in the economic growth and development of the Western capitalist nations. The ardent supporters of the *laissez faire* principle were against any interventions in the affairs of the market by the government as it will affect the effective functioning of the market. However, market as a key actor of economic growth and development failed to provide solution to the economic crisis of the Great Depression which the capitalist countries of America and Europe were facing during 1929–36. Adding to this crisis, the independence of the impoverished Third World countries of the East from the colonial rule and the sundry of socio-economic problems they were facing at the time of their independence were beyond the capacity of the market with the private player to solve all these problems of these underdeveloped countries. Therefore, the intervention of the state in the economic growth and development affairs of both the developed as well as underdeveloped countries was called for. Later on, with the establishment of the Bitten Woods System, the international organizations, i.e World Bank, IMF, and other bilateral and multilateral organizations like Asian Development

Bank (ADB), African Development Bank, UNDP, DFID, USAID, UNESCO, and UNICEF, to name a few among many, were embarked to play an important role in providing financial and technical support to the socio-economic development of the underdeveloped countries. The failure of both the market and state to promote effective grassroots development and the inability of the international organizations to directly deal with the people, has led to the emergence of other actors, i.e. non-governmental organizations (NGOs) and civil society organizations (CSOs), that are playing a proactive role in the implementation of development projects and programmes at the grass-roots level. Of late, with the advent of the democratic decentralization processes in many countries, the local self-government institutions are also playing supplementary and complementary roles in providing support to the government and NGOs. Broadly, the actors involved in the growth and development processes of a nation are the market, state, bilateral, and multilateral organizations, NGOs/CSOs, and local self-government institutions.

After reading this chapter, you will be able to:

(i) Describe the role of market in economic growth and development and discuss the reasons of failure of market in the underdeveloped countries.
(ii) Analyze the role of state in development and describe how the public–private partnership is promoting development.
(iii) Explain the role of various sectors in the economic growth and development.
(iv) Distinguish between the organized and unorganized sectors and explain how the unorganized sector is responsible for underdevelopment of the underdeveloped countries.

THE MARKET

The classical as well as neo-classical economists were staunch supporters of *laissez faire* market economy with minimum state interventions. They were of the view that the economic growth and development can be better accelerated through the free play of the market forces of demand and supply. According to Adam Smith, growth can be promoted through the market institutions and through the activity of competition. In Smith's view, the ideal economy is a self-regulating market system that automatically satisfies the economic needs of the people.

A free market economy which is also called the capitalist economy has the following features:

(i) Individual actions are regulated by the forces of self-interest and competition.
(ii) Production is organized by private individuals with a profit motive.
(iii) All goods and services produced with the help of various factors of production are brought for sale in the market and the invisible hand helps to maintain equilibrium between demand and supply.
(iv) There is minimum interference of the government in the affairs of the market.

The perfect market runs on the principle of Say's law of market, that is, 'every supply creates its own demand' ensures equilibrium. Besides Smith, J.S. Mill, an ardent supporter of *laissez faire* economy, advocated a limited role of government in a country's economic affairs. According to David Ricardo, the tendency to accumulate capital is the prime motive force in the process of economic growth. According to classical economists, the key agents of economic growth and development are the farmers, producers, and businessmen, and it was the free trade, enterprise, and competition that led farmers, producers, and businessmen and their motivation for rent, profit, and interest entices them to expand the market, which in turn, made economic development possible.

The important forms of markets are perfect competition, monopoly, monopolistic competition, and oligopolistic competition. In the perfect competition, there are many sellers and many buyers and this type of market is also featured with freedom of entry and exists; products are homogenous and normal profits are earned by the firms as price is determined by demand and supply. Monopoly is a market form characterized with a single firm selling a particular product and there are many buyers for it. However, under the monopolistic competition which is largely seen in the market, a large number of firms are found selling closely related but not homogeneous products; other characteristics being freedom of entry and exists, lack of perfect knowledge about the market, and firms having full control over the price. The other important form of market is oligopoly where there are a few firms in the market producing either homogenous products or products which are close but not perfect substitutes. Other important features of oligopoly are price rigidity, and the elements of monopoly and interdependence among the firms and advertisement and selling cost play a considerable role in the market. There are also other forms of market like financial markets which deal with the exchange of liquid asset (money); the stock market relating to exchange of shares between buyers and sellers and the bond market dealing with the exchange of debt securities in the form of bonds.

The famous Say's law of market, admired by most of the classical economists, says that 'supply creates its own demand'; ardently supports market and its forces and dynamics. Say's law implies three things: (a) money is a veil, and its only function is to serve as a medium of exchange; (b) general over-production or market glut is impossible; and (c) full employment equilibrium is automatically ensured. The market economy approach argues that the free market economy will always automatically attain full employment equilibrium in the long run. The market mechanism to achieve social optimality, the condition of 'perfect competition' must be satisfied. All the participants in market transactions must have perfect information on the prices and qualities of commodities and no one can have monopolistic power to influence market prices (Hayami and Godo, 2005). However, in general, developing countries will not be able to rely on the market mechanism to the extent that the industrial countries did during their early stages of development and in many developing countries, producers are often unsure about the size of local markets, the presence of other producers and the availability of inputs, both domestic and imported (Todaro and Smith, 2012).

Market operation in the developing countries is highly imperfect in nature. The market failure and its incapability to provide distributive justice have led to miseries of the poor in developing countries. The economic exploitation and urge for the profit motive among the entrepreneurs in the market featured with imperfect competition posed challenge to the capitalist system based on free market principle.

The imperfect market in the underdeveloped countries has the following features:

(i) Operation of monopolistic and oligopolistic markets where a single seller and a group of sellers, respectively are dominating the market.
(ii) Because of lack of skill and other human development factors, there is poor immobility of factors of production, particularly from the agriculture to the industrial and service sectors and from the rural to the urban sector. Due to the mobility of labour force from the rural to the urban sector seen in developing countries because of high speed of urbanization, the rural workforce is placed in low quality of jobs and is enjoying a low standard of living in urban areas.
(iii) There is imperfect knowledge about the market as both the buyers and sellers are ignorant about the market conditions.
(iv) There exists a rigid price system in low profit, low investment, and low employment.
(v) The middleman who appropriate benefits both from the sellers and the buyers by resorting to hoarding play an important role.
(vi) Agriculture in the developing countries of Asia, Africa, and Latin America is largely subject to an imperfect market. It is argued that the size of the government is determined by the degree of market failure in a society. The market is a mechanism to promote economic efficiency but not to improve income distribution and provide social justice as profit motive is the main driving force. As in the underdeveloped countries, a gigantic percentage of population is poor and economic inequality is pervasive, the social justice motive is more important than the profit motive, so market is not able to provide redistributive justice to all. Cypher and Dietz (2006) have, therefore, rightly said that in the society where there are pervasive monopoly or oligopoly forces, government action is clearly called for to reconstitute competitive forces.

In the Western world, despite the failure of the market in a few circumstances, market is playing a key role in the growth and development of the developed countries, i.e. Europe and America. Stiglitz, one of the mainstream neo-classical economists and staunch supporter of market forces, viewed that developing nations would move ahead if they would simply adopt a 'package' whereby state-owned enterprises were privatized, all subsidies were eliminated, all tariffs and other restraints on foreign trade were eliminated, and the government policy was limited to budget balancing and the control of inflation (Cypher and Dietz, 2006). However, the market in the neo-liberalized era has not been effective enough to overcome the economic problems of the developing countries. Hayami and Godo (2005) said that the doctrine of neo-classical liberalism, where free market is the controlling mechanism for economic activities, was criticized since the beginning of 1990s, on the basis of several observations: (a) that Latin American economies were not able to sustain economic growth after their recovery for the debt crisis; (b) that East Asian economies were plunged into crisis in the late 1990s due to a major disruption in regional financial markets; and (c) that structural adjustment programme (SAP) had failed to achieve economic growth and reduce poverty in low-income economies, especially in Africa. The SAP reforms of liberalization, deregulation, and privatization not only fail to improve such economies but often make them less efficient with an increased incidence of market failure (Hayami and Godo, 2005). Ishikawa (1994) and Stiglitz (2002) among others argued that while the SAP approach may be effective in middle-income economies with relatively well-developed market organizations, it is ineffective in 'customary economies' characterized by an underdeveloped market, where markets are highly imperfect or even non-existent under severely imperfect information available.

THE STATE

After the Second World War and the 'Great Depression' of 1929–36, the market economy driven by the capitalists and entrepreneurial imperialistic model faced a great jolt, and interventions of state for development was called for to provide a panacea to economic slowdown and depression. Even the protagonists of the market were also of the opinion that there is a fear of stagnation or stationary state in market economy. According to Adam Smith, "The stationary state is dull, the declining melancholy. Life is hard in the stationary state for different sections of the society and miserable in the declining state". The stagnation as well as declining stage in a capitalist economic system is a situation where market failed to promote economic growth and development; this has resulted in intervention of the state to correct the market distortions. In the view of Keynes, during the situation of economic depression, there is lack of effective demand in the market which creates economic glut, and the producers are reluctant to continue production, resulting in market failure to control the economic crisis, and here the intervention of the State was resorted to, raising the effective demand through government investment.

Therefore, the formation of post-colonial nation-states following the Second World War had at its core, a belief in the merit of an 'extensive state' (Batley and Larbi, 2004). By 1945, 'development' as a process was State-directed and in large part implemented by the State (Jenning, 2006). The 1950s and 1960s, saw a strong consolidation of State power and an emphasis on socio-economic service delivery in both capitalist- and socialist-oriented States through government investment. The term 'developmental state' profusely used in the 19th and 20th centuries envisages the role of state in the development process. According to Leftwich (2000), the developmental state is a state in which politics has concentrated sufficient determinations, power, autonomy, capacity, and legitimacy at the centre to shape, pursue, and encourage the achievement of explicit developmental objectives, whether by establishing, promoting, and protecting the conditions of economic growth (in the capitalist development state) by organizing it directly (in the socialists variants) or varying combinations of both. A development state divests its resources and energy not only in maintaining internal and external security and law and order, but also for improving the quality of life of its people by reducing poverty and hunger, making provision for employment, education, health care, sanitation, safe drinking water, roads, communication, energy, and other developmental facilities.

The development strategies advocated by ADB (2000) in which role of the State is vital promote the following:

(i) Pro-poor development: Sustainable economic growth to reduce poverty by generating income among the poor and fostering equitable development with and for the poor.

(ii) Social development: Ensuring comprehensive social protection and providing access to basic necessities, such as education, primary health care, water, and sanitation, and promoting social institutions and social capital of vulnerable groups.

(iii) Good governance: Public policies that encourage the inclusion of the poor and other vulnerable groups in the development process.

This involves pro-poor public expenditures, social services that are nearer to the users and have more relevance for the poor, policies that generate equity and access to socio-economic assets, and enhanced social relations, including gender equity and the improved status of women. The role of the state is pronounced in building up of social overhead capital in primary and secondary sectors and making provision of social goods, such as education, health care, housing, sanitation, and all other basic needs to the disadvantaged. A few highlighted areas where public sector has played important role in most of the Third World countries of Asia, Africa, and Latin America are (a) social justice, (b) community development, (c) infrastructure development in agriculture and rural development (popularly called Bharat Nirman programme in India), (d) rural employment and poverty alleviation, (e) ensuring basic needs to the disadvantaged, and (f) regional and backward area development, which are not priority areas of the private sector or market.[1] In the same vein, citing the example of the developed nation like United Kingdom, Begg (1993) viewed that the post-war expansion of public sector services was a significant contributor to inter-regional economic stability and employment due to both in scale and its relative geographical evenness throughout the regions of the UK.

The role of the State in the development process has been critically analyzed by the developmentalists, who preferred a strong State as against weak State for faster decision-making, good governance, as well as effective and efficient implementation of developmental projects and programmes. Mentan (2004) was of the view that the quest for a 'strong State' in the development process was a dominant feature of the 'modernization literature'. Gunnar Myrdal, who was one of the strong supporters of the developmental State, said that the soft States are those States, that have neither the administrative capacity nor the political wherewithal to push private investment; control market imperfections and effectively implement industrial policy, etc. According to Lindeke (1995), State softness usually connotes a condition in which the institutions of the state have limited autonomy in carrying out defined normal state functions and this set of problems is often regarded as the primary cause of authoritarian personalism, corruption, and the demise of democratic practices. The fallout of the weak state in African countries has been as follows: the economic crisis of the 1970s; the demise of the argument for state intervention; the ideological hegemony of neo-conservatism in key funding institutions or donor countries; the failure of development planning in many countries; religious strife and stagnation (Mentan, 2004). The Indian Constitution which provides three lists, i.e. Union List, State List, and Concurrent List for functional convenience of the central and provincial governments, however, has given enough leverage and excuses to both central and provincial governments with regards to the formulation and enforcement of rule of law and resulted in weak governance at both the levels. Besides, rise and capture of political power by the regional political parties at the provincial government has changed the approach to the Indian democratic federalism and coalition politics of compulsion and compromises has ramshackled the governance, which resulted in corruption and scams, and poor enforcement of rule of law. The soft States are featured with weak law, poor willpower to initiate effective social and economic reforms, social indiscipline, corruption, scams, poor governance, and weak enforcement of rule of law. Political and bureaucratic establishments in a soft State lack deterministic willpower to take firm decisions on the economic front to strengthen the economy and put it on a higher growth path. Democracy will remain healthy only when there is efficient State machinery both at the centre and provincial levels, both of them work in tandem with full cooperation and coordination, there is effective implementation and enforcement of rule of law, and the government provides safety and security to common men. Therefore, strong State which can effectively guide both the state as well as market machineries is sine qua non for faster development.

THE MARKET VIS-À-VIS STATE PARTNERSHIP

During the 1970s and 1980s, the era of central planning was under attack leading to the 'rolling back of the state' and resurgence of market and growth-based notions of development. The role of State has not been effective enough to bring faster development of the underdeveloped countries because of bad governance, i.e. corruption, poor application of rule of law, and lack of transparency and accountability. Therefore, the public sector reform emphasizing on the downsizing of the role of the State and disinvestment of public sector enterprises all over the world is called for to deal with the development during the 20th century. It is remarked that the recent global phenomenon of public sector reform has been in the opposite direction, i.e. reversing the traditional role of government, the state, and public administration institutions into one that promotes a private, corporate-driven market place, dominated by the big business elite (Farazmand, 2006).

The two international institutions that ardently propagated economic reforms to overcome the failure of the state and suggested liberalization and privatization to promote growth and to overcome economic crisis in the 1980 are the World Bank and the IMF. Both the institutions popularized the principles of the 'Washington Consensus' which called for economic liberalization and a reduction of the role of the state for increased efficiency. The liberalization process which started in the beginning of the 19th century in most of the developing countries has enhanced the role of market resulting in reduction of the role of government in many sectors largely through disinvestments in public sectors and encouraging investment by the corporate sectors and through the FDI in the economy. The World Bank, a staunch supporter of liberalization, encouraged the role of market in the process of development by stating, "...state to let markets work where they can and to step in promptly and effectively where they cannot". The World Bank World Development Report 1983 argued that governmental policies lead to large price distortions and those distortions negatively affected the growth process. Polanyi (1957) was of the view that markets are an essential component of any well-functioning economy and the more efficient such markets are, the better the role of government will likely be; less when markets work well. However, many developmentalists still consider that although market can augment economic growth, yet it would not be able to ensure social justice and equity. Here, it is befitting to quote the Human Development Report, 1999 which envisaged that "competitive market may be the best guarantee of efficiency, but not necessarily of equity. Liberalization and privatization can be a step to competitive market-but not a guarantee of them. And market is neither the first nor the last word in human development". The sometimes artificially created market imperfections and the costs of modernization inflicted by the capitalists, landlords, and businessmen have created hardships for the common men even in their access to basic needs. The government interventions to provide subsidized food through PDS (public distribution system) in India is an illustrious example of resultant market failure and government interventions to upkeep social justice and equity. However, both in developed as well as developing countries in recent years, the market mechanism is a powerful player of the economic system and the process of globalization further enhanced its role in the process of economic development. The market and the state are playing a balancing role in the development of the developing countries, the former needed to be engaged in growth promoting activities, while the latter can create social overhead capital and is also best suited for the development and welfare activities. In recent years, in the developed as well as developing countries, government has created a mechanism of sharing responsibilities between the public and private sectors so that both of them can effectively engage themselves in both growth and development activities, which is popularly known as 'public–private partnership'.

The concept 'public–private partnership' is a popular concept in the developing countries that have accepted the neo-liberal ideals and given adequate space to the private and corporate sector to play an important role and offer a helping hand to the government in their drive for achieving higher economic growth rate and development goals. The market provides 'private goods and services' with profit motive, while the State provides 'public goods and services' with welfare motive and also builds social overhead capital which is beneficial both for the public as well as private sector. The economic reform process adopted by the developing economies in recent years tilts towards marketization of public goods. The post-liberalization era has led to four major changes in the economies: (a) disinvestment of the public sector units; (b) foreign direct investment in various development sectors; (c) outsourcing of the production of public goods to the private sector; and (d) public–private partnership leading to corporatization and marketization of the public goods.

The gradually shrinking role of the State in various sectors, particularly in the service sector, and the proliferation of the market without appropriate strengthening of the primary and secondary sectors in the highly populated and agriculturally predominating developing economies has created more instability and these economies are losing their internal strength to meet the challenges of economic ups and downs. Economic reform is seen as a stimulant for growth of service sector and has forced the contribution of the primary sector to GDP to decline and has halted the pace of contribution of secondary sector to the economic growth, making their economic growth and development more unstable. Stiglitz (2002) apprehended that reforms to reduce government control and intervention will be ineffective or even damaging in low-income economies. The so-called 'mark-gov', market + government, economic reform strategy is the new model of development promoted in recent years by the developing countries under the economic reform strategy. The two illustrious examples of market and government partnership are: Japan's 'Guided Capitalism' under the Meiji emperor, from 1986 to 1912 and reliance on state initiatives for large investment in infrastructure in China's 'Market Socialism' where economic system combines state ownership of the means of production with use of market to allocate resources (Nafziger, 2006). India, through its new initiative of public–private partnership, intends shared arrangements of responsibilities between the public and private sectors and the role of market vis-à-vis State in promoting development.

As far as functioning of both the market and the state is concerned, the desire to accumulate more and more profit and add more amenities to their comfort and luxuries has defamed the capitalistic market economic system; and likewise bad governance, corruption, and congregation of non-performing assets in the public sector has resulted in the malfunctioning of the State or government mechanism. However, both market and government are the key players of economic growth and development and should coexist by creating their own space for functioning, the former is for provisioning private good and the latter for the social and public goods and through partnership both these two actors can cooperate and coordinate for provisioning essential services efficiently and effectively in the underdeveloped countries. However, crony capitalism, which is a marriage between State and private special interest through which the State protects the private special interest by giving them sops in terms of distribution of legal permits, government grants, tax concessions, and similar other forms of State favouritism, has created apprehensions in the minds of the people that this unholy alliance between the corporate and the State may benefit the former and bring miseries to the poor and common man in the underdeveloped countries who are exclusively dependant on State welfaristic measures.

THE INTERNATIONAL AGENCIES

Since the establishment of Bretton Woods System, the international organizations are playing a pivotal role in the economic and social development of the developing countries of Asia, Africa, Latin America, and Caribbean and also providing support to the developed countries in many areas of social, political, cultural, and economic development. They are offering technical and financial help to the member countries in the effective implementation of various projects and programmes in different sectors of the economy. Over the years, they have proved themselves powerful actors in development arena, exerting tremendous influence on development projects in the developing world (Kurain, 2004). They play an important role in today's world and are active in the allocation of resources in the form of global or international public goods and services; the distribution of income and the stabilization of global economy (Frey and Stutzer, 2006). The international development organizations promote development in many ways: (a) build government capacity and public governance framework; (b) build the capacity of local private sector, labour, and CSOs including intermediaries, advocates, technical advisors, whistle-blowers, and pressure groups; (c) build up environment for development; and (d) invest in human capacities and leaderships (Fox and Prescott, 2004).

The international agencies can be broadly categorized into the following six types:

(i) Multilateral agencies
(ii) Bilateral agencies
(iii) International NGOs
(iv) International foundations
(v) Public–private partnerships
(vi) Networks

The multilateral agencies, i.e. World Bank, UNDP (United Nations Development Programme), UNIDO (United Nations International Development Organization), UNICEF (United Nations Children's Fund), European Union (EU), etc. provide technical and financial assistance to the nation-states in various sectors of development and are found involved in the effective implementation of development projects and programmes, such as eradication of poverty, illiteracy, ill health, and unemployment and attainment of MDGs. The bilateral agencies, for example CIDA (Canadian International Development Agency), SIDA (Swedish Agency for International Development Cooperation), JICA (Japan International Cooperation Agency), etc. are involved in similar types of developmental activities on country-to-country basis. The third and fourth categories of international agencies are international NGOs, i.e. Oxfam, ActionAid, Family Planning International (FPI), and so on and the international foundations such as Ford Foundation, MacArthur Foundation, and Bill and Melinda Gates Foundation are found to be engaged in various developmental activities such as health, education, slum rehabilitation, and gender empowerment and are providing technical and financial inputs to the government and non-governmental organizations in developing countries. Besides these organizations, the other two categories of international agencies involved in developmental activities are the international public–private partnerships, such as GAID (Global Alliance for ICT and Development), GAIN (Global Alliance for Improved Nutrition), and GWP (Global Water Partnership) and networks such as GDN (Global Development Network), GKN (Global Knowledge Network), and ILC (International Land Coalition). The liberalization and globalization process which started in the developing countries during the beginning of the 19th century has widened the role of international agencies in the development process of the developing countries. Over the period of time, these agencies have proved themselves as indispensable actors of development. The dependency and neoliberalism era in development has provided enough space to these international agencies to play a proactive and constructive role in the development process of the developing economies. It is a fact that the developed countries have been found to propagate and push their growth and development ideals through these organizations and have created another form of dependency of underdeveloped countries on the developed countries indirectly through the international organizations because the donors of these agencies are primarily the developed nations.

THE NON-GOVERNMENTAL ORGANIZATIONS (NGOs) AND CIVIL SOCIETY ORGANIZATIONS (CSOs)

The CSOs and the NGOs are the important actors of development, which in real terms are working at the grass-roots level in the implementation of projects and programmes formulated by the government, private, and international agencies. They are the go-between the people and the State. Therefore, it is rightly remarked that the civil society is not only a 'contested concept' but in Asia it is also 'very much a received concept' and is conceptualized in various ways: "a civil society opposed to the state, a civil society assisting a minimal state and a pluralistic civil society demanding an accountable state" (Zarsky and Tay, 2000). In the late 1970s and 1980s, 'the NGO decade' took place amidst the Western pursuit of neo-liberal agendas, with NGOs emerging as a promising development alternative (Banks and Hulme, 2012). The 1990s witnessed the increased significance and active participation of NGOs in the aid and development nexus (Feldman, 1998). The new languages of development, i.e. 'participation, empowerment, and equity' adopted by both development institutions and international financial institutions are actually the languages embraced by NGOs (Eade and Ligteringen, 2001).

According to the London School of Economics Centre for Civil Society's working definition:

> Civil Society commonly embraces a diversity of spaces, actors, and institutional forms, varying in their degree of formality, autonomy and power. Civil societies are often populated by organizations such as registered charities, development non-government organizations, community groups, women's organizations, faith based organizations, professional associations, trade unions, coalitions, and advocacy groups.[2]

According to Aisha Ghaus Pasha, "Civil Society is a broader concept, encompassing all organizations and associations that exists outside the state and market". Civil Societies have been well recognized as an important actor of development after market and State. NGOs are the leading institutions among the civil society groups involved in a host of developmental activities at the grass-roots level. They have become important stakeholders in the management of development at the global, national, and sub-national levels (Zafarullah and Huque, 2006). According to Clarke (1998), NGOs are private non-profit professional organizations with a legal character. NGOs are found to be actively involved in the formulation, implementation, monitoring, and evaluation of many socio-economic development projects and programmes. Being closer to the people and less constrained by the rules and regulations of the state machinery, they are more effective at the grass-roots level as compared to other state apparatus. NGOs are the institutions that are closer to the people and are in a better position to carry out development programmes effectively as per the need of the community and with the full participation of the community. As they are bound by the rules and regulations like the government official, they are in a better position to formulate appropriate strategies and community-specific activities for the grass-roots development. Therefore, government is looking up to the NGOs to provide 'delivery services', i.e. implement local development programmes rather than supplement government programmes in their areas of operation (Planning Commission, Government of India, 1994).

Apart from NGOs, the CSOs are also playing equally significant roles at the grass-roots level development. Per se in India, youth clubs, *mahila mandals*, self-help groups, farmers, cooperatives, etc. are providing support both to the government as well as the non-governmental organizations in their endeavour to implement various development projects and programmes at the grass roots. The government and the non-governmental organizations are also taking their help while implementing, monitoring, and evaluating developmental programmes and projects. According to Zafarullah and Huque (2006), total development demands include civic participation and people's empowerment through decentralization structures and the continued interplay between the state and the people.

Some of the important developmental activities in which the CSOs are found to be involved in the developing countries are:

(i) Providing extension and education programme in the agriculture and allied sectors.

(ii) Getting involved in the income-generating and employment-creating activities in the agriculture and allied sectors.
(iii) Promoting self-employment in the marginal, small, and medium manufacturing sectors.
(iv) Strengthening the self-help groups to undertake self-employment activities in both rural and urban areas.
(v) Getting involved in the sanitation and safe drinking water projects funded by the government and bilateral and multilateral agencies.
(vi) Streamlining of the public distribution system, mid-day meal schemes for the school children, prevention of child labour, and management of old age homes, schools, and care centres for orphans and even differently abled children.
(vii) Monitoring and evaluating various rural and urban development projects and programmes.
(viii) Undertaking innovative action research projects in the area of primary education and primary health care.
(ix) Undertaking various developmental works, including awareness programmes in the area of education, health, housing, sanitation, drinking water, etc. for the disadvantaged sections of the society.
(x) Undertaking welfare activities for the physically challenged people.
(xi) Undertaking welfare activities for the aged and construction and management of old age homes.
(xii) Undertaking many cultural activities and heritage development programmes.
(xiii) Creating political awareness among the people.
(xiv) Involved in many women empowerment projects and programmes.
(xv) Involved in poverty alleviation programmes.

However, it is observed that in the underdeveloped countries, most of the powerful NGOs are being owned by the politicians and the retired bureaucrats who get projects from the government and the international agencies through influences. This is again another form of crony capitalism where the State supports the NGOs owned by the economically, politically, and bureaucratically powerful people.

THE LOCAL SELF-GOVERNMENT (LSG) INSTITUTIONS

The local self-government institutions are the backbone of grass-roots political system in decentralized democracies. The last two decades of the 20th century witnessed a significant rise in the scope of local democracy throughout the developing world, with increasing devolution of political, economic, and administrative authority to the local government (Bardhan and Mookherjee, 2007).

This increase in importance and interest in the local governments throughout the world has happened because of the following reasons:

(i) Transparency: The desire for greater democratic involvement.
(ii) Subsidiary: The notion that public activities should be carried out at the lowest level of government possible.

(iii) Competitiveness: Increased and more effective access and use of local knowledge and assets to derive economic development.
(iv) Heterogeneity: Adaptation of policies to local circumstances, since 'one size does not fit all'.
(v) Cost saving: The economies of scale from larger units (Bryden, 2005). As the elected representatives of this political system are more closer to the people as compared to the State legislatures and parliamentarians, they can better understand people's problems relating to development and work closely with the State and NGO functionaries to implement them effectively for the well-being of the people. The local government is generally seen as an important agent of development and grass-roots participation in the democratic process.

According to Shah (2006), local government refers to specific institutions or entities created by national constitutions (Brazil, Denmark, France, India, Italy, Japan, and Sweden), by state constitutions (Australia, the United States), by ordinary legislation of higher level of central government (New Zealand, the United Kingdom, most countries), by provincial or state legislation (Canada, Pakistan), or by executive order (China) to deliver a range of specified services to a relatively small geographically delineated areas. India has two types of local self-government institutions, one for the urban areas known as urban local bodies (ULBs) and another for the rural areas known as the Panchayati Raj Institutions (PRIs). These organizations in India are recognized as the third-tier democratic institutions and now are being treated as important actors of development after market, government, and NGOs. The 73rd and 74th Constitutional Amendment Acts of Government of India have assigned these bodies with duties and responsibilities for carrying out developmental activities.

The key features of the 73rd Constitutional Amendment are:

(i) Establishment of a three-tier structure: village panchayat (also known as gram panchayat), intermediate panchayat (also known as block panchayat/mandal panchayat/panchayat samiti), and district panchayat (also known as zilla parishad).
(ii) Reservation of seats for Scheduled Castes and Scheduled Tribes in proportion to their population.
(iii) Reservation of one-third seats for women.
(iv) Establishment of State Finance Commission to recommend measures to improve the finances of panchayats.
(v) Establishment of State Election Commission for conduction of election for PRIs.
(vi) Establishment of District Planning Committee (DPC) to prepare the draft development plans for the district.
(vii) Establishment of gram sabha (village assembly) and its empowerment as a decision-making body at village level.
(viii) Rotation of memberships in accordance with the reservation of seats for women, Scheduled Castes and Scheduled Tribes in PRIs.

Democratic decentralization and involvement of LSGs in development process has made development need-based, demand-driven, participatory, and people-friendly.

As these institutions are closer to the people, their empowerment will make development projects and programmes more focused, people-centred, and target-oriented and, in a way, democratize development.

The devolution of power to village panchayats in India has enabled these grass-roots level local self-government institutions to perform many developmental activities:

(i) Construction of roads and household and community toilets, and provision of safe drinking water and electricity.
(ii) Distribution of books and scholarships to backward caste students.
(iii) Construction of school building, toilets, drinking water, and playground facility in schools.
(iv) Supervision of ICDS centres and monitoring of mid-day meals in primary schools and ICDS centres.
(v) Implementation of various rural development schemes such as NREGA, SGSY, IAY, TSC, etc.
(vi) Implementation of social security schemes, i.e. old age pension, handicap pension, and widow pension.
(vii) Promotion of rural energy through the installation of *gobar (cowdung)* gas plants and solar energy system.
(viii) Providing support to government in the effective implementation of various flagship programmes such as Sarva Shiksha Abhiyan (SSA) and National Rural Health Mission (NRHM).
(ix) Construction of and reparation of irrigation projects.
(x) Preparation of village development plan either by themselves or with the help of NGOs.
(xi) Implementation and monitoring of public distribution system.
(xii) Monitoring of the primary schools and health sub-centres and activities of teachers, health workers and other staffs working in these institutions.

Haque (1977) believed that decentralization is a way of increasing the effectiveness of development programmes by making them more relevant and responsive to local needs and conditions, allowing greater flexibility in their implementation, thus making the state more participatory, more acceptable, and more effective and efficient. Around 95 per cent of democracies now have elected sub-national governments. The experience of the last 15 years shows that devolution of powers affects political stability, public service performance, equality, and macro-economic stability (World Development Report, 2000). Decentralization and devolution of functions, functionaries, and funds from the central and state governments to the local self-government institutions is perceived as a paradigm shift of responsibilities which has veered centre and state governments as facilitators and the local governments as gadgets of development at the grass-roots level. However, because of the division of rural community on the basis of caste, class, and ethnicity, the economically more powerful and the creamy layers are virtually the de facto and de jure heads of the local self-government institutions, and social justice is found to be negated in many places. Further, the indulgence of these elected representatives, in general, and the heads of these institutions, in particular, in corruption in nexus with the State machinery has resulted in poor performance in the targeted goal of development.

THE SECTORS OF DEVELOPMENT

Effectively, from the point of view of economic growth and development, there are three sectors in an economy, i.e. primary, secondary, and tertiary sectors. The primary sector consists of extraction of resources from the earth, primarily agriculture; the secondary sector consists of industry and manufacturing; and the service sector consists of services. The primary sector which comprises agriculture and allied activities like fisheries, dairy, horticulture, etc. was playing a significant role in the GDP of the developing countries of Asia, Africa, and Latin America, during the initial phase or pre-liberalization phase of economic planning and development. Modern development economists mostly agree that in the post-Second World period, the role of agriculture and rural development is absolutely an integral part of the process of nation building and healthy development (Johnston, 1970). According to FAO estimates, some 1.3 billion people work in agriculture around the world, 97 per cent of them in developing countries (Fechter, 2012). Economists now explicitly identified strong growth linkages and multiplier effects of agricultural growth to the non-agricultural sectors (Mellor, 1969). The several traditional roles essential to overall economic growth, which agriculture plays are:

(i) It provides food and nutritional security to the increasing number of population.
(ii) It supplies raw materials to growing and diversifying domestic industrial sectors, particularly to the food processing and other agro-based industries established both in the public as well as private sector.
(iii) The transformation of labour from the agriculture to the industrial and service sector as well as from the rural to the urban areas fulfils the labour requirement need of these two upcoming sectors in the developing countries and a feeder manpower support to urban infrastructure development activities.
(iv) Growth and mechanization of agriculture enlarges the size of the market for the domestic industrial sector.
(v) It provides employment and livelihood for a large percentage of rural population and helps in rural poverty reduction.
(vi) Income from agriculture promotes rural savings and investment.
(vii) Accumulation of domestic saving and investment in agriculture promotes rural capital formation and provides employment to a large number of women.

According to Schultz (1964), agriculture is important for economic growth in the sense that it guarantees subsistence for society without which growth is not possible. While agriculture accounts for around 2 per cent of GDP and less than 4 per cent of employment in developed countries, its share in the GDP of low-income countries is as high as 24 per cent. Developing countries consider domestic self-sufficiency in food grains as an important element of food security. The World Development Report, 2008 on 'Agriculture for Development' highlights that in much of the Sub-Saharan Africa, agriculture is a strong option for spurring growth, overcoming poverty, and enhancing food security. The report envisaged that from 1980 to 2004, the GDP of agriculture expanded globally by an average of 2.4 per cent a year, more than the population growth of 1.6 per cent a year. Livestock expansion has contributed to the high agricultural growth rates, and it is one of the fastest growing sub-sectors in developing countries, where it already accounted for one-third of agricultural GDP. Still in developing countries, agriculture and allied activities play an important role in development by providing employment to the less educated and less skilled population which constitutes the gigantic percentage of total manpower and livelihood to the countryside men and women. The Africa Human Development Report, 2012 has envisaged that increased agricultural productivity would end the ravages of hunger and malnutrition and will nurture capabilities and conditions for human development.

The secondary sector or the industry sector was the key stimulant of growth and development of the developed countries during early phase of their development. Because of lack of infrastructure and capital formation in the industrial sector, the contribution of industrial sector in the underdeveloped countries is low. Economists like Arthur Lewis, Rosenstein Rodan, Ranger Nurkse, Hirschman, and Leibenstein viewed that economic development is a growth process that requires the systematic allocation of factors of production from a low productivity, traditional technology, decreasing returns, mostly primary sector to a high productivity, modern, increasing returns, mostly industrial sector (Adelman, 1999). The more advanced economies have more diverse industrial sectors and economies that export more sophisticated products grow faster (UNIDO, 2009). Therefore, in the 21st century, manufacturing development remains relevant for poor countries trying to catch up with more advanced economies and provide increasing standards of living for their populations (Naude and Szirmai, 2012). According to UNIDO (2007), "Industrialization is proving a potent force for economic growth in countries of Asia, most recently China and India". The role of manufacturing sector in the Chinese economy is clearly more significant than that of agriculture and service sectors, whereby the sector contributes the highest to growth in China. The industrial sector is broadly categorized into four sub-sectors:

(i) Mining covers the activities of extraction of natural resources such as metals, coal, and oil and those like stone quarrying.
(ii) Manufacturing covers manufacturing of various products such as food products, like flour, processed tea, and aerated drinks; wood products, like furniture; textile products, like yarn, cloth, and garments; leather products, like tyres, tubes, and toys; mineral products, like cement and glass; chemical products, like synthetic, fibres, fertilizers, and pharmaceuticals; metal products, like steel, utensils, machinery, equipment, and apparatus, like machinery, transformers, television, and computers; and transport equipment, like bicycles, cars, trains, trucks, etc.
(iii) Electricity, gas, and water activities relating to generation, transmission, and distribution of electricity; manufacturing and distribution of gas; and the activities associated with collection, purification, and distribution of water.
(iv) Construction activities relating to construction of building and civil engineering works.

In the developed countries, industrialization played an important role in the initial phase of their economic growth and development. Still in emerging Asian Giants, i.e. Japan, Singapore, South Korea, Hong Kong, and also in China, the industrial sector is playing an important role in their economic growth and development. The industrialization process triggered off in the developing countries Asia, Africa, and Latin America only after the liberalization process which they initiated during 1990s, that too when the market forces played important role in establishing industries in various sectors.[3] Industrialization has enabled a nation to achieve a variety of socio-economic objectives, such as higher employment rate, poverty eradication, raising standard of living of labour, and greater access to education and health care of the population employed in industrial sector.

The tertiary sector is popularly known as the service sector. The service sector produces intangible goods and some of the well-known service sectors are health, education, banking, insurance, and the other emerging service sectors in the economies across the world are communication and information, hotel and hospitality, tourism, retail business, real estate, etc. Customarily, service sector requires more human capital than the natural capital as usually demanded by the primary and secondary sector. The service sector largely consists of the 'soft' parts of the economy.

The National Classification of Economic Activities (NCEA) uses the methodology of classification of services defined by International Standard Industrial Classification (ISIC) formulated by the United Nations. It includes four categories of services:

(i) Distinctive service: It includes the physical distribution of goods, wholesale and retail trade, distribution of people and cargo (transport), and distribution of information (communications).
(ii) Non-profit services: These are public administration and other organizations, such as unions, religious temples, welfare institutions, and clubs.
(iii) Business Services: Consisting of intermediary services to other sectors, these include financial activities, advisory services, legal, accounting, information technology, and real estate brokerage.
(iv) Customer services: These services consist of a wide range of social and personal services offered to an individual, mostly to emphasize the quality of life, such as for health care, education, restaurant, leisure, and other services for personnel and family (UN, 2008).

In National Income Accounting in India, service sector includes the following:

(i) Trade, hotel, and restaurants
(ii) Transport, storage, and communication
(iii) Finance, insurance, real estate, and business
(iv) Community, social, and personal services

The service sector makes a direct and significant contribution to GDP and job creation and provides crucial inputs for the rest of the economy, thus having a significant effect on the overall investment climate, which is an essential determinant of growth and development (Cali et al., 2008).

Historically, service industries have been at the heart of economic growth, stimulating and facilitating production for the market rather than simply for self-sufficiency (Riddle, 1986). Many services are key inputs to all or most other business, e.g. infrastructure services, such as energy, telecommunications, and transportation; financial services, which facilitate transactions and provide access to finance for investment; health and education

Table 6.1 *Contribution of Different Sectors to GDP (in percentage), 2009*

Countries	Agriculture	Industry	Manufacturing	Services
Low income countries	26	24	12	50
Middle income countries	10	35	21	55
High income countries	1	25	16	74

Source: World Development Report (2011).

services, which contribute to a healthy, well-trained workforce; and legal and accountancy services, which are part of the institutional framework required to underpin a healthy market economy (Cali et al., 2008).

Table 6.1 exhibits that the contribution of agriculture to the GDP is higher in the low-income countries, while the contribution of industry and manufacturing sector to GDP is higher in the middle-income countries. As far as the contribution of service sector to the GDP is concerned, although it is on rise in low, middle, and high income countries, the percentage contribution of service sector to the GDP is the highest in the high income countries as compared to the other two categories of economies. Even in the fastest growing economy of China, service sector enjoys high priority. One of the reports envisages that developing the service sector is a strategic priority in China's optimization and upgradation of its industrial structure, improving the quality and efficiency of public services, and strengthening the sector's role in generating more jobs.

Other prominent parallel actors, functioning mostly in the underdeveloped countries, both in rural as well as in urban areas, are the formal and informal sectors. The large chunk of workforce in the developing countries is working in the informal sector, otherwise also known as the unorganized sector. Therefore, distinction between the formal and informal sectors holds the key to the development analysis of the developing countries. The formal sector is the regulated sector, while informal sector is the unregulated sector or unregistered sector which does not follow any government rules and regulation. In fact, the main reason of low income and plight of the poor in the underdeveloped countries is the existence of 'informal sector' which is also otherwise called 'informal economy'. The early literature on the informal sector has mostly focused on the Third World countries and has, wittingly or not, assumed that as a social type, such sectors are not to be expected in advanced industrialized countries (Feige, 1979; Gutmann, 1977). Some of the early phrasings of 'informal sector' are the 'bazaar-economy' and the 'firm-centred economy' (Geertz, 1963) and the wartime notion of 'black market' (Smithies, 1984). The actors in the informal sector are petty businessmen, household industries, construction companies, and petty contractors. The definition of unorganized sector runs as "It consists of all unincorporated private enterprises owned by individuals or households engaged in the sale and production of goods and services operated on proprietary or partnership basis and with less than ten total workers". The prominent features of unorganized sector are lower real wage rate, poor working and living conditions, absence of social security, preponderance of casual and contractual employment, and poor human capital base. In India, more than 90 per cent of workers are working in the informal sector. The existence of informal sector in the primary sector is the main reason of preponderance of disguised employment and underemployment in this sector in most of the underdeveloped countries. The urban informal sector is a cause of poverty, inequality, and growth of slums in the underdeveloped countries.

Some of the features of informal sector in the developing countries are:

(i) They are not subject to the law and regulation.
(ii) The number of employees in a unit is small but on the whole, a large percentage of unskilled workforce is working in the informal sector.
(iii) It pays low wage rate to its employees.
(iv) There is no job security.
(v) Usually there isn't any provision of life security, i.e. medical facilities, old-age pension, etc.
(vi) It is largely operated by individual entrepreneurs and even by marginal and small entrepreneurs.
(vii) Primary sector is the largest employer of the informal workers in the developing countries.

The challenge before the underdeveloped countries is to regulate the unorganized sector, in order to provide job and social security to the people working in this sector and also to curtail the size of this sector.

The Sum Up

Many institutions and stakeholders of development are functioning in both developed as well as developing countries to promote growth and multidimensional development. Among all of them, market and state are the key institutions and actors of development. However, over the period of time and after the Britten Woods, many international institutions have been established to provide financial and technical support to the developing countries to effectively formulate, implement, monitor, and evaluate developmental projects and programmes in the developing countries in order to achieve developmental goals. Besides, in recent years, NGOs and the local self-government organizations are found to be playing need-based supplementary and complementary roles in facilitating and implementing developmental projects and programmes at the grass-roots level. The other aspects discussed in this chapter are the sectors of development. Worldwide primary, secondary, and tertiary sectors are the three key sectors of development. However, the unorganized sector is a gigantic player in the economic affairs of the underdeveloped countries. The forceful presence of informal or unorganized sector or the 'informal economy' in the developing countries is considered as one of the important factors responsible for the underdevelopment of these countries.

Keywords market, Say's law of market, stationary state, weak state, public–private partnership, crony capitalism, civil society organizations, non-governmental organizations, Britten Woods, informal sector, service sector.

REVIEW QUESTIONS

1. Explain how market is an important player in economic growth and why imperfect market is responsible for the underdevelopment of the developing countries?
2. Describe why market failed and justify your argument as to how the State has overcome the weakness of the market.
3. What is an imperfect market? Explain the role of various types of imperfect market in an underdeveloped country.
4. Why did the State fail to promote economic growth and development? Explain with examples why a public–private partnership is a viable alternative.
5. Distinguish between organized and unorganized sectors. Explain the reason for the growth of unorganized sector in the underdeveloped countries.
6. What is civil society organization? Explain the role of civil society organization in the development process of the underdeveloped countries.
7. Explain how local self-government organizations are playing an important role in the development of the underdeveloped countries.
8. Service sector is an important player in the development of both developed and underdeveloped countries. Explain.
9. Write short notes on the following:
   (i) Say's law of market
   (ii) Public–private partnership
   (iii) Service sector
   (iv) Crony capitalism
   (v) Unorganized sector
   (vi) Civil society organization

NOTES

1. Mohammed and Farooq from the Pakistan experience remarked that public sector has assumed greater responsibilities in backward areas because the private sector is unable to perform due to greater uncertainties, low level of profit, and hostile social forces.
2. The London School of Economics and Political Science, Centre for Civil Society (2006) Report on Activities, July 2005 to August 2006.
3. Indian planning process gave an important role to small-scale and cottage industries along with that of the large-scale heavy industries. The Second Five Year Plan of government of India emphasizes the role of small scale and cottage industries on the following grounds: (i) generation of employment opportunities; (ii) an equal distribution of national income; (iii) mobilization of capital; (iv) mobilization of entrepreneurial skills; and (v) regional dispersal of industries.

REFERENCES

ADB. 2000. *Fighting Poverty in Asia & the Pacific*. Manila: Asian Development Bank.

Adelman, I. 1999. "The Role of Government in Economic Development." Working Paper No. 890, Department of Agriculture and Resource Economics and Policy, Division of Agricultural and Natural Resources, University of California, Berkeley.

Bahl, R.W. and Smoke, P., eds. 2003. *Restructuring Local Government Finance in Developing Countries: Lessons from South Africa*. Cheltenham, UK and Northampton, MA: Edwaged Elgar.

Banks, N. and Hulme D. 2012. "The Role of NGOs and Civil Society in Development and Poverty Reduction." BWPI Working Paper 171, Brooks World Poverty Institute, University of Manchester.

Bardhan, P. and Moorkherjee, D. 2006. *Decentralization and Local Governance in Developing Countries*. Cambridge, MA: MIT Press.

Batley, R. and Larbi, G.A. 2004. *The Changing Role of Government: The Reform of Public Services in Developing Countries*. Basingstoke Hampshire: Palgrave Macmillan.

Begg, I. 1993. "The Service Sector in Regional Development." *Regional Studies,* 27: 817–25.

Bryden, J. 2005. "Horizontal Coordination at Local and Regional Levels." Mexican Ministry of Social Development and OECD International Conference, "Designing and Implementing Rural Development Policy." Oaxaca, Mexico, 7–8 April 2005.

Cali, M., Ellis, K., and Willem te Velde, D. 2008. "The Contribution of Services to Development and the Role of Trade Liberalization and Regulation." Working Paper 298, Oversees Development Institute, London.

Clarke, G. 1998. *The Politics of NGOs in South East Asia: Participate and Protest in the Philippines*. London: Rutledge.

Cypher, James M. and Dietz, James L. 2006. *The Process of Economic Development*. New York: Rutledge.

Eade, D. and Ligteringen, E. 2001. *Debating Development*. London: Oxfam.

Farazmand, A. 2006. *Strategic Public Personnel Administration: Building and Managing Human Capital for the 21st Century*. Westport, CT: Praeger.

Feige, E.L. 1979. "How Big is the Irregular Economy?" *Challenge*, 22: 5–13.

Feldman, S. 1998. "Structure and Consistency in Public Opinion: The Role of Core Beliefs and Values." *American Journal of Political Science*, 32(2): 416–40.

Fernando, J. and Heston, A. 1977. "The Role of NGOs: Charity and Empowerment." Introduction to *Annals of the American Academy of Political and Social Sciences*, 554, November: 8–20.

Fox, T. and Prescott, D. 2004. "Exploring the Role of Development Cooperation Agencies in Corporate Social Responsibility." Stockholm, 22–23 March 2004. Available at: http://www.eldis.org/fultext/IIED_CSRI.pdf (accessed on 4 December 2013).

Frey, Bruno S. and Stutzer, A. 2006. "Strengthening the Citizens' Role in International Organizations." *The Review of International Organization*, 1(1): 27–43.

Geertz, C. 1963. *Peddlers and Princes: Social Change and Economic Modernization in two Indonesian Towns*. Chicago: University of Chicago.

Gutmann, P.M. 1977. "The Subterranean Economy." *Financial Analysis Journal*, 33(6): 26–27.

Haque, S. 1977. "Local Governance in Developing Nations: Re-examining the Question of Accountability." *Regional Development Dialogue,* 18(2, Autumn): 4–23.

Hayami, Y. and Godo, Y. 2005. *Development Economics: From the Poverty to the Wealth of Nations,* Third edition. New York: Oxford University Press.

Ishikawa, S. 1994. "Kozo Chosei-Seign Hoshiki no Saiken to (Structural Adjustment: A Reassessment of the World Bank Approach." *Ajia Keizai* (Institute of Developing Economies), 35(November): 2–32.

Jennings, M. 2006. "DFID Yemen Social Fund for Development." Institutional Evaluation, Sara'a SFD.

Johnston, B. 1970. "Agriculture and Structural Transformation in Developing Countries: A Survey Research." *Journal of Economic Literature*, 8(2):10–145.

Leftwich, A. 2000. *States of Development: On the Primacy of Politics in Development*. Cambridge: Polity Press.

Lindeke, William A. 1995. "Democratization in Namibia: Soft State, Hard Choices." *Studies in Comparative International Development*, Spring, 30(1): 3–29.

Mellor, John W. 1969. "Production Economics and the Modernization of Traditional Agriculture." *Australian Journal of Agricultural Economics*, 13(1): 24–34.

Mentan, T. 2004. *Dilemmas of Weak States Africa and Transnational Terrorism in the Twenty-first Century*. England: Ashgate Publishing.

Nafziger, E.W. 2006. *Economic Development*. New York: Cambridge Press.

Naude, W. and Szirmai, A. 2012. "The Importance of Manufacturing in Economic Development: Past, Present and Future Perspectives." Working Paper Series #2012-040, Maastricht Economic and Social Research Institute on Innovation and Technology (UNU-MERIT). Available at: http://www.merit.unu.edu (accessed on 6 February 2014).

Polanyi, K. 1957. "The Economy as Instituted Process." In *Trade and Market in the Early Empires: Economics in History and Theory*, edited by K. Polanyi, C.M. Arensberg, and H.W. Person. New York: The Free Press.

Riddle, D.I. 1986. *Service-led Growth: The Role of Service Sector in World Development*. Westport, CT: Praeger.

Shah, A. 2006. *Local Governance in Developing Countries*. Washington DC: World Bank.

Smithies, E. 1984. *The Black Economy in England since 1914*. Dublin: Gill & Macmillan.
Stiglitz, J.E. 2002. *Globalization and Its Discontents*. New York: WW Norton & Company.
Todaro, M.P. and Smith, S.C. 2012. *Economic Development*. New Delhi: Dorling Kindersley Limited.
UNIDO. 2007. *Industrial Development Report, 2007*, United Nations Industrial Development Organization, United Nations Publications.
———. 2009. *Industrial Development Report, 2009*, United Nations Industrial Development Organization, United Nations Publications.
Zafarullah, H. and Huque, A.S. 2006. "Understanding Development Governance: Concept, Institution and Process." In *International Development Governance*, edited by A.S. Huque and H. Zafarullah, 13–50. New York: CRC Press/Taylor and Francis.
Zarsky, L. and Tay, S.C. 2012. "Civil Society and the Future of Environmental Governance in Asia." In *Asia's Clean Revolution: Industry, Growth and the Environment*, edited by D. Angel and M. Rock. Sheffield: Green Leaf Publisher.

SUGGESTED READINGS

Kurien, T. 2004. *From M S Swaminathan & Pedro Medrano, Towards Hunger Free India from Vision to Action*, East West Book, Chennai 2004, *Front Line*, 14 January 2004.
United Nations. 2008. International Standard Industrial Classification of all Economic Activities (ISIC), Department of Economic and Social Affairs, Statistics Division, New York.
World Bank. 2000. *World Development Report*, 2000. Washington DC: World Bank.

7 Paradigms of Development

The story of development is not one single process, but a series of inextricably entwined discourses, processes and paradigms each feeding off the perceived failure of its predecessor and swinging the pendulum from one theory to another.

— Jennings (2006)

A development paradigm is an in-principle argument for how to conceptualize and overcome the development challenges confronting a nation or region.

— Hurungo (2009)

A 'development paradigm' may be defined as a modality or path to follow for achieving development, based on a codified set of activities and/or a vision regarding the functioning and evolution of a socio-economic system.

— Battaglia et al. (2011)

The dynamic nature of development has encouraged experimentation of various models and formulation of different strategies of development for the multidimensional development of the developing countries. The upshot of these experimentations has resulted in the documentation of different successful models and strategies, which have brought out a paradigm shift in development. Therefore, in the development discourse, it is essential to document various paradigms of development. Macmillan dictionary defines 'paradigm' as a set of ideas that are used for understanding or explaining something, especially in a particular subject. According to another dictionary, 'paradigm' is an adjustment in things which comes about as a result of new discoveries, inventions, or real-world experiences. Kuhn (1970) in his book *The Structure of Scientific Revolution* while talking of 'paradigms' argued that scientific advancement is not evolutionary, but rather is 'a series of peaceful interludes punctuated by intellectually violent revolutions' and in those revolutions, 'one conceptual world is replaced by another.' The 'dominant social paradigm' popularized by Pirages and Ehrlich (1974) described it as a prominent worldview, model, or frame of reference through which individuals in a society interpret the meaning of the external world. The paradigm shift is, therefore, a change from one way of thinking to another and is a revolution, a transformation, a sort of metamorphosis. Being a dynamic concept, 'development' is more conditioned to 'paradigms' than any other subject in social sciences. Bellu (2011) while defining 'development paradigm' noted that development was very rarely considered to be a 'God-given' condition of socio-economic system, implying that policy-makers at national and international level have always thought that some activities were required to promote positive changes. The developmental exponents of different countries as well as the international development community in different periods have formulated and suggested specific ways of achieving development adhering to specific 'development paradigm', i.e. to 'a defined modality or path to follow to achieve development'.

After reading this chapter, you will be able to:

(i) Define development paradigm and explain its importance in the development of the underdeveloped countries.
(ii) Explain the poverty reduction and basic needs paradigm and how it is essential for laying the foundation of development of the underdeveloped countries.
(iii) Describe inclusive development paradigms, what different types of inclusion are, and how inclusive development can be achieved.
(iv) Define sustainable development and its indicator and how it is vital for the development of the underdeveloped countries.
(v) Describe the role of international economic cooperation, particularly FDI and remittances in the development of the underdeveloped countries.
(vi) Discuss how and why decentralized approach is critical to achieve holistic development.

Although there are many paradigms of development, a few generic paradigms of development for the underdeveloped countries are discussed in the following sections.

POVERTY REDUCTION AND BASIC NEEDS PARADIGM

The MDGs had identified poverty as one of the important determinants of development and, therefore, aimed at halving the proportion of the world's population living in extreme poverty by 2015. According to a World Bank figure, more than half of the population in the developing countries, around 2.8 billion, is living on less than US$2 a day and one-fifth, around 1.2 billion people, live on less than US$1 a day. Poverty prevents human and social development. Reduction of poverty is fundamental to the MDGs. In order to scale up measures against global poverty, a new development paradigm for the developing countries has been suggested. Here, scaling up means formulating and implementing programmes, policies, or projects on poverty eradication. Many developing countries have considered poverty eradication as one of their vital strategies for augmenting development process and in this process, they have formulated different policies and programmes and have also launched innovative poverty eradication projects. The drive of *Garibi Hatao* (abolition of poverty) through the launching of Minimum Needs Programmes in 1975 and subsequently many poverty alleviation programmes in different Five Year Plans by the Government of India are illustrious pioneering examples of India's endeavour to fight against poverty. Besides, the National Rural Employment Programme (now the MGNREGA) launched in by the Government of India in 2002, one of the largest employment programmes in the world, aims at reducing rural poverty by guaranteeing 100 days employment to each rural household in a year. During the year 2009, it has provided employment to 40.34 million people, out of which 10.14 million were females. Indonesia's Kecamatan Community Development Programme benefits about 35 million poor people, expanding from 25 villages in 1998 to 20,888 villages in the first decade of twentieth century. The Yemen Social Development Fund provides clean water, education, cultural restoration, and health delivery in rugged rural communities, which decide their own priorities, contribute a percentage of the costs, and play a key role in maintaining the service themselves.[1] According to Dutton, poverty is construed as a disease of sorts that can travel without a passport, transmogrify into various forms and threaten prosperity and the 'war on poverty' should fight poverty as one might fight drugs, diseases, terrorism, migration, or some other epidemiological toxin.[2] Therefore, it is urged that poverty reduction paradigm should be a central priority of development governance. Although China is the pioneer of poverty eradication paradigm, yet it is an important paradigm of development for the nation-states of South Asia, Sub-Saharan Africa, and Latin American countries.

Since 1970s, 'the basic needs' concept has been a dominant element in the development debate. One of the development goals of developing countries and duties and responsibilities of the welfare State is to ensure basic needs to its people so that they do not die of hunger, malnutrition, and miseries. In the real sense, the development process and the development projects and programmes in any country should be triggered off with the provision of basic needs to its people; once it is fulfilled, the economy can be put on higher economic growth and development paths. Grant (1977) defines basic needs as "the minimum standard of living which a society should set for the poorest groups of people". These minimum standards usually include nutrition, health, shelter, clean water, transport, and school (Moller and Schlemmer, 1982). According to Streeten (1979), the objective of a basic need approach to development is to assure that all human beings should have the opportunity to live full lives. From the developing countries' perspective, nine basic needs which are required for a sustainable livelihood can be broadly clubbed under three broad heads:

(i) The primary basic needs, including food, clothing, and shelter.
(ii) The secondary basic needs, including drinking water, sanitation, and surface communication.
(iii) The tertiary basic needs, comprising health, education, and energy for cooking and lighting.

These are the basic requirements for an individual or a household in order to enable the members to have a sustainable lifestyle with dignity. In many developing countries, basic needs are being considered as the determinants of poverty. The best way to put a nation on the higher economic development path is to ensure its population their basic needs, and there are instances where the nation-states having fulfilled basic needs have performed better in socio-economic development indicators as compared to the nation-states which have not done so (for example, in India, Punjab and Kerala, which have fulfilled basic needs of majority of its population can be compared with Bihar, Orissa, and Jharkhand, which are yet to fulfil the quality basic needs for the majority of its population).

INCLUSIVE DEVELOPMENT PARADIGM

Inclusive development has become an important paradigm of development in the countries marred with the obnoxious division of the society on the basis of caste, class, gender, colour, etc. and social and economic inequalities and disparities are widely prevalent across region, ethnic groups, gender, and so on. This paradigm is very crucial for balanced, sustainable, and holistic development of the developing countries of South Asia, Africa, and Latin America, where the society is highly stratified and the intensity of disparities is egregious. Inclusive development believes that everyone must participate and contribute to the process of development and also equally enjoy the fruits of development. It is seen that in developing countries reeling under economic and social inequalities, the poor and unskilled labour contribute significantly towards the development in terms of their hard labour, while the income they earn and the benefit they get are paltry and are being manipulated by the rich contractors, businessmen, industrialists, landlords, and skilled educated employed in white collar jobs. A Commission on Growth and Development set up by the World Bank defines inclusiveness as a concept that encompasses equity, equality of opportunity, and protection in the market and employment transition (World Bank, 2008). According to UNDP (2008), inclusion means that people are part of the social, economic, political, and cultural life of their country and that their voices are heard and that they are able to use their capabilities and access resources, including financial and business opportunities. Miller and Katz (2002) defined inclusion as "...a sense of belonging: feeling respected, valued for who you are; feeling a level of supportive energy and commitment from others so that you can do your best". Inclusive development lays emphasis on the principle of economic equity, distributive and social justice, and equality in participation. Economic growth achieved amid social exclusion cannot be economically and socially sustainable. The UNDP (2008) has defined inclusive growth as the process and the outcome, where all groups of people have participated in the organization of growth and have benefited from it. In inclusive development, contributions made by each individual including disabled, women, and other marginalized people are valued, promoted, and quantified. Inclusive development has several dimensions:

(i) Economic inclusion: Enabling and providing opportunity to the excluded group to have equal opportunity and enhance their capabilities to have access to land, market, employment, and income.

(ii) Social inclusion: No exclusion or disparities on the ground of caste, class, colour, gender, religion, etc. in the use of social assets and common property resources, i.e. public places, recreation places, and religious places; school, hospitals, etc. and also to participate in social gatherings. Social exclusion is deterrent to social development and it also influences other developments, like economic, human, and political. A socially inclusive society is defined as one where all people feel valued, their differences are respected, and their basic needs are met so they can live in dignity (Cappo, 2002). It is a process by which efforts are made to ensure that every one, regardless of their background, experiences, and circumstances can gain access to the services and facilities they need to achieve their own potential in life (Social Inclusion Handbook, Limerick City Council, Limerick City, Ireland).

(iii) Political inclusion: Empowering the marginalized and excluded groups and individuals to have access to political power and fully participate in the democratic process, i.e. cast their vote, contest elections, and get involved in the political decision-making process. According to Schmidt et al. (2002), the full incorporation into democratic politics involves:

(a) Full access to participation
(b) Representation in important decision-making processes and institutions

(c) Influence in/power over government decisions
(d) Adoption of public policies that address group concerns or interest
(e) Socio-economic parity

(iv) The emergence of caste-based political parties in India is an effort to enhance political inclusion. Moreover, affirmative action in reservation of seats in the parliament and State legislative assemblies and even in the local self-government institutions in India through constitutional provisions is intended towards promotion of political inclusion.

(v) Cultural inclusion: The cultural practices of different communities and religious groups need to be respected and valued and be integrated into the national mainstream, and there should not be any exclusion on the basis of cultural belongingness. The endeavour to promote cultural heritage, dance, song, folklores, food, etc. by the government of different states in India is an endeavour to promote cultural development. Holding of cultural trade fairs and promotion of the marketing of cultural products are steps towards cultural integration and strengthening of culture-based economic production and practices.

(vi) Regional inclusion: All regions, particularly the socio-economically backward regions, i.e. hilly and dry land areas, must be integrated into the mainstream and be empowered through policy measures to contribute towards development of the nation-state (an illustrious example is BRGF programme launched by the government of India for the development of backward districts of various states). These regions should not be treated as parasite and dependant on subsidies, rather be enabled to become an engine of growth and development.

(vii) Sectoral inclusion: The inclusive development process must place equal emphasis on all sectors, i.e. primary, secondary, and tertiary sectors. The neglect of primary sector will affect basic needs and those of secondary sector can affect employment, income, and growth rate; and neglect of the tertiary sector can affect social and holistic development. The fluctuation in growth rate observed in recent years in most of the developing countries is largely because of excessive dependence on service sector and poor performance of primary and secondary sector. The reduction in the contribution of agriculture sector towards GDP in developing countries, particularly in India and the policy measures of the Government of India to augment agricultural productivity through farm mechanization, provision of irrigation facilities, and other research and training methods is an example of sectoral inclusive measures.

(viii) Last but not the least, in the inclusive development process, each and every individual should feel that he or she is included. Every individual irrespective of caste, class, gender, and creed must be integrated into the process of growth and development and they must feel that they are the partners and stakeholders of development, not just the beneficiaries but the contributors towards growth and development. Burchardt (2004) said the each society and sub-group within the society must be involved in debate and reflection about which capabilities are important.

The process of liberalization, privatization, and globalization has elongated the chasm between the rich and poor, the have-nots are found to be largely excluded from the mainstream development. Lack of adequate knowledge and skill as demanded by the privatization and globalization process has marginalized the impoverished in the global market. Internationally, inequity groups that have been historically excluded include Blacks, Latinos, Asian/Pacific Islanders, American Indians, women, persons with disabilities, Scheduled Castes and Scheduled Tribes in India, and the economically disadvantaged. And now, there is an enlarged list of groups that include other groups, most prominently gays, lesbians, and bisexuals, who are frequent targets of exclusion and discrimination. Inclusive development has been promoted by many developed as well as developing countries through affirmative actions. Affirmative action intends to ensure that no person is denied opportunity because he or she belongs to a certain section of population and happens to be born into a particular type of marginalized community. It provides preferential treatment to the underprivileged sections of population, who are the victims of exclusion. Affirmative action, popularized by the United States in 1960, assures equality of opportunity to all Americas and intends to prevent discrimination against members of certain groups that have been historically subject to a great deal of discrimination, mostly African-Americans. Jencks (1992) maintains that the American government pressurized private employers to hire disadvantaged people in occupations that had traditionally been reserved for advantaged groups. South Africa's Employment Equity Act (1998) as an affirmative action wants to "redress the disadvantages in employment experienced by designated groups are Blacks (including African, Indian, and other coloured minorities), women, and the disabled". The Employment Equity Bill requires all companies with 50 employees or more to implement the quota-based Affirmative Action Policy failing which companies have to pay a fine to be imposed by the department of Labour, Government of South Africa. As affirmative actions, the Indian constitution has a few inclusive clauses which intend to prevent discrimination. Article 15 of the Constitution of India prohibits discrimination on the ground of religion, race, caste, sex, or place of birth. Article 16 lays emphasis on equal opportunities, which reads as, "No citizen shall, on grounds only of religion, race, caste, sex, descent, place of birth, residence or any of them, be ineligible for, or discriminated against in respect or, any employment or office under the state". While Article 16(4) proclaims that:

> ...nothing in this article shall prevent the State from making any provision for reservation in matters of promotion to any class or classes of posts in the services under the State in favour of the Scheduled Castes and the Scheduled Tribes which, in the opinion of the State, are not adequately represented in the services under the State.

The reservation for the Scheduled Castes and Scheduled Tribes in government jobs and reservation of seats in the Parliament and State Legislative Assemblies and even in the local self-government institutions are the result of such constitutional provisions and because of these provisions, many people belonging to the backward communities are in government jobs and have been elected to the Parliament, State Legislative Assemblies, and local self-government institutions. It can be said that the greatest challenge facing today's government of the developing nations is to present a united front to address shared problems. Inclusive development veritably means development for all and all for development. Total development can be a reality when all sectors and actors, stakeholders, and beneficiaries of development are included and contribute equitably and effectively towards development.

SUSTAINABLE DEVELOPMENT PARADIGM

Sustainable development became an important paradigm of development during 1987. It came in the wake of a situation where economic growth and development process was resorted to by the nation-states by distorting natural resources and causing harm to the environment. The Brundtland Commission for Environment and Development, in its report, *Our Common Future* called for application of sustainability as a criterion for all development initiatives. The Commission envisaged that "in order for development to be sustainable, it must meet the needs of the present without compromising the ability of future generations to meet their own needs". Sustainable development necessitates maintaining a balance between the three pillars of development, i.e. economy, ecology, and society (Figure 7.1): (a) it should ensure basic needs, i.e. food, clothing, shelter, safe drinking, sanitation, and social security to its human beings; (b) it must maintain ecological balance and there must be a proper balance between population and ecology and population growth should not be a factor for deterioration of ecology; and (c) the societal goals for sustainable development are removal of illiteracy, reduction of infant and maternal mortality, reduction of fertility and diseases, and social upliftment of women and marginalized must be taken of.

Figure 7.1 *Components of Sustainable Development*

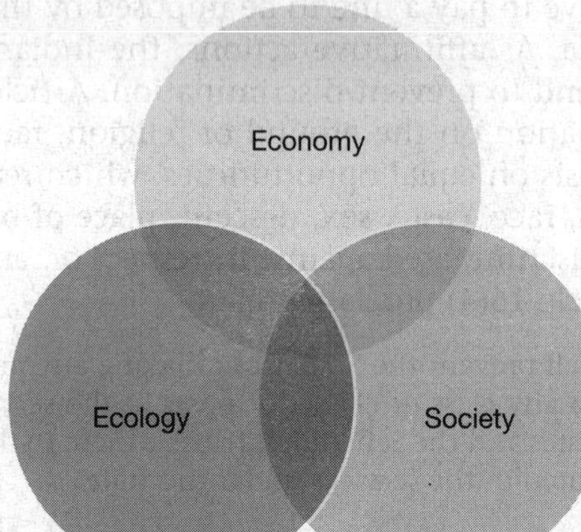

Sustainable Development Goals

On 25 September, 193 countries of the United Nations General Assembly adopted the 2030 Development Agenda named Transforming Our World: The 2030 Agenda for Sustainable Development. The 17 identified Sustainable Development Goals associated with 169 targets and 304 proposed indicators are as follows:

1. End poverty in all its forms everywhere.
2. End hunger, achieve food security, and improved nutrition and promote sustainable agriculture.
3. Ensure healthy lives and promote well-being for all at all ages.
4. Ensure inclusive and equitable quality education and promote lifelong learning opportunities for all.
5. Achieve gender equality and empower all women and girls.
6. Ensure availability and sustainable management of water and sanitation for all.
7. Ensure access to affordable, reliable, sustainable, and modern energy for all.
8. Promote sustained, inclusive, and sustainable economic growth, full and productive employment and decent work for all.
9. Build resilient infrastructure, promote inclusive and sustainable industrialization, and foster innovation.
10. Reduce inequality within and among countries.
11. Make cities and human settlements inclusive, safe, resilient, and sustainable.
12. Ensure sustainable consumption and production patterns.
13. Take urgent action to combat climate change and its impacts.
14. Conserve and sustainably use the oceans, seas, and marine resources for sustainable development.
15. Protect, restore, and promote sustainable use of terrestrial ecosystems, sustainably manage forests, combat desertification, and halt and reserve land degradation, and halt biodiversity loss.
16. Promote peaceful and inclusive societies for sustainable development, provide access to justice for all and build effective, accountable and inclusive institutions at all levels.
17. Strengthen the means of implementation and revitalize the global partnership for sustainable development.

The nations are urged to sincerely attain these goals.

Source: https://en.wikipedia.org/wiki/sustainable_Development_Goals

Sustainable development can be looked at from a variety of perspectives such as environmental, economic, social, political, cultural, and technological. Brundtland (1987) envisaged that sustainable development requires the following:

(i) A political system that secures effective citizen participation in decision-making.
(ii) An economic system that is able to generate surpluses and technical knowledge on self-reliant sustained basis.
(iii) A social system that provides for solutions for the tensions arising from disharmonious development.
(iv) A production system that respects the obligations to preserve the ecological base of development.
(v) A technological system that can search continuously for new solutions.

(vi) An international system that offers sustainable pattern of trade and finance.
(vii) An administrative system that is flexible and has the capacity of self-correction.

Sustainable development gives emphasis on not only the process of present development but also its implication on future development per se. Continuous exploitation of natural resources for the present gain is a scourge not only on present but also on future development. The impact of over exploitation of ground water, vehicle emissions, cutting of forests, digging of hills, converting agricultural land to housing projects, etc. is visible in the form of climate change, which is ultimately affecting productivity and human health. Besides, unbridled population growth in developing countries has profound impact on sustainable development. The international agencies are, therefore, putting emphasis on sustainable development as an important paradigm of development. Brundtland (1987) has rightly envisaged:

> ...in essence, sustainable development is a process of change in which the exploitation of resources, the direction of investments, the orientation of technological development and institutional change, are all in harmony and enhance both current and future potential to human needs and aspirations.

The United Nations in 1995 has framed social indicators for sustainable development. These indicators are as follows:

(i) Poverty: Income poverty, income inequality, sanitation, drinking water, access to energy and living conditions.
(ii) Governance: Corruption and income inequality.
(iii) Health: Mortality, health care delivery, nutritional status and health status, and risks.
(iv) Education: Educational level and literacy.
(v) Demography: Population growth and dependency ratio (United Nations, 2007).

Poverty

Poverty is considered as one of the key indicators of sustainable development. Nations having high percentage of people living below the poverty line would find it difficult on their part to attain sustainable development, as sustainable development desires to have a sustainable level of income in order to meet the basic necessities of life. The sub-themes as well as the core and other indicators to be covered in the area of poverty are given in Table 7.1.

Governance

Governance, in general, and good governance, in particular, is an important indicator of sustainable development. The issues and challenges like corruption, red-tapism, and favouritism benefit a few and deprive many. Moreover, crimes constantly occurring in the developing countries' society also have adverse impact on the development. The identified sub-themes of the governance in sustainable development are corruption and crime. The indicators are given in Table 7.2.

Table 7.1 *Poverty Indicators for Sustainable Development*

Sub-themes	Core Indicators	Other Indicators
Income poverty	Proportion of population living below poverty line	Proportion of population average income below $1 a day
Income inequality	Ratio of share in national income highest to lowest quintile	—
Sanitation	Proportion of population using an improved sanitation	—
Drinking water	Proportion of population using an improved water sources	—
Access to energy	Share of household without electricity or other modern energy services	Percentage of population using solid fuel for cooking
Living conditions	Proportion of urban population living in slums	—

Source: *Indicators of Sustainable Development: Guidelines and Methodologies,* United Nations, New York, 2007.

Table 7.2 *Governance Indicators for Sustainable Development*

Sub-themes	Core Indicators	Other Indicators
Corruption	Percentage of population having paid bribe	—
Crime	Number of international homicides per 100,000 population	—

Source: *Indicators of Sustainable Development: Guidelines and Methodologies,* United Nations, New York, 2007.

Health

Health and development are intimately interconnected and good health status of a nation is an important indicator of sustainable development. A country can never be able to attain sustainable development if its population suffers from morbidity and the mortality rate is very high. Further, expenditure on health will toll away a gigantic percentage of its investment required to be spent on other sectors, and thus will not only hamper development investment in all other sectors but also hamper holistic and sustainable development. The key indicators of sustainable health care are mortality, health care delivery, nutritional status, and health status and risks. The core areas of these health care themes are delineated in Table 7.3.

Education

Education has been identified as one of the important social indicators of sustainable development, and literacy rate, level of education, and gross enrolment ratio are the effective indicators of educational development. Nations having population with higher level of

Table 7.3 *Health Indicators for Sustainable Development*

Sub-themes	Core Indicators	Other Indicators
Mortality	Under five mortality, life expectancy at birth	
Health care delivery	Percentage of population with access to primary health care facilities, immunization against childhood diseases	Contraceptive prevalence rate
Nutritional status	Nutritional status of children	—
Health status and risks	Morbidity of major diseases such as HIV/AIDS, malaria, tuberculosis	Prevalence of tobacco use/suicide rate

Source: *Indicators of Sustainable Development: Guidelines and Methodologies,* United Nations, New York, 2007.

Table 7.4 *Education Indicators for Sustainable Development*

Sub-themes	Core Indicators	Other Indicators
Education level	Gross intake ratio to last grade of primary education, net enrolment rate in primary education Adult secondary (Tertiary) schooling attainment level	—
Literacy	Adult literacy rate	—

Source: *Indicators of Sustainable Development: Guidelines and Methodologies,* United Nations, New York, 2007.

education will better understand the relationship between the population, economy, and environment and behave ethically. The core indicators of education are given in Table 7.4.

Demography

The two important demographic indicators as identified by the United Nations for sustainable development are population growth and the dependency ratio, that is, number of children and old people, in the total population. The demographic indicators for sustainable development are given in Table 7.5. The high fertility rate and higher dependency ratios influence not only the economic but also the social health of the family and the nation. Therefore, sustainable development aims at low fertility rate and a lower dependency ratio.

Table 7.5 *Demography Indicators for Sustainable Development*

Sub-themes	Core Indicators	Other Indicators
Population growth rate	Total fertility rate	Ratio local residents to tourists in main tourist regions and destinations
Dependency ratio	Dependency ratio	—

Source: *Indicators of Sustainable Development: Guidelines and Methodologies,* United Nations, New York, 2007.

Sustainable development is an important development agenda of the 21st century and is one of the vital paradigm shifts in the development process of the developing countries. Countries have to take appropriate measures for improvement of indicators of sustainable development. Therefore, the United Nations has emphasized its institutional framework for sustainable development. In its institutional framework for sustainable development, it has mentioned that for the attainment of sustainable development, good governance and sound economic policies, social democratic institutions responsive to the needs of the people, and improved infrastructure are the basis for sustained economic growth, poverty eradication, and employment generation. Ironically, the present political economy of the developing countries discounts the future value of natural resources, ecology, and environment at the cost of gluttony for achieving higher economic growth rate.

INTERNATIONAL ECONOMIC RELATIONSHIP PARADIGM

The globalization process that started during 1990s has established and hastened the economic and trade relationship not only between the developing and developed countries but also between the developing nations. It is widely recognized that in the globalized era, the development of developing countries is intrinsically interlinked with the relationship that it has with the developed countries. Sapru (1994) was of the view that the progress of development in the developing countries in the present decade cannot be achieved by the action of the developing world alone, as the effect of import competition in industries in Chile and Turkey and the effect of greater competition in export markets on firms in Brazil, Japan, and Republic of Korea are examples to confirm that linking domestic economy with international economy increases the prospects of development in developing countries. A report by OECD (1998) states more open and outward-oriented economies consistently outperform countries with restrictive trade and (foreign) investment regimes. According to IMF (1997), policies towards foreign trade are among the more important factors promoting economic growth and convergence in developing countries. Fischer (2000) was of view that integration into the world economy is the best way for countries to grow. The impact FDI on development is visible in many countries, and China, India, and a few African and Latin American countries are illustrious beneficiaries (see Table 7.6). At present, there are 214 million migrants in the world and if they lived in one country,

Table 7.6 *Comparison of FDI Inflows to China, India, and Developing Economies*

(Amount in US$ millions)

	Year				
Country	**1990–2000**	**2002**	**2003**	**2004**	**2005**
China	30,104	52,743	53,505	60,630	72,406
India	1,705	5,627	4,585	5,474	6,598
Developing countries	134,670	163,583	175,138	275,032	334,285
World	495,391	617,732	557,869	710,755	916,277

Source: UNCTAD, World Investment Report, 2006 (www.dnctad.org/wir).

Figure 7.2 *Top Ten Beneficiaries of Remittances*

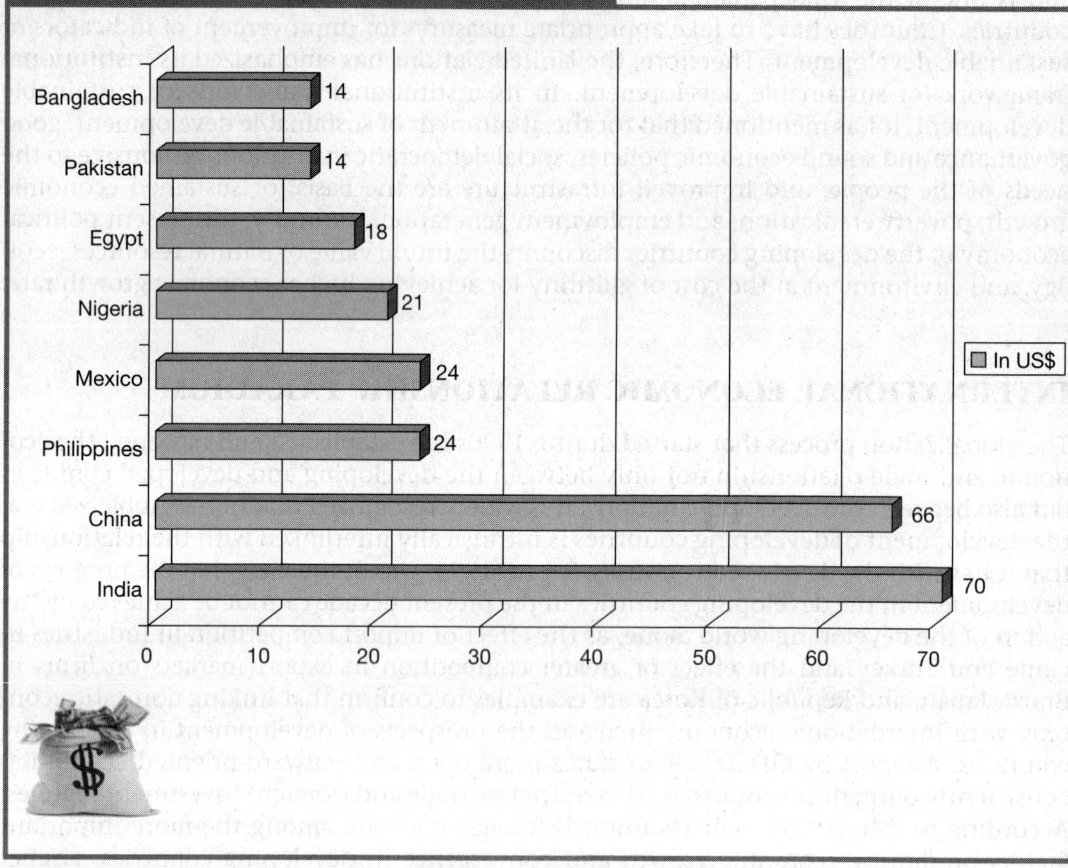

Source: *Hindustan Times*, New Delhi, 1 February 2013, p. 17.

it would be the fifth most populous, after China, India, US, and Indonesia (Provost, 2013). According to World Bank (2013): "The developing world is expected to receive $41 billion in migrant remittance in 2013, an increase of 6.3 percent over 2012. Globally, the world's 232 million international migrants are expected to remit earning worth $550 billion". The largest beneficiaries of remittances in 2012 are India, China, and Philippines (Figure 7.2).

Karras (2006), a study on correlation between foreign aid and growth in per capita GDP using annual data from the 1960 to 1997 for a sample of 71 aid-receiving developing countries, found that the effect of foreign aid on economic growth is positive, permanent, and statistically significant. According to Ray (2012), the effect of FDI in the host economy is usually believed to lead to increase in the employment level, augment productivity, boost exports, and amplify the pace of transfer of technology. Like the FDIs and foreign aids, remittances also produce positive impact on host country's development. One of the illustrious examples is Kerala, one of the socio-economically developed states of India, which is popularly called the 'money order economy', where remittances contribute one-fourth to the state GDP (Kerala Calling, 2012). Many believe that it has been called the

'Money Order Economy' for the skewed nature of the state economy (Biswas, 2010). It is said that for many developing countries, remittances represent a major part of international capital flows, surpassing FDI, export revenues, and foreign aid (Giuliano and Ruiz-Arranz, 2005). Stahl and Arnold (1986) argued that the use of remittances for consumption may have positive effect on growth because of their possible multiplier effect. It was found that remittances have a positive effect on the growth of Latin American countries where the financial systems are less developed by providing an alternative way to finance investment and helping overcome liquidity constraints (Fayissa and Nsiah, 2010). Moreover, the international agencies and organizations are funding various developmental projects on agriculture, electricity, education, health and family welfare, women empowerment, strengthening of grass-roots democracy, and so on for the multidimensional development of the developing countries.

However, many exponents believe that reforms should be devised and developed by developing countries themselves, rather than being imposed by outside agencies and countries. Dogmatic imposition of free market reforms by the international institutions, especially with regard to the free movement of capital, threatens the growth prospects of developing countries. According to Gupta (2010), the present economic relations are mostly parasitic and exploitative or these are based on exploiter–exploited relationships. In this structure, the poor nations are dependent on the rich, while the rich exploit the poor nations in order to hasten their own development. However, in spite of all these debates, the relationship between aid flows and development is stronger after liberalization, privatization, and globalization adopted by various countries, since the beginning of the 1990s. The flow of financial capital from the developed countries to the developing countries in the form of 'outsourcing' and FDIs has led to capital formation in specialized areas, ultimately percolating to the development of other allied areas. The international economic relation between developed and developing countries and also among the developing countries is one of the important paradigms of development that cropped up in the nineteenth and twentieth centuries leading to collaborative development of the developed and developing countries and also among the developing countries themselves. The recent declaration of launch of 'Make in India', which is intended to attract foreign countries as well as international investors to invest in India, is an illustrious example of international economic relationship and development.

DECENTRALIZATION AND PARTICIPATORY DEVELOPMENT PARADIGM

Democratic decentralization of development processes and strategies has proved to be the successful model of promoting grass-roots development being experimented by many nation-states, particularly belonging to the categories of developing countries. Decentralization of functions, functionaries, and funds to the local units of governance is one of the best alternative ways for empowering people, promoting public participation, and increasing efficiency in service delivery. It is remarked that decentralized service delivery is now a key determinant of the scope for less developed countries to achieve the MDGs, and many governments across the developing world are engaged in ambitious efforts to devolve power and resources to local bodies which are increasingly assuming responsibility for managing the delivery of health, education, and other essential services to poor people (Robinson, 2007). The Local Self-government Declaration to the World Summit on Sustainable Development held in 2002 maintains that "...we live in an increasingly inter-connected, interdependent world. Local government cannot afford to be insular and inward looking". The democratic decentralization is premised on the assumption that local governments will be more responsible to the needs of the citizens and take their preferences into account in determining the services to be provided, the level of resources required, and the optimal means of ensuring effective delivery (Robinson, 2007). Haque (1977) argued that the decentralization is a way of increasing the effectiveness of development programmes by making them more relevant and responsive to local needs and conditions, allowing greater flexibility in their implementation, thus making the state more participatory, more acceptable, and more effective and efficient.

The top-down centralized approach is more instructive and less participatory as compared to bottom-up approach. The bottom-up decentralized approach is more persuasive and democratic, as the development process here is made 'of the people, by the people, and for the people'. According to Lewis (1997), localism–grass-rootism development from the bottom up has been enjoying one of its periodic surges in the realm of development policy discourse in the past couple of decades. According to WHO (2002), Community participation is:

> A process by which people are enabled to become actively and genuinely involved in defining the issues of concern to them; in making decisions about factors that affect their lives; in formulating and implementing policies; in planning, developing and delivery services and in taking action to achieve change.

One of the illustrious examples of popular participation is the 'group planning of births' at the village level in the People's Republic of China, where the villagers decide how many babies they should have each year and who should have them. Another illustration of decentralized participatory development could be given as Tanzania, where social mobilization activities by the political party, army, and by radio listening groups help provide mass motivation for local participation in development activities (Rogers, 1976). The involvement of people through their elected representatives from the beginning of the development projects' formulation and also their participation during its implementation and at the time of monitoring and evaluation creates a feeling of ownership among them. This participatory process makes people active agents of development and not mere passive beneficiaries which they generally feel in the top-down centralized approach. Another important advantage of decentralization approach is that it facilitates convergence of technical inputs offered by the government and donor agencies and participatory inputs available at the grass-roots level by the people and their elected and selected representatives, which lead to the convergence of efforts and endeavours. The constitutional 73rd and 74th Amendments of India have assigned 29 and 18 duties and responsibilities to the PRIs and ULBS, respectively, relating to development rural and urban areas.[3] For example, devolution of untied fund directly to the village panchayats in Kerala has enabled them to formulate need-based development projects, programmes, and activities at the grass-roots level and implement them with full community participation. One of the reasons for the success of rural urban continuum in Kerala is the effective democratic decentralization.

However, true participation has not become a reality because of many reasons and a few of them are:

(i) Poor development governance
(ii) Ineffective participatory development administration
(iii) Lack of effective system of democratic decentralization
(iv) Poor attitude towards inclusive participation due to prevalence of traditional beliefs and values
(v) Poor recognition and involvement of CSOs in the development process
(vi) Last but not the least, supremacy of 'top-down' approach over 'bottom-up approach' because of lack of strong political and bureaucratic will.

The Sum Up

'Development paradigms' are the documented development 'outcomes', 'strategies', and 'models' derived from the experimentation of various actions, research and development practices by the governments, NGOs, bilateral and multilateral agencies, and also by the private actors of development in different nation-states, which if replicated and adopted with modification, depending on local-specific conditions, is believed to help a country to augment its multipronged development. Many action research projects conducted in the areas of poverty eradication have helped the poverty-stricken people to come out of poverty. The inclusive development is an instrument to reduce inequality and promote holistic development of a country. While sustainable development practices have not only promoted development but also helped the nation to raise the quality of living of its population and are internationally recognized as a suitable paradigm of development of the underdeveloped countries, the decentralization and participatory development paradigm has enabled Kerala, one of the states of India, to achieve higher human and social development. The remittances coming to Kerala and Punjab through their diaspora have enabled these two states of Indian Union to offer a better quality of life and reduced poverty and hunger in the rural areas of these states. Development paradigms are the noted developmental pathways which developing countries can follow in order to achieve the MDGs.

Keywords development paradigms, basic needs, National Rural Employment Programme, poverty, inclusive development, sustainable development, remittances, FDI, democratic decentralization, top-down, bottom-up approach.

REVIEW QUESTIONS

1. What is a paradigm of development? Explain its significance in the context of undeveloped countries.

2. Poverty reduction and ensuring basic needs are important paradigms of development. Explain how the developing countries are attempting to achieve it with suitable examples.
3. Define inclusive development. Explain how inclusive development is crucial for holistic development.
4. What do you mean by sustainable development? Explain how an underdeveloped country can achieve sustainable development.
5. FDIs and remittances are important means of development of the underdeveloped countries. Explain with suitable examples.
6. Decentralization and community participation are important means of grassroots development. Explain.
7. Write short notes on the following:
   (i) Poverty trap
   (ii) Basic needs approach
   (iii) Inclusive development
   (iv) Sustainable development
   (v) Foreign direct investment
   (vi) Affirmative measures
   (vii) Marginalization
   (viii) Exclusion
   (ix) Remittance and development
   (x) Bottom-up approach

NOTES

1. For Indonesia and Yemen example, see "China through A Lens, A New Paradigm in Poverty Reduction." Available at: http://www.china.org.cn/English/2004/may/96261 (accessed on 11 December 2015).
2. Dutton's view on poverty is expressed in his paper "Subjects of Development: The United Nations Programme as Technology of Neo-liberal Imperialism." Available at: http://www.languageandcapitalism.info/wp-content/
3. The 73rd Constitutional Amendment of Government of India has assigned 29 duties and responsibilities to the PRIs under 11th Schedule (Article 243G), which are: agriculture, including agriculture extension; land improvement, implementation of land reforms, land consolidation, and soil conservation; minor irrigation, water management, and watershed development; animal husbandry, dairying, and poultry; fishery; social forestry and farm forestry; minor forest produce; small-scale industries, including food processing industries; *khadi*, village, and cottage industries, rural housing, and drinking water; fuel and fodder; roads, culverts, bridges, ferries, waterways, and other means of communication; rural electrification including distribution of electricity; non-conventional energy sources; poverty alleviation programme; education, including primary and secondary schools; technical training and vocational education; adult and non-formal education; libraries; cultural activities; market and fairs; health and sanitation, including welfare of the handicapped and mentally retarded; welfare of weaker sections, and in particular of the Scheduled Castes and the Scheduled Tribes; public distribution system and maintenance of community assets. The 74th Constitutional Amendment has assigned 18 duties and responsibilities to the ULBs, which are: urban planning including town planning; regulation of land use and construction of building; planning for economic and social development; roads and bridges; water supply for domestic, industrial, and commercial purposes; public health, sanitation conservancy, and solid waste management; fire services; urban forestry, protection of the environment, and promotion of ecological aspects; safeguarding the interests of weaker sections of society, including the handicapped and mentally retarded; slum improvement and upgradation; urban poverty alleviation; provision of urban amenities and facilities such as parks, gardens, and playgrounds; promotion of cultural, educational, and aesthetic aspects; burials and burial grounds, cremations, cremation grounds, and electric

crematoriums; cattle pounds, prevention of cruelty to animals; vital statistics including registration of births and deaths; public amenities including street lighting, parking lots, bus stops, and public conveniences; and regulation of slaughter houses and tanneries.

REFERENCES

Battaglia, L., Bellu, L.G., Deing, C., Tedesco, I. 2011. *Development Paradigms and Related Policies* (draft), EASYPoL Resources for Policy Making, Food and Agriculture Organization, Rome. Available at: http://www.fao.org/fileadmin/user_upload/tcas/project (accessed on 31 January 2014).

Bellu Lorenzo, G. 2011. "Development and Development Paradigms: A (Reasoned) Review of Prevailing Visions." *FAO Policy Assistance Support Service*. Available at: www.Fao.org/easypol

Biswas, S. 2010. *Conundrum of Kerala's Struggling Economy*. Available at: http://news.bbc.co.uk/2/hi/south_asia/8546952.stm (accessed on 15 February 2016).

Brundtland, G. 1987. *Our Common Future: World Commission on Environment and Development*. Oxford: Oxford University Press.

Burchardt, T. 2004. "Capabilities and Disability: The Capabilities Framework and the Social Model of Disability." *Disability and Society*, 19(7): 735–51.

Cappo, D. 2002. "Social Inclusion Initiative, Social Inclusion, Participation and Empowerment." *Address to Australian Council of Social Service National Congress*, 28–29 November 2002, Hobert.

Fayissa, B. and Nsiah, C. 2010. "Can Remittances Spur Growth and Development? Evidence from Latin American Countries (LACs)." Department of Economics and Finance, Middle Tennessee State University, Murfreesboro.

Fischer, S. 2000. Lunch address given at the conference on "Promoting Dialogue: Global Challenges and Global Institutes." Washington American University.

Giuliano, P. and Ruiz-Arranz. 2005. "Remittances Financial Development and Growth." IMF Working Papers, 2005. Available at: WP/05/234. Available at: https://www.imf.org/external/pubs/ft/wp/2005/wp05234.pdf (accessed on 15 February 2016).

Grant, J. 1977. "Forward." In *Employment Growth and Basic Needs: A One World Problem*, Prepared for the International Labour Office and the Decisions of the 1976 World Employment Conference. New York: Praeger Publishers.

Gupta, B.L. 2010. *A New Paradigm of Development: Sumangalam*. New Delhi: Gayan Publishing House.

Hurungo, J. 2009. "Alternative Development Paradigms: Analysis of India, China and Brazil Models of Development." Prepared for Trades and Development Studies Centre. Available at: www.tradescentre.org.zw/index.php?option%3Dcom/docman%

Haque, S. 1977. "Local Governance in Developing Nations: Re-examining the Question of Accountability." *Regional Development Dialogue*, 18(2): 4–23.

Jencks, C. 1992. *Rethinking Social Policy: Race, Poverty and Underclass*. London: Harvard University Press.

Jennings, M. 2006. *Institutional Analysis of Social Fund for Development, Republic of Yemen*. London: DFID.

Kerala Calling. 2012. *Emerging Kerala*, August 32(10). See "Kerala Remittances Economy: Bursting Bubble?" Available at: http://www.nriachievers.in/kerala-remittance (accessed on 24 December 2015).

Kuhn, Thomas S. 1970. *The Structure of Scientific Revolutions*, Second edition. Chicago, IL: The University of Chicago Press.

Lewis, John P. 1997. India's Political Economy: Governance and Reform. New Delhi: Oxford University Press.

(Lewis was the head of the USAID Mission to India in the mid-sixties and consultant to various international organizations including Ford Foundation.)

Miller, F.A. and Katz, J.H. 2002. *The Inclusion Breakthrough: Unleashing the Real Power of Diversity*. San Francisco, CA: Berrett-Koehler Publisher.

Moller, V. and Schlemmes, L. 1982. "Quality of Life in South Africa: Towards an Instrument for the Assessment of Quality of Life and Basic Needs." *Social Indicators Research*, 12: 225–79.

Pirages, D. and Ehrlich, P. 1974. *Ark-II: Social Response to Environmental Imperatives*. New York: Viking Press.

Ray, S. 2012. "Impact of Foreign Direct Investment on Economic Growth in India: A Co-integration Analysis." *Advances in Information Technology and Management*, 2(1): 187–201.

Robinson, M. 2007. "Introduction: Decentralizing Service Delivery? Evidence and Policy Implications." *IDS Bulletin*, 38(1): 1–32.

Rogers, E.M. 1976. "Communication and Development: The Passing of the Dominant Paradigm." In *Communication for Social Change Anthology: Historical and Contemporary Readings*, edited by A. Gumucio-Dagron and T. Tufte. Communication for Social Change Consortium, USA, 110–26.

Sapru, R.K. 1994. *Development Administration*. New Delhi: Sterling Publisher Privated.

Schmidt, R., Hero, R.E., Aoki, A., and Alex-Assensoh, Y. 2002. "Political Science, the New Immigration and Radical Politics in the United States: What Do We Know? What Do We Need to Know?" Paper presented at the American Political Science Association, Annual Meeting, 29 August–1 September, Boston.

Stahl, Charles W. and Arnold, F. 1986. "Overseas Workers' Remittances in Asian Development." *International Migration Review*, 20(4): 899–925.

Streeten, P. 1979. "From Growth to Basic Needs." *Finance and Development*, 16(3): 28–31.

UNDP. 2008. "A Million Dollar Question: What is Inclusive Growth?" Report prepared by Uyanga Gankhuyag from a learning event organized by the UNDP Learning Resource Centre, Poverty Reduction News Update, Issue # UNDP and also see UNDP Economic and Social Inclusion. Available at: http://www.in.undp.org/content/albania/en/home (accessed on 31 January 2014).

World Bank. 2008. "Growth Report: Strategies for Sustained Growth and Inclusive Development." Commission on Growth and Development, The World Bank.

———. 2013. "Remittances." Available at: www.worldbank.org/en/news/press-release/2013/10/02/developing-countries-remittances-2013-world-bank (accessed on 15 February 2016).

WHO. 2002. *Community Participation in Local Health and Sustainable Development Approaches and Techniques*. European Sustainable Development and Health Series 4, World Health Organization Regional Office for Europe.

SUGGESTED READING

IMF. 1997. *World Economic Outlook*, Washington, DC.

8 Development Administration

Primary obstacles to development are administrative rather than economic...Countries generally lack the administrative capability for implementing plans and programmes.

— Stone (1965)

It would be disastrous, if the importance of public administration were not recognized by those responsible for national development or if public administration were not fully developed and made to contribute its utmost to the development of the developing countries.

— United Nations (1975)

Development administration is one of the vital arms of development as the effective implementation of development projects, programmes, and activities for the achievement of the development goal depends on the efficiency and effectiveness of the development administration. The development administration that is at the helm of affair in the implementation of development projects and programmes at the grass-roots level is being castigated both by the political set-up as well as by the stakeholders and the people for any procrastination and shortcomings in the execution of any developmental projects and programmes. Development administration is the kingpin to streamline the processes, approaches, and strategies of development and facilitate effective implementation of development activities, projects, and programmes undertaken at various levels for the accomplishment of developmental goals. It gives administrative and financial approval and is the ultimate authority and decision-makers in sanctioning development projects. Good development governance primarily depends on the efficiency, effectiveness, accountability, and transparency of the development administrative system and its upright relationship with the legislative system. Bhambri (1980) was of the opinion that the bureaucracy plays a decisive role in nation-building in modern societies and that on its performance and capacity depend the success or failure of various programmes of socio-economic development. The colonial bureaucracies inherited from the Japanese provided both South Korea and Taiwan with effective state organizations in the post-colonial period (Cummings, 1984). In the South Korea and Taiwan, high quality of economic management is being provided by the civil service with merit-based recruitment and promotion, compensation competitive with the private sector, and economic policy-making that is largely insulated from political pressure (Nafziger, 2012). In case of South Korea, a deep sense of corporate loyalty within the bureaucracy inherited from the colonial period made it possible to combine decentralization of administrative decision-making with overall coordination of state intervention (Michell, 1984). While emphasizing on the importance of the development administration, the United Nations (2007) has advocated that an effective government, in turn, requires a sound and efficient public administration that has the managerial and administration capacities and capabilities required to fulfil its responsibilities.

After reading this chapter, you will be able to:

(i) Describe the meaning and scope of development administration.
(ii) Explain the role of development administration in development.
(iii) Discuss the challenges of development administration.

CONCEPT AND MEANING

Development administration emerged as an important concept after the Second World War and was invigorated between the 1960s and 1970s when development programmes and projects were profusely carried out by the developing countries with the help of international agencies. In recent years, development administration and the public administration system is well recognized as an important instrument in the hands of the nation-state to facilitate effective implementation of developmental policies and programmes at least in developing countries of Asia, Africa, and Latin America. According to United Nations (1975), the main focus of development administration is on the building and improvement of public administration system as part of total effort of national development. It is desired that through development administration, the administrative machinery at various levels will be geared up and can be actively engaged in the implementation of development programmes, projects, and activities to fulfil the goals and objectives of development. According to Hsueh (1970), development administration lays emphasis on that role of public administration, which is to develop the activity of the government especially in economic, political, and social fields. While Weidner (1970) was of the view that development administration is concerned with maximizing innovations for development, according to Hope (1984), development administration is a contextual and operational term that implies efficient organization and management of the development activities of a nation to attain the goals of development. According to Riggs (1971), development administration is an organized effort to carry out programmes or projects thought by those involved to serve developmental objectives. In the words of Sapru (1994), "development administration is the process of carrying out development programmes and projects in the direction of nation-building and socio-economic progress through a developed administrative organization". Development administration is that branch of public administration which deals with various developmental issues and challenges at different levels of administrative set-up, including: (a) implementation of various developmental projects and programmes in various sectors of development with the help of different factors of development; (b) to assess and deal with various indicators of development such as poverty, employment, literacy, morbidity, mortality, and availability of basic human needs; and (c) to facilitate inter-sectoral coordination and community participation and encourage the involvement of CSOs at various levels for the attainment of development goals. According to Zafarullah and Huque (2006), bureaucracy is a vital component in the development machine. The key characteristics of bureaucratic administration as outlined by Weber are: (a) a bureaucratic administration presupposes a chain of command that is hierarchically organized; (b) in a bureaucracy, a system of impersonal rules governs the rights and duties of positional incumbents and adherence to rules prevails over sentiment; (c) the rights and duties of officials are explicitly prescribed and proscribed in written regulations which have properly 'enacted'; (d) officials receive contractually fixed salaries and do not own their positions or the means of production; (e) a bureaucracy presupposes a system of impersonal guidelines for dealing with and defining work responsibilities; (f) a bureaucracy is predicated on a clearly defined division of labour, based upon functional specialization of tasks and a well-defined hierarchy of authority; (g) within bureaucracy, norms of impersonality govern interpersonal relation; (h) officials treat people in terms of 'cases' rather than as individuals and remain impersonal in their contacts with the public; (i) written documentation and orientation to files is a precondition to legitimate decision-making; (j) in a bureaucratic administration, the discharge of responsibilities is based on calculable rules which are carried out 'without regards for persons' (Morrison, 1995).

ROLE AND FUNCTIONS OF DEVELOPMENT ADMINISTRATION

Development administration is one of the very vast and challenging branches of public administration, as it deals with the government and its relation with various stakeholders such as NGOs, private and corporate sectors, bilateral and multilateral agencies, and people at large while formulating and implementing various developmental projects and programmes for the attainment of development goals. Moreover, it has to effectively coordinate with the political system, i.e. parliamentarians, legislatures, and elected representatives of the local self-government institutions, while implementing developmental programmes and projects in their constituencies and areas at the grass-roots levels. A huge responsibility lies on the shoulder of the development administrator to implement these programmes through effective inter-sectoral coordination and community participation at the grass-roots level through its line department functionaries. It educates people about various aspects of sectoral development programmes, their aims and objectives, sources of funding, activities to be undertaken, and strategies of implementation, and it also benefits the people and monitor and oversee its impact at the community level. In a holistic sense, development administration deals with the change in social, economic, political, human, cultural, and environmental aspects of development. As development is a changing process, the knowledge, attitude, and skill of the development functionaries has to be updated from time to time as per the requirement of the development programmes and projects through capacity building. According to Fainsod (1963), "improvements in the effectiveness of development administration ultimately depends on the quality and training of the public servants who man it and on a social and political environment which liberates their energies". The capacity building of the administrators and administrative functionaries and the stakeholders as well as those of the beneficiaries on various issues and challenges of development is an important function of development administration.

In the era of globalization, international cooperation constitutes the cornerstone of many sectoral developmental endeavour, i.e. education, health, environmental protection, agriculture, and so on. According to Sharma and Sharma (2002), the development administration in the state includes activities performed by the government concerned about social, political, economic, industrial, and administrative development. The international and bilateral agencies are funding several projects in different areas of development particularly in the developing countries of Asia, Africa, and Latin America, and it is the duty and responsibility of the development administration to ensure that developmental projects are effectively formulated and implemented and their impacts are assessed and disseminated so that there is no hurdle in the flow of funds for developmental activities from the multilateral and bilateral agencies. Effective management of these projects is vital to the achievement of project development goals, which lies on the shoulder of the development administration. The globalization has also injected the inflow of FDI into the economy and the onus of their effective utilization and management at the provincial and grass-roots level falls on the shoulder of the development administration at these levels.

The key role of development administration is to strengthen the process of decentralized development planning. According to Thanace (1971), development planning is a process of organizing national economic and social effort for the promotion or achievement of clearly defined national development goal. The development planning is a complex process that involves organized efforts of government to achieve specific economic and social goals and aims at judicious utilization of physical, human, and financial resources for achievement of set goal and objectives through formulated strategies. It is essential on the part of the development administrator to keep in touch with the ground realities and developmental happening at the grass-roots level by conducting development need assessments from time to time, both formally and informally with the help of grass-roots development functionaries, as the development condition and priorities vary from area to area and also from one community group to that of the other. According to Sapru (1994), developing countries which are very heterogeneous, with large differences between cities and rural areas, or between different ethnic and socio-economic groups, development administrators are expected to be in constant touch with the rapidly shifting social realities. The decentralized district administration must be flexible, accommodative, and people centred while preparing local area development plans. According to Subramanian (1975), a people's plan cannot be a people's plan, unless it has an inbuilt flexibility so that adjustment and mid-term corrections are possible in the light of several factors and circumstances which cause to the fore during the implementation of the programme. The realistic process of development is to keep in touch with the ground realities and interaction with the stakeholders and the plausible beneficiaries of the developmental projects and programmes so that the benefit of development reaches the poorest of the poor and the real beneficiaries and not grasped by the well-ups and the creamy layer among the poor. White (1981) emphasized on involvement of the local population actively in the decision-making concerning development projects or in their implementation.

One of the vital roles of development administration in recent years is to strengthen social and political infrastructure in their administrative region and area. The social institutions playing critical role in social and cultural development at the grass roots, for instance, in India, are *mahila mandals*, youth clubs, religious and cultural organizations, farmers' associations, cooperative societies, farmers' clubs, etc. These organizations along with other CSOs, NGOs, and local self-government institutions not only influence but also play a decisive role in the formulation and effective implementation of development plans. The district administration has to take appropriate measure to build up the knowledge, attitude, and practices of the elected representatives and functionaries of the local self-government institutions on various developmental challenges and state role in launching various development projects and programmes to overcome these issues and challenges. The capacity building of the elected representatives of the local self-government institutions at various levels should be a continuous process as the election to these bodies takes place at fixed intervals. The fabric of social and political institutions at the grass roots must be build up with inclusive character bereft of discrimination and prejudices.

Environment and development are intimately related. The developmental projects such as construction of dams, hydro-electricity projects, establishment of industries and housing complexes, etc. undertaken in hill and forest areas are putting tremendous pressure on the environment and in the agriculturally fertile areas would affect food grain productivity. Cutting of forest, excessive use of ground water, use of chemical fertilizers and pesticides in agricultural lands, and emission of toxic fumes from industry and pollution from vehicles are a few among many casting shadows on environmental protection. The development administration, therefore, has to act upon for the protection of environment, which will not only affect the life of present generation but would also prepare a ground work of good environment for the future generation. Development administration's role in environmental protection is important for sustainable development.

It is the responsibility of the development administration to promote e-Governance for the effective and transparent implementation and monitoring of various development projects and programmes. It is a well-established fact that information and communication technologies (ICTs) have the potential not only to improve the delivery system of government services but also enhance development outcomes through greater transparency, ease of access, and engaging people in development process and through cost reduction and time minimization. Bali (2004) has remarked that ICT is being used to contribute to poverty reduction by building the leadership capacity of poor women, increasing their opportunities to participate in the media and decision-making, strengthening their livelihoods, and helping to secure greater access to social services. The World Bank (2002) has stated that:

> Information and communication technologies are a key input for economic development and growth. They offer opportunities for global integration while retaining the identity of traditional societies. ICT can increase the economic and social well-being of poor people and empower individuals and communities. Finally, ICT can enhance the effectiveness, efficiency and transparency of the public sector including the delivery of social services.

The digital divide between urban and rural areas is one of the important reasons for rural backwardness and the effective and equitable use of e-development strategies by development administration will fasten the development process in both rural and urban areas. Dutta et al. (2004) emphasized that the measures of success of ICT in development will not focus on the spread of technology but on overall progress towards economic growth and ultimately towards the MDGs. ICTs can play an important role in providing underserved communities access to critical information (Weigel and Waldburger, 2004). The role of development administration is vital to augment the use of ICT in the administrative system.

The role of development administration is to promote balanced development of both urban and rural areas. The objective of provision of urban amenities in rural areas (PURA) is to make provision of urban amenities and livelihood opportunities in rural areas available to common masses residing in the countryside to bridge the rural–urban divide, thereby reducing the forced migration from rural to urban areas. Through public-private partnership, PURA aims to provide 'add-on' revenue-earning facilities such as village linked tourism, integrated rural hub, rural market, agri-common services centre and warehousing, etc. in rural areas. The development manager needs to act for achieving a balanced rural–urban development through PURA.

Administrative reform is one of the important components of development administration and is a tool or process directed towards improving the efficiency and effectiveness of development administration. According to Riggs (1971), administrative reform is a problem of dynamics balancing. Caiden (1976) opined that administrative reform is concerned not only with organizational performance per se but with improving the performance of the whole public sector. While Baimyrzaeva (2012) noted that the administrative reform has to be country specific and is more than changes in management. The main aim of the administrative reform is to simplify the complex activities and procedures and to evolve those methods which would enable the development administration to achieve maximum productive results by engaging minimum amount of money and manpower. Government of India, from time to time, has constituted administrative reform committees for this purpose. According to Arora (2006), the performance of public administration in India has come under close scrutiny in the last few years. Rampant corruption, inefficiencies, wastages, and irresponsiveness to the needs of citizens are some of the commonly acknowledged problems afflicting the development administration. Alexander (1984), while lamenting on the distressing trends of the civil service in India, said that the present civil servants: (a) lack involvement in their work; (b) are hyper-critical and have cynical attitude about everything; (c) lack the responsibility for decision-making; (d) are reluctant to meet the members of the public, and (e) keep every file secret and confidential. The administrative reform aims at enhancing the efficiency and effectiveness of development administration in order to achieve development goal and objectives. The development administration through administrative reforms from time to time improves its functioning and enhances its dynamism.

CHALLENGES OF DEVELOPMENT ADMINISTRATION

The development administration is countered with a lot of challenges, while implementing developmental projects, programmes, and activities particularly at the grass-roots level for the attainment of development goal and objectives. At the outset, physical geography imposes vital challenges before the development administration as there are a lot of inter- and intra-regional variations, i.e. there are hilly areas, desert areas, waterlogged areas, wetland areas, forest areas, land-locked areas, coastal areas, and so on, which requires different developmental approaches and strategies. Development administrators posted in disadvantaged and underdeveloped areas, i.e. hilly and tribal areas would face greater challenge compared to their counterparts in the plains while implementing various developmental projects, programmes, and activities. However, the hunger for development is more pronounced in tribal areas and geographically knotty areas compared to non-tribal areas. Besides geographical area, the quantum and quality of population is an influencing factor of development. The challenge before the development administration is to stabilize population on the one hand and use the potential of population in development process on the other. The situation in high population growth developing countries of Asia, Africa, and Latin America veritably differ from those of European and North American nation states. Demographic number, ethnic, social, and religious groups are projected as item agenda of development and vote bank politics in India.

In recent years, regional political outfits are growing in various provinces day-by-day, which are redefining the federal structure of a country. The dichotomy between centre and provincial political system and their political agendas and priorities are affecting the development processes and strategies of the nation-state. The regionalism can also take different forms, i.e. trade and money (economic regionalism), security (security regionalism), constitutional issues referring to institutional norms, rules and procedures (political regionalism), and socio-cultural policy including sustainable development, health, social security, and culture (socio-cultural regionalism) (Borzel, 2011). Adding to this, coalition politics at the national and provincial level and implementation of fragile coalition political compulsion agendas has posed challenge to development administration. The coalition politics has created a cloud of political instability and coalition compulsions creating the risk of uncertainties, corruption, mal-governance, etc. The development administration has to act according to the whims and wishes of the political parties in power while implementing various development programmes. The reshuffle in administration during the transition of political power from one party to that of the other is an illustrious example of political 'vendetta' and bureaucratic victimization contentions. It is well remarked that political uncertainty is a serious impediment to development in underdeveloped countries (Palekar, 2012).

One of the objectives of development administration is to improve the management capacities of the development managers at various levels. At the grass-roots level, the development administrators act not only as administers but also as managers of various development projects, programmes, and activities launched by various agencies both government and non-government organizations in various sectors of the economy for the attainment of development goal and objectives. They virtually monitor and evaluate money, men, and materials deployed in different developmental projects and programmes and oversee their impact on the development targets. Lack of managerial capabilities can lead of the wastage of resources, i.e. material, financial, and human. Therefore, it is observed that the development administrators are being given training on management from time to time to enhance their efficiency and effectiveness. For example, two development managers with different degrees of managerial capabilities will operate in two different levels of development achievement as shown in Figure 8.1.

The focus of the development administration is to improve the knowledge, attitude, and practices of development-oriented managers so that they are able to respond to the growing need of the people. Generally, some of the common features of maladministration in most of the development administration are red-tapism, corruption, irresponsibility, and lack of accountability and transparency. The willful violation of rules and regulations and protracted process of decision-making has contributed to ineffective administration in underdeveloped countries. Most of the developing countries in Asia are

Figure 8.1 *Managerial Capability*

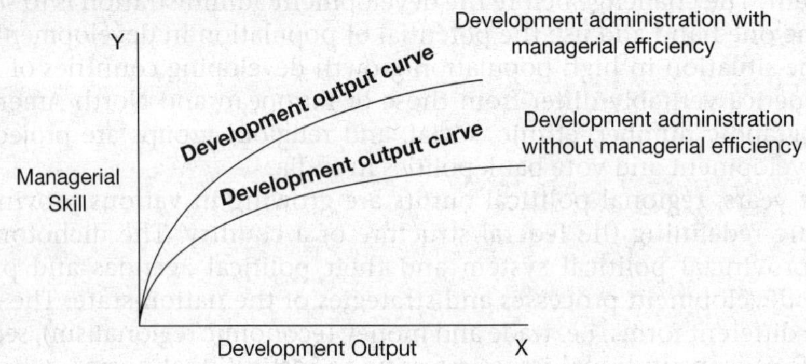

poorly scoring in transparency index developed by Transparency International. A recent civil society movement (Anna Hazare movement for Jan Lok Pal) in India against corruption and demand for bringing bureaucracy and political system at all level under the ambit of 'Lok Pal' is an illustrious example of civil society movement against inefficient and corrupt political system and bureaucratic practices. The development administration has to be accountable to people while implementing development projects and programmes. Lack of transparency and accountability is a case for public resentment against inefficient public administration. According to Jain and Chaudhuri (1982), development bureaucracy needs a framework which is: (a) flexible in its operation; (b) is pragmatic, that is, it is able to take into consideration the exigencies of circumstance from a practical point of view; (c) encourages open decision-making processes; (d) centred around a client-oriented philosophy; and (e) laden with human values of services and dignity for all.

The most stupendous task, the development administration in developing countries faces is the challenge to act under political pressure. Suleiman (2008) has rightly remarked that all bureaucracies have been under political pressure in recent years to reduce not only their size but also their effectiveness, and all have experienced growing de-professionalism and politicization. There seems to have developed a kind of partnership between politicians and bureaucrats within the community (Sapru, 1994). Because of too much political interference, the development administration is finding difficulty to act independently and take unbiased decision with regard to implementation of development projects and programmes. It is being observed sometimes that when they go against the wish of their political boss, it results in transfer, unnecessary harassment, and even face suspension. Thus, the development administrators face a daunting task of resisting political pressure and it is seen that as if they are sandwiched and found to being suffocated between the political leadership and common men. Therefore, even sometimes honest bureaucrats unwillingly are being compelled to succumb to the political pressures and increasingly indulge in corrupt practices and give support to corrupt practices.

Increase in the number of NGOs and parallel bodies in recent years and their engagement in development activities and in the implementation of development projects in various sectors with the funding from the government and other international agencies has posed challenge before the development administration. The parallel bodies are the heterogeneous organizations involved in the implementation of various development programmes, projects, and activities at the grass-roots level parallel to the constitutionally empowered local self-government institutions. In India, NGOs and other parallel bodies like village forest committees, water user groups, *gram vikas samitis*, village vigilance committees, water and sanitation committees, and so on, functioning in different states are not only providing helping hands to the government in the implementation of development schemes and programmes formulated by the government, but also creating substantial hurdles for development administration. In democratic countries, these bodies have a say in the development process. Assigning development projects to NGOs and their monitoring is a problematic affair as most of these NGOs use pressure tactics to get grant from development administration and have nexus with the local politician and in fact many of them are being directly or indirectly owned by the politicians. Government and NGOs interface has become an additional but cumbersome headache for the development administration. Likewise, the parallel these are mostly informal in nature and are found working parallel to the local self-government institutions at the grass-roots level. These are in fact in many cases performing the duties and responsibilities constitutionally assigned to the local self-government institutions. The scuffle between the parallel bodies and the elected representatives of PRIs in India has created additional headache for the development administration functioning at below the state level.

Since 1970s, many alternative development models have been tested in various countries and also in different regions of the same country and are being suggested for replication in similar conditions. It is a challenge before the development administration to select the befitting one and adopt it with modifications and as per the requirements of the development conditions of the local area. In India, the moderate growth and high social development model of Kerala; NGO-led participatory development model in Tamil Nadu and the public–private partnership model of Gujarat are a few among many development models available before the development administration for practice. Besides, several sector-specific models in the area of education, health, sanitation, water supply, housing, slum development, etc. have been successfully documented and suggested for replications. An inquisitive development, administration has to search for such development alternatives and adopt them with modification according to local situation for raising the quality of life of people. Therefore, it is said that development is one of the easiest terms for argument and deliberation, but the most intricate stipulation for implementation and accomplishment. It is a dynamic, a multi-sectoral, and the most versatile concept having many alternatives available for execution. In other words, there are many paradigms of development; however, putting them into practice is an arduous task before the development administration.

World Development Report 2009 has rightly envisaged that "...paradoxically, a world which is rapidly globalizing, one of the most important determinants of well-being is still where a person is born: in which country, in what province within the country and whether in a city or the countryside within that province". In developing countries, development disparities are widely perceived across the region and state and even within the state from one district to that of the other, and between urban and rural areas and in India across the gender, caste and ethnicity. It is also said that inter-state variation in the content and quality of governance, degree of efforts towards mobilization of resources, level of effectiveness of decentralized democratic institutions and community-based organizations (CBOs) have now emerged as factors strongly influencing the movement of the concerned state towards achieving higher level of development (Dreze and Sen, 1995). There are also wide variations among the regions and states in India in terms of achievement of various development indicators such as poverty, literacy rate, infant mortality, maternal mortality, housing, sanitation, and many more. Reducing disparities and brining parity and driving the nation-states towards holistic inclusive development are challenges before the development administration.

One of the challenging tasks before the development administrator is to manoeuvre development dualism conspicuously prevalent in developing countries. To Higgins and Boeke, dualism in less developed countries to a large extent is a sine qua non of their backwardness (Jain and Malhotra, 2010). Dualism in the sense of persistent and increasing divergences exists at various levels, internationally in relations between richer and poorer countries and internally within the developing countries themselves (Singer, 1970). The dualism existing in the form of traditional and modern sector, agriculture and industrial sector, urban and rural sector, formal and informal sector, and so on posit an arduous task before the planners, policy-makers, and the development administration to facilitate balanced inclusive and sustainable development of the interfacing sectors. The globalization has further escalated the differences between these interfacing sectors and these differences are elongating rather than soothing. The existence of a rich country like USA and a poor nation like Ethiopia in the globe and in same vein the coexistence of rich states like Haryana, Punjab, and Kerala on the one hand and Jharkhand, Chhattisgarh, and Bihar on the other in India are illustrious examples of inter- and intra-national dualism. The role of development administration is more challenging in the dualism scenarios. According to Kelley et al. (1972), dualism is not confined to the production alone, but often reflects differences in "social systems, racial or ethnic backgrounds, demographic behaviour, consumer expenditure and consumer savings behaviour and the domestic and foreign sectors". In the stratified society of South Asian nation-states, dualism is veritably as well as present in economic, social, political, and cultural sphere which create hurdles in the path of development and it becomes a herculean task before the development administration to deal with the dualistic situation.

Mobilization of local physical, human, and financial resources particularly at the grass roots is a vital necessity for participatory development. Because of lack of financial resources, it is observed that in India, the local self-governments are fully dependant on the state and central government apparatus for funding to carry out various developmental activities in different sectors. Moreover, there is also lack of willpower among the elected representatives of the local self-government institutions to mobilize community resources for local development, one of the reasons being their familiarity and closeness to people. They are reluctant to impose taxes and collect fee from the people, as a result the own sources of revenue of PRIs many States of India is low. Besides, there is also lack of political and bureaucratic will to mobilize local resources for local area development. For example, the taxable revenue of village panchayats of Kerala in India is many times higher than that of Orissa and Bihar. Iben Nathan said, "local resources mobilization is the effort of the local administration to raise finances from a locality in order to fund activities within that area (Blair, 1989)". Finance is the key to development, and the task before the development administration is to generate as much local revenue as possible for implementation of local area development programmes. Here, they have to convince the grass-roots political system and motivate the people regarding the importance of local revenue generation for local area development. The rural local government revenue generation in developing countries is always a great challenge and the mechanisms, by which local financial resources can be mobilized, have raised some pertinent issues like revenue raising ability, effects on economic efficiency, equity implication, and administrative feasibility (Bahl, 1984).

The development administration is facing many more challenges apart from the above-mentioned few, while discharging their duties and responsibilities at various levels. Therefore, it posits that the development administration has to be creative, industrious, innovative, flexible, accountable, and cooperative in order to overcome the challenges of development.

The Sum Up

Development administration is an inseparable arm of 'development'. Customarily, development administration executes the development process and strategies as finalized by the legislative organ of the government. Development nowadays is not only an economic agenda but also a vital political and social agenda of the nation-state. It is remarked that once development is recognized as the centre of politics, the functions of government grow not only in size, magnitude, and importance but also in complexity. The economics of public administration is becoming an important asset for achievement of development goals and objectives. The public administration has to be fully developed in the developing countries in order to contribute effectively and efficiently to the process of development. However, the development administration is not functioning effectively and efficiently in the developing countries. Caiden (1976) commented that "It seems after killing many myths in the field and experimenting with a variety of models, development administration has in recent years lost its impetus without making any significant intellectual breakthrough or coming to proper grips with the complexities of the subject". As development is a multidimensional concept, the approach of development administration must be pragmatic to deal with the nitty-gritty and complexities of development processes adopted by the developing countries. The dynamics and challenges of development administration are manifold as the actors and sectors of development are many. As development study is an emerging academic area in recent years, the institutions and individuals associated with 'development' have to consider development administration not only an important component of public administration but also of any subject having relationship with development.

Keywords development administration, decentralized development, political infrastructure, e-Governance, PURA, administrative reforms, development alternatives, dualism, development management, regionalism, parallel bodies, development disparities.

REVIEW QUESTIONS

1. What is development administration? Discuss the role of development administration in development.
2. Dualism and development disparities are important challenges before development administration in the developing countries. Explain.
3. What is administrative reform? Why is administrative reform important?
4. Discuss two important challenges of development administration.
5. Mobilization of resources for development at the grass-roots level is a critical challenge before the development administration. Explain.
6. What is a parallel body? Why is the management of parallel bodies vital for the development administration?
7. Write short notes on the following:
   (i) Role of bureaucracy in development
   (ii) Parallel bodies
   (iii) Development alternatives
   (iv) Development dualism
   (v) Development management efficiency
   (vi) Administrative reform
   (vii) Development disparities

REFERENCES

Alexander, P.C. 1984. "Role of Civil Service: Then and Now." *Indian Management*, 23(7): 6–18.

Arora, P. 2006. "Administrative Reforms in India: Need for System Approach to Problem-solving." *International Public Management Review*, 7(2): 83–96.

Bahl, R. 1984. "Mobilizing Local Resources in Developing Countries." *Public Administration and Development*, 4: 215–30.

Baimyrzaeva, M. 2012. *Institutional Reforms in the Public Sector: What Did We Learn?* Bingley, UK: Emerald Group Publishing Limited.

Bali, N. 2004. "Using ICT for Reaching the Millennium Development Goals: Moving from Rhetoric to Action." In *ICT4D-Connecting People for a Better World*, edited by G. Weigel and D. Waldburger. Berne: Swiss Agency for Development Cooperation & Global Knowledge Partnership.

Bhambri, C.P. 1980. "Bureaucracy in India: Challenges of the Eighties." *The Indian Journal of Public Administration*, 26(3), July-September: 520.

Blair, W. Harry. 1989. "Research Findings." In *Can Rural Development be Financed from Below? Local Resource Mobilization in Bangladesh*, edited by Blair W. Harry. Study sponsored by Like Minded Group, 50. Dhaka: University Press Limited.

Borzel, Tanja A. 2011. "Comparative Regionalism: A New Research Agenda." Working Paper, No. 28, WFG the Transformative Power of Europe, Ferie University of Berlin. Available at: http://userpage.fu-berlin.de/~kfgeu/kfgwp/wps (accessed on 18 January 2014).

Caiden, Gerald E. 1976. "International Consultants and Development Administration." *International Review of Administrative Science*, 42(1): 1–7.

Cummings, B. 1984. "The Origins and Development of the Northeast Asian Political Economy: Industrial Sectors, Product Cycles and Political Consequences." *International Organization*, 38(1): 1–40.

Dreze, J. and Sen, A. 1995. *India Economic Development and Social Opportunity*. New Delhi: Oxford University Press.

Dutta, S., Lanvin, B., and Pana, F., eds. 2004. *Global Information Technology Report 2003–04*. Oxford University Press. Available at: http://www.weforum.org

Fainsod, M. 1963. "The Structure of Development Administration." In *Development Administration: Concepts and Problems*, edited by I. Swerdlow. New York: Stracuse University Press.

Weigel, G. and Waldburger, D. (eds). *ICT4D-Connecting People for a Better World*. Swiss Agency for Development Cooperation & Global Knowledge Partnership, p. 103.

Hope, K.R. 1984. *The Dynamic of Development and Development Administration*. Westport, CT: Greenwood Press.

Hsueh, Shou-Sheng. 1970. "Technical Cooperation in Development Administration in South and South-East Asia." In *Developemnt Administration in Asia*, edited by W. Edward Weidner. Durham, NC: Duke University Press.

Jain, R.B. and Chaudhuri, P.N. 1982. *Bureaucratic Values in Development*. New Delhi: Centre for Policy Research.

Jain, T.R. and Malhotra, A. 2010. *Development Economics*. New Delhi: VK Publication.

Kelley, A.C., Williamson, J.G., and Cheetham, R.J. 1972. *Dualistic Economic Development: Theory and History*. Chicago and London: University of Chicago Press.

Michell, T. 1984. "Administrative Traditions and Economic Decision-making in South Korea." *IDS Bulletin*, 15(2): 32–37.

Morrison, K. 1995. *Marx Durkheim Weber Formations of Modern Social Thought*. London: SAGE Publications.

Nafziger, E.W. 2012. *Economic Development*, Sixth edition. New York: Cambridge University Press.

Palekar, S.A. 2012. *Development Administration*. New Delhi: Raj Press.

Riggs, Fred W. 1971. "The Context of Development Administration." In *Frontiers of Development Administration*. edited by W. Fred Riggs. Durham, NC: Duke University Press.

Sapru, R.K. 1994. *Development Administration*. New Delhi: Sterling Publisher.

Sharma, U. and Sharma, S.K. 2002. *Public Administration*. New Delhi: Atlantic Publishers and Distributors.

Singer, H.W. 1970. "Dualism Revisited: A New Approach to the Problems of the Dual Society in Developing Countries." *Journal of Development Studies*, 7(1): 60–75.

Stone, Donald C. 1965. "Government Machinery Necessary for Development." In *Public Administration in Developing Countries*, edited by M. Kriesberg. Washington DC: The Brookings Institution, 53.

Subramanian, V. 1975. "The Citizen and Planning." *The Indian Journal of Public Administration*, 21(3), July–September: 357.

Suleiman, E. 2008. *Dismantling Democratic State*. Princeton, NJ: Princeton University Press.

Thanace, T.T. 1971. "Planning for Development." In *Accelerated Development in South Africa*, edited by John Barrat, S. Brand, David S. Collier, and K. Glaser. London: Macmillan, 451.

United Nations. 1975. *Development Administration: Current Approaches and Trends in Public Administration for National Development*. New York: United Nations, 189.

———. 2007. *Indicators of Sustainable Development: Guidelines and Methodology*. New York: United Nations.

Weidner, Edward W., eds. 1970. *Development Administration in Asia*. Durham, NC: Duke University Press.

White, A. 1981. "Community Participation in Water and Sanitation: Concepts, Strategies and Methods." The Hague: IRC.

World Bank. 2002. *Information Communication Technology: A World Bank Group Strategy*. Washington, DC: World Bank.

Zafarullah, H. and Huque, A.S. 2006. "Introduction: Challenges of Governing Development." In *International Development Governance*, edited by A.S. Huque and H. Zafarullah. London: Taylor & Francis, 3–12.

9 Development Governance

The development governance is the governance, oriented to solve common national development problems and create new national development opportunities and achieve common national development goals.

— United Nations (2009)

Sound development governance is about harmonizing and integrating economic growth, human advancement and sustainable development.

— Zafarullah and Huque (2006)

Governance is the hottest and a mooted concept in the cookbook of 'development'. The 'governance', in general, and 'good governance', in particular, has become one of the demanding agendas of development in the competitive politics of developing countries. As 'governance' is a debatable concept, particularly in the developing countries, therefore, there are differences of opinion about the meaning of the concept 'governance' between the conservatives and liberals, between the socialists and communists; bourgeois and proletariats; democrats and authoritarians, and even between the legislatures and the activists involved in the process of development of the developing countries. It is well said that 'governance' understood as a concept and 'governance' understood as a practice, is an ambiguity that could be described as a slippage between concept and practice (Jose, 2009). According to ODI (2006), governance refers to the nature of rules that regulate the public realm the space, where state and economic and societal actors interact to make decisions. According CONCORD (2008), governance can be defined as the way in which societies develop rules and processes and behaviours necessary for their accomplishment, emphasizing that governance is a cross-cutting issue that needs to be incorporated in all sectors and at all policy levels. Governance plays an effective role in the management of various affairs of the nation-states and is an indispensable instrument for facilitating faster development. A country that improves its governance from a relatively low level to an average level could almost triple the per capita income of its population in the long run (Kaufmann, 2005). The World Bank[1] currently uses 11 per cent of its lending to support government institutions and the rule of law, which is just one part of its broader governance work. The DFID[2] uses approximately 18 per cent of the DFID overall spending on governance and civil society programmes. According to OECD,[3] overall, about 11 per cent of total official development assistance is devoted to the area of government and civil society. Thus, governance is a way the legislative, executive, and judiciary system of the government has to function to ensure social and economic justice to the common masses. Governance aims at accountability, transparency, efficiency, effectiveness, and application of rule of law into the system of functioning of the different wings of the public service delivery system. Therefore, governance is vital to the development of the underdevelopment countries.

After reading this chapter, you will be able to:

- (i) Define development governance and why it is essential for development.
- (ii) Discuss various attributes of development governance.
- (iii) Explain various dimensions of development governance and how they are important from the point of view of development.
- (iv) Describe challenges of deployment governance and think how they can be overcome.

WHAT IS DEVELOPMENT GOVERNANCE? WHY IS IT ESSENTIAL FOR DEVELOPMENT?

Social scientists, development practitioners, CSOs, and the international development organizations are nowadays advocating the adoption of development governance principles and practices as an instrument for the effective implementation of development policies and programmes in the developing countries facing the problems of corruption, red-tapism, and maladministration. It is also believed that use of development governance will accelerate the pace of economic growth and development in the developing countries. According to Zafarullah and Huque (2006), development governance is a dynamic process encompassing vertical and horizontal linkages within public organizations and exchanges with non-state entities. The development governance aims at efficient and effective use of political and bureaucratic machinery in a responsive, accountable, and transparent manner for the achievement of development goals. The UNDP Human Development Report has aptly envisaged that each element of governance is both a means and goal of development and lends insight into how development efforts are succeeding (or not succeeding) in securing choices of the people of a nation. There is strong evidence that governance matters in accelerating development and in reducing poverty in developing countries (Khan, 2006).

There is immense importance of development governance in the development process of the underdeveloped countries. It facilitates effective and efficient public and private participation in development-oriented decision-making process. One of the principles of the development governance is to bring transparency in development administration and this can be promoted only through popular participation of all stakeholders as well as beneficiaries in the development process. Development governance expects that the political parties ruling the nation state must respect the sentiments of the people and initiate debates and discussions in the national parliament or assembly and arrive at a conclusion through consensus before implementing any policy decision. Implementation of law through ordinances is not a sign of good governance. The development governance principle helps and promotes participatory development.

Development governance helps in the effective implementation of development projects and programmes. The managers and implementers of development projects and programmes need to apply development governance principles during the process of project and programme implementation. It is seen that because of non-adherence to governance principles, the outcomes of many developmental projects implemented by the government and non-government agencies are not satisfactory and have failed to achieve their targeted goals. There are complaints of corruption, delay in project completion and siphoning of public money, and also lack of community participation in the development project affairs which matters to them.

According to Tan See Hua[4] some of the benefits of project governance are:

(i) Effective utilization of resources
(ii) Increased project visibility
(iii) Effective and timely decision-making
(iv) Apparent competing project dependencies
(v) Focused leadership team
(vi) Project value is tied directly to strategic goals

Effective governance of development projects results in economic use of all types of resources, i.e. human, financial, and material and fulfilment of projects and programmes, goals, and objectives.

Good governance checks corruption and ensures transparency in the political and administrative system. The governance intends to make institutions and rules more effective and efficient, in order to achieve equity, transparency, participation, responsiveness, accountability, and the rule of law (United Nations, 2012). Development governance expects the capacity building of the elected representatives and the functionaries of the development administration in development governance so that they discharge their duties and responsibilities accountably and in a transparent manner. Development governance is a prerequisite for the development administration to make it effective, efficient, and people centred. Development governance, if put into practice, will serve as an apparatus to check the involvement of politicians, bureaucrats, and other office bearers of the government machinery of the developing countries in corrupt activities.

It will make the development process more inclusive. Development governance by applying principles of good governance aims at achieving inclusive development. In the developing countries stratified on the basis of class, caste, gender, religion, and ethnicity, it is seen that the fruits of development are being grasped by the rich and the creamy layers. The neo-liberalization process has further elongated the gap between the haves and have-nots and between the socio-economically advanced and the laggards, and therefore, inclusive growth and development has become an important development agenda in the developing countries trying to achieve holistic development through the adoption of good governance practices. It is remarked that governance is a continued process of aggregation and articulation of public demand and subsequent conversions into deliberate policies and therefore can provide the 'enabling environment' for inclusive growth (Rahman, 2010).

Governance practices can be helpful in strengthening the functioning of the civil society and other grass-roots level democratic organizations. In fact, implementation of the principles of governance by the political and bureaucratic system presupposes the prevalence of the strong and honest CSO base in the developing countries. Therefore, the use of the word 'good governance' is found to be more popular among the activists of the CSOs. Per se, the recent civil society movement, in India (popularly started by Anna Hazare) for the Jan Lok Pal, is a movement for implementation of good governance practices in legislative and executive system of the government. The good CSOs are the torch bearers of the society and if they adopt good governance practices, they could definitely influence the minds and hearts of the elected representatives and development administration functionaries at the grass-roots level through education and training and motivate them to adopt good governance practices in their administration and functioning. Both are mutually beneficial to each other's effectiveness. The Reality of AID Africa[5] Network has rightly noted:

> Legitimate governance is valuable, because it helps creates norms and information that enable our governments and other actors to coordinate their behavior in mutually beneficial ways. They create opportunities for states and other actors to demonstrate credibility, thereby overcoming issues like commitment problems that are likely to crop up.

Orienting CSOs on good governance will not only strengthen their functioning but also be helpful to the State actors for the effective implementation of good governance practices at the grass roots.

Development governance can improve and strengthen the functioning of the decentralized democratic institutions. In recent years, many of the development programmes and schemes are being implemented by or with the help of the local self-government institutions. The devolution of functions, functionaries, and funds to these institutions has placed the onus on their shoulders to discharge their duties and responsibilities in an accountable and transparent manner by applying rule of law and official procedures. Because of poor governance, many of the elected representatives of the local self-government institutions are found to be indulging in corrupt practices and are unable to perform their duties and responsibilities diligently due to which development process at the grass-roots level is largely hampered. Resorting to development governance principles and practices is the sole answer to make these bodies accountable, transparent, effective, and efficient and involve them effectively for the attainment of development goals.

DIMENSIONS OF DEVELOPMENT GOVERNANCE

Three important dimensions of development governance are: (a) decentralized governance, (b) e-Governance, and (c) participatory governance.

Decentralized Governance

Most of the countries in the world are nowadays shifting emphasis from a centralized towards a decentralized system of governance not only to make development people-centred, but also to promote development through participatory process. Bardhan (2002) argued that the logic behind decentralization is not just about weakening the central authority, nor is it about preferring local elites to central authority, but it is fundamentally about making governance at the local level more responsive to the felt needs of the large majority of the population. While Bardhan and Mookherjee (2000) opined that decentralization by shifting central rights from the central bureaucrats to a local government typically tends to expand service deliveries as authority goes to those more responsive to user needs. The decentralization process initiated by the governments of various countries in recent years is largely intended towards strengthening development governance at the grass roots. In India, Kerala model of decentralization has successfully empowered local self-government institutions to be effectively engaged in local development. The rural–urban continuum in Kerala is an illustrious example depicting effective functioning of decentralized democratic system in the State. Three important forms of decentralization are devolution, delegation, and deconcentration. In case of devolution, both the authority and functions are transferred from the higher level of government to the lower level of governments, while in delegation, the power and sometimes the authority is not transferred, and if transferred, it can be taken away and by deconcentration only the functions and responsibilities are transferred from the higher to the lower government, but not the authority.

Four important elements of decentralization are:

Political Decentralization

Under political decentralization, powers and responsibilities are devolved to various levels of political institutions, and more particularly to the elected representatives of local self-government institutions. This is popularly known as democratic decentralization. Per se in India, political decentralization means decentralization of the decision-making power from the Members of Parliament and Legislative Assemblies to the elected representatives of zilla parishads (district panchayats), block samitis (intermediate panchayats), and gram (village) panchayats in rural areas, and to nagar panchayats (municipalities and municipal corporations) in urban areas. In other words, transfer of responsibility from the parliamentarians and legislatures to the elected representatives of PRIs and ULBs. According to the World Bank[6] (The World Bank Decentralization Thematic Team), political decentralization aims to give citizens or their elected representatives more power in public decision-making. In fact, political decentralization enhances political education among the elected representatives of the grass-roots level political institutions. The hurdles in the path of decentralized political governance are mainly created by the elected members of the central and state level political institutions which are largely reluctant to decentralize power to the lower bodies, that is, to the elected representatives of the local self-government institutions.

Administrative Decentralization

Here, the administrative functions performed by the central government are transferred to geographically and administratively distinct administrative units. It aims at transfer of policy-making authority as well as managerial responsibilities from the central to local self-government. In context of Indian democracy, it means sharing of duties and responsibilities among functionaries at various levels of administration, i.e. central, state, district, subdivision, block, and village level administration. The administrative decentralization presupposes that there should not be any duplication or replication of functions and a clear-cut activity mapping at each level is desired. The demand for transfer of functions from the district-level bureaucracy to the functionaries of local self-government institutions is on the rise in developing countries, particularly in India, where the elected reprehensive of local self-governments are demanding transfer of administrative functionaries under them. Except for a few states, for example, Kerala, in most of the other states, the functionaries supposed to work under the village panchayats have not been transferred to them. According to the World Bank (The World Bank Decentralization Thematic Team), administrative decentralization seeks to redistribute authority, responsibility, and financial resources for providing public services among different levels of government.

Fiscal Decentralization

Fiscal decentralization aims at transfer of funds directly to the lower level of democratic institution, that is, local self-government institutions either from the state government or from the central government and their empowerment to levy taxes and fees and disburse salaries to their employees. In many European countries, the local governments are empowered to impose and collect taxes in their municipal areas and also pay salaries to their own employees from their generated revenues and grants received from the central and provincial governments. This is a way of fiscal empowerment of local bodies and fiscal decentralization to lower level of governments. In Kerala, 40 per cent of their State budget is directly transferred to the village panchayat in the form of untied fund to implement need-based village development programmes. The village panchayats are also effectively empowered to collect taxes and fees from the local area and the won sources of revenue of the Kerala village panchayats are many more times higher than the village panchayats of many states of the Indian union. But in many States, the own sources of revenue of the village panchayats are meagre; therefore, these institutions are solely dependent on the grants from the government, which affects their local area development. The reluctance of village councils to raise revenues locally has been pointed out to be one of the main reasons for failure of fiscal decentralization in India (Jone, 1992). However, it is being feared that devolution of fiscal responsibilities in a non-transparent atmosphere and where the elected representatives do not have adequate knowledge and capabilities to handle budgeting could lead to widespread corrupt practices and misappropriation of funds. The capability building of the local self-government institutions on financial management, i.e. in the preparation of budget, utilization procedure of tied and untied funds, auditing, and issuance of utilization certificate will be an add-on to their financial empowerment skill. Lin and Liu (2000), from their study, concluded that fiscal decentralization positively contributed in the process of economic growth and the economic growth significantly influenced by rural reforms, capital accumulation, and the development of the non-state sector.

Manpower Decentralization

Transfer of manpower according to the principle of subsidiarity so that they are posted and work under a system for which they are supposed to work. In other words, manpower decentralization means transfer of functionaries to the local self-government institutions so that they work under the direct control of local self-government institutions and not under the supervision and control of the provincial administration.

Decentralized Participatory Budgeting—A Case Study of Porto Alegre, Brazil

Porto Alegre is a backward city of Brazil with a population of 1.5 million. Nearly one-third of its population was living in areas lacking in clean water, sanitation, school, and medical facilities. This is because, for a long time, Porto Alegre had invested less amount of its budget in public amenities. A reform process was initiated in Brazil in 1986, in which a policy decision was taken to involve the community by guaranteeing representations from the poor in deciding about expenditures to be made at the grass-roots level. In accordance to this reform, the local government expressed its willingness to share budgetary information and the political commitment of the elected mayors to give priorities to proposal submitted by the poor people. As a result, representatives from relatively poorer areas could pressurize the local government to prioritize their needs so that they could obtain access to basic amenities which all other areas have. As a result, clean water coverage increased from 75 to 98 per cent. The number of schools in the area quadrupled and the spending on health and education in the area increased from 13 to 40 per cent of the total budget.

The overall process empowered the poor to be more active citizens and decreased the domination of bureaucracy in budgetary decision-making. The success of Porto Alegre has inspired many governments to apply participatory budgeting system.

Source: http://siteresources.worldbank.org/INTEMPOWERMENT/Resources/14657_Partic-Budg-Brazil-web.pdf (accessed on 21 February 2016).

Besides, the local self-government institutions must be effectively empowered and involved in the recruitment, career advancement, and other disciplinary action processes of these functionaries. Deficiency of manpower is severely affecting the functioning of the village panchayats in many states of India. For example, in Kerala, a village panchayat has nearly, on an average, 10–15 functionaries, while in Punjab and Haryana and some other states a panchayat secretary looks after the affairs of five to six panchayats. Dhaka (2002) from a field study in panchayats of Haryana, a state in India, opined that technically, panchayats do not have adequate expertise, manpower, and skill to plan and implement developmental schemes and projects, thereby further increasing their dependence on the state apparatus.

e-Governance

The World Summit on the Information Society (WSIS), held in 2003, declared to harness the potential of ICT to promote the development goals of the Millennium Declaration along with a commitment to the achievement of sustainable development. e-Governance is commonly defined as the application of electronic means in the interaction between government and citizens and government and business as well as in internal government operations to simplify and improve democratic government and business aspects of governance (Backus, 2001). According to Heeks (2001), e-Governance is the use of ICTs to support good governance.

e-Governance embraces the following aspects:

(i) e-Administration improves government processes by cutting costs, by managing performance, by making strategic connections within government, and by creating empowerment.
(ii) e-Citizens and e-services connect citizens to government by talking to citizens and supporting accountability, by listening to citizens, by supporting democracy, and by improving public services.
(iii) e-Society builds interaction beyond the boundaries of government by working better with business, by developing communities, by building government partnerships, and by building civil society.

The sole aim of e-Governance is to integrate ICT with the governance initiatives for development. Integrated approach to e-Governance in given in Figure 9.1.

Some of the important contributions of e-Governance towards development are:

(i) Economizing expenditure and cost reductions
(ii) Quick decision-making and service delivery
(iii) Building up capacity of the functionaries of the government, private, NGOs, and CSOs
(iv) Improving the quality and responsiveness of decision-making and service delivery
(v) Enabling innovative approach to governance
(vi) Building up database for quick decision-making
(vii) Promoting easy accessibility and transparency
(viii) Enabling effective implementation of development projects and programmes

Figure 9.1 *Integrated e-Governance for Development*

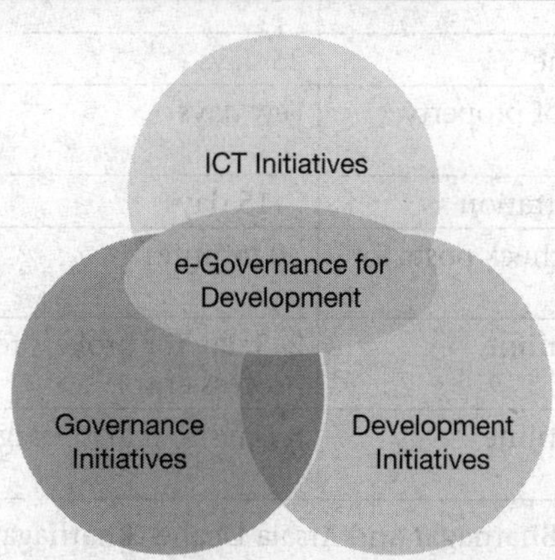

The WSIS which emphasizes on Internet governance (i-governance) intends "the development and application by governments, the private sector, and civil society in their respective roles of shared principles, norms, rules, decision-making in procedures, and programmes that shape the evolution and use of the Internet." The WSIS declaration principles expressed:

> A common desire and commitment to build a people-centred, inclusive, and development-oriented information society, where everyone can create, access, utilize, and share information and knowledge, enabling individuals, communities and peoples to achieve their full potential in promoting their sustainable development and improving their quality of life.

e-Governance and good governance go hand-in-hand, as it makes procedures of governance more transparent and also help in rapid decision-making. It has been observed that effective use of e-Governance by the local self-government institutions has benefited them in different ways, i.e. speedy redressal of public grievances, information sharing about different programmes and projects, issuance of various certificates, i.e. birth and death certificates, electronic payment of user charges, such as electricity, water, and telephone bills, and last but not the least, e-education to countryside people about various development programmes and projects. Castillo (2004) said, "e-service can help to have a more efficient government, they can provide services quicker and with more transparency. By trying to systematize some procedures and services that the government provides, we can have a better government and reduce corruption". The benefits which some of the countries have received through the application of e-Governance in some of their functions is given in Table 9.1.

Table 9.1 *Benefits of e-Governance*

Country	Type of Government Application	Time to Process before Application	Time to Process after Application
Brazil	Registration of 29 documents	Several days	20–30 minutes per document, one day for business licences
Chile	Taxes online	25 days	12 hours
India, Andhra Pradesh (AP)	Valuation of property	Few days	10 minutes
India, (AP)	Land Registration	7–15 days	5 minutes
India, Gujarat	Interstate check posts for trucks	30 minutes	2 Minutes
Jamaica	Customs online	2–3 day for brokers to process entry	3–4 hours
Philippines	Customs online	8 Days to release cargo	Between 4 hours to 2 days to release cargo

Source: (i) Based on Subhash Bhatnagar and Arsala Deane (Bhatnagar and Deane, 2003).
(ii) e-Governance: Initiatives in India. Available at: http://arc.gov.in/11threp/arc_11threport_ch4.pdf (accessed on 27 July 2015).

Gram Sampark: A Rural Development e-Governance Initiative of Madhya Pradesh

Gram Sampark is a flagship ICT product of the government of Madhya Pradesh, India. Through *Gram Sampark*, a complete database of the available resources, basic amenities, beneficiaries of government programmes, and public grievances of all the 51,000 villages of Madhya Pradesh can be obtained by accessing the website Gram Sampark. It has three sections: (a) *gram paridrashya* (village scenario), (b) *samasya nivaran* (grievances redressal), and (c) *gram prahari* (village sentinel). An 11-point monitoring system has been put in place whereby programmes are monitored village-wise every month.

Sampark Centres: An Urban e-Governance Initiative of Chandigarh

The Union Territory of Chandigarh has established electronic service centres known as 'Sampark' in different locations of the city. These centres provide different government services, such as payment of taxes, payment of water, sewerage, and electricity bills, payment of sticker/postal challans, issue of bus passes, issue of senior citizen cards, issue of birth and death certificates, space bookings, tenant registrations, domestic servants registrations, passport application, and payment of selected telephone bills under a single roof. It has reduced the cost of travel and also has saved a lot of time of the customers.

Participatory Governance

The Declaration of the Right to Development adopted by the United Nations in 1986 says:

> The right to development is an inalienable human right by virtue of which every human person and all peoples are entitled to participate in, contribute to and enjoy economic, social, cultural and political development, in which, all human rights and fundamental freedoms can be fully realized. (UN, 1986)

In the same vein, article 25 of the International Covenant on Civil and Political Rights states that "Every citizen shall have the right and the opportunity...to take part in the conduct of public affairs, directly or through freely chosen representatives". The universality of the right to participate in the development process has been well recognized. When people are able to exercise their voice in the conduct of public affairs, they will find an opportunity to reveal their true preferences and choices. In the participatory development governance process, people govern themselves for their own development, the government and other development agencies only play a catalyst role. The success of participatory governance depends on many factors, such as prevailing conditions, the number and quality of the people involved, the representation of women and people

Ralegan Siddhi—An Epitome of Participatory Governance for Development

Before 1975, when Anna Hazare visited the village Ralegan Siddhi, the condition of the people was very bad, there was poverty and illiteracy and people of the village had poor access to sanitation and safe drinking water. Because of lack of water, only 55 acres of land was cultivated in the village. There was no rainwater conservation system and most of the rainwater was wasted. Anna with the help of community participation, i.e. with the help of elected representatives of PRIs, *gram sabha,* and other civil society organizations triggered off a water conservation movement. Several committees were formulated to look into various issues such as water, irrigation, education, rationing, women, and youth empowerment. With these initiatives, the community took charge of their own governance and development. With peoples' initiatives, 31 water *nalla* bunds were constructed for the conservation of rainwater. As a result, 700–800 acres (90% of the total) were brought under the cultivation. This was achieved with the people's participation and with the mobilization of voluntary labour called *shramdaan*. With the availability of water, a lot of trees were planted and many acres of land was brought under the cultivation of fodder, as a result, the number of livestock increased and the milk production in the village went up. Other benefits were: (a) provision of safe drinking water; (b) rise in literacy; (c) better nutrition and reduction of drudgery and dowry problem; (d) prohibition of alcoholism and adoption of small family norms by the families; (e) food security; and (f) community marriages and social inclusions. As Anna Hazare told that the dream of India as a strong nation will not be realized without self-reliant, self-sufficient villages; this can be achieved only through social commitment and involvement of common man.

Source: www.hydratelife.org/?=1765 (accessed on 12 December 2015); www.fao.org/docrep/x5669e069.htm (accessed on 12 December 2015).

belonging to different social groups, the overall social–political environment prevailing at the grass-roots level, the level of socio-economic development, and so on. The participatory governance gives voice to the voiceless, thus it provides 'opportunity' and is a great 'capabilities enabler'. Through the participatory governance, development can become more democratic, equitable, and people centred. The Development Assistance Committee of OECD (1997) has concluded that "Participatory, accountable, and efficient governance harnesses the activities of the state and its citizens to the objectives of sustainable social and economic development".

ATTRIBUTES OF GOOD DEVELOPMENT GOVERNANCE

Good development governance is one of the key determinants of development, as it facilitates and fosters faster development. According to Acemoglu et al. (2003), good governance is not only critical to development but it is also the most important factor in determining whether a country has the capacity to use resources judiciously and effectively to promote economic growth and development. Former UN Secretary General Kofi Annan said, "Good governance is perhaps the single most important factor in eradicating poverty and promoting development". Improving governance is one of the vital cornerstones of development. Each element of good governance can be understood both as a means and as goals of development (Canada Crops, 2005). According to Sachika and Durwood (2005), good governance promotes accountability, transparency, efficiency, and rule of law in public institutions at all levels and allows for sound natural, economic, and financial resources for equitable and sustainable development. The World Bank (1992) veritably linked good governance to sound development management. According to the World Bank, "the importance of good governance has now become an article of faith with multilateral organizations, donors, and lenders, increasingly basing their aid and loans on the condition that policies which ensures good governance are adopted". The IMF has also announced that good governance is important for countries at all stages of development. Wolf (2005) argued that political corruption and malgovernance are among the principal barriers to economic development and social betterment in the Third World. The Office of the High Commission for Human Right in its Resolution 2001/72 emphasized that "the strengthening of good governance at the national level including through the building of effective and accountable institutions for promoting growth and sustainable human development is a continuous process for all governments regardless of the level of development of the countries concerned". Good governance has several advantages, such as it saves cost and time, brings transparency in the process of governing, helps in better decision-making process, and checks corruption.

The United Nations Economic and Social Commission for Asia and Pacific has envisaged eight characteristics of good governance, viz. participatory, responsive, consensus-oriented, accountable, transparent, effective efficient, equitable and inclusive and follows the rule of law. Similarly, a 'White Paper on European Governance 2001' of European Commission has mentioned five good governance principles: Openness, participation, accountability, effectiveness and coherence. It has envisaged that minimum good governance requires a fair legal framework that is enforced impartially by an independent judiciary and its decisions and enforcement are transparent or carried out in a manner that follows established rules of law. Following are some of the attributes of good development governance.

Accountability

Good governance necessitates accountability on the part of the political and bureaucratic system to the needs of the people. Accountability means to be liable or answerable or responsible towards assigned activities. It implies that one should not, be it government or non-governmental organization, shy away from its role and responsibilities. The elected representatives as well as the development administration and functionaries of the government should not shy away from their responsibility. Besides government, all other stakeholders, like private undertakings, CSOs and NGOs dealing with developmental activities at the grass-roots level, need to be accountable to people for their development actions. To circumscribe, the principle of good accountability means, the executor or the leader must accept the responsibility of failure and share the credit for success with his or her team members and the people. Shifting the responsibility of failure from one person to another and fighting for taking the credit for success are contrary to accountability. Development programmes have failed largely because of poor accountability on the part of organizations responsible for implementation of these projects and programmes.

Transparency

Etymologically, transparency means 'openness'. The actors of governance such as government, private sector, NGOs, and the CSOs must be well-intentioned and open to public scrutiny. This is a vital ingredient in preventing corruption. The lack of transparency particularly in financial matter is considered one of the leading causes of mistrust and barriers to development. Transparency presupposes that rules and regulations and procedures must be simple, clear, and understandable with fewer contradictions. Transparency also necessitates democratic decision-making and sharing of information among the partners, stakeholders, and largely with the beneficiaries. Honesty is an important ingredient of transparency. It is generally observed that honest leaders are more transparent than their counterparts, who are dishonest and do not hesitate to share information with the partners, stakeholders, and beneficiaries.

Responsiveness

The dictionary meaning of the word 'responsiveness' is quick to react in a way that is needed, suitable, or right for a particular situation. Responsiveness in governance implies that institution and institutional processes have to demonstrate concern or responsiveness to the hopes and aspirations of the people. The development agencies and institutions engaged in various development projects, programmes, and activities needed to elucidate receptivity to the views, complaints, and suggestions from citizens and service users. Delay in reply is an indication of an attempt to conceal a fact or showing callousness towards a genuine problem. Therefore, institutions and processes try to respond to the queries of stakeholders and beneficiaries of development within a reasonable time. The other meaning of responsiveness is commitment towards one's responsibility. Punctuality is one of the important characteristics of responsiveness.

Equitable and Inclusive

The equity dimension of governance seeks to ensure that development is inclusive. Equitable means dealing fairly or in a right and just manner with all concerned and presupposes that there should not be any discrimination. People irrespective of caste, sex, gender, and ethnicity must enjoy equally various benefits of the fruits of development. They should not feel excluded and discriminated from the mainstream for their economic, social, cultural, and physical laggardness and disability. A nation-state giving affirmative benefits to certain laggard groups of population for their socio-economic and political upliftment is to be considered as one of the inclusive agendas of development. Good development governance believes in social, economic, political, and cultural inclusion for achieving holistic development. To be equitable means assigning preferential benefits to the unequal or have-nots over haves.

Effectiveness and Efficiency

Effectiveness and efficiency are the two important pillars of development governance. Efficiency is a productivity metric which means how fast one can do anything. While effectiveness is a quality metric meaning how good a person is in doing anything. In management terminology, efficiency means doing the things in a right manner, while effectiveness is doing the right things. In other words, efficiency focuses on 'means' whereas effectiveness focuses on achieving the 'end' goal. Good governance means devising a system which produces results that meet the needs of society with the best use of manpower and financial resources. Being efficient means you spend less time, less money, and less effort on doing something, while being effective means, you perform well in doing something. Both these concepts are two important sides of the coin of development governance and one is meaningless without the other.

Rule of Law

The good governance must apply rule of law in the development process. Rule of law presupposes a fair and predictable legal framework where individuals and businesses may have access to opportunities without fear of any interferences or expropriation. According to Sachiko and Durwood (2007), the term 'rule of law' is used to mean independent, efficient, and accessible judicial and legal systems, with a government that applies fair and equitable laws equally, consistently, coherently, and prospectively to all of its people. The key elements of rule of law are fair, impartial, and accessible justice system used for the common good of the people. According to Canada Crops (2005), the rule of law is also something that resides in the consciousness of the citizens of society, how they understand, use, and value the law. UN (2005) acknowledged that good governance and the rule of law at the national and international levels are essential for sustained economic growth, sustainable development, and the eradication of poverty and hunger. Because of hapless rule of law and measly application of rule of law, the benefits of development are siphoned of by the middlemen (touts) and are hardly delivered to the poor who deserve it.

Participatory

Good governance emphasizes on participatory development process in which decisions are not imposed, but are rather followed and accepted through popular participation. Participatory means to take part or getting involved in an activity. Participatory approach to governance desires to make governance process both supply and demand driven, where the government functionaries is the supply side and the people are the demand side and both participate together in the decision-making process. According to Huque and Zafarullah (2006), one of the critical elements of development governance is empowerment of the people, particularly the poor and those marginalized at the grass roots, by expanding their capabilities and enlarging the domain of their participation and their influence over the process of development. People-centred approach to development views an individual not as a subject but as an actor who defines goals, controls the resources, and directs processes affecting his or her life (Korten, 1984). Participation can happen directly or through people's representatives. For example, at the grass-roots governance in India, 'gram sabha' or 'village assembly' is the institution of participatory governance. Another well-known term used for participatory governance is 'decentralized governance'. According to Blackman (2005), participation can happen: (a) by attending a meeting even though one does not say anything; (b) by taking part in decision-making process; (c) contributing material, money, and labour; (d) providing information; and (e) answering questions for a survey. Participatory development governance is a healthy governance process and it is considered to be 'of the people, by the people and for the people'. Participatory governance to be effective must be inclusive in nature and take appropriate action for inclusion of the excluded and marginalized in the decision-making process and also during implementation and monitoring of development projects and programmes.

Consensus Oriented

The term 'consensus oriented' conventionally means decisions should not be imposed, rather should be emerged. Consensus means to agree to the majority sentiment and in the consensus-oriented process all the parties look forward to reach an agreeable situation, which is acceptable to all. Different stakeholders involved in the development process must be consulted before taking a final decision. Here the government, private, and civil societies must be oriented towards consensus-building behaviour rather than resorting to confrontation. It believes in democratic process rather than authoritarian nature of decision-making. UNESCAP (2009) envisages that good governance requires mediation of the different interests in society to reach a broad consensus in society on what is in the best interest of the whole community and how this can be achieved. The consensus-oriented approach is more inclusive and encourages collective decision-making. It promotes democratic communication and development action.

Pluralistic

Good governance believes that a nation needs to recognize and respect pluralistic character of its society. Plural means many or not single, pluralism means respecting the value of diversity of views or opinions rather than equivocally sticking to a single approach or accepting the dominance of a particular view or opinion. Pluralism presupposes that all the people of nation, inside and outside the nation, all religious groups, majority as well as minority, and all ethnic groups of population either residing in the plains or in the hills or forests, are its own and all are equal before law. India represents a unique character of pluralism, having attributes of unity in diversity. Pluralism believes in the energetic engagement with diversity and active seeking of understanding across differences. In a pluralistic country like India, which is a land of many languages, cultures, traditions, religions, festivals, castes, etc. any development-governance strategy must take into consideration pluralistic character of the society in order to achieve holistic development. Pluralism believes in peaceful coexistence and universal brotherhood. Unilateralism is detrimental to holistic development. Pluralism is an integral and important characteristic of good governance.

India Is Home, but Happier Away

A survey conducted by using e-mail on Indian respondents from Hong Kong, Singapore, Sri Lanka, UK, France, Germany, and US found that on an 8-point scale NRIs gave a thumbs down to the Indian Government's performance on various issues vis-à-vis their resident countries.

Table 9.2 *NRI's Perception of Indians about Good Governance in India and Abroad*

Statements	India	Abroad
1. Good quality policy formulation and implementation	3.5	7.2
2. Policies to promote economic growth	4.2	7.2
3. Policies to promote economic equality	3.8	6.2
4. Policies to promote industrial growth	4.5	7.1
5. Policies to promote gender equality	3.7	7.5
6. Implementing measures to control corruption	3.0	7.5
7. Punishing the corrupt	2.3	7.5
8. Freedom to the civil servants from political pressures	4.3	6.6

Source: *Hindustan Times*, February, 2/2014 p. 12.

ISSUES OF DEVELOPMENT GOVERNANCE

It is always easy to talk, confabulate, and offer suggestions on good governance, but very difficult to put various principles of good governance into practice. It requires a lot of courage and conviction on the part of the individual as well as organization and also on the part of the various wings of the government to implement and uphold the sanctity of governance and apply them for the socio-economic development of the nation. Principles of governance are largely linked to the application of conscience, heart, mind, and wisdom. However, putting the principles of good governance into practice is a Herculean task. It is rightly remarked by Harlow (2006) that good governance has been highly influenced by European structural models such as French Administration Law, the English Common Law, the German Principles of Proportionality, and the Scandinavian Ombudsman Institution.

The following paragraphs describe some of the issues before the development governance for its effectiveness.

Upholding the sanctity of governance requires strong political and bureaucratic willpower. It is remarked that most decentralization policies and programmes falter during implementation because they are introduced with political hesitation, bureaucratic resentment, and suspicion or incomprehension from the general society (Kauzya, 2005). Formulation of stringent rules and procedures and their adherence without fear and favour requires strong political and bureaucratic will. In developing countries, where corruption has taken deep roots, these principles are found to be grossly violated at every sphere at the national, state, and societal level. For example, issuing tickets to politicians with corrupt and criminal records for contesting elections and getting them elected to the parliament and assemblies is a blot on governance. Indulgence of political and bureaucratic machinery in corruption is against the ethics and ethos of good governance and a big challenge for development governance. Leadership in a country has a key role to play in combating corruption (Alatas, 1999).

The investigating agency is the teeth of governance. To have a responsive and impartial investigating agency is a challenge before a nation-state. The issue of 'Lok Pal' in India is one of the illustrious examples of demand for good governance by the CSOs and common man. At a minimum, good governance requires fair legal frameworks that are enforced impartially by an independent judiciary and its decisions and enforcement are transparent or carried out in manner that follows established rules and regulations (Sharma, 2007). Speedy and timely redressal of grievances and appointment of ombudsman or *lokayukta* with a clean image is an attribute of good governance. Effective and efficient investigating and judicial system is a precondition for effective development governance.

Corruption at various levels is a common challenge faced by development governance. Removal of corruption in political and administrative sphere will calibrate development governance and enhance its efficiency and effectiveness. Because of corruption at various levels, only a meagre percentage of colossal amounts of money earmarked for development activities reach to the real beneficiaries and the rest are siphoned of by the middlemen. Corruption is one of the greatest enemies of development and is a scourge on development governance. Jagmohan (2005) has remarked that corruption distorts economic growth, undermines social stability, kills the faith of the people in fairness and justice, weakens the overall moral fabric of the nation, and takes it to decline and destruction. In developing countries, democratization, public sector 'downsizing' and deregulation are not only desirable goals in themselves but also a useful means to reduce extensive corruption (Doig and Riley, 1998). Myrdal (1984) noted that in Singapore, economic development proceeded to a certain degree, because it was one of the few states in underdeveloped world which actively fought against corruption.

CSOs have emerged as an organized pressure group on state and unresponsive governments in matters of democracy and development (Pillai, 2006). Efficient CSOs are sine qua non for the propagation of development governance principles and practices among the common masses. Honest and dedicated CSOs are the watchdogs of democracy and development and do not hesitate to expose political and bureaucratic corruption. OECD (2000) has noted that good governance requires a broad approach to partnership extending beyond government and parliaments to include civil society and private sector. According to Ghaus-Pasha (2005) civil society can further good governance, first, by policy analysis and advocacy; second, by regulation and monitoring of state performance and the action and behaviour of public officials; third, by building social capital and enabling citizens to identify and articulate their values, beliefs, civic norms, and democratic practices; fourth, by mobilizing particular constituencies, particularly the vulnerable and marginalized sections of masses, to participate more fully in politics and public affairs; and fifth, by development work to improve the well-being of their own and other communities. However, the disgruntled CSOs having lust for grabbing money are the bane of development and headache for development governance.

Exclusion on the basis of caste, class, gender, etc. is a challenge for development governance. Development governance believes in the principle of equity, equality and inclusiveness. Denial of 'opportunities' and underestimating 'capabilities' on the basis of above-said criteria are against the ethics of good development governance. Affirmative actions in lieu of promoting socio-economic equality are a conjecture of development governance. Addressing caste, ethnic, gender, regional, and economic inequalities is seen as an important priority by poor people, being treated with respect and dignity would significantly lessen their sense of exclusion and make a significant contribution to their experience of well-being (Jones et al., 2009). Exclusion creates inequality and, therefore, is detrimental to good governance which believes in equity.[7]

Engaging citizens in policy-making allows government to tap new sources of ideas, information, and resources at the time of decision-making (Caddy, 2001). Good citizenry is an asset for the nation's development and a means to good governance. Oxfam[8] holds the view that citizens are able to tell power-holders about the issues they face and hold the government accountable for its decisions and allocation of resources, power holders benefit from feedback and inputs from citizens and from the push to be more accountable. Citizens as a whole need to practice certain ethics in their public life and their decision not to give bribe and accept bribe are signs of good development ethics. It must come from within; self-governance is the best governance. The Committee on Standards in Public Life set out seven core principles: (a) selflessness, (b) integrity, (c) objectivity, (d) accountability, (e) openness, (f) honesty, and (g) leadership and these principles have been incorporated into the codes of conduct of numerous government institutions, including the parliament (Nolan, 1998).

Knowledge and information are essential for the people to avail opportunities and respond successfully to challenges of development. Development communication is an important issue essential for the successful transaction of knowledge, skill, and developmental practices with the common men, particularly belonging to the countryside. Communication for development is about seeking change at different levels including listening, establishing trust, sharing knowledge and skills, building policies, debating, and learning for sustained and meaningful change (WCCD, 2006). Access to information helps to enhance food security, improve rural livelihood, and foster new development opportunities (WCCD, 2006). The basic objective of development communication is to place communication and media technology in the service of development. Development communication is not only advertisements, propaganda, entertainment, and establishing public relations and image building but is an instrument for serving the needs of the people to attain development. Effective development communication system is important for the Third World countries, where people belonging to rural, far-flung, and backward areas do not have adequate knowledge about the developmental projects and programmes, their process of implementation, sources of funding, community participation mechanism, etc. It is generally said that one of the important reasons for which majority of development programmes or projects fail to reach to the real beneficiaries because of lack of awareness and knowledge about the project and programmes, for whom they are targeted, who are the possible beneficiaries, how it can be accessed, who are the implementing agencies, and so on. Propagation of development education is one of the important challenges before development governance in the developing countries. According to Caddy (2001), citizens are not government, they elect it and want to be served by it. But if they are to participate more than just via the ballot box, they need proper access to information, meaningful consultation, and opportunities to take an active part in policy-making. Today, there are widespread efforts to put more government information online and open up portals for online consultation, like the America Speaks Citizens' Electronic Forum in the US, the UK's discussion and information portal, Citizen's Space or Finland's Share Your Views with Us (Caddy, 2001). According to Myint (2000), it is the responsibility of the press to gather, analyze, organize, present, and disseminate information and is considered vital to create greater public awareness and to provide the momentum for undertaking reforms to overcome corruption. Effective communication is the torchbearer of effective governance.

The Sum Up

Governance has a key role to play in development and is a fundamental requisite for the effective implementation of development projects and programmes. Good governance principles, such as transparency, accountability, equality, consensus building, etc. are deeply relevant in development administration and management. Corruption and bad governance in developing countries are the factors responsible for underdevelopment. Participatory and inclusive governance, which takes everyone, and particularly includes the excluded in the development process, will promote sustainable and holistic development in the developing countries. Good governance is an ornament, and if properly adorned would magnify the credentials of a country in the international arena.

Keywords development governance, e-Governance, participatory governance, transparency, accountability, good citizenry, development communication, decentralized governance, rule of law, fiscal decentralization.

REVIEW QUESTIONS

1. What is development governance? Why is it important for the developing countries?
2. Participatory governance is an important dimension of development governance. Explain.
3. What is e-Governance? Explain the importance of e-Governance in development by giving suitable examples.
4. What is good governance? Explain four important attributes of good governance.
5. What is governance? Explain the role of governance in development.
6. Explain three important challenges of development governance. How can they be overcome?
7. What is decentralized governance? Explain the role of decentralized governance in the development of the underdeveloped countries.

8. What is democracy? Discuss the role of good governance in a democratic underdeveloped country.
9. Write short notes on the following:
   (i) Decentralized governance
   (ii) Rule of law
   (iii) Good governance
   (iv) e-Governance
   (v) Participatory governance
   (vi) Good citizenry
   (vii) Development communication
   (viii) Transparency and accountancy

NOTES

1. World Bank, "Issue Brief: Governance and Anti-Corruption," July 2011. Available at: http://siteresources.worldbank.org/INTEMPOWERMENT/Resources/14657_Partic-Budg-Brazil-web.pdf (accessed on 15 February 2016).
2. DFID: Department for International Development, Statistics on International Development 2005/06-2–9/10., October 2010.
3. OECD: Development Cooperation Directorate "Creditor Reporting System." Available at: http://stats.oecd.org/Index.aspx (accessed on 12 December 2015).
4. Tan See Hua "Project Governance." Available at: carnegieendowment.org/files/aiding_governance.pdf (accessed on 15 February 2016).
5. The Reality of Aid 2004 Africa, "Governance and Promotion of Human Rights in International Cooperating." Available at: www.realityofaid.org/wp-content/uploads/2013/02/ROAHYPERLINK "http://www.realityofaid.org/wp-content/uploads/2013/02/ROA_2004_part2.pdf"_2004_part2.pd (accessed on 15 February 2016).
6. For more detail see http://www.annahazare.org/ralegan-siddhi.htm (accessed on 22 July 2015)
7. World Bank Decentralization Thematic Team. "What is Decentralization?" The online Source Book on Decentralization and Local Development. Available at: www.czesin.org/decentralization/English/General/Different_forms.html (accessed on 15 February 2016).
8. Ratan Tata has said that India's greatest weakness is inequality in enforcement of governance and the country is yet to achieve a transparent position. He said that whether you are a billionaire or a street vendor you are governed in the same manner. If we achieve that in our every large and diverse country, governance will take a more transparent position. We are not there as yet (quoted from *Indian Express,* Friday, 19 June 2015, 20).

REFERENCES

Acemoglu, D., Johnson, S., Rohinson, J., and Thaicharoen, Y. 2003. "Institutional Causes, Macro-Economic Symptoms: Volatility, Crises and Growth." *Journal of Monetary Economics*, 50(1): 49–123.

Alatas, Hussain S. 1999. *Corruption and the Destiny of Asia*. Singapore: Simon and Schuster (Asia).

Bardhan, P. 2002. "Decentralization of Governance and Development." *Journal of Economic Perspectives*, 16: 185–205.

Bardhan, P. and Mookherjee, D. 2000. "Corruption and Decentralization of Infrastructure Delivery in Developing Countries." Working Paper, University of California, Berkeley.

Bhatngar, S. and Deane, A. 2003. "Building Blocks of e-Government: Lesson from Developing Countries". Washington DC: World Bank; quoted from Hanna Nagy, K. 2010. Transforming Government and Building the Information Society, Challenges and Opportunities for the Developign World, Bethesda, USA, 157.

Blackman, R. 2005. *Project Cycle Management*. Teddington, UK: Terfund.

Caddy, J. 2001. "Citizens as Partners: Information, Consultation and Public Participation in Policy Making, OECD. Available at: http://www.oecdobserver.org/news/archivestory.php (accessed on 14 February 2014).

Canada Crops. 2005. "Guide to Key Concept in Governance and Development." Governance_WebFINAL_EN.doc

Castillo, R. 2004. "How can ICT Make a Difference in National Development Effort? Development Policies, ICT and the Shaping of the Future." In *ICT4D-Connecting People for a Better World*, edited by G. Weigel and D. Waldburger.Berne: Swiss Agency for Development Cooperation & Global Knowledge Partnership, 91.

CONCORD (Confédération Européenne des ONG D'urgence et de Développement). 2008. PCP-EU Joint Parliamentary Assembly Ljubljana (Slovenia), 15–20 March 2008. Available at: http://www.concordeurope.org (accessed on 15 February 2016).

Dhaka, R.S. 2002. "Panchayati Raj Institutions in Haryana: A Field Study." *Kurukshetra*, January.

Doig, A. and Riley, S. 1998. "Corruption and Anti-corruption Strategies: Issues and Case Studies from Developing Countries." In *Corruption and Integrity Improvement Initiatives in Development Countries*, by UNDP. New York: UNDP, 45–62.

Echeverri-Gent, Jone. 1992. "Public Participation and Poverty Alleviation: The Experience of the Reform Communists in West Bengal." World *Development*, 20(10): 1401–22.

Ghaus-Pasha, A. 2005. "Role of Civil Society Organization in Governance." The Global Forum on Reinventing government towards participatory and transparent governance, 24–27 May 2005. Seoul: Republic of Korea.

Harlow, C. 2006. "Global Administration Law: The Quest for Principles and Values." *The European Journal of International Law*, 17(1): 187–214.

Jagmohan. 2005. *Soul and Structure of Governance in India*. New Delhi: Allied Publisher.

Jones, N., Bhatta, B., Gill, G., Pantuliano, S., Singh, H. B., Timsina, D., Uppadhaya, S., and Walker, D. 2009. "Governance and Citizenship from Below: Views of Poor and Excluded Groups and their Vision for a New Nepal." Working Paper 301, ODI, London.

Jose, J. 2009. "Concept, Dammed Concept and Governance." Paper presented at Newcastle Symposium on Governance, University of Newcastle, August, 24.

Kaufmann, D. 2005. "10 Myths about Governance and Corruption." *Finance and Development*, 42(3): 41–43.

Kaul, V. 2011. "Development Communication in India: Prospect, Issues and Trends." *Global Media Journal—Indian Edition*, Winter Issue, 2(2).

Kauzya, J.M. 2005. *Local Governance Capacity Building for Full Range Participation: Concepts Framework and Experiences in African Countries*. Department of Economic and Social Affairs, United Nations Headquarter, New York.

Khan, Mushtaq H. 2006. "Governance and Anti-corruption Reforms in Developing Countries Policies, Evidence and Ways Forward." G-24 Discussion Paper Series, United Nations Conference on Trade and Development, 42, November 2006.

Korten, D.C. 1984. "Rural Development Programmes: The Learning Process Approach." In *People Centred Development: Contributions Towards Theory and Planning Framework*, edited by D. Korten, K. Cand Klauss. Hartford: Kumarian Press.

Lin, J.Y. and Liu, Z. 2000. "Fiscal Decentralization and Economic Growth in China." *Economic Development and Cultural Change*, 49(1): 1–21.

Myint, U. 2000. "Corruption: Causes, Consequences and Cures." *Asia-Pacific Development Journal*, 7(2): 33–58.

Myrdal, G. 1984. "International Inequalities and Foreign Aid in Retrospect." In *Pioneers in Development*, edited by G. Meier and D. Seers. London: Oxford University Press.

Nolan, L.M. 1998. "Just and Honest Government." *Public Administration Development*, 8(5): 447–57.

ODI. 2006. "Governance, Development and Aid Effectiveness: A Quick Guide to Complex Relationship." *Odi Briefing Paper*, March 2006, ODI, London.

OECD. 1997. *Evaluation on Programs Promoting Participatory Development and Good Governance*, Development Assistance Committee, OECD, Paris.

———. 2000. *Partnership for Poverty Reduction: From Commitment to Implementation*, Statement by the Development Assistance Committee (DAC) High Level Meeting, Paris, 11–12 May 2000.

Pillai, P.P. 2006. "Democratic Decentralization Participatory Development and Civil Society: The Story of People's Campaign for Decentralization Planning in India." Institute of Planning and Applied Economic Research, Thrissur, Kerala. WS Focus_Pillai.pdf (accessed on 12 December 2015).

Rahman, N. 2010. "MDGs Inclusive Growth and Governance." One World Foundation India, New Delhi. Available at: www.borjournals.com/a/index.php/jbmssr/article/view/126 (accessed on 19 February 2016).

Sachiko, M. and Durwood, Z. 2007. "Rule of Law, Good Governance and Sustainable Development." Available at: http://www.inece.org/conference/7/vol1/05Sachiko Zaelke.pdf (accessed on 12 December 2015).

Sharma, S.D. 2007. "Democracy, Good Governance and Economic Development." *Taiwan Journal of Democracy*, 3(1): 29–62.

UNESCAP. 2009. Available at: http://www.unescap.org/pdd/prs/Project Activities/Ongoing/gg/goverance.asp (accessed on 12 December 2015).

United Nations. 2009. *The Least Developed Countries Report, The State and Governance*, 2009, UNCTAD, 15.

———. 2012. "United System Task Team on the Post-2015 UN Development Agenda, Governance and Development." Available at: www.un.org/millenniumgoals.pdf/…/7_governance.pdf (accessed on 15 February 2016).

WCCD. 2006. "Communication for Development." World Congress on Communication for Development, Rome. Available at: http://www.fao.org/3/a-ai143e.pdf (accessed on 17 February 2016).

Wolf, M. 2005. "Aid is Well Worth Trying." *Financial Times*, 5 July.

World Bank 1992. *Governance and Development*. Washington, DC: The World Bank.

Zafarullah, H. and Huque, A.S. 2006. "Introduction: Challenges of Governing Development." In *International Development Governance*, edited by H. Zafarullah, and A.S. Huque. London: Taylor & Francis, 3–12.

10 Development Planning

Development planning relates to a teleological-determined manipulation of policy measures and instruments devised so as to stimulate the actors of the socio economic scene to act in the way most conducive to the achievement of the national socio-economic development objectives and goals.

— United Nations (1974)

Development planning as a process of organizing national economic and social efforts for the promotion or achievement of clearly defined national development goals.

— Thahane (1974)

With the scanty resources available in the hands of the post-war underdeveloped nations to tackle sundry of socio-economic problems, i.e. poverty, unemployment, inequality, illiteracy, ill health, and so on, and, simultaneously, to achieve higher growth rate and development, most of the developing countries resorted to development planning process for the effective utilization of their scanty resources among different sectors of the economy. Planning for development is an important feature of socialistic and mixed economic system. As most of the developing countries are mixed economies in nature with the combined features of capitalism and socialism, development planning is also an important development strategy of many of these countries. Development planning tries to cover many key aspects such as objectives of the development plan, resources available with the nation, sectoral allocation of resources with priority, programmes to be initiated and implemented in each sector, strategies and delivery mechanism, and output and outcome to be achieved during the plan period. The plan document is a cookbook of the development plan of a nation which gives an account of development vision, mission, goals, objectives, action plans, activities' formulation, and resource allocation prepared in each and every plan period, be it annual plan, five-year, plan or long-term ten-year plan.

After reading this chapter, you will be able to:

(i) Define development planning and discuss the need for development planning.
(ii) Discuss the role of development planning in development.
(iii) Explain different types of development planning and the various principles of development planning.
(iv) Narrate various useful steps necessary for the preparation of a development plan.
(v) Describe decentralized planning process in India and the people's planning process of Kerala.

MEANING OF PLANNING

'Planning' is defined as a process of setting of goals, formulation of objectives, development of strategies, outlining activities and tasks, and sector-wise allocation of resources in order to accomplish the developmental goals and objectives within a particular time period. For Cole (1993), planning is an activity which involves decisions about ends as well as means and about conduct as well as result. Ivancevich et al. (1994) perceived planning as embracing all the activities that lead to the determination of objectives and the appropriate courses of action that lead to their achievements. Planning is in essence an organized, conscious, and continual attempt to select the best available alternatives to accomplish specific goals (Waterston, 1971). 'Development plan' is a dynamic professional exercise that is undertaken by the government of a nation-state in order to improve the quality of life of the people by placing thrust on various sectors and development of various regions through proper allocation of resources, appropriate strategies and action plan formulation, and placing effective implementation, monitoring, and evaluation mechanisms for the achievement of developmental goals and objectives. To Marcellus (2009), development planning comprehensively involves predetermining a nation's visions, missions, policies, and programmes in all facets of life, such as social, human, political, environmental, technological, etc. and the means of achieving them. Dickinson (1939) defines economic planning as the making of major economic decisions, i.e. what and how much is to be produced and to whom it is to be allocated by the conscious decision of a determinate authority, on the basis of a comprehensive survey of the economic system as a whole. Development planning helps a nation to strategically allocate financial resources towards performing different activities, projects, and programmes in various sectors of development in order to achieve overall development goals and objectives. Planning, therefore, is a process in which all organs/departments should be engaged and a process where competing demands are ironed out, adjusted, and reconciled in as rational a way as feasible (Sapru, 1994). The United Nations (1975 a, b) has rightly said, "A plan is a programme of action for achieving definite objectives or goals. In this sense, a plan is a policy statement and planning means policy making". In short, planning maybe defined as conceiving, initiating, regulating, and controlling economic activity by the state according to set priorities with a view to achieving well-defined objectives within a given period (Dewett, 1978).

Although development planning has not enabled all developed as well as developing nations to overcome their development bottlenecks, it has been helping them to systematically work out their strategies and action plan, effective use of their scanty resources and monitoring the progress and taking corrective measures from time to time in the implementation of various development programmes in various sectors of the economy. The plan document is a prodigious source of information about a nation's developmental achievement and would guide action in various fronts. However, planning cannot be treated as the sole panacea to developmental ills of the developing countries, and it can only help them to systematically assess development needs, initiate development action, and allocate precious limited resources for development of various sectors. It is remarked that there are countries which have achieved development without much planning, and there are planned countries that do not achieve much development (Waterston, 1971). The need for planning is widely felt; however, its success depends on its effective formulation and efficient implementation; political and administrative governance; effective monitoring and evaluation mechanism; and peoples' participation at the grass roots, and an efficient impact assessment and follow-up system. One can never be certain what contribution planning has made to the socio-economic development of a country, as the development planning of a country rests on a number of factors as technological, environmental, economic, social, cultural, and political considerations (Sapru, 1994). However, planning has become an inexorable instrument in the hands of the nation-states of developing countries having socialist and mixed economic system for achieving their development goals and objectives.

ROLE OF DEVELOPMENT PLANNING IN DEVELOPMENT

Development planning provides a direction to the government regarding its development goals, thrust areas, and action plan and strategies of implementation of various developmental programmes and projects to achieve the development goals. A nation without development planning is like a ship without harbour. An unplanned economy according to Lerner is like "an automobile without a driver but in which many passengers keep reaching over to the steering wheel to give it a twist. It will be a miracle indeed if the automobile reaches its destination safely" (Dewett, 1978). Without proper planning, a lot of imbalance may happen in terms of sectoral activities and regional development. In a way, planning minimizes the chances of uncertainties and inadvertent errors and gives an opportunity to the planners to initiate corrective measures through mid-term evaluation. The development plan is central to achieving greater balance in regional development and enabling all areas to develop to their maximum potential (Government of Ireland, 2007). Planning helps a nation in the judicious allocation of strategic and scarce resources in the best possible manner for achieving sustainable and inclusive development. Effective allocation of resources to various regions in terms of their population and socio-economic backwardness and various sectors in accordance to their strategic importance and possible direct and indirect contribution towards economic growth and development is vital trajectory to economic growth and development. While emphasizing the need for planning, Singh (1966) said that the change in ideology of the people, their growing social consciousness, and the realization of the social and economic evils of maldistribution of income and wealth have drawn attention to the need for directing economic growth in a manner that would bring about not only increased production but would also ensure more equitable distribution for the larger output. Egalitarian measures have, therefore, been called for, and regulation of economic mechanism has become necessary to ensure social justice and equality. Planning aims at achieving socio-economic equity and balanced development. It is remarked that planning is an appropriate development path to improve the life of common people (Shakya, 2007).

Planning enables a nation-state to work out, examine, and analyze alternative courses of action after doing proper need analysis, problem identification, and understanding of their likely consequences. Continuous planning after every five years gives an idea to the development planners, comprising various subject and technical experts, to exercise their judgement and proceed cautiously to choose the most feasible and favourable course of action. Therefore, development planning implies deliberate control and direction of the economy by a central authority for the purpose of achieving definite targets and objectives within a specified period of time (Jhingan, 2005). Planning document provides the guidelines to the legislatures, executives, and the technocrats to effectively run the affairs of the government. The continuous monitoring of planned actions would enable to identify any delay, deviation, and lapses in the implementation of planned action and thereby to take corrective measures. It makes development tasks and activities more appropriate and systematic, and as a result sporadic, eccentric, and erratic actions are avoided. Planning makes economic and social development easier by providing for explicit analysis and evaluation of alternative policies, and it can systematically resolve competing demands and conflicts (Sapru, 1994).

Effective planning is considered an action towards adaptive responses. As a nation moves on, a lot of internal and external changes take place, and globalization is one among them. Planning in a way tends to improve the ability of a nation to effectively adopt and adjust its activities and directions in response to the changes taking place in the internal as well as external environment. Per se, developing countries preparing planning in the globalized world have to take into consideration the inflow and outflow of resources which play important role in the socio-economic development at the national, provincial, and grass-roots level and also the role of FDIs and remittances on economic development of the nation. According to Lewis (1951):

> The State now claims to know better than its citizens for how many years they should send their children to school, between what hours they should drink, what proportion of income should be saved, whether cheap houses are better than cigarettes and so on.

Planning in the mixed economy is essential not only to work out strategies and action for the government, but also to deal with market imperfections and take into consideration functioning of the gigantic structure of the informal economy, mostly prevalent in the developing countries. To Sapru (1994), "In developing countries, operation of the market is generally imperfect because of lack of competition or absence of appropriate institutions. In these cases planning complements the market mechanisms".

As Galbraith (1962) said:

> There is much that market can usefully encourage and accomplish. But the market cannot reach forward and take great strides when these are called for. As it cannot put a man in space, so it cannot bring quickly into existence a steel industry when there was little or no steel making capacity before... To trust the market is to take an unacceptable risk that nothing or too little will happen.

Government through planning tries to fulfil a large number of development objectives, which is beyond the reach of the vast informal sector to accomplish.

Planning is an important exercise to bring out effective integration of diverse sectors and activities and also the development actions of various actors of development not only at a point of time, but also over a period of time. Various aspects relating to different sectors are strategically integrated through planning in order to facilitate holistic development of an economy. The integrated development planning helps a nation to achieve effective use of scarce resources, speeds up delivery system with cost effectiveness, attracts additional resources at the community level, and strengthens decentralized democracy. A planned document gives a holistic picture of futuristic targets of different sectors and their direct and indirect contribution to or effect on social and economic development of the nation. The planning process is a response to the issues arising from growing cultural diversity and should seek where possible to actively affirm and support the needs of the new local communities which are emerging (Government of Ireland, 2007). It helps a nation to achieve sustainable development through judicious allocation of resources to various sectors. The development plan will set out policies for the protection of the environment and heritage and is an important source of information for landowners, developers, communities, and members of the public (Government of Ireland, 2007). A country can achieve sustainable development by emphasizing on the development of the economy, society, and environment and tries to maintain close coordination among these three important dimensions of development, for the attainment of sustainable development. It is now realized that lack of coordination, recurrence of business cycles, economic inequalities, social parasitism, economic insecurity, wastes of competition, absence of industrial peace and huge social costs, which characterize an unplanned economy, can be done away with by resorting to planning (Dewett, 1978). Development planning also emphasizes upon inclusive development. It must work out special action plan and programmes for the socio-economically weaker sections of the society, to enable them to be in the mainstream. It is only the State and its development plan mechanism which can provide justice to the poor, down-trodden and backward people. Moreover, allocation of resources for the backward, hilly, desert, tribal, and other regions lagging behind must be given special allocation of resources in the planned document to enable these regions to contribute towards the economic growth and development. Development planning controls the affairs of both public as well as private enterprises, and in recent years the action of the NGOs and the actions of the local self-government institutions at the grass roots for the attainment of national goals. It sets priorities which both the public and private sectors and other actors of development have to follow in order to attain national goals. In a way, it assimilates individual goals with the national goals in order to attain sustainable national development. To Lewis (1951), the word 'planning' is sometimes used to describe the means which the government uses to try to enforce upon private enterprises, the targets which have been previously determined.

WHAT ARE DIFFERENT TYPES OF DEVELOPMENT PLANNING?

Development planning is of many different types, as mentioned here.

Planning by inducement and planning by direction: In planning by inducement, the State tries to achieve the objectives of development planning indirectly by giving inducement to the market forces. This type of planning is largely adopted in the capitalist economies where private enterprises and market mechanism are in full operation. The State adopts inducement mechanism by giving subsidies and tax benefits to the private enterprises for the initiation and augmentation of development action. In other words, in this type of planning, government tries to influence and control economic and investment decisions indirectly through its fiscal and monetary policies. It is also known as planning by persuasion not by direction. This form of planning presupposes that there is freedom of enterprises, free play of market forces of demand and supply in the economy, and freedom of consumption and production. However, there is some degree of regulation and control by the government. On the contrary, planning by direction is State-formulated and dictated planning, where the State is in full command and is the sole authority of planning. It formulates, directs, and executes the plan. The government through its plan document orders and directs the private entrepreneurs, market forces, producers, and consumers to carry out the instruction of the government in order to fulfil the planned developmental goals and objectives. This type of planning is largely perceived in the socialist economies and also in the mixed economies where State is playing a predominant role. Planning by direction is authoritarian and totalitarian in nature, where State directive is the sole guiding force and it covers the entire economy. The government gives directives to the ministries and line department functionaries and also to the enterprises carrying out the planned endeavours of the line departments and orders them to execute planned activities for achieving the targets of the national plan. The private enterprises and other stakeholders of development carry out their activities as per the direction of the government and as per the guidelines of the plan document and government order.

Physical planning and financial planning: Physical planning is an input–output exercise and takes in to consideration the size of real resources in terms of land, labour, capital, and organization required to implement the plan activities. The Second Five Year Plan of Government of India defines physical planning as, "an attempt to work out the implications of the development effort in terms of factor allocations and product yields so as to maximize incomes and employment". On the other hand, financial planning takes into account the financial dimension and it is a narrative of the amount of finances required for the implementation of plan activities in order to attainment of plan goals and objectives. Financial planning provides clues to the government for the mobilization of resources required for investment during the plan period. India's Second Five Year Plan has stated that "The essence of financial planning is to ensure that the demands and supplies are matched in a manner which exploits physical potentialities as fully as possible without major and unplanned changes in the price structure". A good development plan is a convergence of physical and financial planning, as both of them are vital to development, one without the other is unfinished.

Centralized planning and decentralized planning: The centralized plan is prepared at the centre level or by the central government and the regional and local governments are directed to carry forward and implement the designed plan as formulated by the central government. In this type of planning, regional and local governments have hardly any say in the planning process. In other words, it is not a participatory method of planning, rather an authoritarian planning process and believes in top-down approach. On the contrary, decentralized planning is the planning, where at the outset, plans are prepared at the various lower levels of governments and finally the national plan is prepared taking into consideration all the plans prepared at various lower levels. Here, in this type of planning, local aspirations are included in the national plan. Of late, Government of India has encouraged a decentralized planning process, where a plan prepared at the village level is called 'village plan', at the intermediate level is called 'block plan', at the district level is called 'district plan', and at the state level is called 'State plan'. The State plan is an aggregate of the aspirations of all plans prepared at various lower levels such as district, block, and village levels. The decentralized planning process is also variously known as participatory planning or democratic planning or bottom-up planning or integrated planning. Decentralized planning has become popular in many developing countries of the world.

Fixed plan and rolling plan: The fixed plans are prepared for a fixed time period, most of the developing nations prepare plan for a fixed period of five years called 'Five Year Plan'. While the rolling plans are those prepared at intervals usually one year and these rolling plans are mostly annual plans where planning process rolls from one year to the other. A rolling plan is flexible and allows for revision and modification. In rolling plans, review of the plan becomes a continuous exercise. The Government of India adopted rolling plans during the period 1961 to 1963 because of the 1961 war and this period is popularly known as 'plan holiday'.

Short-term, medium-term, and long-term plans: Short-term plans are prepared for a short period, usually for one year, and are therefore known as 'annual plans'. They are also known as 'controlling plans'. The medium-term plans are prepared for the period of 3 to 7 years. The Five Year Plans in vogue in most of the developing countries are the medium-term plans prepared with judicious allocation of financial and physical resources for raising per capita income, standard of living, employment, and economic growth and reducing inequalities in the country. The long-term plan usually lasts for a period of 10–30 years. These plans are known as 'perspective plans'. The origin of long-term planning goes back to USSR where GOELRO Plan 1920–35 was first formulated and implemented in 1920.[1]

Plans vertically prepared at various levels, such as at the national, provincial, and local levels are called national plan, regional plans, and local plans, respectively. The national plan is made for the entire nation being formulated by the central government where the aspirations of different regions are taken into consideration. On the other hand, regional plans are those plans which are being prepared by the provincial governments. In India, each State prepares its own development plan, taking into consideration its geography, population, and socio-economic situation. Local plans are the outcome of the decentralized planning process being followed by many countries. Local plan begins at the village level called village development plan being approved by the village panchayats in their respective gram sabhas. All the village plans are finally merged with the district plan and becomes local plan and is approved by the district development committee. If the plans prepared at the provincial and local level are integrated with the national plan, then it is known as the integrated planning and on the other hand, if these three plans are separately prepared and implemented at respective levels then it is an example of independent planning.

Finally, planning also differs from one economic system to the other, i.e. capitalism, socialism, and mixed economy. In capitalism, private enterprises play a predominant role in the development of the economy. There is no single authority governing the planning activity. In other words, capitalism does not follow the instruction of any single planning authority, as the economic activities are controlled by the private sector. On the other hand, under socialism where government is the key decision-making authority and public sector plays a dominating role in economic system, the central planning authority formulates the plan, which covers all the sectors of the economy. In the mixed economy, where both public and private sectors play an important role, planning is primarily formulated by the government, and the private sectors are advised to follow central planning in order to achieve the development goal. The developing countries, having mixed economic system, in recent years mostly followed decentralized planning process, where plans are prepared by the central, regional, sub-regional, and local self-governments for the holistic development of the nation. For developing countries having limited financial resources, proper economic planning will have far-reaching impact on development.

PRINCIPLES OF DEVELOPMENT PLANNING

The plan document should clearly spell out the vision, mission, goals, and objectives by making use of available information gathered from various levels. It should clearly delineate the sector-wise thrust areas, achievements, future strategies, and expected outcomes.

It should formulate a clear strategic framework for the holistic and balanced development of various sectors such as primary, secondary, and tertiary sectors and dimensions of development, i.e. economic, social, human, cultural, and so on.

Development planning is essentially required to be flexible and amenable to change, which will enable it to adapt to the changing situation. It should have scope for mid-term evaluation so that corrective measures during the plan period could be taken for the achievement of the targeted outcome as envisaged in the plan document.

Development plans should put emphasis on the development of the backward regions, on diverse community needs, and on sectors having strategic importance in the holistic development of the nation. A well-designed and unbiased formula for the allocation of resources to different provinces needs to be put in place. Moreover, special schemes and programmes are needed to be launched for uplifting socio-economically laggard sections of population.

Development plans need to have an in-built monitoring mechanism so that performances are continuously monitored and corrective measures are taken from time to time. A participatory monitoring mechanism, where the donors, stakeholders, and the beneficiaries are together involved in the monitoring process in the implementation of the planned development programmes is preferred. Without an in-built monitoring and evaluation mechanism, corrective measures cannot be appropriately initiated and it may lead to wastage of resources.

A development plan has to be simple, logical, and internally consistent and should provide relevant information on development indicators, tasks and activities, and targeted output and outcome. The plan document should be prepared in such a way that a proper sequencing and logical flow of information on objectives, activities, strategies, and allocation of resources for various sectors of the economy is astutely pronounced.

Development plans need to put emphasis on sustainable and inclusive development of the nation. The developmental measures to be envisaged in the plan document should be prepared keeping an eye on its impact on the environment and human health. Besides, it must lay emphasis on the social sustainability aspects, such as population growth, infant and maternal mortality, literacy and level of education, governance, etc. The provision for all the sectors and allocation of special funds for the backward areas and socio-economically backward sections of population needs to be given adequate weightage in the plan document.

Development plans are required to be based on the principle of decentralized planning and must be participatory in nature. Decentralized planning is an appropriate method of democratic planning where planning process starts from the bottom and is amalgamated at the top so that administrative and political representatives of all levels and people at large participate in the planning process. It is also known as peoples' planning. decentralization through the involvement of local-level representative institutions in the formulation as well as implementation of plans for development is being advocated in the interest of efficient utilization of resources for ensuring more equitable sharing of benefits of development (Rao, 1989).

The development plan needs to be formulated on rigorous need-analysis exercise and follow suitable model of development. A proper and effective participatory need assessment is the cornerstone of a good development plan. Plans must be prepared based on grass-roots realities. Development plans prepared without a need assessment with the full participation of the people cannot be successful in fulfilling the aspirations of the people.

DEVELOPMENT PLAN FORMULATION

Preparation of a medium-term and long-term plan document is a tedious process and calls for a systematic course of groundwork much before the preparation of the plan document for implementation.

The main aspects to be taken into consideration in plan preparation are:

(i) Need assessment and identification of the problems
(ii) Formulation of vision, mission, goals, and objectives
(iii) Fixing targets to be achieved and prioritizing activities and programmes to be launched in each sector of the economy
(iv) Mobilization of financial and other resources required for the execution of the plan
(v) Creation of the necessary organization or agency for the execution of the plan
(vi) Formulation of strategies for plan implementation
(vii) Plan implementation as per formulated strategies
(viii) Putting monitoring and evaluation mechanisms in place
(ix) Mid-term assessment of the progress
(x) Injecting correction on the basis of findings of the mid-term assessment and end-term evaluation after the end of the plan period
(xi) Dissemination of the achievement during the plan period and gaps location
(xii) Preparing the groundwork for the next plan based on the identified gap or needs

Proper plan preparation calls for rigorous exercise on the part of the government and any cursory attempt will lead to the wastage of resources and may not enable the nation to achieve the desired goals and objectives. Because of procrastination in plan preparation, sometimes the initiation of subsequent plan period gets delayed by a couple of years. Broadly, the steps being followed in development planning are:

(i) Step I: At the outset, the team being assigned the preparation of development plan has to identify the key developmental issues and problems relating to various sectors of development. If it is a decentralized planning process, all effort has to be initiated to collect information and data on problems and issues prevailing at the grass-roots level, i.e. at the village level through 'village need assessment'. This can be done by conducting systematic need assessment surveys at the grass-roots level with the help of local self-government institutions and other CBOs operating at the grass-roots level. Sector-wise committees and sub-committees and task forces have to be constituted which will provide help to the planners from the beginning till the finalization of the plan document preparation.

(ii) Step II: Prioritization of these problems and issues through the analysis of potentials, opportunities, constraints, and challenges (POCC). This will help to concretize or synthesize and help the planners to properly draw out the vision, mission, goals, and objectives of the plan.

(iii) Step III: Here, the plan document needs to formulate the vision, mission, goals, and objectives of the development plan. The planners have to be realistic while jotting down vision, mission, goals, and objectives of the plan.

(iv) Step IV: After that the planning group and the sub-groups have to formulate sector-wise goals and objectives, strategies, sectoral development programmes, programme of action (POA), verifiable indicators, physical targets, and financial allocations. If it is a medium-term or a five-year plan, then sectoral annual action plan with physical targets and financial provisions have to be stated.

(v) Step V: This step is the plan integration (if any). If a nation is following decentralized planning, then integration of plans prepared at regional, sub-regional, and local levels with the national plan is essential in order to prepare a composite plan, which takes into account the problems and issues existing at various levels, for promoting balanced development. Besides this vertical integration, the horizontal integration of various sectoral plans is also critical to development planning. However, during the process of integration, meticulous attention is called for so that replication and overlapping are avoided to the maximum extent.

(vi) Step VI: In this step customarily may be the formulation of monitoring and evaluation mechanism so that plan performances are monitored from time to time and corrective measures are taken. At the end of each plan and before the initiation of new plan, sectoral evaluation takes place and gaps are identified which become interventional points for the new plan. However, doing a mid-term evaluation is prudent so that necessary corrective actions are taken to achieve the planned goals and objectives during the plan period.

(vii) Step VII: The next step is the preparation of draft plan document by the planning team and putting it before the plan approving authority. In case of India, it is placed before the National Development Council for discussion and valuable comments and suggestions.

(viii) Step VIII: The comments and suggestions gathered during the plan presentation before the apex body (for example, earlier National Development Council in India) are incorporated and handy final plan document came into force.

DECENTRALIZED DEVELOPMENT PLANNING: INDIAN EXPERIENCES

Decentralization of planning process, of late, has become a matter of worldwide concern, whether in socialist or in mixed economies (Rao, 1989). Decentralized planning process customarily adopts multi-level planning procedures and adopts suitable micro–macro linkages and convergence mechanism to integrate the local level plan into the district, state, and national plan.

Some of the merits of decentralized development planning are:

(i) It will effectively accommodate people's felt needs.
(ii) It is democratic in nature, as under decentralized planning, development plans are prepared at different levels and are integrated at the centre.
(iii) It can bridge the gap between people and bureaucracy and thereby government is brought closer to the people.
(iv) It helps mobilization of local resources and can check corruption at grass-roots level.
(v) It involves people at various stages of development, i.e. plan formulation, implementation, monitoring, and evaluation and thereby can promote better utilization of resources and restrict wastages.
(vi) Sustainable development can be better achieved through community participation rather than government working in silos; therefore, decentralized planning can ensure effective community participation for sustainable development.
(vii) Through decentralized planning and involvement of people, people feel empowered and consider themselves as partners of development with the government rather than passive beneficiaries of development.
(viii) Decentralized planning can synchronize regional disparities better than centralized planning can.

A few important objectives of decentralized planning are to promote economic and social development, reduce regional imbalance, promote social justice and human well-being, protect environment and natural resources, and energize community participation and people's involvement in development. Besides, other important objectives of decentralized development planning are to curtail red-tapism, check corruption, and strengthen local governance. Decentralized development planning is largely based on the principles of autonomy; devolution functions, functionaries, and funds; functional clarity at different levels of administration and governance; and public participation and principle of effective integration. However, the law of subsidiarity, accountability, bridging the regional disparities, and capacity building of local self-governance institution in effective plan formulation, implementation, and impact assessment are critical to the success of decentralized planning.

The Government of India has followed the decentralized planning process while preparing 'District Development Plans' for various districts of India. Although it was triggered off with the preparation of District Backward Region Grant Fund called BRGF Plan, yet the other types of district development plans prepared through the decentralization strategy in India are: (a) Comprehensive District Agriculture Plan popularly called C-DAP and (b) District Mahatma Gandhi National Rural Employment Guarantee Act Plan, known as MGNREGA Plan. Besides, the decentralized planning process has been used in the preparation of various sectoral development plans known as District Education Plan for education development and District Health Plan for health development.

The decentralized planning process follows the bottom-up approach. At the outset, village plans for all the villages of the district are prepared with the help of village panchayats. Many state governments have taken the help of NGOs to help village panchayats in the preparation of village plans, and all the village plans of a village panchayat are integrated with the village panchayat plan (if the village panchayat consists of more than one village). The village assembly (the gram sabha) is the statutory body to approve the village plan. Later on, all the village panchayat plans are integrated with the block panchayat plan (the block is the administrative set-up between district and village and the block plan is also known as the intermediate panchayat plan) and an integrated block plan is formulated and approved by the block development committee (the assembly at block level). Finally, all the block plans are integrated at the district level with the district plan. In addition to these rural area plans prepared by the PRIs at various levels, the plans of the ULBs such as those of nagar panchayats, municipal council, and municipal corporation are also being prepared by these bodies and finally all these rural areas plans and urban areas plans are integrated or subsumed in the district plan. In the end, the draft district plan document is prepared and placed before the District Planning Committee, a statutory body for approval. The comments and suggestions of the DPC are being incorporated and then final district plan document is prepared. All these district plans are send to the State Planning Board for inclusion in the state plan. Finally, an integrated State Development Plan is prepared and approved by the State Planning Board. The aspirations of all these state plans were taken into consideration while preparing the national Five-Year Plan. A structure of decentralized planning is given in Figure 10.1

Decentralized planning process is a bottom-up approach, where the planning process is triggered off at the village level and is finally integrated at the national level after successfully being integrated at the block, district, and state levels. Although it is the most tedious and time-consuming process of developmental planning, yet it is a participatory

Figure 10.1 *Structure of Decentralized Planning*

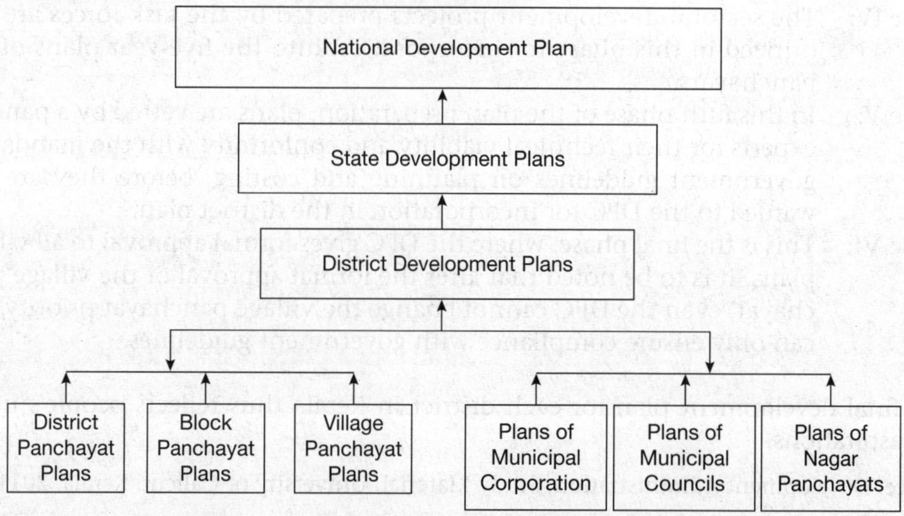

The *bottom-up* approach to decentralized planning in India

People's Planning Campaign—Kerala Model of Decentralized Planning

In Kerala, the 'decentralized planning' at the grass-roots level adopts the following phases for plan preparation.

Phase I: In this phase, gram sabha (village assembly) is convened to identify local development priorities. To ensure popular participation, a volunteer squad visits household to household and explains them the importance of participation in the gram sabha. The gram sabha is the key to the identification of local development aspirations and needs, collection of information on natural resources, and problem identification.

Phase II: During the second phase, 'Local Development Seminars' are being organized to suggest actions to address the identified development priorities identified by the gram sabhas. These seminars are being organized with the help of a group of trained local resource persons, elected PRI representatives, and government officials. This phase produces an extensive local database, a comprehensive survey of the development status of the panchayat, and a list of likely solutions to development problems. In this phase, 'task forces' on various sectors of development are set up to prepare development projects for each development sector.

Phase III: In the third phase, the sector-wise task force prepares projects based on suggestions emerging from the development seminars. All the development sectors have a task force of 10–15 members each and are chaired by an elected representative of village panchayat with an officer from the relevant line department being the convener.

Phase IV: The sectoral development projects prepared by the task forces are prioritized in this phase for incorporation into the five-year plans of the panchayats.

Phase V: In this fifth phase of the plan preparation, plans are vetted by a panel of experts for their technical viability and conformity with the mandatory government guidelines on planning and costing, before they are forwarded to the DPC for incorporation in the district plan.

Phase VI: This is the final phase, where the DPC gives formal approval to all village plans. It is to be noted that after the formal approval of the village panchayat, even the DPC cannot change the village panchayat priority, but can only ensure compliance with government guidelines.

The final development plan for each district in Kerala thus reflects people's needs and aspirations.

Source: Development Administration, Study Material, University of Calicut, Kerala, 2011.

and democratic way of preparing a development plan, where the aspirations of the grassroots democratic institutions, their elected representatives, and of the people are taken into consideration. In the developing countries, having lot of regional and local variations in terms of socio-economic development, decentralization is the most suitable approach to development planning.

The Sum Up

Development planning is an important pillar of development in the developing countries having socialistic and mixed economic system, and is found to be in vogue in these economies. It gives a future direction to the nation regarding the thrust areas and allocation of resources to these areas for materializing balanced sectoral and regional development, improving quality of life of the people, ensuring economic and social justice, and attaining higher economic growth rate. Planning is sine qua non for developing countries with limited resources, large population, vast underdeveloped areas, and many underperforming sectors. However, the success of planning in producing desirable results depends heavily on the economic, political, institutional, and cultural contexts and also on the system of governance in a particular country.

Keywords centralized planning, decentralized planning, rolling plan, strategic plan, planning by inducement, planning by direction, village plan, district plan.

REVIEW QUESTIONS

1. What is development planning and how can development planning be helpful to promote development of the underdeveloped countries?
2. Distinguish between planning by direction and planning by inducement. Which system is suitable for the developing countries and why?
3. What is strategic planning? To what extent is strategic planning useful for developed and developing countries?
4. Explain the role and principles of development planning.
5. What is decentralized planning? Explain various steps in the preparation of decentralized planning giving a suitable example.
6. What is integrated planning? How is it useful for the developing country's development?
7. Write short notes on the following:
   (i) Planning by direction
   (ii) Decentralized planning
   (iii) Strategic planning
   (iv) Bottom-up planning
   (v) Rolling plan

NOTE

1. Quoted from the "Types of Economic Planning." Available at: http://www.oocities.org/znuniverse/Economics_of_Planning/types_of_economic_planning.htm (accessed on 17 February 2016).

REFERENCES

Cole, G.A. 1993. *Management: Theory and Practice*, Fourth edition. London: DP Publications.

Dewett, K.K. 1978. *Modern Economic Theory Micro and Macro Analysis*. New Delhi: Shyam Lal Charitable Trust.

Dickinson, H.D. 1939. *Economics of Socialism*. London: Oxford University Press.

Galbraith, John K. 1962. *Economic Development in Perspective*. Cambridge: Harvard University Press.

Government of Ireland. 2007. *Development Plan, Guidelines for Planning Authority*, Government of Ireland.

Hanumantha Rao, C.H. 1989. "Decentralized Planning: An Overview of Experience and Prospects." *Economic and Political Weekly*, 24(8): 441–16.

Ivancevich, I.I., Lorenzi, R., Skinner, S., and Crosby, P.B. 1994. *Management*. New York: Free Press.

Jhingan, M.L. 2005. *The Economics of Development Planning*. New Delhi: Vindra Publication.

Lewis, W.A. 1951. *The Principles of Economic Planning*. London: Dennis Dobson Ltd.

Marcellus, I.O. 2009. "Development Planning in Nigeria: Reflections on the National Economic Empowerment and Development Strategy (NEEDS) 2003–2007." *Journal of Social Science*, 20(3): 197–210.

Sapru, R.K. 1994. *Development Administration*. New Delhi: Sterling Publisher.

Shakya, R.K. 2007. "Formulation of Development Plans: Planning Techniques." *Administration and Management Review*, 19(2), August, 9–17.

Singh, Bright D. 1966. *Economics of Development with Special Reference to India*. New Delhi: Asia Publishing House.

Thahane, T.T. 1974. "Planning for Development." In *Accelerated Development in Southern Africa*, edited by John Barratt, Simon Brand, David S. Collier, and Kurt Glaser. London: Macmillan, 451.

United Nations. 1974. *Proceedings of the Interregional Seminar on Organization and Administration of Development Planning Agencies*. New York: United Nations.

———. 1975a. *Development Administration: Current Approaches and Trends in Public Administration for National Development*, 189. New York: United Nations.

———. 1975b. *Development Administration Current Approaches and Trends in Public Administration for National Development*, 63. New York: United Nations.

Waterston, A. 1971. *Development Planning: Lessons of Experience*. Baltimore, MD: John Hopkins University Press.

11 Development Management

Development management is a very widely used term in recent development literature.

— Saifullah (2001)

Replacement of administration with management as signifying a stronger emphasis on strategy and proactive style, as opposed to the tasks and tools of routine administration.

— Brinkerhoff and Coston (1999, quoted in Saifullah 2001)

Development management is one of the emerging areas of development in the developing countries as these countries are relentlessly trying to accelerate their pace of development in order to provide better quality of life to its people with the judicious utilization of their scarce resources. The emergence of globalization has enhanced the utility and scope of development management in development process at least in the developing countries. The flow of funds from the developed countries as well as from the bilateral and multilateral organizations in the form of foreign aids and FDI to the developing countries has called for the effective utilization of these with the proper management of development projects and programmes. Moreover, launching of sundry programmes by the government of the developing countries in the area of poverty alleviation, employment generation, education, health, housing, sanitation, drinking water, and development of rural and urban areas has enhanced the role of development management in the developing countries. Besides, development management is also useful to many, i.e. NGO managers, managers of corporate sectors engaged in corporate social responsibilities, and the CSOs involved in the development activities conducted by various sectors of development. Brinkerhoff and Coston (1999) were of the view that the term development management has widened its scope and is no longer restricted to the public sector; development manager can be NGO staffer, members of the community groups, business people, as well as civil servants. Clarke (1996) argued that the term development management includes much of the elements in development administration, is necessarily a broader term, which can include areas of activity that would not come under the heading of development administration. As development is a multidimensional concept having many actors and sectors, development management becomes indispensable for 'development' at least in developing countries. Managing development means focusing on concrete impacts at all phases of the national development process. Harold Koontz has rightly pointed out that "Management is the art of getting things done through and with people in formally organized groups".[1] and to Marry Parker Fallett, "management is the art of getting things done through people."[2] The management development approach embodies generally accepted tents of good governance-setting clear objectives, evidence-based decision-making, transparency, and continuous adoption and improvement.[3]

After reading this chapter, you will be able to:

(i) Define development management and tell why there is a need for development management in development.
(ii) Describe the role and functions of development management.
(iii) Explain the system approach to development project management.
(iv) Discuss critical issues in development project management.

WHAT IS DEVELOPMENT MANAGEMENT?

Development management is not only a question of getting the task done effectively and efficiently by the best available means; however, it also means building the capacity at all levels on how to get the developmental activities done and handle developmental issues and challenges through the formulation of alternative approaches and strategies. Brinkerhoff and Coston (1999) emphasized on four related aspects of development management, i.e. (a) development management is a means of improving efficiency and effectiveness of foreign assistance programmes and furthering international agency's policy agenda; (b) development management is toolkit; it promotes the application of a range of management and analytical tools adapted from a variety of social sciences disciplines, including strategic management, organizational development, psychology, and political science; (c) development management incorporated a value dimension that emphasized self-determination, empowerment and an equitable distribution of development benefits; and (d) development management is a process intervention, where the application of tools in pursuit of objectives is undertaken in ways that self-consciously address political and value issues. According to Seers (1979):

> Development management means managing as far as possible, in such a way, as to enhance potential of those working with directly and development organizations that carry similar values, even if this is not the most straightforward way of getting a particular job done. In the view of Solaiman and Quadir (1998), development management means evaluating change from the present situation into a better situation and it is a process of improving, building, and innovating in order to ensure better quality of life for the present human being without jeopardizing those of the future.

Brinkerhoff and Ingle (1989) defined development management as that branch of public administration that deals with the promotion of socio-economic process in the developing world. The development management is a process of carrying out the development in a systematic way taking into consideration the past, present, and future actions, needs and priorities while formulating, implementing, monitoring, and evaluating developmental activities, projects, and programmes for achieving set developmental goals. In a holistic sense, it refers to effective management of money, manpower, and materials deployed in performing development activities, projects, and programmes in an efficient, effective, systematic, and sustainable way. Allan Thomas (1999) has critically discussed development management in the following manner.

(i) Development management includes:

  (a) First, the management of the specific tasks involved in development interventions called 'management of development'.

  (b) Second, the normative idea of management oriented towards development ideals called 'management for development'.

  (c) Lastly, the more straightforward notion of management in a development context known as 'management in development'.

(ii) According to Thomas, development management is not just a question of getting the task at hand completed by the best means available, it also means simultaneously building the capacity to undertake future tasks and learning how to be able to cope with what at present are unspecified task.

(iii) Management for development implies a style of management in which any and every activity is undertaken in such a way as to enhance development.

The development management aims at effective and efficient management of development activities, projects, and programmes for the achievement of set goals and objectives of development. Some of the characteristics of development management are:

(i) It is a managerial process adopted for the systematic conduction of development projects and programmes.

(ii) Development management intends to achieve results through the involvement of donors, stakeholders, and beneficiaries.

(iii) It is action oriented and pragmatic, and it enables the development manager to effectively achieve the development objectives set forth in the DPR (detailed project report).

(iv) Development management aims at tackling economic, social, cultural, human and political development issues and challenges by applying management principles and practices.

(v) It aims at achieving the developmental project and programme goal and objectives through inter- and intra-sectoral coordination and community participation.

(vi) It aims at applying innovative methods, models, approaches, and strategies for the effective implementation of development projects.

(vii) Development management helps in the appraisal of development project, their monitoring, evaluation, and impact assessment.

(viii) It applies systematic cyclical approach for the effective management of development issues and challenges.

FUNCTIONS OF DEVELOPMENT MANAGEMENT

The development management helps the development administrators and managers of development projects and programmes in the process of the smooth implementation of various development projects and programmes in different sectors of the economy. It intends to apply system approach in the management of development programmes and projects, as a well-formulated project with proper need assessment not only offers good result but also helps in judicious use of resources and curtails wasteful expenditure. Whatever sufficient be the amount of input in terms of physical, financial, and human resources, the output and outcome will not be optimum if these are not effectively and efficiently processed and managed. Further, the development management in general and participatory development management in particular lead to empowerment of the people to manage their development activities either by themselves or with the help of grass-roots level institutions and other stakeholders engaged in either the formulation stages of the development process or in the implementation of development projects and programmes. Development management enables the stakeholders and beneficiaries to share and shoulder the responsibility of formulation, implementation, and monitoring of development projects and programmes, while the participatory development management process empowers the stakeholders and beneficiaries to collectively shoulder the responsibility along with the development managers. According to Chawla and Kelloway (2004), participatory management predicts productivity and organizational change. The participatory management is recommended to prevent low workers' morale, poor-job-related productivity, and high voluntary turnover (Lee et al., 2009).

Development management enables the managers of development projects and programmes to properly formulate, allocate, and judiciously spend the allocated budget on different heads. Proper way of incurring expenditure on the administrative head and on-service delivery activities in development action projects is an arduous task before the development managers and it is in general observed that in most of the development projects, the payment of salaries to the project staffs consumes gigantic share of expenses, while a little is left for service delivery. This is a serious lacuna as it hampers grass-roots development. Development management helps the development managers to make projects and programmes cost effective and produce maximum output with the use of minimum resources.

One of the key functions of development management is to enable an individual or an organization to effectively manage its projects and programmes so that it earns maximum output and outcome with the use of minimum possible resources and produces desirable impact on the development indicators as envisaged in the projects and programmes. The United Nations Administration programme while emphasizing on development management also advocated that the implementation of MDGs requires the overall governance environment, especially those elements that contribute more directly to the planning, budgeting, implementation, and monitoring of public services, require adjusting, repositioning in a way that goes beyond the realm of public administration, and become more citizen based and engaging.[4] To Guide (2004), the work of the project is managed by planning, executing, monitoring, and controlling processes. Effective project management involves repeated performance of these processes (Jafari et al., 2011). The development managers of various development projects and programmes need to apply APOSDCCRBCD: 'A' for appraisal, 'P' for planning; 'O' for organizing; 'S' for staffing; 'D' for directing; 'C' for coordinating, 'C' for controlling; 'R' for reporting and 'B' for budgeting; 'C' for capacity building and finally 'D' for disseminating. All these mechanisms have to be meticulously taken care of in the process implementation of development projects and programmes for the achievement of developmental goals and objectives. According to G.R. Terry, "Management is a distinct process consisting of planning, organizing, activating and controlling to determine and accomplish the objectives by the use of people and resources".

(i) Appraisal: At the outset after the formulation of the project proposal and before going for planning and implementation, a thorough appraisal study on all aspects such as technical, institutional, organizational, managerial, social, environmental, economic, and sustainable has to be done. It will help the organization to assess whether it is viable, appropriate, and logical to go ahead with the project which would incur a huge amount of investment. The technical aspects consider the technical feasibility of the project from input supply side and output delivery side. The institutional aspects take into consideration the administrative step and involvement of other institutions in project input supply and output delivery such as government, corporate sector, financial institutions, NGOs, etc. while the organizational aspects assess the strength and capability of the organization to undertake the project. The social impact assessment is a big issue which takes into consideration the social pattern, customs, traditions, culture, and livelihood to be affected by the project, and the environmental aspects study the impact of the project on the environment. The economic aspect deals with what will be the impact of the project on income, standard of living, employment, land asset, etc. and the sustainable aspect takes into consideration the issue as to how the project effort will sustain after the project interventions is withdrawn from the project areas. Some of the project appraisal techniques used are: accounting rate of return (ARR), net present value (NPV), internal rate of return (IRR), and benefit cost ration (BCR).

(ii) Planning: After a conscious decision is taken for launching the project, the development manager has to do a meticulous planning of the development project implementation. During the process of planning, all the required steps, i.e. need assessment, goals, and objective settings; outcome and activity mapping; implementation strategy; monitoring and evaluation mechanism; and impact assessment must be rigorously exercised and put in place. Customarily, three types of planning mechanism, i.e. short term, medium term, and long term, are widely practiced keeping in view the need and urgency of the programme; depth of the developmental problem; society's level of education and awareness of the issues; and availability of resources at the centre and state level to achieve the development goals. Planning must be realistic and should be prepared by applying participatory method, with the help of all stakeholders and beneficiaries. A realistic planning is the one which achieves the planned objectives within the planned allocated budget and during the plan period. Rao (1992) had stated that "Planning is essential for macro-economic management, for taking care of the poor and the downtrodden who are mostly outside the market system and have little asset endowment".

(iii) Organizing: Effectively organizing the activities of planned development projects is of critical and immense importance for not only the successful implementation of these activities but also the achievement of development goals and objectives. Development managers during the process of organizing various activities have to ask the following important questions to themselves: who will do what, what will be done when, where it will be done, how it will be done, by whom it will be done, and so on. These are some of the important organizational questions that development managers have to seriously look into during the organizational process of the project or the programme. Most of the development plans failed due to poor organization, blame game, and shifting and transfer of responsibility from one person to another, which takes place because of poor organizing capability of the development manager.

(iv) Staffing: Human resources are fundamental to success of any project or programme. It is customarily observed, other things remaining constant, given the same amount of resources, one organization achieves better results compared to the other, and this may be fundamentally due to differences in manpower knowledge, skill, attitude, and practices. Therefore, manpower recruitment or staffing is a crucial function of development management and one of the important determinants of success and failure of development project or programme. Putting right man in the right job is a Herculean task before the development manager. Well-qualified, experienced, and accountable employees are not only assets to an organization, but also vital ingredients to properly understand developmental issues and challenges, formulate appropriate development projects, effectively implement them, and successfully achieve development goal. Recruitment of right person for right job is a challenge particularly for public sector organizations reeling under maladies of nepotism and corruption. Besides, over-staffing will lead to financial burden and understaffing may hamper project and programme implementation activities. Therefore, appropriate staffing as per the need is a challenge and depends on the ingenuity of the development manager.

(v) Directing: The manager of development projects and programmes usually appoints many programme or project directors as per the requirement of the projects and programmes who lead their team with identified objectives, tasks, and development targets. Leading the team in right direction is fundamental to the achievement of set development targets and goals. It can be remarked that direction-less development manager might end up in non-linear achievement, while direction-bound development managers may be able to achieve curve linear outcome. Division of work and placing right man in right job and building their capacities and motivating them to put their 100 per cent endeavour to achieve development goal is one of the vital components of directing.

(vi) Coordinating: Proper coordination among different divisions of development organization and also among different project or programme directors and their members in the team is crucial for effective implementation of development programme or project. Lack of coordination will lead to confusion, controversy, and distractions, which will ultimately lead to the failure of the development projects and programmes to achieve their set goals. By coordinating, it means harmonizing working relationships and unifying individual endeavours for the accomplishments of development goals. According to Waldron, Vasanthakumar, and Arulraj,[5] coordination needs a professional, competent leadership, a democratic style that leads to trust, open communication, and ease of information flow.

(vii) Controlling: Control over the functions, functionaries, and funds is essential for the successful implementation of the development projects and programmes. By controlling, it means tapping the progress and taking corrective measures from time to time. In other words, controlling means keeping an eye on the input, process, output, and outcome of the project or programme and taking corrective measures in case of any deviation from the design. According to Reeves and Woodward (1970), "Controlling refers to the task of ensuring that activities are producing the desired results. Control in this case is limited to monitoring the outcome of activities, reviewing feedback information about this outcome and if necessary, taking corrective actions". To Terry and Franklin (1982), "Controlling is determining what is being accomplished, that is, evaluating performance and if necessary, applying corrective measures so that performance takes place according to plans". Lack of control may create anarchy which may ultimately lead to poor outcome.

(viii) Budgeting: Budgeting is the financial representation of development goals and objectives. The planning of any development activities is meaningless without budgeting or allocation of resources to various planned tasks and activities. According to Waldron, Vasanthakumar, and Arulraj budgeting means making financial plans, maintaining accounting and management control of revenue, and keeping cost in line with objectives. Appropriateness and accuracy in financial estimation for various tasks and activities of the project and programme to achieve the set goals and objectives terms as budgeting, which reflects the financial management skill of the development manager. Judicious allocation of budget on various components of the projects depends on ingenuity of the development manager and over-budgeting may lead to the rejection of the project proposal, while under-budgeting will result in financial deficit to perform the formulated activities, which may invite a lot of criticisms. Therefore, participatory budgeting is largely recommended for the preparation of a realistic budget for the developmental projects.

(ix) Capacity building: One of the important functions of the development management is the capacity building of the project personnel including the stakeholders as well as the beneficiaries at all levels. Development is multidimensional and is the most dynamic concept, and is largely preferred for the successful implementation of development project and programme a multidisciplinary team. As they are from different fields, there capacity building on development mission, vision, goal, objectives, activities, etc. is essential in order to enable them to effectively involve in the various phases of the projects such as during project formulation, implementation, monitoring, evaluation, and impact assessment. Without capacity building, the personnel engaged in the developmental project or programme for performing various tasks may not be effective enough to produce desired output. Capacity building will enable them to do their job effectively and efficiently.

(x) Reporting: The end result of any project or programme is reporting, which is said as, "All is well that ends well". The development manager has to generate monitoring reports on the monthly, quarterly, and annual basis as per the requirement of the project. The various evaluation report, i.e. the mid-term and end-term reports and also the impact assessment reports, the successful case studies, etc. are prepared by the project team under the leadership of the development manager and submitted to the funding agencies. It requires a lot of articulation on the part of the development manager to generate data and information from the development projects and programmes, analyze it and put it in the form of a report. Reports can be represented in graphical or tabular form and in a proper format. Reporting serves the function of highlighting performance (both in qualitative and quantitative terms) against the set goals and objectives and is just like systematically serving the food on a dining table. The development manager must be apt in report writing and well versed in both qualitative and quantitative data analysis technique.

(xi) Disseminating: The result of the project and programme evaluation and impact assessment has to be disseminated by publishing it in the newspaper and journals in the form of articles and research papers so that other stakeholders, researchers, government and other agencies, and civil society, at large, are informed and educated about the project and programme and its impact. It also unfolds the scope of further replication. All the aspects including input, process, output, and outcome are needed to be properly disseminated. A complete detail helps other stakeholders as well as beneficiaries and development managers to interface with the larger audience directly and indirectly interested in knowing about the strength, weakness, opportunities, and threat issues of project and programme. Some of the essential aspects usually covered in dissemination are: (a) goal and objectives; (b) target audiences, activities, and strategies of implementation; (c) stakeholder roles; (d) time management; (e) resource management; (f) training and technical assistance; (g) community participation and intersectoral coordination mechanism adopted; (h) monitoring and evaluation mechanism; (i) impact on the end users or the beneficiaries; and (j) problems encountered in different stages of project implementation; and (k) future scope and plan, if any.

SYSTEM APPROACH TO DEVELOPMENT PROJECT MANAGEMENT

Management of development projects and programmes is the most complex affair, as many actors are involved in the formulation, implementation, monitoring, and evaluation of development projects and programmes. Because of poor management, many developmental projects fail to achieve its targeted goals and objectives, and incur huge loss of resources. Therefore, there is a need on the part of the development manager to apply system approach technique for the effective management of development projects and programmes, and this system approach is popularly known as 'development management cycle or development project management cycle'. The system approach to development management begins with the problem analysis and ends with the follow-up action on development projects. The various steps in systematic management of a project are narrated as follows.

Problem Analysis, Gap Identification, and Goal Setting: At the outset, development goals are formulated after the conduction of development need assessment study, taking into consideration the findings of NAR (need assessment report). Development need is the difference between what is the current development performance and what it should really have been. In other words, it is the gap between performances in different indicators in various areas of development as against the targeted national and state goal. This gap is the development problems or the issues and challenges of development. Development situation analysis and problem analysis are the two key tasks before the manager of the developmental projects for the careful and accurate goal setting and objectives formulation.

Situation Analysis: Understanding the situation or the ground realities is the beginning of designing any development project or programme. Ordinarily, situation analysis means studying what is happening, and if it is not happening as per the expectation, then why it is happening, what the problem is, and what interventions are required for improving the situation. According to McCoy and Bamford (1998), the aim of the situation analysis is to describe an analysis of the situation, to explain what is happening and to identify factors which are facilitating or preventing progress. The situation analysis on development may comprise the analysis of facts and situations pertaining to different dimensions of development such as economic, social, human, cultural, political, and environmental within which the populations live. Some of the development indicators to be used for the data collection during the situation analysis of a development project relating to the 'quality of life of the population of an area' are: composition of population, housing, sanitation, health, employment, drinking water, education, agricultural holding, industry, services, etc. An example of the context and type of information required for the situation analysis is given in Table 11.1.

Problem Analysis: The second step in effective need identification is problem analysis. For understanding a situation to be influenced by a project, it is essential to know the problems and factors responsible for these problems. Problem analysis is of prime importance to developmental project planning as it strongly influences the formulation of strategies for the possible developmental interventions. In fact, the problem identification is a deductive process. It is an analysis relating to the state of affairs, facts, or figures that cause difficulties and sufferings. The problem analysis not only investigates as what is wrong, but it also tries to understand 'why' and 'how' it is wrong in order to assign priority to the problem. The problem tree method is a popular way to conduct problem analysis. According to Food and Agriculture Organization (FAO), the problem tree is a visual problem-analysis tool that can be effectively used by both the field development staff and the community to specify and investigate the causes and effects of a problem and to highlight the relationship between them.[6] The problem tree analysis helps to find out solutions by mapping out the anatomy of cause and effect around an issue.[7]

The problem tree is given in Figure 11.1, where the roots of the tree refer to the causes of the problem; the middle part of the tree or the tree trunk is the main problem, and the tree branches on the upper side of the tree refer to the effects of the main problem.

Formulation of Development Objectives: The second step in system approach to development project management is setting of objectives. Development objectives are drawn out

Table 11.1 *Information for Situation Analysis*

Context	**Type of Information**
Socio-demographic indicators	• Population composition and distribution • Household and family types • Education status • Health services and health profile of the population • Housing conditions • Sanitation and drinking water • Access to communication/energy • Access to basic amenities • Mortality • Morbidity pattern • Dependency ratio
Economic indicators	• Income • Employment/workforce participation • Wages • Expenditure • Debt situation • Standard of living/poverty • Economic inequality • Income from land property • Income from livestock • Land holding pattern • Income from plant and plantation • Irrigation pattern • Role of small-scale and cottage industry • People in hunger • Unemployment status
Socio-cultural and political dynamics	• Political structure • Political participation • Functioning of grassroots level political organization • Role of disadvantaged in grassroots political institutions • Predominant social structure • Gender role in the household • Decision-making pattern • Condition of marginalized • Prevailing social and cultural norms and believes and values • Role of CSO and opinion leaders • Social networking • Role of cultural economy

of the developmental goal. For example, if the development goal is eradication of poverty, the development objectives are: (a) ensuring population with basic needs such as food, clothing, and shelter; (b) providing means of livelihood; and (c) enhancing employment opportunities. Development objectives are the statement of desired end product to be achieved through the effective implementation of development project. These statements

Figure 11.1 *Problem Tree*

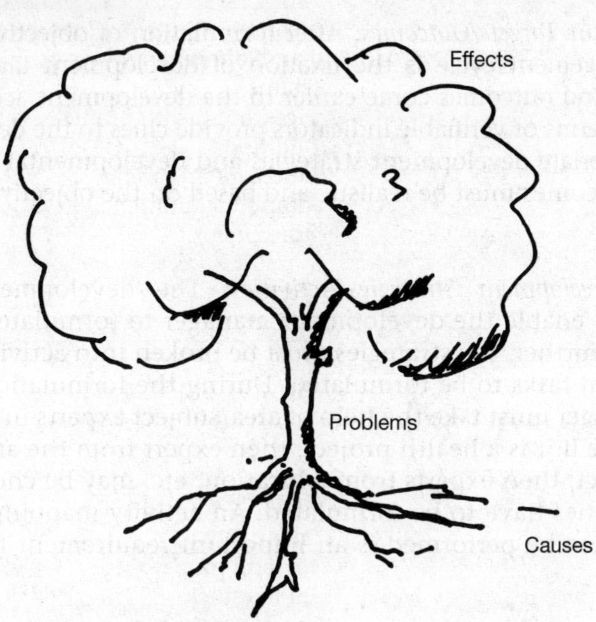

Steps in Problem Analysis

- Describe the identified key problems and their causes and effects.
- Delineate how these problems affect the target group.
- Discuss how addressing the causes will lead to eradication of these problems.
- The description should be clear, specific, and prescriptive.
- For each specific selected problem, develop a problem tree having the description on the causes, problems, and effects.

in development objectives are needed to be clearly spelled out. The development objectives as far as possible should be 'SMART' and must not be too complex or too ambitious. SMART is:

- S–Simple: The statement must be very simple to understand which can also be implementable.
- M–Measurable: It can be measurable in quantitative or qualitative terms.
- A–Attainable: The objectives must be attainable so that at the end of the implementation of activities or projects or programmes, the outcome is visible.
- R–Realistic: The objectives should be realistic which can be put into operation without much difficulty.

- T–Time-bound: The formulated objectives should be such that it can be achieved within the set time period of the development projects or programmes.

Fixing up Development Targets/Outcomes: After formulation of objectives, the next step in development management cycle is the fixation of development targets and outcomes. Fixation of targets and outcomes come earlier to the development activities, because outcomes specified in terms of verifiable indicators provide clues to the development manager to formulate appropriate development strategies and developmental tasks and activities. The targets and outcomes must be realistic and based on the objectives of the projects or programmes.

Formulation of Development Strategies/Activities: The development objectives and expected outcomes enable the development manager to formulate suitable objective-specific strategies. Further, the strategies must be broken into activities and to perform each activity several tasks to be formulated. During the formulation of strategies, the development manager must take the help of area/subject experts in the specified development areas per se if it is a health project, then expert from the area of health; if it is an education project, then experts from education, etc. may be chosen and with their help suitable activities have to be formulated. An activity mapping, with a detail jotting down of tasks to be performed is an important requirement for effective project management.

Allocation of Resources: Judicious allocation of resources on various heads, i.e. salary of hiring personnel, delivery of services, TA/DA, and so on are critical to effective implementation of development project. It is observed that a gigantic share of development fund goes to the administrative side that is for payment to the project staffs and meagre is left for programme activities by the governmental, non-governmental, and private agencies implementing various developmental projects and programmes. This type of imbalance in allocation of resources on various heads will have adverse impact on project output and outcome. One of the important roles of the development manager is to see that resources are allocated properly on various components of projects keeping in view the type of the project, their thrust and priorities, and intended development outcome from the project. Moreover, the community contribution must be resorted to wherever necessary so that the project activities become participatory and sustainable.

Implementation of Development Plan and Activities: The art of preparation and implementation of development plan and activities is a challenge before the implementing agencies. The activity plan with 'gnatt chart' along with activity mapping is needed to be prepared. This should clearly delineate the month-wise activities to be performed with detailed predetermined timeline. It helps the donor agencies as well as implementing agencies to monitor the activities against the set targets and timeline. During the process of implementation, the development manager has to use the controlling and coordinating mechanism for the successful implementation of various activities designed in the projects. Development manager must possess adequate skill to prepare development project plan and activity mapping and effectively implement them with appropriate strategies for the achievement of development goals and objectives.

Monitoring: Monitoring and evaluation are the important management tools to track progress and facilitate decision-making. Monitoring in common sense means keeping an eye on the implementation of the activities, its progress, and identifying problems, if any. Monitoring is to be conducted both internally and, if required, through the external independent agency for the impartial assessment of progress of the development project or programme. Monitoring is not one time activity, but rather a continuous and periodic exercise, in the form of review and surveillance by the development manager at every level of the implementation of the project activity to ensure that input deliveries, work schedules, transacted outputs, and other required actions are proceeding according to plan. To Sera and Beaudry (2007), monitoring is a continuing function that aims primarily to provide the management and main stakeholders of an ongoing intervention with early indicators of progress or lack thereof, in the achievement of results. Availability of an activity plan as discussed in preceding point is a precondition for monitoring. During monitoring, field data are collected, processed, analyzed, and presented to the management as well as donor agencies for decision-making. The project and programme managers must possess adequate knowledge and skill to develop standardized monitoring tools and apply statistical technique to analyze the data collected through monitoring.

Evaluation: Evaluation is a process of systematically and objectively determining the relevance, efficiency, effectiveness, and impact of project activities in the light of the stated objectives. It provides information to the development manager about past or ongoing activities and in a way help the project management team in case there is any need for modification in planned activities. To Sera and Beaudry (2007), evaluation is a systematic and objective assessment of an ongoing or completed project, programme, or policy and its design, implementation, and result. Evaluation is done during the mid-phase of the project called mid-term evaluation and also at the end of the project called final evaluation. Sometimes, in order to have impartial evaluation, external agencies having expertise in evaluation technique, and methodology is being engaged by the project donor agencies. Through evaluation, gaps are identified and solutions are recommended. The development managers and development institutions and organization require to have specialists in preparing and standardizing evaluation tools, sampling techniques and methodology of evaluation, and report writing.

Impact Assessment: Monitoring is a continuous process. Evaluation takes place during the mid-phase and also immediately after the completion of the projects and programmes, whereas impact assessment is conducted after a gap of at least six months in order to know the end result of the project interventions on the target beneficiaries. In its broader sense, impact assessment is the process of identifying the anticipated or actual impacts of a development intervention, on those social, economic, and environmental factors which the intervention is designed to affect or may inadvertently affect.[8] For example, the evaluation of an employment programme may deal with the number of people received employment, wage rate, number of man days used, and assets created, while impact assessment of employment programme is judged whether it has raised the quality of life in terms of their access to nutrition, sanitation, and better education and health care for their children.

Follow-up Action and Close: It is the last, but not the least, step in project management. Any project particularly the action research project, which aims at improving the quality of life of the people, will remain incomplete if it omits the follow-up action. The project implementer after the impact assessment has to identify and locate the gap and has to take appropriate action to overcome the gaps. They have to revisit the project sight and fulfil these identified gaps with active participation of the community. The entire project action and endeavour will remain half-finished or even become futile if this final touch is omitted from the project strategy. Follow-up action believes in the principle "All is well that ends well".

WHAT ARE THE ISSUES IN DEVELOPMENT PROJECT MANAGEMENT?

The project management is becoming a key strategy for managing organizational change in contemporary organizations with corporations, governments, academia, and other organizations recognizing the value of common project approaches and/or educated employees for the execution of projects (Rooij, 2009). The effective management of development project requires careful attention towards the following essential managerial aspects:

(i) Integration management: The development project is a culmination of tasks and activities performed by different actors such as government, NGOs, corporate sectors, CSOs, and also the beneficiaries and the common men. Customarily, effective implementation of project requires an integrated approach, which integrates the action of all these actors of development. The project which integrates the actions of the various service providers and the beneficiaries can better avoid duplication and replication of project endeavour. Every activity of the project must be well coordinated or integrated. There must be proper coordination mechanism at each level from the top and middle management level to down the line workers level. The CBOs and the community as a whole must be integrated into the whole process of project management, starting from project planning, formulation of strategies, implementation, monitoring to controlling of various project activities.

(ii) Scope management: Proper delineation of the scope of the project is an important exercise which the project manager has to do at the outset before the initiation of any project activities and its task. As project is a time-bound activity, its scope must be bounded, taking into consideration the time and resources available at the disposal. The project managers have to limit their action within the scope of the project and should not perform those tasks which are beyond the scope of the project and also should not neglect or leave those work which are within the scope of the project. Any activity undertaken beyond the scope of the project will not only create confusion, but also lead to wastage of time, energy, and resources and will invite a lot of criticisms. According to the PMBOK, project scope management constitutes "the processes to ensure that the project includes all of the work required and only the work required, completing the project successfully". It envisaged that the project scope management has several purposes: (a) it defines what work is needed to complete the project objectives; (b) it determines what is included in the project; (c) it serves as a guide to determine what work is not needed to complete the project objectives; and (d) it serves as a point of reference for what is not included in the project.[9] One of key responsibilities of the project manager is to clearly define the scope of the development project and confine its activities within the scope of the project. The scope feasibly of a project should be ascertained in terms of technical factors, managerial potential, economic factors, environmental issues, political expediency, financial analysis, economic realities, and community impact (Badiru, 2009).

(iii) Time management: A good project always sticks to its time and gets completed within the stipulated time period. Project time management refers to developing a time schedule, which is popularly presented in the form of a 'Gantt Chart' that can be met and then controlling the activities to ensure that it happens. An efficient project manager tries to effectively manage the time and achieve the project tasks within the allocated time period. Taking long time adds to the inefficiency of the project and taking too less time can put question mark on the relevance and reliability of the project. It is well mentioned that:

> Time is a resource, if it is managed effectively; otherwise it will be a constraint. A successful project is the one that is on time, within budget, and deliver what is expected. If project managers cannot control their time, then they will have difficulties controlling team members and consequently the entire project is likely to be late.[10]

(iv) Cost management: Cost management implies that project proposal to be so formulated that it would achieve its objectives and be completed within the formulated budget. Proper estimation of the cost of project expenditures, i.e. manpower, equipment, materials, and other things like travel expenditure and other miscellaneous expenses is a taste of financial management capability of the development project manager. After writing the project proposal, cost is budgeted, and during the implementation phases of the project activities, cost is being tracked and necessary corrective measures are taken from time to time in controlling the expenses for keeping the project within the budget. The project cost must be appropriately budgeted and should not be too high amounting to rejection of the project and also must not be too low which may compel the organization to pay out of their pocket and from its own resources. Sometimes good project proposals are rejected not because of technical deficiencies but due to the financial bid. Therefore, costing is critical to project management. According to Venkataraman and Pinto (2008), effective project cost management is an extremely complex process that begins very early during a project lifecycle and long before it actual starts and among the factors that influence success is a reasonable and accurate system for estimating costs.

(v) Human resource management: Human resources are the key and are supreme of all other resources. Human resources largely refer to the type of personnel deployed in the project, their knowledge, attitude and skill in handling various project activities. It involves identifying and recruiting appropriate personnel needed to do the job, defining their roles and responsibilities. Acquiring efficient people as per the job requirement and imparting them job-specific training is critical to project management. The human resource management also includes the salary packages, leisure, and medical and other benefits given to the selected personnel recruited in the project. Sometimes project staff is less motivated to work for poor benefits, which affects their efficiency, having repercussion of project output. Therefore, many organizations depute their efficient staffs to the project by offering them higher salary package and grade. In the view of Project Management Professional (PMP):

> Project human resource management is multifaced. It is the ability to lead, direct and orchestrate the project team, the customers, project partners, contributors and any other stakeholders to achieve the desired results for the project purpose. Some of the general management skill on which project human resource management relies on are leading, communicating, negotiating, problem solving and influencing.[11]

According to Michael R. Williams, the important processes involved in the project human resource management are: (a) project human resource planning; (b) acquiring the project team; (c) developing the project team; and (d) managing the project team.[12]

(vi) Quality management: The balancing between the quantity and quality of project deliverables is central to effective project management. Maintenance of quality is vital to project and any compromise with the quality will lead to dissensions among the beneficiaries for whom the project is targeted. The quality of inputs divested in project and the output and outcome of the project must be clearly visible and must be disseminated from time to time. The qualified and experienced manpower employed in the project can effectively and efficiently manage the project than their counter parts who are less qualified and less experienced. Nepotism in the recruitment of manpower, and the use of less and low quality inputs would affect the quality of project output. The ultimate success of the project depends on the quality of services it has provided to the targeted beneficiaries. It is well mentioned that "The main principle of project quality management is to ensure the project will meet or exceed the stakeholder's needs and expectations. The quality management is a continuous process that starts and ends with the project".[13]

(vii) Procurement management: Projects need materials, equipment, manpower, training, and many other goods and services. According to Project Management Professional (PMP), "the project procurement management is the process of purchasing the products and services necessary for meeting the needs of the scope of the project. Project management involves planning, soliciting sources, choosing a source, administering the contract and closing out the contract".[14] While the Project Management Institute (1996) viewed that the project procurement management includes the process required to acquire goods and services from outside the performing organization, procurement of good quality materials and services is an essential part of procurement management and is an important aspect of project service delivery for attainment of project goals and objectives. Proper tendering, procurement of good quality materials, and effective use of material will not only make project cost effective but also lead to better project outcomes. While doing all these activities, transparency is called for so that it will not invite any audit objection in future. Corruption largely takes place at this stage of project management.

(viii) Communication management: Communication management refers to planning, executing, and controlling the acquisition and dissemination of all information relevant to the needs of all project stakeholders. According to Anita Mehta, communication is the project manager's sword, as he or she guides the project team through the jungle overcoming the various issues and roadblocks with an eye on the finish line.[15] Transparency in communication and democratic way of communication where all the stakeholders as well as the beneficiaries participate and share their opinion regarding various aspects of project starting from the project formulation up to the impact assessment is critical to a good project management. Maintaining free flow of communication from top-to-bottom and bottom-to-top is essential for effective implementation of the project. Any procrastination and hiding of facts at any stage will have adverse impact on project outcome in the long run. Communication and dissemination of project findings to the larger audience will provide inputs to the policy-makers for policy formulation and others for replication and expansion of project activities to other areas. The Project Management Institute (1996) has nicely described that the project communication management includes the process required to ensure timely and appropriate generation, collection, dissemination, storage, and ultimate disposition of project information.

(ix) Risk management: Risk is the uncertainty or unexpected event or happening that might affect the project during the process of its implementation. Risk management is a systematic process of identifying, quantifying, analyzing, prioritizing, and responding to the anticipated project risk. To Hillson (2001):

> Risk response planning phase is arguably the most important phase of the risk management process, since this is where appropriate actions are developed in the light of identified risks-both threats and opportunities. If effective responses are not developed and implemented, the risk process will fail and the chances of the project achieving it s objectives will be reduced.

Higher is the risk, lower is the efficiency and effectiveness of the project. The efficiency and effectiveness of a project is influenced by the risk factor. According to Lewis (2001), it includes maximizing the probability and consequences of positive events and minimizing the probability and consequences of advance events to project objectives. It is an extremely important aspect of project management. Mitigation of risk is a challenge before the project manager. Hillson (2001) has remarked that the risk management process is not complex and is simply a common sense and structured approach to dealing with uncertainty, ensuring that proper account is taken of every foreseeable risk.

The Sum Up

Developing countries are investing a lot of resources in the form of men, money, and materials for the development of their underdeveloped areas. However, the outcomes are not so sanguine. One of the reasons for poor implementation of development projects and programmes is lack of effective planning and plan implementation and poor management of development projects and programmes. Development management holds the key to effective implementation of development projects and programmes. It will check the duplication and replication of endeavours and enable development managers to judiciously use resources, make project cost effective, enable the development managers to complete development projects in time, and promote public–private partnership and peoples' participation in the process of development. Effective planning and management of development projects and programme will guide the government and development agencies in such a way that the benefits reach the genuine people. Development planning and management is crucial to development particularly in the developing countries having paucity of resources.

Keywords development management, controlling, budgeting, problem tree, scope management, SMART, time management, risk management.

REVIEW QUESTIONS

1. What is development management? Explain the role of development management in the development of the developing countries.
2. Why is there a need for development management in the developing countries? What need does development management fulfil in development of the developing countries?
3. Explain in detail various steps in the development management cycle. Which step in your view is important and why?
4. Cost management and communication management are critical issues in development management. Explain.
5. What is problem analysis? How is it important in development management cycle?
6. Explain four important functions of development management.
7. What is impact assessment? Discuss the role of impact assessment in development management?
8. Explain why development projects and programmes are not properly implemented in the developing countries. Explain the role of development management in development projects.
9. Explain in detail four critical issues in development management and why they are critical for the developing countries.
10. Write short notes on the following:
    (i) Development management
    (ii) Monitoring and evaluation
    (iii) Time management
    (iv) Procurement management
    (v) Principles of development management
    (vi) Impact assessment
    (vii) Situation analysis
    (viii) Need assessment

NOTES

1. Managing for Development Results Information Sheet. Available at: www.oecd.org/development/effectiveness/mfdr.htm (accessed on 17 February 2016).
2. These definitions are quoted from the web: http://kalyan-city.blogspot.com/2010/06/management-functions-process-management.html (accessed on 21 January 2014).
3. Quoted from: www.oecd.org/regional/searf2009/42577005.pdf (accessed on 17 February 2016) title "United Nations Public Service Day" (accessed on 12 December 2015).
4. Quoted from: unpan1.un.org/intradoc/groups/public/documents/un/unpan014159.pdf (accessed on 17 February 2016) title "United Nations Public Service Day" (accessed on 12 December 2015).
5. The definition given by Rajiv Gandhi is given in Waldron, M.W., Vasanthakumar, J., and Arulraj, S. Available at: http://www.fao.org/docrep/w5830e/w5830eOf.htm (accessed on 19 October 2013).
6. FAO Corporate Document Repository, Chapter 2, Situation Analysis Framework in PRCA. Available at: http://www.fao.org/docrep/008/y5793e/y5793e04.htm (accessed on 10 April 2014).
7. ODI Toolkit, Successful Communication, A Toolkit for Researchers and Civil Society Organization. Available at: http://www.odi.org/publications/5258-problem (accessed on 30 January 2015).
8. What is Impact Assessment? Available at: www.forestcarbonportal.com/sites/default/files/doc_191.pdf (accessed on 17 February 2016).
9. Managing the Project Scope. Available at: http://www.euroi.ktu.It/It/images/stories/Paskaitos/Ch05.pdf (accessed on 17 February 2016).
10. Managing Information Systems Project Time and Resources. Available at: docplayer.net/5663748-Managing-information-systems-project-time-and-resources.html (accessed on 17 February 2016).
11. Project Management Professional (PMP): Introducing Project Human Resource Management. Available at: http://www.euroi.ktu.It/It/images/stories/Paskaitos/ch (accessed on 22 February 2014).
12. Michael R. Wlliams. see Project Human Resource Management Overview of PMBOK Basics. Available at: http://www2.parkland.edu/businesstraining/document (accessed on 22 February 2014).
13. Project Management for Development Organization Doing the Right Project Doing the Project Right. Available at: www/pm4dev.co/…/18-the-project-q (accessed on 21 February 2014).
14. Project Management Professional (PMP): Introducing Project Human Resource Management. Available at: http://www.euroi.ktu.It/It/images/stories/Paskaitos/ch (accessed on 22 February 2014).
15. Anita Mehta, "Communication in Project Management." Available at: https://groups.yahoo.com/neo/groups/Migas_Indonesia/conversations/messages/98498 (accessed on 17 February 2016).

REFERENCES

Badiru, A.B. 2009. *Step Project Management, Guide for Science, Technology and Engineering Project*. New York: Taylor & Francis.

Brinkerhoff, D.W. and Ingle, M.D. 1989. "Integrating Blueprint and Process: A Structured Flexibility Approach to Development Management." *Public Administration and Development*, 9: 487–503.

Chawla, A. and Kelloway, E.K. 2004. "Predicting Openness and Commitment to Change." *The Leadership and Organizational Development Journal*, 16: 74–92.

Clarke, R.F. 1996. *What Is Development? In Search of Some Parameters*, IDPM Discussion Paper Series, 45, Manchester: Institute of Development Policy and Management, University of Manchester.

Hillson, D. 2001. "Effective Strategies for Exploiting Opportunities." Proceedings of the Project Management Institute Annual Seminar and Symposium, 1–10 November, Nashville, Tennessee.

Jafari, Mohammad, Ahmed, M., Md Dawal, S.Z., and Zayandehroodi, H. 2011. "The Importance of Project Management in Small and Medium-sized Enterprises (SMEs) for the Development of New Products through e-collaboration." *African Journal of Business Management*, 5(30): 11844–55.

Lee, W. J., Joo, H.J., and Johnson, W.W. 2009. "Effect of Participatory Management on Internal Stress, Overall Job Satisfaction and Turnover Intention among Federal Probation Officers." *Federal Probation: A Journal of Correctional Philosophy and Practice*, 73(1): 55–73.

Lewis, M.A. 2001. "Success, Failure and Organizational Competence: A Case Study of the New Product Development Process." *Journal of Engineering and Technology Management*, 18(2): 185–206.

McCoy, D. and Bamford, L. 1998. *How to Conduct A Rapid Situation Analysis A Guide for Health Districts in South Africa*. Durban: Health Systems Trust.

Project Management Institute. 1996. Project Procurement Management, 12, 130, South State Road, Upper Darby, USA. Available at: www.bus.iastate.edu/nilakant/ProjectManagement/pmbok1.pdf (accessed on 17 February 2016).

Rao, P.V. Narasimha. 1992. "Forewords." In *Eighth Five Year Plan 1992–97, Vol. 1*. Planning Commission, New Delhi.

Reeves, T.K. and Woodward, J. 1970. "The Study of Managerial Control." In *Industrial Organizations: Behaviour and Control*, edited by J. Woodward. Oxford: Oxford University Press, 37–56.

Rooij, S.W. van. 2009. "Scaffolding Project-based Learning with the Project Management Body of Knowledge." *Journal of Computer Education*, 52(1): 210–19.

Saifullah, A.K.M. 2001. *NGOs Capacity in Development Management: Experience from Bangladesh*. Tampere, Finland: Tampere University Press. Available at: https://tampub.uta.fi/handle/10024/67161 (accessed on 17 February 2016).

Seers, D. 1979. "The Meaning of Development." In *Development Theory: Four Critical Studies*, edited by D. Leham. London: Frank Cass, 9–30.

Sera, Y. and Beaudry, S. 2007. "Monitoring and Evaluation." Social Development Department, The World Bank. Available at: http://siteresources.worldbank.org/INTBELARUS/Resources/M&E.pdf (accessed on 17 February 2016).

Solaiman, M. and Nasrul Quadir, S.M. 1998. "Sustainable Development Management Through Growth with Equity by Participatory Forestry in Rural Bangladesh." In *Management of Development (Growth with Equity)*, edited by R. Abudur. New Delhi: Excel Books.

Terry, G. and Franklin, R.G. 1982. *Principles of Management*, Eighth edition. Homewood, Illinois: Richard D. Irwin.

Thomas, A. 1999. "What Makes Good Development Management?" *Development in Practice*, 9–17.

Townsend, J.G. 1998. "Are Non-governmental Organization Working in Development a Translational Community?" *Journal of International Development*, 11: 613–23.

Venkataraman, R.R. and Pinto, J.K. 2008. *Cost and Value Management in Projects*. New Jersey: John Wiley and Sons.

12 Development Communication

The communication could play an important role in the national development and the relationship between development communication and economic growth has been the main guiding paradigm for development programmes of the Third World countries.

— Wibur Schramm (1964)

If information and knowledge are central to democracy they are the conditions of development.

— Annan (1999)

Without communication no society can exist, develop or survive.

— Ayee (1993)

Development communication is an inseparable wing of 'development' for the developing countries, where the level of literacy is low and there is a general lack of knowledge about the development issues, challenges, policies, and programmes, importantly among the countryside population. It is argued that development communication has its origin in post-war international aid programmes to the countries in Latin America, Asia, and Africa that were struggling with poverty, illiteracy, poor health, and a lack of economic, political, and social infrastructure (Waisbord, 2001). One of the estimations reveals that more than 850 million people in developing countries are excluded from a wide range of information and knowledge, with the rural poor, in particular, remaining isolated from both traditional media and new information and communication technologies which would improve their livelihoods.[1] A lot of projects and programmes launched by the government in these countries are not reaching to its targeted population and is being siphoned off by the middlemen, one of the reasons being that there is lack of awareness and knowledge about the aims, objectives, and procedure for availing the benefits of these projects and programmes among the targeted beneficiaries. Further, the information, education, and communication strategies and behavioural change techniques being adopted are many of the times not appropriate to target audiences, lack proper method mix, are not appealing to target audiences, and has lack of trained development educators and multimedia materials at the grassroots level which can orient the people through group and individual communication methods. Communication has the capability to influence development in the developing countries. Many factor-analysis studies have shown communication variables to be significantly correlated with development (Deutschmann and McNelly, 1964). Rao (1966) from his comparative study of two Indian villages found strong correlation between the communication and the social, economic, and political development. Frey (1966), from his survey conducted in 460 villages of Turkey, found a clear correlation between communication and development. Besides, Lerner (1958), through his study comprising about 50 countries, came to the conclusion that media participation is highly correlated with literacy, urbanization, and political participation. Development communication through different methods, i.e. inter-personal, group, and mass communication methods has been playing an important role in creating awareness, changing attitudes and behaviour, and providing necessary strategic inputs to the people regarding various development issues and challenges relating to agriculture, education, health, family welfare, and sanitation and the programme and policy measures formulated by the government to overcome those issues and challenges. A UNESCO (1961) study conducted in Latin America, Africa, the Middle East, and South East Asia found a strong correlation between mass media factors and economic factors in general development. Agunga (1998) said there cannot be development without participation and it is almost impossible to have participation without communication. UNDP (2001) felt that the Internet, wireless telephone, and other ICT enable people to communicate and obtain information in ways which were never before possible, dramatically opening up possibilities to participate in decisions that affect their life. Propagation of informal and non-formal education on development through various development communication methods, approaches, and strategies particularly among the rural masses was discovered as a suitable means to augment development, i.e. economic, social, political, and cultural development in these countries.

After reading this chapter, you will be able to:

(i) Define development communication and tell how it is important for the development of the developing countries.
(ii) Narrate various development communication theories and how they have given thrust on the role of communication in development.
(iii) Describe various principles, approaches, and strategies of development communication.

WHAT IS DEVELOPMENT COMMUNICATION?

The subject 'development communication' became widely popular, since 1950s, in the development process of the developing countries predominated by rural areas and having high illiteracy and low level of literacy. The World Congress on Communication for Development (WCCD) vouches that communication for development is an essential ingredient for meeting today's most pressing development challenges and as such, should be more fully integrated in development policy and practice.[2] Development communication has been defined as the strategic application of communication technologies and processes to promote social change (Wilkins, 2000). According to The United Nations Resolution 51/172, 1997 "communication for development stresses the need to support two-way communication systems that enable dialogue and that allow communities to speak out, express their aspirations and concerns and participate in the decisions that relate to their development" (United Nations, 1997).

The WCCD defined communication for development as

> ...a social process based on dialogue using a broad range of tools and methods. It is also about seeking change at different levels, including listening, building trust, sharing knowledge and skills, building policies, debating and learning for sustained and meaningful change. It is not public relations or corporate communications. (World Bank, 2007)

To FAO (1987) development support communication is the systematic utilization of appropriate communication channels and techniques in increase people's participation in development and to inform, motivate, and train rural population, mainly at the grass-roots level. Development communication consists of two words, 'development' and 'communication' both are multidimensional in nature. Freire (2008) said 'development' and 'communication' are two terms heavily loaded with different conceptions and a richness of uses and functions shaped by their various theoretical underpinnings and such richness often leads to ambiguities and a lack of clarity that affects the fields of development communication. Gibson was of the opinion that the absence of a widespread consensus in defining 'development' and 'communication' reflects the large absence of common vocabulary in the field.[3]

At the annual meeting of the International Broadcast Institute at Cologne in 1973, a report of the working committee on 'Communication in Support of Development' had the following definitions of the key concepts:

(i) Development: The improvement of the well-being of the individual and the betterment of the quality of his or her life.
(ii) Communication: The transfer of information between individuals of groups of individuals by human or technical means.
(iii) Development support communication: The systematic use of communication in the planning and implementation of development (IBI, 1975).

World Bank has remarked that development communication is the integration of strategic communication in development projects.[4] Quebral (1975) defined development communication as the art and science of human communication applied to the speedy transformation of a country from poverty to a dynamic state of growth and makes possible greater economic and social equality and larger fulfilment of human potential. According to Rogers (1962), development communication entailed:

> ...process by which an idea is transferred from a source to a receiver with the intent to change his behaviour. Usually the source wants to alter the receiver's knowledge of some idea, create or change his attitude towards the idea, or persuade him to adopt the idea as part of his regular behaviour.

According to Moemeka (1989), in a very broad sense, development communication is the art and science of human communication to the speedy transformation of a country (economic growth, modernization, and industrialization) and the mass of its people (self-actualization, fulfilment of human potentials, and greater social justice). Rosario-Braid (1979) described development communication as the identification and utilization of appropriate expertise in the development process that will assist in increasing participation of intended beneficiaries at the grass-roots level. To Malan (1998), development communication is "All forms of communication that are used for the improvement of an individual, community or country's material, cultural, spiritual, social and other conditions".

Development communication is basically undertaken with the objective of informing and educating people belonging to both urban and rural areas about various developmental issues and challenges and how to overcome them; also to educate them about various developmental projects and programmes launched by the government in different sectors of development; and the ways and means to avail the benefits of these programmes by applying different communication approaches and strategies. The aim is to effectively educate, encourage, and engage people in the process of development. The ultimate goal of 'development communication' is to raise the quality of life of the population, including increasing income and well-being, eradicate social injustice, promote land reform and freedom of speech, and establish community centres for leisure and entertainment (Melkote, 1991). The success and failure of most development projects are often determined by two crucial factors, i.e. communication and people's involvement (Fraser and Restrepo-Estrada, 1998). To World Bank, meaningful communication is about getting information out to particular audiences, listening to their feedbacks, and responding appropriately.[5] Ironically, the role of development communication has not been taken up seriously in the development process of various sectors except a few (per se in India, agriculture sector) in many developing countries and expenditure on development communication is largely being treated as a wasteful expenditure. The lack of development education which could have been promoted through different development communication methods is one of the important factors of failure in effective implementation of developmental projects and programmes in various sectors, particularly in rural areas of developing countries.

The World Bank Development Communication Division has envisaged that the main goals of development communication are to: (a) strategically integrate communication components into operations to mitigate nonfinancial risks and maximize development outcomes and (b) explore and assess stakeholder's motivations and perception towards reforms and other development initiatives (Mefalopulos, 2008). Communication is the nerve of development and needs to be spread across the body of development.

The objectives of development communication are:

(i) To provide information and knowledge to the people at the grass-roots level regarding the aims, objectives, and benefits of various development projects, programmes, and activities.
(ii) To use various communication methods and media for the successful transaction of development message to the audience.
(iii) To promote peoples' participation in development programmes through various communication methods, such as focus group discussions, seminars, role play, etc. on various development issues and challenges and their solution through popular participation at the local level in cooperation with the local level organizations, i.e. youth club, *mahila mandals*, local self-government organizations, and other civil society groups.
(iv) To see that development communication is an invaluable ingredient in all local area development programmes.

DEVELOPMENT COMMUNICATION THEORIES

The importance of communication in development was triggered off by the modernization theorists (1950s to 1970s) who equated underdevelopment with poverty and lack of material goods (Narula and Pearce, 1986) and development was based on industrialization and economic growth (Agunga, 1998). Modernization theory advocates that the modernization process experienced by the USA and several Western Europe countries provided a model which could be applied to the developing countries in order to enable them to develop through adoption of modernization. Modernization theorists were of the view that traditional beliefs and values and cultural traditions were impediments to development and traditional communication media used in the process of development communication were not considered suitable to convey development messages, and therefore, there is a necessity of modern communication methods and technology, particularly Western type of mass communication system to successfully transmit development message to the countryside people in the developing countries. Daniel Lerner, one of the profound propagators of modernization theory, highlighted the role of media in the modernization of a nation. In his illustrious book, *The Passing of Traditional Society: Modernizing Middle East*, he noted that as people are more exposed to media, the greater is their capability to imagine themselves as strange persons in strange situations, places, and time than did people in any previous historical epoch. Lerner emphasized the need to bring the idea of democracy and modernity to the developing world by adopting the following approach: increase in urbanization which would lead to higher rates of literacy, then disseminate information via the media, which leads to political participation and economic growth (Singh, 2002).

His social development model consisted of the following components:

(i) A core of mobile individuals whose psychological orientation made it easier to accept rapid changes in their personal lives and overall social system.
(ii) An omnipotent mass media system that reinforced and accelerated societal and individual change by disseminating the new ideas and attitudes conducive to modernization.
(iii) Correlations between important indices of urbanization, literacy, media exposure, and economic and political participation to establish a modern Western type of society (Lerner, 1958; Khalid, 2012).

Schramm (1964), another proponent of development communication theory, who was influenced by Lerner, considered that communication tasks need to be utilized in order to realize social change. Firstly, he advocated that at the outset, people must be provided with information about national development and why changes are needed for development. Secondly, there must be opportunities for people to participate in the decision-making process where leaders can lead and people can voice their opinions. Finally, the skills that are needed for the application of development and change must be taught.

Besides, modernization theory, the diffusion of innovations theory propagated by Rogers also highlighted the role of communication in change and development. Rogers noted that the mass media can raise the level of aspiration among the traditional minded people of the developing countries and thus create a climate for change and the adoption of innovation. In Rogers' diffusion of innovation theory, communication is an important element. For Rogers (2003), communication is a process in which participants create and share information with one another to reach a mutual understanding. While, diffusion is the process in which an innovation is communicated through certain channels over time among the members of a social system and adoption is a decision of full use of an innovation as the best course of action available and rejection is a decision not to adopt an innovation. Various communication channels, i.e. mass media and interpersonal and group communication play an important role in the various stages of decision-making process which Rogers categorized into five stages: knowledge, persuasion, decision, implementation, and confirmation. Rogers' diffusion theory holds substantial relevance for the developing countries and is a path to promote the use of development communication in development.

PRINCIPLES OF DEVELOPMENT COMMUNICATION

It is essential to know the various principles of development communication as they are the guiding forces behind development communication. The nine basic principles of development communication identified by the World Bank are: dialogic, inclusive, heuristic, analytical, participatory, contextual, interdisciplinary, strategic, and persuasive (Mefalopulos, 2008).

First, dialogue is the lifeblood of development communication and it helps to overcome obstacles to communication. Communication becomes effective when it becomes a two-way process between the communicator and the listeners. Development communication needs to foster dialogue to facilitate mutual understanding, to assess situation, eradicate hassles, and to seek wider consensus. The development projects and programmes should facilitate continuous dialogue between donors, stakeholders, and beneficiaries in order to create better convergence between project priorities and community problems and needs.

Second, development communication should adhere to the principle of inclusiveness. All, especially the marginalized, those who have not been given a chance and are being left out must be given the opportunity to communicate their developmental concerns. In other words, a two-way communication should always give the required attention to those groups that are marginalized or are excluded from the mainstream and are passive beneficiaries.

The third important principle of development communication is heuristic, which means, development communication process must be investigative in nature so that actual problems are identified and solutions provided. The *Development Communication Sourcebook of World Bank* envisages that the heuristic feature denotes the sharing of information and knowledge, which usually generates more knowledge that in turn can lead to effective collective action (Mefalopulos, 2008).

The fourth principle of development communication is analytical, which perceives that the development communication process is basically an analytical one, and the solution to the development problems can be better found by analyzing the problems with the help of the community rather than in a one-sided prescriptive approach, i.e. straight way providing the solution. The analytical approach through the collection of information and data, by interacting with the civil societies and people at large is an effective way to deal with developmental problems and finding solutions for them.

The fifth one is the participatory development communication process that applies a democratic approach in which all, i.e. actors of development, stakeholders, the people affected with the problems, participate in analyzing the development problems and finding solutions to local problems. Here, people are given a freehand to fully participate in the debate for development. According to Otsyina and Rosenberg (1997), development communication must give preference to horizontal approaches that encourage dialogue centred on problem analysis and a search for solutions, as well as bottom-up approaches that aim to raise the awareness of decision-makers.

Sixth, development communication becomes meaningful if it is focused, problem-centric, and contextual. Development communication will be contextual only when it is based on the communication needs assessment (CNA). A universal and stereotyped approach to all situations, i.e. rural versus urban, socio-economically backward vs. socio-economically advanced, tribal vs. non-tribal, and so on may not be effective enough to spread the message across the stratified developing societies.

Seventh, as development is an interdisciplinary concept and a cross-cutting phenomenon, the development communication principle must be interdisciplinary in nature. The development communication specialists needed to be familiar with various disciplines, i.e. ethnography, sociology, political economy, adult education and extension, public health, rural management, and so on. Therefore, development communication has to follow a team approach consisting of experts from various fields, who can communicate on different aspects to solve local problems, i.e. spread of political education, providing tips on home economics, social tensions and conflict management, quality of life, family life, education, etc.

The eighth principle of development communication is strategic. Development communication specialists need to adopt appropriate strategies to achieve development goals. A strategy could be defined as a plan to achieve set objectives with available resources in a given timeframe and the principle of 'strategic' implies that all parts of the process, from setting the objectives to selecting the media are carefully assessed, triangulated, and, if needed, modified to allow the design and implementation of an effective strategy (Mefalopulos, 2008). The strategy varies from one set of areas to that of the other, and the development communication strategy formulation for the hilly and tribal areas certainly would be different from those of plain and non-tribal areas. There cannot be a universal strategy for all projects and programmes, and it must differ from project to project and from one area to that of the other and from one group of development beneficiaries to that of the other.

Finally, development communication needs to be persuasive in nature. The renowned Greek philosopher, Aristotle considered persuasiveness as an effective way to communicate. Persuasion in the context of development communication is a two-way process, where accurate message is given and mutual discussion takes place for reaching consensus to provide solutions to development problems. The Development Communication Sourcebook of the World Bank has noted that to avoid the manipulation connotations of the past and be ethically appropriate, persuasion should be based on accurate information and within the context of two-way communication. Therefore, as a development communication principle, persuasion must not be thought of as a negative connotation as 'manipulation', 'propaganda', or 'trapping'. Healthy two-way persuasive approaches ensure that the best available options among the various parties are considered and agreed upon, so that sustainable change for development is materialized.

APPROACHES TO DEVELOPMENT COMMUNICATION

Popular approaches to development communication are: (a) development extension, (b) social mobilization, (c) social marketing, (d) multimedia and interpersonal communication, (e) advocacy, (f) educational entertainment, and (g) participatory communication.

Development Extension: Development extension is one of the important approaches to development communication. It aims at getting extension workers (senders) and people (receivers) tuned together for a particular message or series of messages related to development projects, programmes, and activities. In extension work, attempt is made by the extension functionaries and workers to transfer accurate information to people by using different client-friendly communication methods and strategies. According to Leagans (1961), extension education is the process of teaching rural people as to how to live better by learning ways that improve their farm, home, and community institutions. According to van den Ban and Hawkins (1996), extension involves the conscious use of communication of information to help people form sound opinions and make good decisions. Extension education has a significant role in development communication and the main emphasis of extension programme, as identified by Kelsey and Hearne (1967), is to enhance: (a) efficiency in production; (b) efficiency in marketing, distribution and utilization; (c) conversion, development and use of natural resources; (d) management of farm and home; (e) family living; (f) youth development; (g) leadership development; (h) community development and rural area development; and (i) public affairs.

Extension education programme is found to be carried out in different sectors of development such as agriculture, health and family welfare, women and child development, youth development, public health, and so on. The national extension service launched in 1953 in India was integrated with the community development programme in 1958, aimed at carrying out integrated multiphase development such as increasing agricultural productivity, promotion of village, small, and cottage industries, effective delivery of health care services at the grass-roots level, welfare of women and children and the involvement of youth in village development programme, communal harmony and peace education, human rights issues, role of village panchayat in rural development, environmental and sanitation issues, and creating awareness about various rural development programmes. According to Moemeka (1989) the basic tenets of the extension and community development method can be: (a) that there are no solutions to problems that are imposed on local communities from the outside and that local communities must first arrive at the problem definition and then its solution on their own; (b) that social animator—the communicator—is to be as closely identified with the local community as possible; (c) that he/she is to be non-directive in his/her approach; (d) that communication's chief role is to help define the problem, but not to give the solution; and (e) that community participation and social action is the goal and, therefore, feedback from the community is an essential means. The development extension programme must be an important strategy of development communication in the developing countries having

Achievement of the Health Services Extension Programme, Southern Ethiopia

Some of the achievements of the health services extension programme in Southern Ethiopia are:

- Increased family health services coverage
- Increased latrine construction and utilization
- Disease outbreaks are immediately reported
- Maintenance of updated vital statistics at the community level has been increased
- Increased community awareness about their health

Source: Bekele et al. (2008).

Mobile Food and Nutrition Extension Centre, India

Realizing the importance of nutrition education, the Department of Food and Public Distribution has established Mobile Food and Nutrition Extension Units (MEUs) equipped with mobile vans, audiovisual equipment, and technically trained personnel in different parts of the country to impart nutrition education in rural, urban, and tribal areas. The department has 33 Food and Nutrition Extension Centres (FNECs) in different parts of the country to impart education and training to the housewife on nutrition.

Source: Department of Food and Public Distribution, GOI, New Delhi, http://fcamin.nic.in/dfnd/eventdetails.asp

lower adult literacy rate in the effective transaction of knowledge, attitude, skill, and transfer of technological interventions in the implementation of various innovative programmes in different sectors of development.

Social Mobilization: Social mobilization is a comprehensive planning approach that emphasizes on political coalition building and community action (UNICEF, 1993; Wallack, 1989). It is something that happens to a large number of people in areas that undergo modernization, i.e. where advanced, non-traditional practices in culture, technology, and economic life are introduced and accepted on a considerable scale (Deutsch, 1961). Social mobilization has an important role to play in the developing countries, where the society is stratified on the basis of caste, class, ethnicity, and religious and community groups. Under social mobilization of development communication approach, community level institutions, i.e. youth organizations, women groups, local self-government institutions and other grass-roots level parallel bodies, and the people as a whole are mobilized for a certain development cause that may be sanitation, safe drinking water, health, education, family welfare, and so on. According to McKee (2000), social mobilization is the process of bringing all the feasible and practical intersectoral social partners and allies together to determine the felt needs and raise awareness of and demand for a particular development objective. It involves enlisting the participation of such actors, including institutions, groups, networks, and communities, who have to play a constructive role in identifying, raising, and managing human and material resources, thereby increasing and strengthening self-reliance and sustainability of achievement at the grass-roots level. It treats society as a cohesive group irrespective of caste, colour, and creed. It is the process of bringing together all feasible and practical inter-sectoral social allies to raise people's awareness of and demand for a particular development programme, to assist in delivery of resources and services and to strengthen community participation for sustainability and self-reliance (Waisbord, 2001). Social mobilization interventions are empowerment processes through which individuals or communities take direct control over their lives and environment. World Bank's (1992) nutrition and family planning projects in Bangladesh used a social mobilization approach by assigning NGOs the role of mobilizing communities.

Social Marketing: Unlike social mobilization, social marketing is being used as a useful approach and method of development communication particularly in rural areas. Social marketing need not be as it is generally understood to be marketing or selling of a product tactics, rather it must be perceived from the standpoint of selling the development ideas, projects, and programmes for the economic, social, human, cultural, and political development in the community. Many of the development projects or programmes fail with one of the reasons being that they are not marketed properly. The integration social marketing strategies in the development projects and programmes have been

Impact of Social Mobilization

Social mobilization, integrated with other communication approaches, has been a key feature in numerous communication efforts worldwide. Some prominent examples include: (a) Soul City's campaign against domestic violence in South Africa; (b) the UNICEF polio eradication campaign in Uttar Pradesh; (c) HIV/AIDS prevention in Uganda and Thailand; and (d) eliminating the vitamin A deficiency disorder in Nepal (UNICEF, 2005).

Study on Social Mobilization & Micro Credit for Women's Empowerment, A Case Study of Dhan Foundation concluded that social intermediation has contributed to relationship of trusts among each other and access to wider arena of society. This has brought tremendous confidence and awareness of self among women as individuals. As a result, there has been some beginning in changes of position and status of women. Moreover, women themselves perceive these changes as valuable, as extending of financial services and social intermediation through the Community Banking Programme has enabled building of human assets by improving self-esteem, bargaining power, and ability to demand.

Source: www.stoptb.org/.../stop%20TB%2020ACSM%20country%20level%20strategic%20frame (accessed on 21 February 2014).

found to be successful implementation of project and programme interventions. Generally, social marketing aims at marketing and use of selling techniques for education, behavioural change, adoption of goal, objectives and benefits of development projects and programmes, and other developmental interventions launched in various development sectors of the economy for raising the quality of life of the people in different social settings. According to Smith (2006), social marketing is not a science, but rather a professional craft which relies on multiple scientific disciplines to create programmes designed to influence human behaviour on a large scale. Social marketing is the application of commercial marketing technologies to the analysis, planning, execution, and evaluation of programme designed to influence voluntary behaviour of target audiences in order to improve their personal welfare and that of society (Andreasen, 1997). It intends to reduce the psychological, social, economic, and practical distance between the consumer and their behaviour (Wallack et al., 1993). The social marketing technique applies behavioural change communication method to promote socially beneficial practices and products in a target group. According to Andreasen (1997), the fundamental purpose of any social marketing campaign is to change people's behaviour. Social marketing is being used in developing countries in many interventions such as promotion of the use of family planning methods particularly condom use, breastfeeding, and immunization programmes. Variations of social marketing have been applied to promote traffic safety, tobacco control, drug prevention, childhood immunization,

Impact of Social Marketing

1. Mother Against Drunk Driving (MADD) and stronger seat belt laws is a programme that demonstrated the importance of primary seat belt laws combined with effective publicity of enforcement, increased seat belt use in North Carolina from 63 to 80 per cent and went on to become a national model.
2. Florida's first TRUTH anti-smoking campaign reduced teen smoking in one year by 19 per cent.
3. Dozens of HIV/AIDS prevention efforts ranging from the Swiss Stop AIDS Programme, which has increased condom use in casual partners from 50 to 80 per cent, to programmes throughout the developing world in Uganda, Jamaica, Brazil, Thailand, etc. have also shown positive results.
4. *PREMI*, a programme in Ecuador, increased full immunization coverage of the highest risk infants at one year of age from 5 to 28 per cent in 18 months.
5. *Mass Media and Health Practice*, a programme in Honduras, increased the correct use of oral rehydration solution from 9 to 44.8 per cent in five years.
6. *Social Norming Programmes* showed effects in multiple university settings in reducing alcohol abuse among college age students—Florida State University reported a 15 per cent reduction in high risk drinking among male students and 5 per cent among females, Hobart and William Smith Colleges in New York reported a 32 per cent reduction in student athletes drinking more than once per week.

Source: Smith (2006).

improved nutrition, and diet and environmental behaviour, as well as to reduce infant mortality (Smith, 2006). It becomes more challenging when the audience is culturally, religiously, and ethnically from diverse communities.

Multimedia and Inter-personal Communication: The rapid political, social, and economic transition in the Third World countries has been materialized through the creation and use of effective, equitable, and socially acceptable mass communication system that is helping in generating awareness on various social, economic, and political issues and challenges these societies are facing in their march towards multidimensional development. Multimedia in combination with inter-personal communication act as an effective tool of development communication which facilitates behaviour change among the target audience. The multimedia mass communication facilities, i.e. Internet, radio, television, mobile, and so on are being found to be used by the development functionaries for the spread of message across a wide range of audiences on various development issues, such as agriculture, health, sanitation, drinking water, family welfare, and so on. Katz and Lazarsfeld (1955) found that interpersonal relations were crucial in channelizing and shaping opinion and there are two steps of information flow from media to opinion leaders and from leaders to the masses. Both these two methods of development communication supplement and complement each other for the effective transmission of messages on development from the development communicators to the target audiences. The mass communication method which is effective in transmitting awareness is re-enforced through interpersonal communication such as individual to individual and focus group discussion leading to adoption of development interventions for the achievement of development goal. Blending media and interpersonal channels is fundamental for effective interventions (Flay and Burton, 1990).

Advocacy: Advocacy is the act of promoting a cause, idea, or policy to influence people's opinions or actions on matters of public policy or concern (Ranghelli and Craig, 2010). UNICEF (2008) noted that advocacy informs and motivates leadership to create a supportive environment to achieve programme objectives and development goals. At UNICEF, advocacy is defined as the continuous and adaptive process of gathering, organizing, and formulating information and data into argument, which is then communicated to policymakers through various interpersonal and mass media communication channels. According to Michael (2013), advocacy requires gathering, organizing, and formulating information into argument and then communicating it through various interpersonal and media channels to political and social leaders. Smart et al. (2008) said that advocacy is putting a problem on the agenda, providing a solution to that problem, and building support for acting on both the problem and the solution. Some of the advocacy strategies usually adopted in development communications are identification of an issue or challenge, development of advocacy work, identifying audience or target for the advocacy work, development of advocacy message, selection of message for advocacy, selection of influential people for advocacy, conduction of advocacy, and evaluation and impact assessment of advocacy programme on the population. In developing countries, in mass media, film stars, sports persons and famous personalities are being used in advocacy for various development programmes, especially to promote programmes on health, environment, family welfare, education, and poverty eradication. There are numerous communication tools that can be used for good advocacy work, such as lobbying, project visits, petitions, posters, leaflets, newsletters, theatre, engaging artists, and celebrities, working with the media—TV, radio, and the press and more (UN, 2008). According to UNICEF,[6] the audiences of advocacy are many and varied: the president or head of state, prime minister, cabinet, parliamentarians, key public servants, religious and traditional community leaders, social and business leaders, women leaders, NGO leaders, media executives and producers, celebrities, etc. who may have a positive effect on public opinion and donors. It has been noted that successful advocacy depends on the following core principles: (a) clearly define the issue; (b) determine the specific goals and objectives; (c) understand which kinds of evidence are available (quantitative/qualitative/mixed methods); (d) develop an efficient advocacy team; (e) transact the message through advocacy to the target audiences; and (f) monitor, evaluate, and study the impact assessment of messaging on target audiences through participatory approach.

National Sanitation and Hygiene Advocacy and Communication Strategy Framework for 2012–17, India

The Ministry of Drinking Water and Sanitation (MDWS) along with UNICEF and other partners has developed the National Sanitation and Hygiene Advocacy and Communication Strategy Framework for 2012–17. The overall goal is to make sure that people have access to and use a toilet and practice good hygiene, including washing hands with soap after using the toilet and before having food. The strategy focuses on increasing knowledge and perceived importance of sanitation and hygiene practices, with the long-term objective of changing the way society thinks so that open defecation is no longer acceptable in India.

Source: Ministry of Drinking Water and Sanitation, GOI (2012).

HIV/AIDS Advocacy and Communication, UNICEF Bangladesh

The HIV/AIDS Prevention Project—Advocacy and Communication Components (HAPP—ACC) of UNICEF, Bangladesh intends to create common understanding of issues related to HIV/AIDS and ensure involvement of all stakeholders regarding the development of strategic communication designs. The participants of the advocacy workshop were diverse: NGO workers, government officials, adolescents, media representatives, including local and folk media performers, and peers of vulnerable groups such as male sex workers/males having sex with males, brothel-based sex workers, street-based sex workers, hotel-based sex workers, residence-based sex workers, people living with HIV/AIDS, and injecting drug users.

Source: http://www.southbound.com.my/vipp/Vipp_Case_BangladesHAPP.htm (accessed on 28 January 2014).

Educational Entertainment: Educational entertainment refers to the process of purposely designing and implementing a media message to both entertain and educate, in order to increase audience knowledge about an educational issue, create favourable attitudes, and change overt behaviour (Singhal and Rogers, 1999). Like diffusion theory, the entertainment education approach to development communication intends to facilitate behaviour change about development issue through the dissemination of information. It is based on the premises that people learn, change their attitude, and adopt developmental practices by observing role models, particularly projected in the mass media. Besides social learning, entertainment education strategies are based on the idea that expected changes result from self-efficacy, the belief of individuals that they can complete specific tasks (Maibach and Murphy, 1995). The development education on health, education, agriculture, banking and credit, insurance, and so on are being advertised in the educational entertainment channels through television and in the movie halls before the beginning and during intervals of the picture show in the developing countries (in India). This was used as one of the best ways to transact development education through communication media to the countryside people during early phase of development (1950s to 1970s) in India and is still in vogue. The entertainment media plays a proactive role in population education and development in many developing countries intending to restrict their population growth.

Participatory Communication: The participatory development communication was popularized by the international agencies, i.e. World Bank, UNDP, UNESCO, ADB in the Third World countries since 1960s and 1970s for effective implementation of various developmental projects. It is rightly said that the participatory communication is, first and foremost, an alternative to media dominated communication promoted by transnational corporations (Reyes-Matta, 1986). It is defined as a dynamic, interactional, and transformative process of dialogue between people, both individually and collectively, to realize their full potential and be engaged in their own welfare (Singhal et al., 1993). In the participatory

Telenovelas Pioneered the Entertainment: Education Strategy

With the assistance of David Poindexter, the President of Population Communication International, a non-profit organization in New York, the 'technology' of entertainment-education *telenovelas* spread to India in 1984 (where a soap opera called *Hum Log* [We People] was broadcast) and then to Kenya in 1987 (where a radio soap opera, *Usikwapo Shikimana* [When Given Advice, Take It] and television soap opera *Tushauriane* [Let us Discuss]) were broadcast.

Hum Log featured educational messages about women's status, family harmony, and smaller family size norms. It attracted a very large-sized audience, setting a record for television ratings in India (up to 95%) and getting through to the mass population in India as no television series had ever done before.

Source: Singhal et al. (1993).

development communication process, people articulate their own views, identify their common concerns, and seek solution for it along with governmental and non-governmental functionaries and other actors of development engaged in the implementation of developmental projects and programmes. While emphasizing on the importance of participatory communication, Cooper and Goodsmith (2010) said that dialogue and direct interpersonal exchange play an especially crucial role in successful communication for social change programmes, particularly when they address highly sensitive issues. Morris (2003) said that participatory initiative 'focuses on community involvement'. Participatory development communication is a democratic way of propagating education regarding any developmental issue at the grass roots and desires to make the development process of the people, by the people and for the people. It puts people and inter-personal communication and dialogue at the centre of communication strategy. Participatory communication takes place at the community level where various community-level organizations, i.e. youth organizations, women's organizations, farmers' groups, cooperative society members, members of religious and philanthropic organizations, NGO representatives, and the functionaries of the government take part and discuss various development issues and challenges and take a collective decision for their well-being. In the Indian context, gram sabha (village assembly) is an embodiment of participatory development communion mechanism at the grass-roots level for collective decision-making on any developmental issues at the village level, be it approval of village development plan, selection of beneficiaries for various developmental schemes, village needs assessment, and so on. No development project or programme can succeed without the full participation of the local people or client community in the identification of needs, project planning, and involvement in the implementation of the plan to meet those needs (Ayee, 1993). According to Melkote and Steeves (2001), people need to have open discussions, identify their needs and problems, decide on a plan of action, and then use a specific medium of communication and an information database most appropriate to their needs and the need for information, that is the prerogative of the user at the village level rather than an authority at the top.

Participatory Communication and Reproductive Health

Communication for Change, a New York based not-for-profit organization has formed long-term partnerships with leading NGOs in several countries, including Action Health in Nigeria, the Self-employed Women's Association (SEWA) in India and Banchte Shekha in Bangladesh. Their work demonstrates that participatory video activities can play an important role in meeting the reproductive health needs of adolescents, improving women's economic status, opposing violence against women, elevating the status of women in society, and enabling women to become decision-makers in their lives as well as leaders in their communities.

(i) Action Health's video project helps to meet the reproductive health needs of adolescents: At Action Health in Lagos, young people have been producing video programmes for their peers since 1992. To our knowledge, Action Health is the only NGO that produces video programmes on many teen reproductive health issues (e.g. STDs, AIDS, teen pregnancy, pubertal changes) and on related issues like communicating with parents and alcohol consumption. Young people respond positively to the relevance and honesty of Action Health programmes because they present the real issues and problems confronting teenagers.

(ii) The video projects of Banchte Shekha and SEWA help combat violence against women: SEWA and Banchte Shekha's legal aid unit demonstrates the potential of participatory video to expose and combat violence against women. The team has documented cases of domestic violence, shown the tapes to stimulate discussion in villages and used the videos to gain justice through traditional courts. Now, the threat of being exposed on a Banchte Shekha video programme is becoming a deterrent to violence and abuse. No one wants to be embarrassed in front of his neighbours and village leaders. Tolerance of spousal abuse has declined in the areas where Banchte Shekha is working.

Source: http://c4c.org/about/ParticipatoryCommunication.html (accessed on 13 December 2015).

DEVELOPMENT COMMUNICATION STRATEGIES

Development organization has to follow appropriate development communication strategies for the effective transaction of information and knowledge to the people about various developmental projects and programmes and their goal, objectives, and development-related actions, activities, and practices in various sectors of development. The communication strategy for Water Sector Development in United Republic of Tanzania (2006) says:

> The communication strategy provides a foundation for sharing information to broaden stakeholders' role in the process of programme implementation. The strategy is multifaceted, recognizing the need for timely and relevant information at all levels. Information is needed by the government for informed policy dialogue and decision-making. Civil society and politicians also require information to participate in policy formulation issues and guidance on programme implementation.

Application of System Approach to Development Communication (SADC) is a way forward as a communication strategy for the effective transaction of development information among the target audiences. The seven steps of SADC are: (a) constitution of development communication team and their capacity building; (b) Development Communication Need/Problem Analysis (DCNPA); (c) identification of development communication methods; (d) development of communication materials and pre-testing of materials; (e) implementation of development communication programme; (f) monitoring/evaluation of development communication programme; and (g) impact assessment/follow-up of development communication programme.

Constitution of Development Communication Team (DCT) and Its Capacity Building: At the outset, the organization involved in the development communication process has to formulate a DCT before initiating any action on development communication. The composition of DCT needs to be versatile and multidisciplinary in nature, consisting of experts from various disciplines, i.e. media, sociology, economics, rural development, anthropology, development studies, women studies, extension education, journalism, media studies, etc. The team members having experience in handling developmental projects on various sectors, i.e. education, health, rural development, sanitation, drinking water, etc. may be given preference. In other words, the team should be a combination of generalists as well as specialists. After constitution of the team, it should be given appropriate induction training and orientation training from time-to-time on various aspects on how, why, and what development-related issues are to be covered in the development communication campaign and also how to conduct development communication need assessment in different social settings.

Development Communication Need Assessment and Problem Analysis: Needs assessment is a method of assessing what the needs of your community are compared to what already exist (Bates and Jones, 2012). In other words, development communication need refers to the development issues that have to be communicated and have not been communicated to the audience earlier. The first thing the DCT has to do after its constitution is to undertake a development communication need assessment (DCNA) in the proposed area/locality in which development-related projects, programmes, and activities are to be launched. DCNA is the identification of needs and problems relating to any specific development aspect and it is preferable that one issue may be covered at one go. If the development issues are relating to basic needs, information regarding housing, sanitation, drinking water, food, energy for cooking, and other essential household requirements are to be collected, either by conducting surveys in the project area or through focus group discussions with the people to be benefited by the project, and then prioritizing and identifying those issues and problems, which could be addressed through communication. Not only quantitative information but also qualitative data on awareness, attitude, and beliefs and practices has to be collected which is being realized can be better dealt with the help of behaviour change communication. It is pertinent that characteristics of population belonging to different caste, ethnicity, religion, etc. are taken into consideration so that different types of development communication techniques and methods are designed accordingly for the specific group of population.

Setting of Development Communication Goals/Objectives: As development communication is an education and learning process, the learning goal and objectives have to be carefully formulated in behavioural form. Goal is a general statement which broadly delineates the intention of the programme. While learning objectives are statements in specific and measurable terms of what the learners is supposed to do and perform after viewing, attaining, and participating in the learning activity. Learning objective needs to have three essential characteristics, i.e. an action verb, content, and criteria.

Identification of Methods/Strategy of Development Communication: Communication method may vary from one problem to that of the other and from one target group to that of the other, per se in one problem interpersonal communication may be suitable and for the other group mass communication method can be more appropriate. The strategy of effective development communication method has to be problem and issue-specific. The tasks at this stage are as follows: (a) define the specific means of communication for each programme; (b) specify target audience; (c) develop the key messages to be portrayed; (d) identify communication channels and activities; (e) spell out the targeted outreach; and (f) prepare a Gantt chart of timeline.

Preparation of Development Communication Materials (DCM): Once the team is constituted and methods are being identified for various development problems that require the support of development communication, the duty of the team is to prepare, procure, and pretest these DCMs before its final application to large audience. Necessary precautions have to be taken that good quality DCMs must be clear, accurate, interesting, and relevant to the target audience; and appealing and appeasing to the specific caste, ethnicity, gender, religious, caste groups, etc. for whom these materials are aimed at.

Implementation of Development Communication Programme: The implementation process starts after the development of DCMs. The DCT has to involve a group of stakeholders who ultimately can mobilize audiences and target group of people for administration of development communication messages. The team has to take appropriate measures with regards to giving prior information to the target audience, place of organization of development communication programme, and suitable time of display of development communication programmes in consultation with stakeholders and beneficiaries.

Monitoring/Evaluation of Development Communication Programme: Successful monitoring and evaluation will be used to improve the project, highlight its success, and raise the profile of the project in the local community (Bates and Jones, 2012). According to Ramboll (2005), "monitoring and evaluation is the systematic collection and analysis of information to enable managers and key stakeholders to make informed decisions, uphold existing practices and principles, and improve the performance of their projects". Monitoring is the regular gathering, analysis, and reporting of information that is needed for evaluation and/or effective project management, while evaluation is a selective and periodic exercise that attempts to objectively assess the overall progress and worth of the project (Ramboll, 2005). During the time of implementation of development communication programme, the DCT can administer pre- and post-test before and after the conduction of the programme, in case, it is a small audience, on a sample basis, for evaluating and monitoring the effectiveness of the programme. Besides, a question–answer session after the end of the programme will also be helpful to clear doubts among the target audience. Monitoring and evaluation should be made an integral part of development communication strategy. Monitoring report along with the SWOT analysis should be prepared either on a quarterly or a six-monthly basis and necessary steps should be taken for removing the weaknesses. Finally, an evaluation report may be prepared after the end of the development communication project and its result may be widely disseminated. If the project is implemented at the grass-roots level, participatory monitoring and evaluation method may be taken into consideration.

Impact Assessment/Follow-up: The final step of the development communication strategy is the conduction of an impact assessment study, preferably after six months of the conduction of the development communication programme, which may include knowledge, attitude, change in behaviour, and quantitative change in action related to various development issues. World Bank's strategic communication toolkit recommends the following indicators for measuring the outcomes of communication activities: (a) number of communications produced by type, during the reference period; (b) number of communications disseminated, by type, during the reference period; (c) percentage of target audience who correctly comprehended a given message; (d) percentage of target audience who express knowledge, attitude, and beliefs consistent with message; (e) percentage of target audience who acquire the skills recommended by the message; (f) percentage of target audience who discuss message with others, by type of person; and (g) percentage of target audience who engage in recommended practices (Cabanera-Verzosa, 1999). Then an attempt has to be made for the dissemination of results before partners, key stakeholders, the news media, and funding agencies. The key findings and impacts of the project and lessons learned report may be prepared during the impact assessment. During impact assessment, gaps are identified, then, if required, a follow-up development communication programme (DCP) is conducted. The World Bank states that an impact evaluation is intended to determine whether the programme had the desired effects on individuals, households, communities, and institutions and whether those effects are attributable to programme intervention (Baker, 2000).

It is pertinent to mention here that there is no fixed development communication strategy and a good development communication strategy must be flexible and participatory in nature. It is said that drawing up a communication strategy is an art and not a science and there are a lots of different ways of approaching a task (Hovland, 2005). UNICEF (2008) has remarked:

> There is no ideal time in the life of a development programme for writing a communication strategy. Communication strategy development could come at any stage-at initial planning, after a programme/plan has been approved and funded or even while it is being implemented. But regardless of the programme stage, it is important for the communication professional to work closely with programme staff, with partners and stakeholders and to do the analyses together that are the basis of a sound strategy.

The Sum Up

Communication is vital to development, particularly grass-roots development and development of the rural and backward pockets of urban areas. Communication processes are central to broader empowerment practices through which people are able to arrive at their own understanding of issues, to consider and discuss ideas, to negotiate, and to engage in public debates at community and national levels (UNDP, 2011). It is observed that one of the reasons of underdevelopment in the rural areas of the developing countries is not because of lack of availability of resources by the government for development, but because of deficiency of knowledge of people of those areas regarding various developmental programmes, their aims and objectives, processes of implementation, implementing agencies, and modalities associated with those development programmes. An effective development commutation system and proactive and effective operational mechanisms are sine qua non for the need-based development of socio-economically backward areas of the developing countries. Effective communication cannot be brushed aside if rural development is to be accomplished (Adedokun et al., 2010). In the communication for development, rural people are at the centre of any given development initiative and so communication is used in this sense for people's participation and community mobilization, decision making and action, confidence building for raising awareness, sharing knowledge and changing attitudes, behaviour, and lifestyles (Adedokun et al., 2010). An enabling environment is, therefore, a prerequisite for effective Communication for Development planning and implementation. Development projects and programmes can be more effectively implemented if its activities and benefits are effectively communicated to the people, who not only understand their aims and objectives but also develop a positive attitude and cooperate fully in their implementation.

Keywords development communication, participatory communication, social marketing, advocacy, social mobilization, development extension, diffusion of innovation.

REVIEW QUESTIONS

1. Define development communication. Discuss the role of development communication in development.
2. Explain the various theories of development communication. Which theory is more relevant for the underdeveloped countries and why?
3. What is social marketing? Explain how social marketing has been successful in health care development by giving suitable examples.
4. What is communication? Explain how the principles of communication can be applied to development.
5. What is development communication? Explain the various strategies of development communication.
6. What is advocacy? Explain the merits and demerits of advocacy as an approach to development communication.
7. What is development extension? Explain system approach to development extension.
8. What is monitoring and evaluation? Explain the role of monitoring and evaluation in communication development projects.

9. What is impact assessment? Explain why and how impact assessment is vital to successful implementation of communication development programmes.
10. Write short notes on the following:
    (i) Advocacy
    (ii) Social marketing
    (iii) Participatory communication
    (iv) Monitoring and evaluation
    (v) Communication impact assessment
    (vi) Communication need assessment
    (vii) Diffusion of innovation
    (viii) Educational entertainment

NOTES

1. Quoted from the document "Communication for Development," Network on Rural Development and Food Security, UN System. Available at: http://www.rdfs.net/themes/communication_en.htm (accessed on 27 February 2014).
2. World Bank's emphasis on development communication is quoted from "What is Development Communication?" Available at: http://web.worldbank.org/WBSITE/external/TOPICS (accessed on 27 February 2014).
3. Gibson's opinion is quoted in Waisbord, 2001.
4. Quoted from the document "Communication for Development," Network on Rural Development& Food Security, UN System. Available at: http://www.rdfs.net/themes/communication_en.htm (accessed on 27 February 2014).
5. World Bank's emphasis on development communication is quoted from "What is Development Communication?" Available at: http://web.worldbank.org/WBSITE/external/TOPICS (accessed on 27 February 2014).
6. Noted from UNICEF, Communication for Development (C4D), Advocacy. Available at: http://www.unicef.org/cbsc/index_42346.html (accessed on 3 March 2014).

REFERENCES

Adedokun, M.O., Adeyemo, C.W., and Olorunsola, E.O. 2010. "The Impact of Communication on Community Development." *Journal of Communication*, 1(2): 101–5.

Agunga, R.A. 1998. "Communication for Development in Africa: A Clarion Call." *Communicare*, 17(1): 28–48.

Andreasen, A.R. 1997. "Challenges for the Science and Practice of Social Marketing." In *Social Marketing: Theoretical and Practical Perspectives*, edited by E. Goldberg, M. Fishbein, and S.E. Middlestadt, Mahwah, NJ: Lawrence Erlbaum Associates, 3–19.

Annan, Kofi. 1999. "Preventing War and Disaster: A Growing Global Challenge—1999 Annual Report on the Work of the Organization." United Nations.

Ayee, E.S.A. 1993. *A Participatory Communication Approach to Rural Community Development*. Thesis submitted in fulfillment of the requirements for the degree Doctor of Philosophy in Communication, University of Potchefstroom, May.

Baker, Jude L. 2000. *Evaluating the Impact of Development Projects on Poverty: A Handbook for Practices*. Washington DC: World Bank. Available at: http://siteresources.worldbank.org/INTISPMA/Resources/handbook.pdf (accessed on 17 February 2016).

Bates, G. and Jones, L. 2012. *Monitoring ad Evaluation: A Guide for Community Projects*, Centre for Public Health, Liverpool, JMU. Available at: www.cph.org.uk/wp-content/uploads/2013/02/Mointorig-and-evaluation-a-guide-for-community-projects-a-short-guide.pdf (accessed on 17 February 2016).

Cabanera-Verzosa, C. 1999. *Strategic Communication for Development Projects*. Washington DC: World Bank. Available at: http://www.oecd.org/dev/devcom/46388330.pdf (accessed on 9 March 2014).

Cooper, C. and Goodsmith, L. 2010. *Communication, Participation and Social Change: A Review of Communication Initiatives Addressing Gender-based Violence, Gender Norms and Harmful Traditional Practices in Crisis Affected Settings*. Through an Eye, Health Communication Partnership, Uganda. Available at: http://www.arcrelief.org/site/DocServer/Through_Our_Eyes_Desk_Review--FINAL.pdf?docID=1602 (accessed on 17 February 2016).

Deutsch, K.M. 1961. "Social Mobilization and Political Development." *American Political Social Review*, 55(3, September): 493–514.

Deutschmann, P.J. and McNelly, J.T. 1964. "Media Use and Socio-economic Status in a Latin American Capital." *East Lansing*, Michigan, Michigan State University, Series, No.3.

FAO. 1987. *Perspectives on Communication for Development*. Rome, FAO.

Flay, B.R. and Burton, D. 1990. "Effective Mass Communication Strategies for Health Campaigns." In *Mass Communication and Public Health*, edited by C. Atkin and L. Wallack, 129–145. Newbury Park: SAGE Publications.

Fraser, C., and Restrepo-Estrada, S. 1998. *Communicating for Development Human Change for Survival*. London, New York: IB Touris Publishers.

Freire, P. 2008. "Reflections on the Theory and Practice of Development Communication." In *Development Communication Source Book Broadening the Boundaries of Communication*, edited by P. Mefalopulos, 39–77. Washington DC: World Bank.

Frey, F.W. 1966. *The Mass Media and Rural Development in Turkey*. Massachusetts: Massachusetts Institute of Technology, Centre for International Studies.

Hovland, I. 2005. "Planning Tools: How to Write a Communication Strategy." Available at: www.odi.org/publications/5186-communications-strategy-planning (accessed on 17 February 2016).

IBI. 1975. "Communication in Support of Development," IBI Annual Meeting: Report of the Working Committee I (Mimeographe), International Broadcast Institute. Available at: http://www/sunypress.edu/pdf/52881.pdf (accessed on 27 February 2014).

Katz, E. and Lazarsfeld P.F. 1955. *Personal Influence: The Part Played by People in the Flow of Mass Communication*. New York: Free Press.

Kelsey, L.D. and Hearne, C.C. 1967. *Cooperative Extension Work*. New York: Comstock Publishing Associate.

Khalid, M.Z. 2012. "Media and Development Communication: A Perspective." *International Journal of Scientific and Research Publication*, 2(5): 1–5.

Leagans, J.P. 1961. *Some Principles and Concepts of Extension Programme Building*. Ithaca, NY: Cornell University Press.

Lerner, D. 1958. *The Passing of the Traditional Society*. Glencoe, IL: Free Press.

Maibach, E. and Murphy, D.A. 1995. "Self-efficacy in Health Promotion Research and Practice: Conceptualization and Measurement." *Health Education Research*, 10(1): 37–50.

Malan, C. 1998. "Development Communication as Part of Culture." *Communicare*, 17(1): 49–87.

McDivitt, J.A., Zimicki, S., and Hornik, R.C. 1997. "Explaining the Impact of a Communication Campaign to Change Vaccination Knowledge and Coverage in Philippines." *Health Communication*, 9(2): 95–118.

McKee, N. 2000. "Motivation to Act: Effective Communication." In *Involving People, Evolving Behaviour*, edited by N. McKee, E. Manoncourt, S.Y. Chin, and R. Caregie. New York: Penang, 108–109.

Mefalopulos, P. 2008. *Development Communication Source Book Broadening the Boundaries of Communication*. Washington DC: World Bank.

Melkote, S.R. 1991. *Communication for Development in the Third World, Theory and Practice*. New Delhi: SAGE Publications.

Melkote, S.R. and Steeves, H.L. 2001. *Communication for Development in the Third World: Theory and Practice for Empowerment*, Second edition. New Delhi: SAGE Publications.

Michael, G. 2013. "Communication for Development." Available at: www.who.int/water_sanitation_health/dwq/gdwq0506.pdf (accessed on 17 February 2016).

Moemeka, A.A. 1989. "Perspectives on Development Communication." *Africa Media Review*, 3(3): 1–22.

Morris, N. 2003. "A Comparative Analysis of the Diffusion and Participatory Models in Development Communication." *Communication Theory*, 13(2): 225–48.

Narula, U. and Pearce, W.B. 1986. *Development as Communication: A Perspective on India*. Carbondale, IL: Southern Illinois University Press.

Otsyina, J.A. and Rosenberg, D.B. 1997. "Participation and the Communication of Development Information: A Review and Reappraisal." *Information Development*, 13(2): 89–93.

Quebral, Nora C. 1975. "Development Communication: Where Does it Stand Today." *Media Asia*, 2(4): 198.

Ramboll. 2005. *Project Monitoring and Evaluation*, Guideline 7. Water & Forestry Department, Republic of South Africa. Available at: http://www.daff.gov.za/doaDev/sideMenu/ForestryWeb/dwaf/cmsdocs/Elsa/Docs/PFM/PFM%20Guideline7.pdf (accessed on 17 February 2016).

Ranghelli, L. and Craig, J. 2010. *Strengthening Democracy, Increasing Opportunities Impacts of Advocacy, Organizing and Civic Engagement in Los Angeles*. Washington, DC: National Committee for Responsive Philanthropy.

Rao, L.Y.V. 1966. *Communication and Development: A Study of Two Indian Villages*. Minneapolis: University of Minnesota.

Reyes-Matta, F. 1986. "Alternative Communication: Solidarity and Development in the Face of Transnational Exposition." In *Communication and Latin American Society: Trends in Critical Research, 1960–1985*, edited by R. Atwood and E.G. McAnany. Madison, WI: University of Wisconsin Press, 190–215.

Rogers, E.M. 1962. *Diffusion of Innovations*, First edition. New York: Free Press.

Rogers, E.M. 2003. *Diffusion of Innovations*, Fifth edition. New York: Free Press.

Rosario-Braid, F. 1979. "A User-oriented Communication Strategy." In *Communication Strategy for Productivity Improvement*, edited by S. Rosario-Braid. Tokyo: Asian Productivity Organization, 34.

Schramm, W. 1964. *Mass Media and National Development: The Role of Information in the Developing Countries*. Stanford, CA: Stanford University Press.

Singh, J.P. 2002. "Communication Technology and Development: Instrumental Institutional, Participatory and Strategic Approaches." In *International and Intercultural Communication*, Second edition, edited by W.B. Gudykunst and D. Mody. Thousand Oaks, CA: SAGE Publications, 479–98.

Singhal, A. and Rogers, E.M. 1999. *Entertainment–Education: A Communication Strategy for Social Change*. Mahwah, NJ: Lawrence Erlbaum.

Singhal, A., Rogers, E.M., and Brown, W.J. 1993. "Harnessing the Potential of Entertainment-Education Telenovelas." *Gazene*, 51: 1–18.

Smart, H.S.L.P., Heard, W., Sikazwe, A., Nampanya-Serpell, N., and Ross, J. 2008. Consultancy Services to Develop a Strategy for Prevention Mitigation of HIV/AIDS in Public Service Zambia, Advocacy and Communication Strategy, 1.0.

Smith, W.A. 2006. "Social Marketing: An Overview of Approach and Effects." *Injury Prevention*, June, 12(suppl. 1): i38–43.

UNDP. 2001. "Human Development Report," United Nations Development Programmes, New York.

———. 2011. *Communication for Development: Strengthening Effectiveness of the United Nations*, Bureaus Development Policy, Democratic Governance Group, UNDP, New York.

UNESCO. 1961. *Mass Media in Developing Countries*, Paris.

UNICEF. 1993. "We will Never Go Back: Social Mobilization in the Child Survival and Development Programme in the United Republic of Tanzania." New York, UNICEF.

———. 2008. *Writing a Communication Strategy for Development Programmes A Guideline for Programme Managers and Communication Officers*. UNICEF Bangladesh, Knowledge Management Unit, Dhaka.

United Nations. 1997. *United Nations General Assembly Resolution: 51/172*. Available at: http://daccess-dds-ny.un.org/doc/UNDOC/GEN/N97/765/67/PDF/N9776567.pdf?Open Element (accessed on 21 December 2013).

———. 2008. *Advocacy for Sanitation: A Brief Guide Advocating for Sanitation during the International Year of Sanitation and Beyond, International Year of Sanitation 2008*. UN Water. Available at: http://esa.un.org/iys/docs/IYS%20Advocacy%20kit%20ENGLISH/Advocacy%20guide.pdf (accessed on 17 February 2016).

United Republic of Tanzania. 2006. "Water Sector Development Programme (WSDP) 2006–2025," *Programme Implementation Manual*, Vol. 7, Ministry of Water, United Republic of Tanzania.

van Den Ban, A.W. and Hawkins, H.S. 1996. *Agriculture Extension*. Oxford: Black Well Publishing.

Waisbord, S. 2001. *Family Tree of Theories Methodologies, Strategies in Development Communication*. New York: Rockefeller Foundation.

Wallack, L. 1989. "Mass Communication and Health Promotion: A Critical Perspective." In *Public Communication Campaign*, edited by R.E. Rice and C. Atkin, Second edition. New Bury Park: SAGE Publications.

Wallack, L., Dorfman, L., Jernigan, D., and Themba, M. 1993. *Media Advocacy and Public Health: Power for Prevention*. Newbury Park: SAGE Publications.

Wilkins, K.G. 2000. "Accounting for Power in Development Communication." In *Redeveloping Communication for Social Change: Theory, Practice and Power*, edited by K.G. Wilkins. Oxford: Rowman and Littlefield.

World Bank. 1992. "World Bank Report 1992, Development and the Environment," Oxford University Press, 46.

——— 2007. "World Congress on Communication for Development: Lessons, Challenges and the Way Forward," World Bank, Washington DC.

SUGGESTED READINGS

GOI–UN Joint Programme on Convergence. 2012. "Compendium of Innovations and Initiatives, Intercooperation Social Development India." Secunderabad, Andhra Pradesh.

Minkler, M. 1990. "Improving Health through Community Organization." In *Health Behaviour and Health Education: Theory, Research and Practice*, edited by K. Glanz, F.M. Lewis, and B.K. Rimer. San Francisco, CA: Jossey-Bass Publishers, 257–87.

Rogers, E.M. 1976. "Communication and Development: The Passing of the Dominant Paradigm." In *Communication for Social Change Anthology: Historical and Contemporary Readings*, edited by A. Gumucio-Dagron and T. Tufte. South Orange, NJ: Communication for Social Change Consortium, 110–26.

GLOSSARY

Accountability: It means answerability. One has to be answerable for his or her assigned activities and accept responsibility for his or her performance. To circumscribe, the principle of good accountability means that the executor or the leader must accept the responsibility of failure and share the credit of success with his or her team members. Shifting of responsibility from one person to another for failure and fighting for taking credit for success are adversaries to accountability.

Administrative Reforms: Administrative reform is one of the important components of development administration and is a tool or process directed towards improving the efficiency and effectiveness of administration. It is a method of administrative dynamics balancing. Caiden (1976)[1] opined that administrative reforms are concerned not only with organizational performance per se but also with improving the performance of the whole public sector. The aim of the administrative reform is to simplify the complex activities and procedures and to evolve those methods which may be able to achieve maximum productive results by engaging minimum amount of money and manpower. The Government of India, from time to time, has constituted administrative reform committees for this purpose.

Advocacy: Advocacy is the act of promoting a cause, idea, or policy to influence people's opinions or actions on matters of public policy or concern. The United Nation has advocated numerous communication tools that can be used for good advocacy work such as lobbying, project visits, petitions, posters, leaflets, newsletters, theatre, engaging artists, and celebrities working with the media—TV, radio, and the press.

Agency: It is an important component of the human capacity theory propounded by Amartya Sen. According to Sen, agency refers to a person's ability to pursue and realize goals that he or she values and has reason to value. An agent is someone who acts and brings about change. The agency aspect is important 'in assessing what a person can do in line with his or her conception of the good'. Agency in Sen's term is a powerful concept in capability formulation which stresses on self-determination, self-reliance, empowerment, raising voice, etc.

Ascriptive Bond: Sociologically, ethnicity may be defined as an ascriptive bond. There are similarities as well as differences between ethnicity and kinship. Kinship includes blood ties, whereas ethnicity is determined by birth. Ethnic groups try to help each other.

[1] Caiden, Gerald E. 1976. "International Consultants and Development Administration." *International Review of Administrative Science*, 42(1):1–7.

Backward and Forwards Linkages: The 'backward linkages' will enhance the selling of inputs by the entrepreneurs to the industries, while the 'forward linkages' will boost up units that buy output from the industries. For example, establishment of steel industry would enhance the demand for coal and iron ore and related goods. This linkage is called 'backward linkages', which will promote activities and employment in the coal and iron sector. At the same time, expansion of steel industries would also lead to expansion of industries, making use of steel product such as steel furniture, steel home appliances, and steel machines and tools. This linkage is called 'forward linkages'.

Backwash Effect and Spread Effect: The cumulative causation which tends to economically weaken a region was termed as 'backwash effect'. Contrary to 'backwash effects', there are 'spread effects' which tells that the industrial expansion in a more developed region of the underdeveloped countries will have positive repercussion on its less developed region in terms of demand, market avenues, and technology through the transfer of surplus capital from the more developed region to the less developed region. These favourable effects, which the more developed regions produce on the socio-economic development of the less developed regions, are termed as 'spread effects' and the positive impact of the 'spread effects' will help to neutralize the negative impact of 'backwash effects' to a great extent.

Basic Needs: These are minimum requirements of individuals so that they remain healthy and contribute towards the development of their family, society, and nation. Some of the basic needs critical to the stainable level of living are food, clothing, shelter, safe drinking water, sanitation, energy for cooking and lighting, and road and surface connectivity to access to nearest city or town for the fulfilment of other exigencies, particularly education, health care, and employment.

Capital Formation: It is the creation of additional capital stock in an economy. It is augmented through the increase in saving capacity of an economy.

Centralized Planning: The centralized plan is prepared at the centre, by the central government and the regional and local governments are directed to carry forward and implement the designed plan as formulated by the central government. In this type of planning, regional and local governments have hardly any say in the planning process.

Centre and Periphery: The central point on which Perbisch theory revolves around was centre-periphery, at the centre are the rich European countries and the United States and at the periphery are the impoverished Latin America, Asia, and African Nations. According to Perbisch, the centre exploits the periphery to its own advantage or development. In other words, the development of rich centre is built on the exploited resources of the periphery poor.

Civil Society Organizations (CSOs): These organizations are the important actors of development, which in real terms are working at the grass-roots level in the implementation of projects and programmes formulated by the government and private and international agencies. CSOs are largely the registered charities, development non-government organizations, community groups, women's organizations, youth clubs, religious organizations, professional associations, trade unions, coalitions, and advocacy groups.

Corporate Social Responsibility: It aims at the involvement and contribution of corporate sector towards development. In India, the government has made a policy by which the corporate sector has to investment two per cent of its profit on the socio-economic development activities. The corporate sectors are doing this either by themselves or with the help of NGOs and charitable trust established by them.

Crony Capitalism: It is a marriage between the State and private special interests through which the state protects the private special interest by giving them sops in terms of distribution of legal permits, government grants, tax concessions, and similar other forms of State favouritism. This has created apprehensions in the minds of the people that this unholy alliance between the corporate and the State may benefit the former and bring miseries to the poor and common man in the underdeveloped countries, who are exclusively dependant on State welfare measures.

Cultural Development: The cultural identities, i.e. dress code, song, drama, food habits, and languages; tangible and intangible heritage; cultural industries; cultural institutions like marriages and festivals; cultural pluralism; and geo-culture are the fabrics of cultural development. According to Nurse, the areas of culture has grown in salience in global development issues on account of the rising share of cultural goods, services, and intellectual property in world trade as well as the threats to cultural diversities and identities associated with contemporary globalization.

Decentralized Governance: Decentralized system of governance intends to make development people centred and to promote development through participatory process. It aims at shifting of governance from the centre to the lower levels of political and bureaucratic set ups. Three important forms of decentralization are devolution, delegation, and deconcentration. In case of devolution, both the authority and functions are transferred from the higher level of government to the lower level of governments, while in delegation, the power and sometimes the authority is not transferred and if transferred, it can be taken away and by deconcentration, only the functions and responsibilities are transferred from the higher to the lower government but not the authority.

Decentralized Planning: Decentralized planning is the planning, where at the outset, plans are prepared at the various lower levels of governments and finally the national plan is prepared taking into consideration all the plans prepared at various lower levels. Here, in this type of planning, local aspirations are included in the national plan.

Development Administration: Development administration includes administrative activities performed by the government concerning social, political, economic, human, and cultural development of a nation-state. It aims at effective implementation of development projects and programmes.

Development Communication: Development communication is basically undertaken with the objective of informing and educating people belonging to both urban and rural areas about various developmental issues and challenges and how to overcome them, and also to educate them about various developmental projects and programmes launched by the government in different sectors of development and the ways and means to avail the benefits of these programmes by applying different communication approaches and strategies. The ultimate goal of 'development communication' is to raise the quality of life of populations, including increasing income and well-being.

Development Disparities: Disparities among different region, state, caste, class, and ethnic groups in terms of achievements in terms of development indicators is termed as development disparities. For example, the development indicators like percentage of people living below the poverty line, literacy rate, mortality rate, morbidity rate, etc. varies across the regions, state, caste, and ethnic group of population.

Development Extension: It is one of the important approaches to development communication. It aims at getting extension workers (senders) and people (receivers) tuned together for a particular massage or series of massages related to development projects, programmes, and activities. In extension work, attempt is made by the extension functionaries and workers to transfer accurate information to people through communication.

Development Governance: The development governance aims at efficient and effective use of political and bureaucratic machinery in a responsive, accountable, transparent, efficient, and effective manner for the achievement of development goals. According to the United Nations, the development governance is the governance oriented to solve common national development problems and create new national development opportunities and achieve common national development goals.

Development Management: The development management aims at effective and efficient management of development activities, projects, and programmes by the government, NGOs, and other actors of development for the achievement of set goals and objectives of development.

Development Paradigms: The paradigm shift is a change from one way of thinking to another and is a revolution, a transformation, and a sort of metamorphosis. Being a dynamic concept, 'development' is more conditioned to 'paradigms' than any other subjects in social sciences. Bellu, while defining 'development paradigm', noted that development was very rarely considered to be a 'God-given' condition of socio-economic system, implying that policy-makers at national and international level have always thought that some activities were required to promote positive changes.

Development Programme: This programme is a written statement with vision, mission, objectives, activities, and a budget on proposed developmental areas to be completed over a period of time. As compared to project, programme is much broader. A programme may consist of many projects. For example, the National Rural Health Mission, a programme of the Government of India, can consist of projects on maternal health care, child health care, family planning, adolescent health care, HIV/AIDS, etc. The programme is undertaken by the government, while projects are usually undertaken by individuals or organizations. The scope of the programme is much wider than the project.

Development Project: It is a planned piece of work or an activity undertaken by an individual or organization in an area of development with a budget to be completed within a time period. As compared to a programme, the objectives of a project are limited to its budget and time period. Development projects are being formulated on various areas of development such as agriculture, industry, education, health, women empowerment, etc. Projects are of different types such as survey based, empirical, historical, action research, experimental, etc. The scope of project is limited.

Development: It is a dynamic concept and its basic aim is to raise the quality of living of people through various interventions in different dimensions of development, such as economic, social, political, human, cultural, and so on; through the development of various sectors, such as agriculture, industry, and services; and through the efforts of different actors, such as market, state, international agencies, NGOs, and CSOs. Its objective is to reduce poverty, inequality, unemployment, illiteracy, ill health, and insanitation, and to provide access to each and every family healthy housing, safe drinking water, sanitation, energy for cooking and lighting, surface and e-communication, primary education, and primary health care services through good governance. In other words, development is a quantitative and qualitative change in various socio-economic indicators.

Directly Productive Activities (DPAs): These are the consequences of social overhead capitals (SOCs) which add to the flow of final goods and services. As the SOCs are infrastructure-related activities, they have to be provided by the government, which will ultimately boost DPAs by the private investors in agriculture and industrial sectors and also in tertiary sector. The DPAs in the agriculture will enhance food grain productivity and in industrial sector, per se steel industry sector will increase productivity of steel items, which will ultimately boost employment and economic growth rate of the economy and in the tertiary sector, it will enhance education, health, banking, and insurance sector activities.

Division of Labour: This means breaking the total labour effort of an economic activity into different specialized components so that each division will work to the best of its potential. It is believed that the division of labour will enhance productivity in three ways: (i) increases dexterity (skill) of the labourer; (ii) saves labour times: and (iii) helps in the invention of labour-saving machinery.

Dualism: This represents the existence of two types of sectors, one having characteristic features of modernity and the other backwardness; for example, the existence of traditional and modern sectors, agriculture and industrial sectors, urban and rural sectors, and formal and informal sectors in the developing countries.

Economic Development: This means increase in the performance of the economy in various economic indicators, such as rise in GNP, per capita income, reduction in economic inequality, reduction in economic poverty, and reduction in unemployment.

Economic Growth: Increase in the capacity of an economy to produce goods and services from one year to that of another. It is measured by the GNP in a year with that of the GNP in the previous year.

Economic Inequality: This is a result of unequal distribution of income and wealth in a society across its population. Income inequality, which is a form of economic inequality, is measured by Gini Coefficient. The value of Gini Coefficient varies between zero and one. If zero, it is a case of perfect equality and if one, it is a case of perfect inequality.

e-Governance: It is the application of electronic and technological means in the interaction between government and citizens and government and business as well as in the internal government operations in order to simplify and improve government service delivery system and bring transparency in the functioning of the public affairs.

Ethical Development: The ethical dimension of development emphasizes on human happiness. Happiness is something eternal and can be truly gained holistically by doing well-being of all by keeping one's self-interest minimal. The mission of the ethical development is to facilitate development of all and involve all in the process of development, and there is less discrimination and marginalization. According to Cypher and Dietz, development is about realizing very fundamental human values and finding the means to extend the fruits of these values to the greatest majority of the world's population.

Fiscal Policy: It refers to the government's policy on revenue (taxation) collection and spending (expenditure). It intends towards maintaining economic stability and promoting growth rate of an economy.

Foreign Direct Investments (FDI): It refers to those investments in which a company from one country makes direct investment in another country on which the foreign investor has control over the investments. Thus, FDI implies that the investor exerts influence on the management of the enterprise resident in the other country.

Functioning: It is an important component of the human capacity theory propounded by Amartya Sen. To Sen, functioning is 'the various things a person may value doing or being'. The examples of 'being' are being well nourished, being housed in a healthy house, being educated, being part of supportive network, being groomed in an healthy environment, etc. An achievement or outcome will not be treated as functioning if it is not something that is valued by the person concerned, who has achieved the milestone.

Gain Spirit: By 'gain spirit', Weber meant a system of conduct based on ethical norms which govern commercial activity. This brings the economic and religious spheres into a relationship with each other, which was acting as deterrent to free trade and commerce in the Eastern economies.

Gender Development Index (GDI): GDI measures the achievement of women in front of literacy, life expectancy, and income as used in Human Development Index (HDI); however, take cognizance of inequality in achievement between women and men.

Gender Development: Gender development aims at the empowerment of women vis-à-vis men in all aspects of development, such as economic, political, social, and human development. The economic empowerment of women aims at reducing income inequality, poverty, and labour market discrimination against women. The social empowerment measures intend to raise women education and health care status, and the political empowerment aims at raising the political participation of women in legislature. As women constitute nearly 50 per cent of the total population, gender development is vital to development.

Gender Empowerment Measure (GEM): GEM is being calculated by using three important indicators such as proportion of seats held by women in national parliament; percentage of women in economic decision-making positions; and female share of income.

Gender Inequality Index (GII): GII is a measure propounded by UNDP that uses three dimensions of women's backwardness for the calculation of GII—these are reproductive health, empowerment, and labour market participation. The two important indicators used in the determination of reproductive health are maternal mortality rate (MMR) and adolescent fertility rate (AFR); and indicators used in the measurement of empowerment of women are share of parliamentary seats held by men and women and higher education attainment level (secondary education and above) of women.

Governance: Commonly, 'governance' refers to the action and process by which authority is exercised and decisions are taken and implemented. The UNDP has defined governance as "The exercise of economic, political and administrative authority to manage a country's affairs at all levels". Some of the features of good governance are transparency, accountability, efficiency and effectiveness, participatory, consensus oriented, equitable and inclusive, and follows the rule of law.

Gram Sabha: It is known as the 'village assembly'. All voters are the members of the gram sabha. Article 243(b) defines gram sabha as, "A body consisting of persons registered in the electoral rolls relating to the village comprised within the area of the panchayat at the village level". While Article 243A says that "A gram sabha may exercise such powers and perform such functions at the village level as the legislature of a state may, by law provide". It provides forum to the village people to gather and discuss their common problems and understand the needs and aspirations of the people. Gram sabha is held one to four times in a year. All important decisions on the selection of the beneficiaries for the various rural development schemes are being taken in the gram sabha.

Great Depression: The great depression refers to the economic slump which had occurred during the period 1929–39 and affected the developed economies of the Northern America, Europe, and other part of the world. It also has a moderate impact on the developing countries. It caused drastic decline in productivity, severe unemployment, and acute deflationary pressure.

Gross Domestic Product (GDP): GDP measures the total value for final output produced by an economy, by both its residents and non-residents. In other words, GDP is the total income created within the borders of a country, regardless of whether the ultimate recipient of that income resides within or outside the country.

Gross Happiness Index: The concept of development as happiness believes that the GDP-based approach is outdated and a nation should be seen as succeeding not if its citizens are financially well-off but rather if they are healthy and happy (Helliwell et al., 2013). The World Happiness Report 2013 has used variables, like healthy life expectancy, perceptions of corruption, GDP per capita, freedom to make life choices, social support and generosity in the calculation of Gross Happiness Index.

Gross National Product (GNP): GNP measures the money value of total annual domestic product of a country plus income earned from abroad by its residents, minus payments made to non-residents and foreign institutions. In other words, GNP is equal to Gross Domestic Product + import – export.

Human Development: Human development of a nation is measured by Human Development Index (HDI). HDI measures the average achievement of a country in three basic dimensions of human development: (i) a long and healthy life, as measured by life expectancy at birth; (ii) knowledge as measured by the adult literacy rate; and (iii) a decent standard of living as measured by GDP per capita in purchasing power parity (PPP) terms in US dollar. The formula used in the calculation of each dimension of human development is as follows:

Inclusive Development: Inclusive development believes that everyone must participate and contribute towards the process of development and also equally enjoy the fruits of development. It lays emphasis on the principle of economic equity, distributive and social justice, and equality in participation and believes that the economic growth achieved amidst social exclusion cannot be economically and socially sustainable. The UNDP has defined inclusive growth as the process and the outcome, where all groups of people have participated in the organization of growth and have benefited from it.

Inflation: It means persistent rise in prices of goods and services. The inflation rate in an economy is calculated by the wholesale and consumer price indexes. Inflation leads to fall in the purchasing power and the value of money in an economy.

Informal Sector: The large chunk of workforce in the developing countries working in the informal sector is also known as the unorganized sector. The informal sector is the unregulated sector or unregistered sector, that is not subject to any government rules and regulations. In fact, the main reason of low income and the plight of the poor in the underdeveloped countries is the existence of 'informal sector' which is also called as 'informal economy'.

Invisible Hand: According to Adam Smith, market has an inherent property called as 'invisible hand'. The invisible hand of the market operates through the forces of demand and supply and the free play of demand and supply would ensure an efficient level of production, consumption, and distribution of goods in the society. It is the 'invisible hand' which creates automatic equilibrium between demand and supply in the perfectly competitive market.

Jan Lok Pal: It is an anti-corruption bill being drafted by the civil society activists in India aiming at the appointment of a Jan Lok Pal (citizen ombudsman) an independent body to investigate the corruption charges against the public servant. It aims at checking corruption due to which the common man suffers a lot.

Laissez Faire: The *laissez faire* means left alone, which advocates that the state should have minimum interference in the functioning of the market. The policy of left alone or *laissez faire* allows the producers to produce as much they like, earn as much income as they can and save as much as they wish. It allows the producers to make judicious use of the factors of production, i.e. land, labour, capital, and organization in the process of economic development.

Marginalization: Marginalization means some groups of population are at the margin and are vulnerable to be excluded. With globalization, the intensity of marginalization and exclusion has elongated. Marginalization and social exclusion are factors responsible for inequality and inequity in development. The marginalized and socially excluded groups are being deprived of the fruits of development. Their level of participation in the development process, i.e. in the formulation, implementation, and monitoring of developmental projects and programmes, which are intended to improve their livelihood and development indicators is low. They are socially, economically, and politically marginalized.

Mechanical Solidarity: The concept 'solidarity' refers to the system of social bonds which link individual to society and widen the individual's vision. The characteristic features of underdeveloped nations are akin to mechanical solidarity, while those of advanced nations are in proximity to organic solidarity. A few features of mechanical solidarity are: (i) a homogenous population which is small and isolated and the density of population is high; (ii) division of labour based on social cooperation, with little or no specialization; and (iii) a system of social institutions in which religion is dominant and people are guided by religious beliefs and values.

Monetary Policy: It deals with the money supply, credit, and interest rate and is prepared by the central bank of the country. It aims to control inflation through the regulation of money supply and interest rate in the country. In India, monetary policy is prepared by the Reserve Bank of India.

Morphology of Backwardness: According to Baran, the backwardness of the underdeveloped countries is largely due to exploitation by the developed countries as well as their internal conditions. The potential surplus of the underdeveloped economies is appropriated by a group of dominant classes, i.e. landlord, money lenders, and small and monopolistic industrial bourgeoisie. Because of all these conditions, the potential surplus of underdeveloped countries is being plundered and appropriated by the dominants from within and also from outside the nation, is what he termed as 'the morphology of backwardness'.

Nai Talim: Gandhi advocated *Nai Talim* (New Education) a novel approach to education which emphasizes on total personality development of an individual, including body, mind, and spirit. The basic principles of *Nai Talim* are:

(i) Education or learning should be in one's mother tongue and should include handicraft work.
(ii) Work should be linked with most useful vocational needs of the locality.
(iii) Learning should be linked with vocational work.
(iv) Work should be socially useful and productive needed for living.

Neo-liberalism: Neo-liberalism is a political economic theory, committed to *laissez faire* market fundamentalism and a minimalist role for state intervention in the economic affairs of the nation. Some of the features of neo-liberalism are:

(i) Market is the key economic player and its proper functioning would hasten economic growth and development in developed as well as developing countries.
(ii) Neo-liberal policies aim at privatization, liberalization, and globalization.
(iii) Privatization of public sector units will enhance their efficiency and raise their contribution to economic development.
(iv) The role of government in the process of economic development must be minimal and its action in correcting market imperfection will act as stimulant to economic development.

Non-governmental Organizations: NGOs are private non-profit professional organizations and registered bodies with a legal character engaged in various sectors of the economy. Besides their own funding, they also receive grant from the government and other international agencies. NGOs are found to be actively involved in the formulation, implementation, monitoring, and evaluation of many socio-economic development projects and programmes. Being closer to the people and less constrained by the rules and regulations of the state machinery, they are more effective at the grass-roots level, as compared to other state apparatus.

Organic Solidarity: The concept 'solidarity' refers to the system of social bonds which link individual to society and widen the individual's vision. The characteristic features of underdeveloped nations are akin to mechanical solidarity, while those of advanced nations are in proximity to organic solidarity. A few features of organic solidarity are:

(i) Large populations spread over broader geographical areas and the density of population is low.
(ii) Complexity of division of labour and the economic functioning is guided by the division and specialization of labour.
(iii) Individuals are linked to each other by contract or through social net working rather than by sentiment and obligation.

Panchayati Raj Institutions (PRIs): Panchayati Raj Institutions are the third-tier democratic bodies, after the parliament at the centre and assemblies at the state level in

India. The three tier PRI institutions such as zilla parishad at the district level, block samities at the intermediate level, and gram panchayat at the village level are the local self-government institutions for the political governance of rural areas. The 73rd Constitutional Amendment of India has assigned 29 development-related duties and responsibilities to PRIs. The election to these bodies is held every five years, which is being conducted by the State Election Commission constituted for the purpose. Thirty-three per cent of seats are reserved for women in these bodies. There is also reservation of seats for Scheduled Castes, Scheduled Tribes, and Other Backward Caste people. There are more than 232,278 village panchayats, 5905 intermediate panchayats, and 499 district panchayats being manned by 2.92 million elected representatives.

Parallel Bodies: The bodies and the organization running parallel to the government as well as the local self-government institutions are largely called- parallel bodies. Examples of such organizations operating at the grass-roots level are, village forest committees, water user groups, *gram vikas samitis*, village vigilance committees, water and sanitation committees, and so on, formulated in different states in India.

Participatory Communication: It is a dynamic, interactional, and transformative process of dialogue between people, both individually and collectively, with the actors and stakeholders of development to realize their full potential and be engaged in their own welfare. In the participatory communication process people articulate their own views identify their common concerns and seek solution for it along with governmental and non-governmental functionaries and other CSOs engaged in the implementation of developmental projects and programmes.

Participatory Governance: In participatory governance people exercise their voices in the conduct of public affairs. It also means that people govern themselves for their own development, while the government and other development agencies only play a catalyst role. The success of participatory governance depends on many factors such as the prevailing state of affairs, the number and quality of the people and their representatives and their willingness to involve in the development process, the balance of forces between different social groups, the overall social-political environment, and the level of economic development.

Perspective Plan: The perspective plans are otherwise called short-term, medium-term and long-term Plans. Short term plans are prepared for a short period, usually for one year and therefore known as 'annual plan'. They are also otherwise known as 'controlling plans'. Medium term plans are prepared for a period of 3 to 7 years. The five year plans in vogue in most of the developing countries are the medium term plans prepared with judicious allocation of financial and physical resources for raising per capita income, standard of living, employment, and economic growth and reducing inequalities in the country. The long term plan usually lasts for the period of 10–30 years.

Pluralism: Pluralism means recognition and affirmation of diversity. Pluralism presupposes that all the people of nation and outside the nation, all religious groups, majority as well as minority, and all ethnic groups of population are its own and all are equal before law. Pluralism believes in the energetic engagement with diversity and active seeking of understanding across the line of difference.

Political Development: Political development implies that the political system needs to be mature enough to deal with economic growth and development of a country. It emphasizes on the development of pluralistic political systems, strengthening developmental education among the parliamentarians, legislatures, and elected representatives of the local self-government institutions, the creation and empowerment of local political units though capacity building, encouragement of effective public interest groups, democratic decentralization, political modernization, equalization of power, protective discrimination in political empowerment of disadvantaged, gender political empowerment and good governance, and recognition of political federalism.

Political Governance: It implies adherence to governance principles, of transparency, accountability, and rule of law by the political parties in the process of running the affairs of the nation-state.

Political governance needs to ensure: (i) free and fair election and transition of power; (ii) effective and constructive political opposition and representative government; (iii) absence of political corruption and misuse of political power for personal and family gains; (iv) dereliction of political pressure on executive, judiciary, and other investigating agencies in their function for political and personal gains; and (v) transparency and accountability in the implementation of development projects and programme.

Positive-sum Incentives and Zero-sum Incentives: The actors involved in the economic growth process, i.e. the entrepreneurs, the inventors, the discoverers, and the innovators have to be given positive-sum incentives including productive investment, use of technical know-how, exploration and exploitation of new markets, and use of scientific discoveries and innovations. The positive-sum activities are those which raise savings, investments, income and employment opportunities in the economy; while the zero-sum activities are those which do not produce conducive effect on national income and growth rate, therefore, needs to be given zero-sum incentives. The zero-sum incentive consists of trading risks, non-trading or speculative activities, and transference of income and profit from one section of people to another.

Poverty: A person in poverty is one who is incapable to afford the basic necessities of life, such as: (i) food, clothing, and shelter; (ii) safe drinking water and sanitation; (iii) rudimentary requirements of primary health care and elementary education; (iv) basic form of energy for cooking and lighting; and (v) certain amount of basic household amenities such as bed, utensils, and other accessories of minimum sustainable living. UNDP termed it as constrained choices and unfulfilled capabilities and according to World Bank it is the inability to attain a minimum standard of living.

Primary Sector: The primary sector consists of extraction of resources from the earth, primarily the agriculture and other allied activities, like fisheries, dairy, horticulture, etc.

Provision of Urban Amenities in Rural Areas (PURA): The programme of Provision of Urban Amenities in Rural Areas popularly known as 'PURA' is one of the endeavours aimed at raising the quality of living in rural areas at par with that of urban areas. The aim of the PURA is to provide livelihood opportunities and urban amenities in rural areas to bridge the rural–urban divide. Through public–private partnership, PURA aims to provide 'add-on' revenue-earning facilities such as village-linked tourism, integrated rural hub, rural market, agri-common services centre warehousing, etc. in rural areas. APJ Abdul Kalam who was a strong votary of PURA, said that sustainable rural development can be achieved with the mission of PURA through creation of three connectivities, namely physical, electronic, and knowledge, leading to economic connectivity.

Public–Private Partnership: The 'public–private partnership' is a popular concept in the developing countries that have accepted the neo-liberal ideals and given adequate space to the private and corporate sector to play an important role and offer a helping hand to the government in their drive for achieving higher economic growth rate and development goals. Under public–private partnership, the market or the private or corporate sector provides 'private goods and services' with profit motive; while State provides 'public goods and services' with welfare motive and the convergence is built for the effective and efficient delivery of good quality services.

Razor's Edge Equilibrium: Any divergence from the equilibrium of natural growth rate, warranted growth rate, and actual growth rate will lead to state of instability which according to the Harrod–Domar model is called as 'knife-edge equilibrium'.

Remittances: Sending of money by a person residing or working in a foreign country or other than his or her State to his kith and kin in home country or own state.

Rolling Plan: The rolling plans are plans prepared at intervals usually one year and these rolling plans are mostly the annual plans where planning process rolls from that of one year to that of the another. A rolling plan is flexible and allows for revision and modification. In rolling plans, review of the plan becomes a continuous exercise.

Sarvodaya: According to Gandhi, *sarvodaya* is an important means of development and it intends to make development process 'of the people, by the people and for the people' and promote the welfare of all. By welfare of all, Gandhi did not mean the greatest good of the greatest number, but prioritizing the welfare of 'the last man', the most deprived and the weakest, and the poorest of the poor. He advocated that it is the duty of the society, to give priority to the care of the poorest of the poor. In the *sarvodaya* system, basic needs always get precedence over other needs that are not so basic, largely the needs for attainment of comfort and luxury.

Scheduled Castes: Indian society is largely a stratified society on the basis of caste, class, ethnicity, and religion. The Scheduled Castes in Indian society occupy the lowest status in the caste hierarchy. The Scheduled Castes are primarily known as 'depressed classes'. The Indian Independence Act 1947 defined the term 'the scheduled castes', to mean such castes, races, tribes, parts, or groups, which appear to the governor general to correspond to the classes of persons formerly known as the 'depressed classes'. They suffer from all sorts of deprivation, such as social, economic, and political deprivations. The Scheduled Castes constitute one-seventh of the total population in India.

Scheduled Tribes: They are the most socio-economically backward group of population in India. In India, they are largely known as adivasi (original settlers), girijan (hill dwellers), vanya Jati (forest caste men) and Anusuchit Janjati (Scheduled Tribes). They constitute eight percent of the total population of the states, such as Madhya Pradesh, Orissa, Gujarat, Maharashtra, Jharkhand, and Chhattisgarh that have sizable number of tribal population. There are more than 600 tribes in India.

Secondary Sector: The secondary sector is the industrial sector. The industrial sector is broadly categorized into four sub-sectors, i.e. (i) mining that covers the activities of extraction of natural resources, such as metals, coal, and oil and those like stone quarrying; (ii) manufacturing that covers manufacturing of various products, such as food products, like flour, processed tea and aerated drinks; wood products, like furniture; textile products, like yarn, cloth and garments; leather products, like tyres, tubes and toys; mineral products, like cement and glass; chemical products, like synthetic, fibres, fertilizers, and pharmaceuticals; metal products, like steel, utensils, machinery, equipments and apparatus, like machinery, transformers, television and computers, and transport equipment, like bicycles, cars, trains, truck, etc.; (iii) electricity, gas and water- activities relating to generation, transmission, and distribution of electricity; the manufacturing and distribution of gas and the activities associated with collection, purification, and distribution of water; and (iv) construction activities relating to construction of buildings and civil engineering works.

Service Sector: The tertiary sector is popularly known as the service sector. The service sector does not produce tangible goods, however, it has the capacity to generate income and employment and some of the well-known service sectors are health, education, banking, insurance, and other emerging service sectors in the economies across the world are communication and information, hotel and hospitality, tourism, retail business, and real estate.

Social Capital: The World Bank has remarked on the role of social capital in development as: (i) social capital can 'bridge' different groups by enabling cross-cutting and inclusive ties; (ii) social relationships and networks are a form of capital that may bring benefits to their members; (iii) the interplay of kin and communal bonding and bridging social relations shapes cross-cutting social capital and social cohesion. Thus, an investment in social capital is an important requisite for not only raising social capital formation but also for the promotion of human, economic, social, and political development.

Social Development: Social development emphasizes on the role of social aspects such as education, health, women empowerment, social inequalities, social exclusion, marginalization, social networking, and social capital formation in development. World Bank emphasized that for social development, people should be put in the centre of development (inclusion), strengthening the social fabric of communities so that their members can work together (cohesion), and finding ways for people to exercise their voices to authorities (accountability).

Social Marketing: Social marketing aims at the use of marketing and selling techniques for the education, behavioural change and adoption of goal, objectives, and benefits of development projects and programmes and other developmental interventions launched in various development sectors of the economy for raising the quality of life of the people in different social settings.

Social Mobilization: The social mobilization intervention is an empowerment process through which individuals or communities are effectively mobilized to take direct control over their lives and environment. Social mobilization keeps different community organizations and various communities at the grass roots bound together and enables them to solve community level development issues and challenges through joint action.

Social Over-head Capitals (SOCs): The SOCs includes all public services, i.e. law and order, education, public health, road transportation, communications, power, water supply, irrigation, drainage, etc. which are required for the development take off of the economy. The SOCs are to be provided by the government, as private sector will be least interested to invest in SOCs. However, the investment in SOCs by the public sector will boost direct productive activities (DPA) by the private investors in agriculture and industrial sectors.

Soft State: Soft States generally feature weak law, poor willpower to initiate effective social and economic reforms, social indiscipline, corruption, scams, poor governance, and weak enforcement of rule of law. Political and bureaucratic establishments in a soft State lack deterministic willpower to take firm decision on the economic front to strengthen the economy and put it on a higher growth path.

Steady State: At the stage of 'steady state' of the economy, any further increase in the application of capital will not lead to growth of income; rather it will start to diminish. The 'steady state' situation customarily takes place when input–output combination is at equilibrium.

Stimulant Forces and Forces of Shocks: Stimulant forces give impetus and generate drive which increases level of savings, investments, income, and output in an economy, while, the 'forces of shocks' act as distractors to development which reduce the level of output, income, savings, and investments of an economy. The former are treated as income-generating forces and the latter as income-depressing forces.

Surplus Value: Surplus value is the extra labour of the worker for which the worker does not get wage. This surplus value which is over and above the wage is appropriated by the capitalists. In other words, 'surplus value' is a means of exploitation adopted by the capitalist to exploit labour.

Sustainable Development: Sustainable development considers that development process sustainable when it meets the needs of the present without compromising the ability of future generations to meet their own needs. Sustainable development necessitates maintaining a balance between the three pillars of development, i.e. economy, ecology and society.

Take-off Stage: At this stage, growth becomes a normal process of development in a society. This becomes possible because of agricultural and industrial revolution and application of scientific and technological innovations into the agricultural and industrial sectors of the economy, corroborated by the supportive international environment. The economy marches towards self-sustaining growth and the obstacles and resistances to steady growth are being removed and the forces of economic development dominate the society.

The HDI is the simple average indices of all the above three dimensions.

Third World Countries: These countries are otherwise known as underdeveloped or developing countries. The term, 'Third World' was used by the developed countries, i.e. USA and Europe, in order to distinguish them from the first world, consisting of the rich capitalists or the world of advanced market economies and the second world, the centrally planned economies of Eastern Europe and the Soviet Union. These countries largely consist of economically poor nations of Asia, Africa, Latin America, and Caribbean nations.

Transparency: Etymologically, transparency means 'openness'. It is otherwise being quoted as 'much is known by many'. The actors of governance, such as government, private sector, NGOs, and the CSOs must be well-intentioned and open to public scrutiny. Transparency presupposes that rules and regulations and procedures must be simple, clear, and understandable with fewer contradictions.

Trusteeship: Gandhi propounded the doctrine of trusteeship as a way to realize social change and development through non-violent means. Gandhi was critical of both capitalism and socialism, as he believed that the former relies on private ownership, while the latter advocates state ownership of means of production and distribution. He advocated a new method that would substitute both capitalist and socialist forms of ownership, which is called 'trusteeship'. Some of the features of trusteeship are: (i) It does not recognize any right of private ownership of property except in as much as it may be permitted by society for its own welfare. (ii) It does not exclude legislative regulation of the ownership and use of wealth. (iii) Under state regulated trusteeship, an individual will not be free to hold or use his wealth for selfish satisfaction or in disregard of the interest of society.

Unemployment: Generally, unemployment refers to a situation where people are willing and are capable to work but are unable to find suitable paid employment. The unemployment condition of a nation is usually calculated by the unemployment rate. The formula for unemployment rate is as follows:

Unemployment Rate (UR): Unemployment Rate (UR) is defined as the number of persons unemployed per 1,000 persons in the labour force (employed and unemployed).

$$\text{UR} = \frac{\text{Number of unemployed persons}}{\text{Labour force}} \times 1000$$

Urban Local Bodies (ULBs): The three-tier ULBs are the municipal corporations, municipal councils and nagar panchayats, based on the population of the cities. They are the local self-government institutions for the political governance of urban areas. The 74th Constitutional Amendment of India has assigned 18 development related duties and responsibilities to these bodies. The election to these bodies is held in every five years, which is being conducted by the State Election Commission constituted for the purpose. Thirty-three per cent of seats are reserved for women in these bodies. There is also reservation of seats for Scheduled Castes, Scheduled Tribes and other backward classes. There are 4,041 ULBs manned by more than 70,000 elected representatives in India.

Vicious Circle of Poverty: The underdeveloped economies are vexed with vicious circle of poverty from both demand as well as supply side. Because of the vicious circle, the circular constellation of forces tends to act and react upon one another in such a way as to keep a poor country in a state of poverty. On the demand side, low demand for goods leads to low investment, low investment leads to low production, low production results in low employment, low employment leads to low income, and low income finally leads to low demand. On the other hand, the supply side runs as, low supply of capital leads to low investment, low investment leads to low production, low production results in low employment, low income and low savings, and low savings ultimately results in low investment, and low investment will lead to low capital formation.

INDEX

access to energy, 135
accountability, 169
accounting rate of return (ARR), 199
achievement, need for, 54
ActionAid, 113
actors in development state, 41
actual growth rate, 22
ADB
  development strategies advocated by, 108
administrative decentralization, 163
administrative reform, 150
adolescent fertility rate (AFR), 91
advanced countries and poor countries, difference between, 43
advanced societies
  structure of, 53
advocacy, 227
affiliation, 65
African countries
  features of development state, 41
agency, 64
age of high mass consumption development process, 37
agricultural labourer, 9
agricultural productivity, 9
  enhancement of, factors to, 18
agriculture
  contribution in GDP of developing countries, 10
  role in economic development, 77
agriculturist, 9
Amin, Samir, 58
ancient slave stage, 36
Anna Hazare movement for Jan Lok Pal, 152
Annan, Kofi, 169
appraisal, 199
appraisal, planning, organizing, staffing, directing, coordinating, controlling, reporting, budgeting, capacity building and disseminating (APOSDCCRBCD), 198
Aristotle, 63
arithmetic progression, 19
ascriptive bonds, 53

backward linkages, 34, 35
backwash effect, 42
balanced growth, Gandhian model of, 70
balanced growth theorists, 29
balanced growth theory, 33
basic needs, 14
basic needs, concept of
  definition of, 128
  from developing countries perspective, 128
  objective of, 128
Bauer, Peter, 61
bazaar-economy, 121
benefit cost ration (BCR), 199
benevolent capitalism, 96
Bharat Nirman programme, 109
Bhudan Movement, 67
big push approach, 30
big push investment, 30
big-push theory / approach, 31
Bihar
  growth rate of, 7
bilateral agencies, 112
Bill and Melinda Gates Foundation, 113
block plan, 185, 191
bodily health, 65
bodily integrity, 65
bottom-up approach, 140, 141
brahmacharya (celibacy) practice, 71
Bretton Woods System, 112
budgeting, 201
bureaucracy, 146
bureaucratic administration
  characteristics of, 147
business process outsourcing, 94

Canadian International Development Agency (CIDA), 113
capabilities, 64
capacity building, 201
capital accumulation, 17, 18, 21
  impact of increase in population, 19
  source of promotion, 17
capital formation, 6, 11, 17, 29, 31, 33, 38, 39, 78
capitalism, 8, 16, 36
  analysis of growth, 51
capitalist development in periphery countries, 59
capitalist economic system, 108
capitalist economy, 20, 21

capitalists class, 20
capitalist sector of economy, 38
capitalist system
  classes of, 20
capital-output ratio, concept of, 22
capital stock, 22
Cardoso, F. H., 59
centralized planning, 185
centre countries, 58
civil service in India,
  distressing trends of, 150
civil society organizations (CSOs), 115, 148, 159
classical liberalism, 60
classical theories of economic growth and development, 16
classical theories of development, 19
coalition politics, 151
colonialism, 59
communication, 217
communication for development, 216
communication management, 211
communication needs assessment (CNA), 221
community development, 109
community participation, 140
comprador (trading) bourgeoisie, 58
Comprehensive District Agriculture Plan popularly (C-DAP), 190
confirmation, 220
consensus oriented decision, 172
consumerism, 96
controlling, 201
control over one's environment, 66
cooperative societies, 148
coordinating, 200
Corn Law, 18
corporate social responsibility (CSR), 9, 96
corruption, 151
cost management, 209
creative capitalism, 96
critical minimum effort theory, 32
crony capitalism, 112, 115
cultural development dimension, 88
cultural paradox of developing countries, 12
cultural taboos in developing countries, 12
cultural tourism, 87
cumulative causation, 42
custodian role of developmental state, 41
Das Capital (Karl Marx), 20
decentralization, 89
decentralization paradigm, 141
decentralized development, 148
decentralized development planning, 192
decentralized district administration, 148
decentralized governance, 161, 172
decentralized planning, 185
decision, 220
decision making process, 220
declining state, 18
Delhi Human Development Report 2013, 79
demiurge role of developmental state, 41
democracy, 88
democratic decentralization, 139
demography, indicators for sustainable development, 137
dependency
  meaning of, 56
dependency theory of development, 60
dependent capitalism, 59
developed economy, 26
developing countries, 148
  reasons for, 13
developing countries market, 60
developing economies
  characteristics of, 12
developing nations, 10
developing societies
  guided by traditional believes and values, 53
development
  in capitalist system, 16
development, 95, 98, 217
  chain of disequilibria, 34
  continual discourse on, 10
  discourse, 126
  dynamic nature of, 126
  equated with economic growth, 6
  factors for, 18
  goal of, 97
  indicators of, 7
  is a learning process, 55
  meaning of, 76
  methods to achieve, 19
  of economy, 17
  paradigm, 126
  paradigms, 141
  realization of fundamental human values, 95
  sectors of, 122
  stages of, 36
  strategies, 29
  strategies and investments in developing countries, 35
development administration, 146, 155
  challenges of, 155
  meaning of, 147
  role and functions of, 150
developmentalism, 29
developmentalist theorists, 29
developmental projects, 149
developmental state, 29, 39, 43, 108
development alternatives, 153
development bureaucracy, 152
development communication, 175, 215, 216
  approaches to, 230
  definition of, 218
  goals of, 218

objectives of, 218
principles of, 222
strategies of, 233
theories of, 220
development communication materials (DCM), 232
development communication need assessment (DCNA), 231
development communication programme, 232
development communication team (DCT), 232
development disparities in developing countries, 154
development extension, 223
development governance
aim of, 159
as apparatus to check corruption, 160
attributes of, 172
benefits of, 160
decentralized democratic institutions, 161
dimensions of, 168
importance of, 159
issues of, 176
meaning of, 159
principles of, 159
development management, 195
aims of, 197
aspects of, 196
characteristics of, 197
definition of, 196
functions of, 202
development managers, 198
development of an economy
meaning of, 25
development plan, 181
development planning, 148, 193
aim of, 181
definition of, 180
formulation of, 189
principles of, 188
role in development, 184
types of, 186
development practitioners, 159
development project management
issues in, 211
system approach to, 208
development state, 43
development state theory, 43
development support communication, 217
diffusion of innovation theory, 220
diffusion process, 220
directing, 200
directly produced activities (DPAs), 34
directly productive activities (DPAs), 34
disseminating, 202
district administration, 149
District Development Committee, 186
District Planning Committee (DPC), 191
division of labour, 17, 18
dominant social paradigm, 126
drinking water, 135
drive to maturity, 36
dualism, 154
dualism scenario in developing countries, 11
Durkheim, Emile, 50, 52

Eastern economies, 51
economic activity, 17
economic crisis of 1970s, 109
economic development, 18, 35, 98
aim of, 95
factors of, 67
importance of, 77
influenced by market imperfection, 78
meaning of, 77
measures of, 77
policies programmes, 79
economic dimension of development, 79
economic empowerment, 92
economic empowerment, women, 92
challenges before, 93
economic exploitation, 106
economic governance, 77, 79
economic growth, 16
factors for, 18
stages of, 36
economic growth, mechanisms of, 78
economic growth of economy, 17
economic growth rate, 7, 11, 17
economic indicators, 204
economic liberalization, 110
economic planning, 181
economic reform process, 111
economic regionalism, 151
economic system and planning, difference between, 186
economic variables, 6
economy
challenge of, 17
sectors in, 38
educational entertainment, 228
education, indicators for sustainable development, 136
education of women, benefits of, 95
effectiveness, 171
efficiency, 171
efficiency of developmental state, 41
e-Governance, 149, 167
embedded autonomy, 41
embedded state, 41
emotional neutrality over affectivity criteria in modern societies, 54
emotions, 65
employment
competition for, 18
environmental sustainability, 81
equity dimension of governance, 170
ethical development, 95
ethical dimension of development, 97

ethics of development, 95
European Union (EU), 60, 113

Family Planning International (FPI), 113
farmers associations, 148
farmers clubs, 148
farmers cooperatives, 114
feudalism, 36
finance, 154
financial planning, 185
firm-centered economy, 121
First World nations, 10
fiscal decentralization, 163
fixed plan, 186
fixing up development targets and outcomes, 206
forced labour, 8
forces of shocks, 32
Ford Foundation, 113
foreign direct investment (FDI), 78, 111, 148, 195
 impact on development, 137
forward linkages, 34, 35
Frank, Andre Gunder, 57
free trade, 18
Friedman, Milton, 61
full employment growth rate, 23
functioning, 64
functioning economy, 62

gain spirit, 51
Gandhian theory, 72
gap identification, 203
Garibi Hatao (Abolition of Poverty) programme, 127
Gates, Bill, 96
GDP, 6, 7
Gender Development Index (GDI), 91
gender development, measurement of, 91
gender dimension, 95
Gender Empowerment Index (GEI), 91
Gender Empowerment Measure GEM), 91
Gender Inequality Index (GII), 91
Gender-Related Development Index (GDI), 91
gender sensitive service sectors, 94
geometric progression, 19
Global Alliance for ICT and Development (GAID), 113
Global Alliance for Improved Nutrition (GAIN), 113
Global Development Networks (GDN), 113
Global Knowledge Networks (GKN), 113
Global Water Partnership (GWP), 113
gross national product (GNP), 6, 8, 95
goal setting, 203
good citizenry, 175
good governance, 29, 109, 160
governance, concept of
 aim of, 159
 definition of, 158
governance, indicators for sustainable development, 135
government
 functions of, 62
Grameen Bank, 92
gram sabha, 191
Gram Swaraj for total development, 69
gram vikas samitis, 153
Great Depression (1929–1936), 108
gross domestic product (GDP), 77
gross national income (GNI), 77
growth
 and development,
  difference between, 9
 meaning of, 6
guided capitalism, Japan, 111
Gujarati diasporas, 79

happiness, 95, 96, 97
Harris–Todaro model of labour migration, 46
Harrod–Domar model, 24
 benefits for developed
  countries, 23
 capital-output ratio, 22
 criticism against, 23
 economy dependence, 22
 growth rates, types of, 22
 impact of increase in savings, 22
 investment in economy, 26
 knife-edge equilibrium problem, 23
 prediction on equilibrium economy, 23
Hazare, Anna, 161
health, indicators for sustainable development, 136
heterodox economics, 49
heterodox theory of development
 emphasises on non-economic aspects, 49
Hind Swaraj, 95
Hirschman, Albert, 29
human capabilities theory, 66
human capital
 role of, 19
human development
 dimension, 81
Human Development Index, 12
Human Development Index indicators, 79
Human Development Report 1999, 110
human resource management, 210
husbandry role of developmental state, 41
imagination, 65
International Monetary Fund (IMF), 60, 110
imperialism, 59
implementation, 220
inclusive development, 141, 160
inclusive development paradigm, 131
inclusive dimension of governance, 170
income inequality, 134, 135
income poverty, 135
Indira Awas Yojana, 9

individual in society, role of, 53
individualism, 53
industrial development, 78
industrial enterprise, 96
industrialization, 29, 119
  task of, 31
industrial reserve army, 21
informal education, 216
informal sector, 121
information and communications technology, 149, 164, 216
infrastructure development, 29, 109
intermediate panchayat plan, 191
intermediate state, 39, 40
internal rate of return (IRR), 199
international agencies, 113
international development organizations, 112, 159
international economic relationship paradigm, 139
international foundations, 112
International Labour Organization, 3, 93
International Land Coalition (ILC), 113
international NGOs, 112
internet, 216
inter-personal communication, 226
irresponsibility, 151

Jan Lok Pal, 161
Japan
  growth rate of, 8
Japan International Cooperation Agency (JICA), 113
job creation
  in secondary and tertiary sector in developing countries, 11

Kecamatan Community Development Programme, Indonesia, 127
knowledge, 220
Kripalani, J.B., 66
Kudubashree, programme of women empowerment for development, 93
Kuhn, Thomas, 126
Kurihara, K.K., 23

labour, 17, 38
labourers, 20
labour intensive agriculture-based economies, 10
labour market participation indicators, 91
labour productivity
  technological change for, 21
labour saving tool technology, 21
laissez faire, 18, 23, 60, 62
LDCs, 59
Lerner, Daniel, 50, 55
less developed, 10, 13
Lewis, Arthur, 29
Libenstein, 29
liberalism, 60
life, 65
living conditions, 135
localism–grass-rootism development, 140
local plan, 186
local self-government
  Declaration to the World Summit on Sustainable Development (2002), 140
local self-government (LSCs) institutions, 117
long-term plans, 186

Mac Arthur Foundation, 113
macro-economic management, 199
Mahatma Gandhi, 66–68, 95
Mahatma Gandhi National Rural Employment Guarantee Plan (MGNREGA), 190
Mahatma Gandhi Rural Employment Guarantee Act, 9
mahila mandals, 83, 114, 148
mainstream development, 9
maladministration in development administration, 151
Malayali diasporas, 79
Malthus, T.R., 16, 25
management, definition of, 195
management for development, 197
management in development, 197
management of development, 197
manpower decentralization, 164
market, 53, 108
  invisible hand of, 18
  vs state partnership, 112
market imperfection, 78
market operation in developing countries, 106, 183
mark-gov market, 111
Marshall Plan (Europe), 23
Marxian theory of economic development, 21
Marxist approach to dependency, 56
Marx, Karl, 20, 36, 63
mass media system, 219
maternal mortality rate (MMR), 91
mature democracies, 89
McClelland, David, 50
media role in development process, 55
medium-term plan, 186
metropolis, 57
Millennium Development Goals (MDGs), 89, 127, 139, 149, 198
Mill, J S, 16, 18, 25
Minimum Needs Programmes (1975), 127
minorities, 83
mobile individuals, 219
modern capitalism, 96
modernization, 29
modernization theory, 219
modernization theory of development, 56

modern liberalism, 60
money, 53
more developed, 13
morphology of backwardness, 57
multilateral agencies, 112
multimedia communication, 226
municipal corporation, 191
municipal council, 191
Myrdal, Gunnar, 41, 61

nagar panchayats, 191
Nai Talim, Gandhi
  methodology for development, 69
nation
  internal dynamics of, 59
National Classification of Economic Activities (NCEA), 120
national plan, 186
National Rural Employment Programme (MGNREGA), 127
National Rural Health Mission, Swajal Dhara, 9
nation development
  non-economic factors for, 51
natural growth rate, 22
need assessment report (NAR), 203
neo-classical liberalism, doctrine of, 107
neo-classical theories of economic growth and development, 16
Neo-classical theory, 26
neo-liberalization process, 160
neo-liberal theory, 63
net present value (NPV), 199
networks, 112
non-formal education, 216
non-governmental organizations (NGOs), 115
Nurkse, Rangar, 29, 31
Nussbaum, Martha, 63, 65

organic solidarity, 52, 53
organizing, 199
output
  increase in, factors for, 17
Oxfam, 113

Panchayati Raj Institutions, 140, 191
paradigm
  basic needs of, 128
  definition of, 126
  shift, 126
parallel bodies, 152, 153
Parsons, Talcott, 50, 53
participatory communication, 230
participatory development paradigm, 141
participatory development process, 171
participatory governance, 168
party identification, 89
People's Planning Campaign, Kerala Model of Decentralized Planning, 192
Perbisch, Raul, 58
Perbisch theory, 58
per capita income, 6, 77
perceived planning, 181
periphery countries, 58, 59
  centre exploits, 58
  industrialization of the, 59
persuasion, 220
physical planning, 185
plan holiday, 186
planned document, 183
planning, 199
  meaning of, 182
planning by direction, 184, 185
planning by inducement, 184, 185
play, 66
pluralistic over universalistic criteria
  modern societies, 54
pluralistic society, 172
political decentralization, 89, 162
political democracy, 88
political development
  dimension, 90
political development in developing countries, 13
political dynamics, 204
political governance, 12, 89, 90
political governance, deficiencies in developing countries, 90
political inequality, 89
political infrastructure, 148
political interference, 152
political leadership, 88
political power, congregation in elites hands, 89
political regionalism, 151
political repression, 8
political values, 89
poor economy, 26
population and development, Gandhian model of, 72
population growth, 18
population growth and economic growth, relationship between, 33
population theory, 19
Porto-neoliberalism, 60
positive checks, 19
positive-sum activities, 33
positive sum incentives, 33
post-colonial nation states, 108
post Second World War approach towards development, 29
poverty, 134
  indicators of sustainable development, 135
  reduction of, 128
poverty alleviation, 109
practical reason, 65
pre-condition of take-off development process, 36
predatory state, 39, 40
pre-Newtonian societies, 36
preventive checks, 19
primitive society, 36
private enterprises, in capitalism, 186
problem analysis, 203, 208
problem tree method, 203, 205

procurement management, 210
production
  factor of, 18
productivity
  on existing land, 18
profit, higher, 17
pro-poor development, 108
public administration,
  performance in India, 150
public distribution system
  (PDS), 111
public–private partnership,
  112, 150
public–private partnership,
  concept of, 111
public sector role in third
  world countries, 109
Punjab agriculture
  benefits for migrant
    labourers, 9
Punjabi diasporas, 79
PURA, 150

quality management, 210
quantitative aspects of
  development, 7

rate of investments and
  savings, 6
rate of profit
  decline of, 21
realistic process of
  development, 148
red-tapism, 151, 190
Regan, Ronald, 60
regionalism, 151
regional plan, 186
regional political outfits, 151
remittances
  to Kerala and Punjab
    through diasporas, 141
remittances, beneficiaries of,
  138
reporting, 202
resources drainage, 8
responsiveness, 170
Ricardo, David, 16, 18, 25
rich economy, 26
Ricrado, David, 17
right to recall, 88
right to reject, 88
risk management, 211
Robert Solow model of
  economic growth, 25
Rodan, Paul Rosenstein, 30
rolling plan, 186
Rosenstein-Rodan, Paul, 29
Rostow's stages of economic
  growth, 37
Rostow, W.W., 29, 36, 50
rule of law, 171
rural areas development, 29
rural employment, 109

Sabake Sath Sabka Vikas
  (development of all with
  the cooperation of all), 82
sanitation, 134, 135
Sarva Shiksha Abhiyan, 9
Sarvodaya system, 68
satellite nations, 57
Say's law of market, 106
Scheduled Caste, 83
Scheduled Tribes, 83
scintillating sector of
  economy, 38
scope management, 208
secondary sector, contribution
  in GDP, 120
Second World nations, 10
Second World War, 108
security regionalism, 151
self-help groups, 83, 114
Sen, Amartya, 63, 64
senses, 65
service industries, 120
service sector, 78
short-term plan, 186
simple, measurable,
  attainable, realistic and
  time bound (SMART), 206
Singapore, ethnic, cultural
  diversity and development
  in, 86
situation analysis, 204
Smith, Adam, 16–18, 25, 36,
  63, 108
social backwardness, 53
social capillarity thesis
  (Dumont), 33
social capital
  characteristics of, 84
  components of, 85
  importance of, 84
  role in development, 84
social capital role in
  development, 82
social development, 53, 109
social development analysis
  in development,
  importance of, 53
social development
  dimension, 85
social development indicators
  of developing countries, 12
social development model,
  55, 219
socialism, 36, 186
social justice, 109
social marketing, 225
social mobilization, 224
social overhead capitals
  (SOCs), 34, 35
social pathology, 53
social scientists, 159
society
  influence on individual, 53
  stages in, 36
socio-cultural dynamics, 204
socio-cultural regionalism, 151
socio-demographic indicators,
  204
sociologically ethnicity
  definition of, 53
solidarity, concept of, 52
South Africa's Employment
  Equity Act (1998), 131
specific over diffused criteria\
  modern societies, 54
spread effects, 42
staffing, 200
state, 110
  Bauer's criticism on
    intervention by, 61
  claim for its citizens, 183
  definition of, 39
  prepared own development
    plan, 186
  role in developmental state,
    43

role of, 61
through welfare measures, 96
types of, 39
state softness, 109
stationary state, 18, 19, 25, 108
steady state, 24–26
stimulant forces, 32
structural adjustment programme (SAP), 107
structuralist approach to dependency, 56
subsistence sector of economy, 38
surplus value, 21
sustainable development, 13
sustainable development, Gandhian model of, 71
sustainable development paradigm, 137
Swachh Bharat Abhiyan, 9
Swedish Agency for International Development Corporation (SIDA), 113

take-off development process, 37
Tata, JRD, 96
technological advancement, 29
technological progress, 18
tertiary sector, 120
Thatcher, Margaret, 60
Third Development Decade, United Nation, 90
Third World, 10
Third World countries, 43
thought, 65
tickle down effect, 9
time management, 209
top-down centralized approach, 140
traditional sector of economy, 38
traditional society, 36
transfer of labour, 29
transparency, 170
trusteeship, Gandhian doctrine of, 69

unbalanced growth theory, 35
unbalanced theories, 29
underdeveloped, 10, 13
underdeveloped countries
paucity of resources, impact of, 30
common characteristics of, 57
institutional metamorphosis in, 43
internal conditions of, 57
political power, 43
poverty and miseries in, reason of, 57
reasons for poor, 61
underdeveloped economies, 32
underdeveloped economy, 26
underdeveloped nation suffers from dualim, 42
underdeveloped nations characteristic features of, 53
underdeveloped society features of, 53
undeveloped countries meaning of, 10
UNDP Human Development Report, 159
UNESCO Declaration on the Principles of International Cultural Cooperation, 87
United Nations Children's Fund (UNICEF), 113
United Nations Development Programme (UNDP), 79, 113
United Nations International Development Organization (UNIDO), 113
unorganized sector, features of, 121
unproductive consumption, 17
urban local bodies, 116, 140, 191

vicious circle of poverty, 31–33, 46
village economy, 67
village forest committees, 153
village panchayat plan, 191
village vigilance committees, 153
villagism, Gandhian, 69

wage fund theory, 19
wage rate in capitalist sector, 38
W.A. Lewis theory of unlimited supply of labour, 39
warranted growth rate, 22
Washington Consensus, 60, 110
water and sanitation committees, 153
water user groups, 153
weak State, 109
Weber, Max, 50, 51
welfarism, 96
Western capitalism, 51
Western economies, 51
wireless telephone, 216
women
as legislatures, 94
women economic participation in workforce, 90
women role in development, 90
World Bank, 60, 110, 113, 158, 217
World Congress on Communication for Development (WCCD), 217
World Development Report 2008 on Agriculture for Development, 118
World Development Report 2009, 153
World Trade Organization (WTO), 60

Yemen Social Development Fund, 127
youth clubs, 114, 148
Yunus, Mahammad (Dr), 92

zero sum game for periphery underdeveloped nations, 59
zero-sum incentive, 33